Alice Munro's Late Style

Four Laidlaw Generations, Summer 1954, Wingham Ontario (left to right, standing): Robert Eric Laidlaw (1901–76), Sheila Munro (1953–), Alice Laidlaw Munro (1931–); (seated): Sarah Jane "Sadie" Code Laidlaw (1876–1966). Photograph: Ianville Hammerton Studio, Wingham, Ontario.

Alice Munro's Late Style

"Writing is the Final Thing"

Robert Thacker

BLOOMSBURY ACADEMIC
LONDON • NEW YORK • OXFORD • NEW DELHI • SYDNEY

BLOOMSBURY ACADEMIC
Bloomsbury Publishing Plc
50 Bedford Square, London, WC1B 3DP, UK
1385 Broadway, New York, NY 10018, USA
29 Earlsfort Terrace, Dublin 2, Ireland

BLOOMSBURY, BLOOMSBURY ACADEMIC and the Diana logo
are trademarks of Bloomsbury Publishing Plc

First published in Great Britain 2023
Paperback edition published in 2025

Copyright © Robert Thacker, 2023

Robert Thacker has asserted his right under the Copyright, Designs and
Patents Act, 1988, to be identified as Author of this work.

For legal purposes the Acknowledgments on pp. xiv–xv constitute an
extension of this copyright page.

Cover design: Rebecca Heselton
Cover image © Sheila Munro

All rights reserved. No part of this publication may be reproduced or transmitted
in any form or by any means, electronic or mechanical, including photocopying,
recording, or any information storage or retrieval system, without
prior permission in writing from the publishers.

Bloomsbury Publishing Plc does not have any control over, or responsibility for, any
third-party websites referred to or in this book. All internet addresses given in this
book were correct at the time of going to press. The author and publisher regret
any inconvenience caused if addresses have changed or sites have ceased
to exist, but can accept no responsibility for any such changes.

The author and publisher gratefully acknowledge the permission granted to reproduce
copyright material in this book. The third-party copyrighted material displayed in the pages
of this book are done so on the basis of fair use for the purposes of teaching, criticism,
scholarship or research only in accordance with international copyright laws, and is not
intended to infringe upon the ownership rights of the original owners.

A catalogue record for this book is available from the British Library.

ISBN: HB: 978-1-3502-7038-1
PB: 978-1-3502-7042-8
ePDF: 978-1-3502-7039-8
eBook: 978-1-3502-7040-4

Typeset by Integra Software Services Pvt. Ltd.

To find out more about our authors and books visit www.bloomsbury.com
and sign up for our newsletters.

*To our daughters Alison and Melissa,
To their husbands Jakob and Dan,
And especially to their children, our grandchildren:
Theo and Nora, Willa, Cameron, and Zoë.*

Contents

Preface: "I Want to Do This with Honour, If I Possibly Can"	viii
Acknowledgments	xiv
Introduction: Of Late Styles and Alice Munro	1
1 "*Maybe* I Can Do Something Unexpected with It": Imagining *The View from Castle Rock*	11
2 "It Is Difficult to Decide What Works in a Book of This Sort": The Making of *The View from Castle Rock*	41
3 "It Has Some Real Munrovian Highlights": "The View from Castle Rock" and *The View from Castle Rock*	71
4 "And Then Another Little Story Comes along and That Solves How Life Has Got to Be": The Recursions of *Too Much Happiness*	101
5 "It Seemed as If We Had Gotten Time Back, as If There Was All the Time in the World": The Gathering of Stories before the "Finale" in *Dear Life*	127
6 "Simple Truth": "Too Much Happiness" and the "Finale" to *Dear Life*	155
Epilogue: "To Have Got My Chance to Do It, as well as I Could": Alice Munro *Finis*	181
Notes	183
Works Cited	207
Index	216

Preface:
"I Want to Do This with Honour, If I Possibly Can"

My first meeting with Alice Munro for the purposes of *Alice Munro: Writing Her Lives: A Biography* (2005, revised 2011) happened in Clinton, Ontario during late August 2001. She was then seventy years old, was awaiting heart surgery that fall, and explained that she was spending the waiting time working on small jobs, not writing new stories. One of those jobs was a revision of her memoir story "Home" (1974) which, as it happened, would again appear in its revised form in Britain in *The New Statesman* just as 2001 ended. Describing the work of its revision, Munro was quite keen about excising the author's metafictional commentary included in its first appearance in *74: New Canadian Stories*. The day before our meeting, Munro's author copies of her latest book, *Hateship, Friendship, Courtship, Loveship, Marriage* (2001), had arrived there in Clinton, but she had not opened them yet. One of her daughters, then visiting, had been threatening her with opening the parcel herself and staging a public reading. A joke, but apt. In 2003 after her successful surgery, Munro referred to this time in her life, telling a journalist from the *Guardian* that before she went into the hospital that October she "rewrote everything that hadn't been published [in a book], so it would be around in a better version, and now I've rewritten some of it again. I'm really working out what will be here when I'm not here. As if it mattered!—but it does. It does to some extent" (Edemariam).

Awaiting that surgery, Munro knew that her father, Robert Eric Laidlaw (1901–76), had undergone a similar procedure himself and had not survived. His worsening heart problems are at the center of "Home," so as she awaited her own surgery and worked on its revision she again shared communion with him, and in her rewriting of it she knew too that as he awaited his surgery he was also working on revisions of his pioneer novel. *The McGregors* (1979) draws upon the circumstances of his own family's settlement of Huron County; his daughter Alice saw to its posthumous publication by Macmillan of Canada just after the same firm brought out her own *Who Do You Think You Are?* (1978). Among the stories included in the first version of that book, a version Munro famously pulled from the press at the last minute in order to revise it, was one entitled "The Moons of Jupiter" (1978). Like the first version of "Home," which Timothy Findley singled out as "an elegy in prose," one "beyond compare," "Moons" derives from the circumstances of her father's heart problems and decline. It too is "an elegy in prose."

At the time of her father's death Munro had been living again in Huron County for less than a year. She had returned from British Columbia to live in Ontario after she left her marriage by 1973; at the time she said that she did not know whether or not she would keep writing. The return to Ontario was a shock of recognition: the 1974 "Home," with its metafictional first-person commentary ("*I don't know how to end this*"; "*I want to do this with honour, if I possibly can*" [151, 153; original emphasis]) on her descriptions of her father and stepmother living in Wingham during a 1972 visit there, is key; it is an urtext marking Munro's return to Huron County after over twenty years away. "Home" begins the process of Munro's rediscovery of her home place as her central subject and prime focus, a place she rediscovered in her forties, then already a writer of note and repute. Writing of Huron at this time too Munro asserted that "everything here is touchable and mysterious." Yet equally there is biographical evidence that Munro knew that the aesthetic path she was embarking on, having returned home to live in Huron, was in some ways fraught. When "Home" was published in 1974 she asked J. R. (Tim) Struthers, then a graduate student and a reviewer of literary titles in the London *Free Press*, not to review *74: New Canadian Stories* there—her father and stepmother might see the review in the paper and so become aware of the memoir story which, among other portrayals, offers a characterization of Munro's stepmother in an unflattering light (Struthers email). In the same vein, though years later, in a letter to her friend and agent Virginia Barber who had just "gone home to see" her parents, Munro makes a surprising comment that will prove to resonate here in myriad ways:

> I woke up this morning thinking of my mother's death & wishing I had been there. I wasn't—partly lack of money but also the hard-hearted anti-hypocrisy pride of youth & plain detestation of the culture I came out of. In a way, with the burden, its a blessing when they live long enough for you to outgrow that (I don't mean that you had to, just that I wish I had).
>
> (February 15, 1994; 883/11.5.1.5)

I begin here with the biographical Munro at seventy awaiting heart surgery, revising "Home," because that memoir proved to be the earliest piece included in *The View from Castle Rock* (2006), her "kind of a family book" (as she referred to it in a letter to her Canadian editor Douglas Gibson on October 13, 1980; Macmillan 429.4). Seen now, "Home" proved also to be the first step on the imaginative and compositional path that led not only to *Castle Rock* but also to its two successor volumes, *Too Much Happiness* (2009) and *Dear Life* (2012). Taken together, these three books form Munro's late-style progression, one that begins with the sustained and long-meditated inclusion of new historical writing and revised but previously published pieces like "Home" in *Castle Rock*, and culminates with the four "Finale" stories in *Dear Life*. This grouping revealed Munro's recursive return to her first material and, most clearly, asserted them as a final statement.

"Writing is the final thing," Munro told two interviewers in December 2010 (Lehey and Jernigan 52). With the three books that form the substance of Munro's recursive late style, most especially the whole of *Castle Rock*, the title story to *Too Much Happiness*, and the finale stories of *Dear Life*, Munro demonstrates that for her this is so: writing *is* the final thing. One of the reviewers of *Castle Rock* saw as much in it, asserting that book as "a work of dizzying originality," "one that creates an entirely new category of book into which only it can fall" (Eisenberg). The same must be said of all three books that best and most dazzlingly display Munro's late style.

Since I begin here with biographical facts—Munro in August 2001, waiting, revising, her own copies of her latest book just arrived, a key moment in the development of her late style—I would like to say a few more things of that nature. As already mentioned, when Munro returned to Ontario in 1973 she wondered if she would keep writing; she even said that she might need to go out and find a regular job, and that was no joke. In August 2001 with *Hateship, Friendship, Courtship, Loveship, Marriage* finished, revising "Home" and other pieces which had not yet appeared in a book in the face of her upcoming surgery, Munro commented:

> [Y]ou know, the thing about writing is—I don't know about other writers—but other professions, like I'm sure if you're a surgeon you learn how to do operations and after a while you get in there and you just do them, and you're confident you'll do them right. Writing isn't like that at all. It isn't like that all. It's just constant despair. I mean it can hit you at any time.
>
> (Thacker interview August 2001)

This is a sense Munro has expressed throughout her career, and her reluctance to open that parcel of author copies she had just received in August 2001 was an expression of genuine doubt about her work, strange though that seems to others now. Submitting her stories, Munro had long refrained from signing manuscripts until the last possible moment, since that signature signified that she was finished with it. That, and Munro's habit of perpetually revising endings, became a running joke among her "literary triumvirate"—her agent Barber and her editors Ann Close at Knopf in New York and Douglas Gibson at McClelland & Stewart in Toronto. Barber once commented that Munro "said that she was written out, but then came *The Love of a Good Woman*" (1998) while Close, just days before Munro's Nobel Prize in Literature was announced, wrote that Munro "has been trying to 'end' her writing career for the past several books" (Barber interview November 20, 2000; Close email September 6, 2013). When *Castle Rock* was published in 2006 Munro created a stir by publicly announcing that it would be her last book while Gibson, for his part, was quoted just after her announcement asserting that was not so (Thacker *Alice* 532). Having worked closely with this author since the mid-1970s, Gibson knew the issues and the likelihoods. She would go on to say the same thing about the next two books.

Altogether these facts define an author well aware of endings and final forms. That Munro spoke frequently of *Castle Rock* as her last book—she did so, certainly, to me when I interviewed her in April 2004—shows her a prolific author bringing a long career to a close as she contemplated final things. That she did so through what the excellent Munro critic Robert McGill calls her "poetics of recursion" lends foundation to the biocritical approach I am undertaking here, or as McGill also writes, "a poetics of review that repudiates the presumption of amelioration" (McGill 140-3, 142; see also York, Cox). In 1998, introducing a volume of critical essays on Munro, and writing then too about "Home," I wrote that Munro's "Everything Here Is Touchable and Mysterious" was "prescient: her art since then has largely been one of visiting and revisiting the same places, the same people, shifting emphases, altering structures, moving in time, 'rescuing one thing from the rubbish,'" quoting then from the ending of Munro's "Meneseteung" (1988) (Thacker *Reading* 150). So Munro continued to do as she moved on into the 2000s, refining a late style which critics saw as poetic.

Charles E. May, a noted expert on the short story form, begins a close analysis of Munro's "Powers" in *Runaway* (2004) asserting that

> the short story, as practiced by Munro and other great short story writers, does not depend on plot or character, but rather on some significance by means of reiteration through pattern. If the short story does not hold together by plot or action, but rather reiteration through pattern, then the short story is not a narrative form at all, but rather a poetic form.
>
> (180–1)

And Dennis Duffy, author of one of the best single analyses on the historical narratives Munro has made, in this case the unique "Too Much Happiness," comments that writers, "as everyone knows, do not always confine themselves to familiar practices, especially as they proceed toward the ends of their careers" (379). Each of these critics will be returned to in what follows here, along with Edward Said and those responding to his *On Late Style* (2006). Following all of them, my purpose through the biocritical approach I have taken is to see Munro's final three collections, as Eisenberg wrote of *Castle Rock*, as the "dizzyingly original" triad that they are. Munro may well have been in earnest when she told me as her biographer and announced publicly that *The View from Castle Rock* would be her last book, but through recursion and review, the other two came along on their own through her long practice. This book offers that story, one borne of archival evidence, of biography, and of the critical effects of the books themselves.

A last prefatory word about "Home" and about Munro's relation to her home place as she has responded to and written it throughout her long career—her first story was published in 1950—is needed. When she came to place the revised "Home" in *The View from Castle Rock* (the evidence confirms that the book's structuring was a protracted process), that memoir story lent its title to the whole of the book's second section and, itself, appeared between "The Ticket," the only fictionalized memoir story Munro wrote explicitly for *Castle Rock*, and "What Do You Want to Know For?" (1994), a piece she has identified as straight memoir. Given this structure, the section entitled "Home" offers a progression of narrators from girlhood ("Fathers" [2002]), through adolescence ("Lying under the Apple Tree" [2002], "Hired Girl" [1994]), to young adulthood ("The Ticket"), to middle ("Home") and old age ("What Do You Want to Know For?"). Taken together, this "Home" structure moves Munro from the Laidlaw ancestors she focuses upon in the first section, "No Advantages," to the life she has lived at home herself. Owing to its provenance as a fictionalized memoir story written explicitly for *Castle Rock* without prior publication, "The Ticket" is especially indicative of Munro's recursion. It is focused on the time just before Munro's marriage in December 1951, when she was twenty years old. It is shot through with the narrator's awareness of the tensions borne between the culture and relatives she is about to leave and the new life that awaits her in Vancouver, where she will be moving after the wedding with her upper-class husband. Recalling, Munro writes:

> And yet the town was enticing to me, it was dreamy in these autumn days. It was spellbound, with a melancholy light on the gray or yellow brink walls, and

a peculiar stillness, now that the birds had flown south and the reaping machines in the country round about were silent. One day as I walked up the hill on Christena Street, towards my grandmother's house, I heard some lines in my head, the beginning of a story.

All over the town the leaves fell. Softly, silently the yellow leaves fell—it was autumn.

And I actually did write a story, then or sometime later, beginning with these sentences—I can't remember what it was about.

(261; original emphasis)

That story was "The Yellow Afternoon." It does begin with language quite close to Munro's recollection here ("All over the town the leaves fell; it was autumn. Carelessly, softly, the leaves fell, for there was no wind" [37.16.34.f1]), and it is about a talk between a high-school teacher encouraging a bright student to attend university and the student, for her part, telling the teacher that she will not do so, that she will soon marry a young farmer.[1] Munro dated it to the summer of 1951; it was read on *Anthology*, a national Canadian Broadcasting Corporation (CBC) radio program, in February 1955.

Here Munro returns to herself in 1951 when she was twenty and about to very consciously leave the only home she had known—leaving too her family and especially her mother, who by then was deep within the Parkinson's disease which would take her in early 1959—to become the writer she became. Munro returns in memory in "The Ticket" to "The Yellow Afternoon," and in so doing she was continuing an imaginary process which has characterized the whole of her career. One of Munro's most avowed influences, Eudora Welty, once wrote of another of Munro's influences, Willa Cather, in a phrasing that resonates within both of their oeuvres: "She made this work out of her life, her perishable life, which is so much safer a material to build with than convictions, however immutable they seem to the one who so passionately holds them. It is out of our own lives that we, in turn, reach out to it" (House 60). Welty's reliance on the short story was key to Munro early on, when everyone expected a novel and she was struggling to produce one—she told this to Ann Close (Close to Thacker June 19, 2018). But more than Welty as a model to emulate, Munro held her close as a reader, just as she did Cather. A. S. Byatt, reviewing Munro's first volume of *Selected Stories* (1996), pointed to Cather herself where, in Munro's story "Dulse" (1980), she "appears as a riddling object of contemplation … and I would guess that Munro has learned something about the shocking, the paradox of the formed and the formless, from that other local writer who transcended her local preoccupations without betraying them. But really she is unique; there is no one quite like her" (D18).[2]

Before taking up late style as a concept and then addressing just how that notion applies to Munro in her last three books, I want to say a few further words about this book as very consciously a biocritical analysis. As *Alice Munro: Writing Her Lives: A Biography* and other writings I have published demonstrate, I am fundamentally an archive-based scholar and critic. As it happened, I first published my Munro biography in late 2005, the year before Munro herself published *The View from Castle Rock*. When I was able to revise and update that book in 2011, I discussed *Castle Rock* and

Too Much Happiness, foresaw some of the stories which would appear in *Dear Life*, but effectively missed that book. And notably too I missed Munro's Nobel Prize in Literature announced in October 2013.

Since the 2011 iteration of my biography I have interviewed Munro two more times and visited with her in 2016 on the occasion of that year's Alice Munro Festival of the Short Story in Wingham; we have talked several times on the phone as well. I have talked also with Munro's longtime agent, the late Virginia Barber, with Munro's book editors Ann Close at Knopf and Douglas Gibson of McClelland & Stewart, and with Deborah Treisman, her editor at the *New Yorker*. Throughout these years too I have been gathering materials connected to the production of many of the stories included in the last three books; those from her agent and book editors have largely made it into archives (the University of Calgary and McMaster University), but those from the *New Yorker* have not yet. Many of these materials are used here for the first time.

What all this means is that the critical discussion of Alice Munro's late style I offer here is informed—and probably at times to a reader, infused—with archival evidence as the basis for critical judgments. And at the same time, since I missed treating the whole of these three books and the Nobel Prize in my biography's two appearances, if I err here toward biography over criticism, I do so only because timing and circumstances and personal abilities warrant such emphasis.

Robert Thacker
Fort Collins, Colorado
November 2022

Acknowledgments

This book began in an email conversation with my friend and fellow longtime Munro reader and critic Tracy Ware. The two of us have been going back and forth about Munro, about Canadian literature, and about many other shared interests since at least the late 1980s. Our frequent exchanges have been a delight, always informative and useful. From time to time we've shared one another's company over the years but, mostly, we lived about 100 miles apart with the Canada–US border, the St. Lawrence River, and (aptly here) the Frontenac Axis between us. Sometime early in 2020, just as Covid-19 was breaking out, I told Tracy of my desire to write on *The View from Castle Rock*. He immediately responded, suggesting that I might think about a book on Munro's late style with *Castle Rock* as the anchor and the last two books, each one her "last," Munro said, we both knew, following after. As soon as he wrote that I realized he was right, a better path than what I had had in mind. I am deeply grateful for the initial suggestion and, even more, for Tracy's interest in and support of this book as it was being researched and written. He was here all the way through.

Another person central to this book has been Ann Close, Senior Editor at Alfred A. Knopf and Munro's editor there from *The Beggar Maid* (1979) on. Along with Douglas Gibson, Munro's Canadian editor, and the late Virginia Barber, her longtime agent, Ann was among the group I have long called Munro's "literary triumvirate"—that is, the core group that helped make her books with her from the late 1970s to *Dear Life* (2012). That all of them traveled to Stockholm in late 2013—sadly Munro was unable to go herself—to share in the joy of the Nobel presentation there was as joyfully appropriate as anything I might imagine. And, as the text of what follows here shows, each of them contributed significantly to this book's making. Ann did so most especially with regard to *Too Much Happiness* and *Dear Life*—we wrote back and forth constantly while I was researching and writing, and we talked often. And Doug Gibson's impress is evident throughout here too, most especially in the making of *The View from Castle Rock*. Munro's dedication of that book to him, with its deep sincerity and wry humor, captures the essence of his dedication to her as a person and a writer, an unwavering editorial support I know something of myself, though nothing equal to, nor as longstanding, as Munro's.

Some words about Virginia Barber, who died early in 2016. Like the other members of Munro's triumvirate (and Munro herself), she became a friend through our various contacts. Her generous responses to a pre-publication version of my biography remain the most edifying I have ever gotten as a scholar and writer, and her determination to see to it that her Munro papers got into the Alice Munro Fonds was daunting—as a scholar herself, she well knew their importance. As this book shows, she got them there. But most of all Barber's dedicated, always professional, shepherding of Munro's career—"a gallop at full speed" if there ever was one—and their deep friendship is an edifying story to itself. She was a singular person.

Deborah Treisman, Fiction Editor at the *New Yorker*, has continued here to contribute significantly to my work on Munro. She saw to it that I had access to the magazine's accrued Munro materials after my biography was done. Whenever I posed a question, and I often did, she responded with alacrity and precision. Her contributions to this book are many, and I know it would not tell the story it tells without her. She, along with her predecessors in the fiction department at the *New Yorker* as well as the entire editorial staff there, is deeply proud of their association with Munro. Well they would all be, of course, but Deborah's was the editorial hand most involved with *The View from Castle Rock* and its successor volumes. I am grateful for all she has done for this work.

Two others have made key contributions to this story: Sheila Munro provided me with the photograph I have used here as a frontispiece—she is in it herself still in her own first year, of course—and I very much appreciate her willingness to allow its use here. As an image this photograph makes vivid the familial connections infusing *Castle Rock* which Munro imagined and thought over for decades before that book was assembled and written. Reg Thompson, long a good friend to Alice Munro and Gerald Fremlin both, provided critical information about Huron County and the Ottawa Valley, also both, and he directed Munro and Fremlin, and then me, to that crypt in Sullivan Township, Grey County. Its image is here too.

Along the way other Munro scholars, most of them quoted here, have been encouraging and supportive: Dennis Duffy, Christopher Gittings, Robert McGill, Eric Reeves, J. R. (Tim) Struthers. And Lorraine York, reviewing two Munro books I published in 2016, deftly pointed me toward Munro's recursions, as did McGill. I am very grateful to them all. At the University of Calgary, Annie Murray confirmed holdings and file numbers with enthusiasm and precision, along with her colleague Allison Wagner.

In a less direct way, too, I want to acknowledge and thank the far-flung members of the Alice Munro Book Club, Zooming through Covid-19 (2020–), still going strong. Having a weekly Munro discussion with such a range of enthusiastic and thoughtful readers, mostly relatively new to Munro, was a real tonic for me during pandemic isolation while I read for, researched, and wrote this book. Of these people I have met only a few, yet our weekly gatherings on Zoom created lots of human connections ranged about this great author.

Finally, as I worked through my Munro materials for this book I returned, often, to files made when I was at work on my biography during the early 2000s and before. There I frequently found notes from the late Joan Larsen, a great friend, a wonderful colleague, and a sharp researcher. These are reminders of just how deeply she valued and supported my Munro work. Though she is gone now as well—just as Munro in her late style reminds us we shall all be—the notes, comments, and extra copies of the *New Yorker* Joan passed on to me during those gathering years, most of which I have lately been rediscovering anew, are yet a happy reminder of the efficacies of the critical spirit and of the life of the mind. And that I was lucky enough to discover Alice Munro in 1973, and to have kept on reading her work and writing about it over all these years, remains for me the most happy joy itself.

Introduction:
Of Late Styles and Alice Munro

We passed through a village. I saw the backs of house[s], mostly red brick, their black screened porches, and the vegetable gardens, all the back yards stretched out wet and dark from the night. I knew that I had not really seen any place at all like this and that I had not really been able to remember what it was [I saw] here was the exact, inimitable country where I was born and lived, a landscape less distinctive, perhaps, than most I had seen since, and the only one that could move me to pain—not the same thing as nostalgia, nothing even a little bit comfortable [,] a recognition final and uninstructive as death.

(37.19.39)

This passage is from a single-page fragment typescript, the beginning of an abandoned story Alice Munro wrote sometime in the 1960s or even the 1970s. It begins, "I live on the west coast of North America, in British Columbia." The narrator is on an eastbound passenger train; she is looking out her window at the scene she finds south of Parry Sound, Ontario, adjacent to Georgian Bay, a part of Lake Huron, as the train presumably makes its way to Toronto. She sees this landscape, as she says, as "the only one that could move me to pain," "a recognition as final and uninstructive as death."

Munro's image here is one of return, the return to Ontario she may have already effected when she wrote this, although she may also have been imagining her eventual return from British Columbia to Ontario as she completed, as she would later write in a different phrasing, the "long necessary voyage from the house of marriage" (*Hateship* 169). Married at twenty in December 1951, Munro and her new husband left their native Ontario on this transcontinental train to start their new life together in Vancouver. After their first daughter Sheila was born, Munro and her husband James took their baby back to Ontario in 1954 to visit the families, hers in Wingham and her husband's in Oakville (see frontispiece). During the two decades she lived in British Columbia there were other trips east on that train until, during 1972–3, she left her marriage and returned to Ontario for good. Among the writing Munro did during 1973 was the memoir story "Home" which also features a return. It was first published in 1974 and, revised in 2001, became the anchor story in the first of the three volumes treated here as emblematic of Munro's late style, *The View from Castle Rock*. There, on her third bus heading home to Wingham from Toronto where she was then living,

Munro has trouble getting "an unobstructed view" because of the bus's windows; she has to crane her neck and, as she writes, "I find this irritating, because the countryside here is what I most want to see—the reddening fall woods and the dry fields of stubble and the cows crowding the barn porches. Such unremarkable scenes, in this part of the country, are what I have always thought would be the last thing I would care to see in my life" (*Castle Rock* 286). Not an exact echo of the fragment typescript epigraph, but this is close: both offer an author alluding to final things, and to death.

Such travel as figures here appears often in Munro's writing. While yet an undergraduate at the University of Western Ontario (1949–51), she wrote a story called "The Man Who Goes Home" which features a protagonist who repeatedly takes a train to Maitland, the town he is from, each time refusing to venture farther into the town; he has a cup of coffee at the station and then takes the next train back to the city (Sheila Munro 8). During the 1950s and early '60s Munro worked on an unpublished novel, often called "The Boy Murderer," featuring a character named Franklin returning home from service in the Second World War who jumps off the train just before it reaches his hometown, Goldenrod. Throughout Munro's stories there are several other instances of train travel and, when she reached her last book, *Dear Life*, the opening story "To Reach Japan" (2012) is structured by the same eastbound transcontinental trip Munro's fragment narrator takes. The story which follows it there, "Amundsen" (2012), has two revelatory train journeys while a later story in that book, "Train" (2012), finally brings the long-ago character Franklin from Munro's unpublished novel into print—although late in the publication process his name was changed from Franklin to Jackson (March 2012 *Dear Life* Manuscript). As that story ends, Jackson concludes yet another train trip, one allowing him another transformation of his life, arriving in Kapuskasing, Ontario. And just before *Dear Life*, Munro's final collection, an extended train trip figures in Sophia Kovalevsky's final journey in "Too Much Happiness" (2009) where, ill, she journeys toward her own imminent death.

I begin here with these continuities in Munro's writing clustering around train travel because they evidence this writer's recursive late style. Throughout her career, Munro has repeatedly used such trips—returning home or setting out—as means of approaching her subjects, as a way of confronting what she wants to examine in her stories. In recent years some critics have complained over the sameness of Munro's characters, that they are always people connected to or living in her home place, Huron County, Ontario. That is, people like Munro herself. Such complaints point toward my subject here: Munro's constant return home through yet another go at a situation or a circumstance that she has written about in different ways before, offering characters in situations which echo stories she had published previously. See, for example, "Fiction" (2007) in *Too Much Happiness*: it echoes "Material" (1973), the second story in *Something I've Been Meaning to Tell You* (1974). Such echoings are not by way of repetition but rather by way of dissatisfaction: Munro wanted to approach a story's circumstances again to go further, to dig deeper, to imagine more fully what is there. To recreate, through her writing, what she once described as "the rest of the story" (*Selected Stories* xvii).

Nowhere is this recursion more evident than in Munro's last three books. While I might point to many early attempts in Munro's papers at the University of Calgary archives to use recollections of Wingham and family circumstances in writing done in British Columbia (1952–73), Munro's contemplation of *Castle Rock*—what she called "a kind of family book" in her letter to Gibson—likely really began with "Home," its anchor story. One of three memoir stories in *Castle Rock*—the others are "Working for a Living" (1981) and "What Do You Want to Know For?" (1994)—"Home" is borne of first real return, approach, and recognition as Munro reacquainted herself with the sights, culture, and mores of her home place when she returned to Ontario. And, owing to her subsequent reconnection with Gerald Fremlin—he was among an audience in London when Munro read "The Man Who Goes Home" in the spring of 1951—Munro made an ultimate move in 1975 to Clinton in Huron County, where she lived until quite recently.

The point here is that Munro's return to Ontario and then to Huron County was critical to her career. Returned to Huron a middle-aged writer of accomplishment and recognition, she saw her home place anew, and her writing refocused on it in imaginatively complex ways, through aesthetically charged techniques. First there were three particular stories, "Home" among them and all first published in 1974, that treated Munro's family history in new ways (the others are "The Ottawa Valley" and "Winter Wind," each in *Something*). Then there was a descriptive text focused on rural Ontario scenes, "Places at Home," that Munro initially worked on in 1975 but ultimately abandoned, though many of its vignettes were ultimately used in *Who Do You Think You Are?/The Beggar Maid*. The complex history of the making of that book (or, truly, those books) is critical to the new path its author was embarked upon. Munro's decision in 1978 to take *Who*, then in production at her new publisher Macmillan of Canada, off the press for a radical restructuring and revision, suggests a writer's intent on the exact shape of the work; this act, and the US version published by Alfred A. Knopf in 1979, further revealed Munro as the consciously precise writer she is. Together, these acts define a writer well able to forge a unique style of her own through the home-place materials she rediscovered during the mid- to late 1970s and, ultimately, to shape the "kind of family book" she envisioned for so long into a recursive late style all her own beginning with *The View from Castle Rock* (see Thacker *Alice* 257–67, 294–301, 336–65; "Alice Munro Country").

Of Testamentary Acts and Late Styles

Throughout Munro's career she has been repeatedly "discovered" by literary types, mainline and academic alike, in the United States, Britain, and elsewhere. A recent instance is a book by Lee Clark Mitchell, *More Time: Contemporary Short Stories and Late Styles* (2019); there, he treats Munro's *Dear Life* as the first of four summative chapters focused on selected story writers whom he sees as "brilliant practitioners" of the short story form (3). Each figure, he holds, may be seen "refining a style carefully honed over a lifetime" (3), and he purports to treat the whole of each writer's career since "any understanding of individual late style requires reviewing the whole career" (26). I point to Mitchell's book here both as acknowledgment of its precedence on the subject of Munro's late style and to say something too about that critical notion itself, one attributed most often to Edward Said's *On Late Style* (2006) (see also Said "Thoughts"). Be that as it may, Said's book is less foundation for the analysis offered here than is an earlier one, Michael Millgate's *Testamentary Acts* (1992). Its title is useful phrasing for the analysis of Alice Munro's late style, one that is closer to just what she was doing when she finally reached *The View from Castle Rock* and its two successor volumes. A salient point in this progression was that in late 2003 Munro contracted with Knopf for not one but two books, the first *Runaway* and the second, though untitled at the time, *Castle Rock*.¹ But what the archival and textual evidence demonstrates is that Munro's final three books are borne of both their author's perpetual recursion and that their succession is itself a long-envisaged testamentary act; indeed, that is so in just the ways Millgate defines the phrase in relation to the histories of his subjects, Robert Browning, Alfred, Lord Tennyson, Henry James, and Thomas Hardy. Reminding at the outset of his study that one of the OED definitions of "'career'" is "'a short gallop at full speed,'" Millgate sets about examining the actions taken by his four authors regarding their work as each of their careers concluded and ultimate demise loomed (2). With Munro, *Castle Rock* begot further testamentary acts in *Too Much Happiness*—most especially the title story which ends that penultimate book—and, even more emphatically, the "Finale" of four personal stories that end *Dear Life*. Following as they do "Dolly" (2012), a story in which the narrator and her partner look very much like Alice Munro and Gerald Fremlin about 2010, the four girlhood stories circa the 1930s and '40s in the "Finale" telescope Munro's own "dear life" back to the time of her essential beginnings as an author, when she lived amid her birth family on a fox farm along the Maitland river in Lower Town Wingham, Huron County, Ontario (1931–49). Testamentary acts in fact.

Millgate's analyses of his four cases in *Testamentary Acts*, most especially James and Hardy, prepare the ground here for a brief consideration of late style itself. He notes the older Hardy's "intensification of habits of creative reverie which he had adopted, or fallen into, much earlier in his career" (136). That phrasing applies equally and fully to Munro's practice, both before and during the composition of her last three books. Concluding his chapter on Hardy before taking up his widow's actions after her husband's death in January 1928, Millgate offers a passage that, while he is writing about Hardy, applies equally in most respects to Munro:

> It was not simply that he rose, so remarkably, from a position of rural obscurity to one of scarcely equalled national and international renown, but that he realized his genius in such a variety of literary forms and presented, by the time of his death, a model of a life lived to the limits of its creativity, active and even innovative to the very end and yet leaving no substantial literary tasks undone.
>
> (138)

Concluding, Millgate asserts his thesis once more—that the "immediately pre-posthumous years of writers" deserve more attention than they have gotten—and rather sees those years, based on the analyses he has offered, "as the locations of deliberate, comprehensive, and effectual rewritings of both texts and lives—as well as of testamentary acts with profound and often unanticipated consequences for both future scholarship and for the long-term prosperity of the author's own work and reputation" (205). That this is so regarding the four authors examined in *Testamentary Acts* is without question, but also certainly Millgate has set the stage for a discussion of late style as it applies to Alice Munro.

Said's *On Late Style*, a collection of essays shaped and published by other hands after its author's death in 2003, developed a long critical reach after it appeared and is still being debated and written about. His notion of a thing called "late style" shared by long-lived artists had real attraction, so serious engagement with the book appeared at once. John Updike published a review essay of it in the *New Yorker* as it was out, "Late Works: Writers Confronting the End," and academic discussions ensued. In the years since a consensus has emerged—and Mitchell's book is very much part of this—that it is more a matter of "late styles," not any single late style. Each older artist develops a unique late style. Thus Updike, who was writing as he confronted his own end a few years later, aptly treats Said and his book with sharp insight. Of academic critics, Gordon McMullen in *Shakespeare and the Idea of Late Writing* (2007) hypothesizes what he calls the *caesura*, "the point at which the mid- or mature period style stops and the late style begins" (65), an identifiable moment in an artist's career when the shift occurs and late style is evident (see also Hutcheon, Delbanco). Altogether this criticism impinges here, but I am writing about Alice Munro's late style as it emerged throughout her long career and came to an evident clarity in her last three books as a testamentary act: "'Writing,'" as she said, "'is the final thing.'"

"A Form of Creative Repetition and Reliving": Alice Munro's Late Style

I want to return briefly to that day in August 2001 which I described at the outset of the preface here: this was a *caesura* moment in Munro's career—it was so biographically certainly, given what she told Edemariam from the *Guardian* in 2003—but this was so stylistically as well. When I introduced the critical volume of essays published by Bloomsbury in 2016 focused on three of Munro's last five books, *Hateship, Friendship, Courtship, Loveship, Marriage*, the first of the three and the one whose author copies Munro had refrained from opening when they arrived, I identified it as a repository of late Munro, writing that with it she "burst into what we are here calling late Munro" (Introduction 22). I especially noted "The Bear Came Over the Mountain," which I called "an urtext," but I also made mention of "Nettles," "Post and Beam" (2000), and "What Is Remembered" (2001) as stories offering narrators who remind readers of Alice Munro at different stages in her life. There too I remarked that "Late Munro was disrupted some in her next collection, *The View from Castle Rock*." This comment is recanted here, for *Castle Rock* is no disruption, but now I recursively return to and reassert another comment which followed: it is both utterly so and also the fundamental basis of this book: "*Castle Rock* will likely ultimately be seen as among Munro's most important—it offers too much of what she sees as narrative to be otherwise and shows too well what she has learned about the writer's life." There too I called it "audacious," something I still think it is (Introduction 3). As will be seen in the three chapters here treating *Castle Rock*, given the length of time Munro spent contemplating that book and the complexity of its making, it is both an initial testamentary act and, as a preliminary to the two books that follow, an embodiment of Munro's late style writ large.

While there is no doubt that biographically Munro was at a *caesura* moment in August 2001, defining just when her late style began is difficult and, ultimately, probably not categorical anyway. The great fact of Alice Munro's initial stylistic shift was her return to Ontario. The first years after were about re-seeing and re-discovering her home place, the site of her material. That is what the stories she first did upon her return to Ontario were all about. By the time the stories in *Who Do You Think You Are?/The Beggar Maid* were completed, Munro was hitting her stride through the processes involved in having connected with an agent, with editors at the *New Yorker*, and with two book editors weighing in. The period was particularly fecund—more memoir was emerging—"Working for a Living," for instance, started as fiction but ended as memoir in *Castle Rock*.

Two fugitive pieces from this period figure in the question: having been passed over twice for inclusion in a book, "Wood" (1980) was being considered for *Friend of My Youth* (1990), as was "The Ferguson Girls Must Never Marry" (1982).[2] Neither made the cut for that book. The latter has never been included in a book, though Munro worked on it perpetually throughout the years, and "Wood" was passed over repeatedly until it was used, very much revised and expanded, to precede "Too Much Happiness" in 2009. By *Friend of My Youth* few close readers would dispute that with it, and with its predecessor volume, *The Progress of Love* (1986), Munro had reached an entirely different level of complexity and of narrative indeterminacy. In *Progress* the title story came in for particular consideration, along with "White Dump" (1986), its last. And with *Friend* the title story—one of two in that book which pointed toward her growing interest in Scotland and in her father's Laidlaw ancestors that would culminate in *Castle Rock*—was so seen. But more especially was "Meneseteung," a complex historical narrative study in indeterminacy, one that also presaged Munro's authorial position in *Castle Rock*: there the narrator is a person doing biographical research into the life of the story's protagonist. Throughout the 1990s with *Open Secrets* (1994) and *The Love of a Good Woman* (1998), there is no doubt that a late style was emerging, one seen most especially in the massively complex title story of the latter volume, and that fictive late style carried on into the 2000s with *Hateship, Friendship, Courtship, Loveship, Marriage* and with *Runaway*, probably Munro's most complete indeterminate book.[3]

Yet paired with *Runaway* and long imagined, *Castle Rock* was Munro's first and most thoroughly considered testamentary act. For a time after it was published in 2006, when she was seventy-five, she said it was her last book yet, with her imagination and recursive memory well still alive, it was not. Two more volumes emerged and each one, upon publication, was said by its author to be the last as well. So *Dear Life* has proved to be. With it, Munro's testamentary acts reached their apogee with the "Finale" that ends *Dear Life*. That they do is apt, for as the conclusion of Alice Munro's recursive career "Dear Life" returns once more to Anne Chamney Laidlaw, her mother who died in early 1959 after an almost twenty-year struggle with Parkinson's disease, her mother whom she left in Wingham when she married at twenty and moved away to Vancouver, her mother who escaped from the hospital into the snow just before her death, her mother who is perpetual presence in Munro's stories. She published her first story about her mother's suffering and death in "The Peace of Utrecht" in 1960 and wrote her throughout until Munro herself reached her "Finale" amid her own "Dear Life."[4]

Just before Munro made her first trip to Europe in early 1982, a trip which included her first visit to Scotland and to the Ettrick valley there, the place from which her Laidlaw ancestors first emigrated to Canada in 1818, she wrote an essay entitled "What Is Real?". It was twice published that year, in *Making It New*, an anthology of contemporary Canadian short stories edited by her friend John Metcalf and, in connection with that book's publication, in the *Canadian Forum*. Metcalf had asked the authors to write about story technique but, when Munro sent her essay to him she noted that she did not really do that, remarking that "[a]ll that can be said is, its about writing, & does relate to a story being used" (January 26, 1982; John Metcalf Fonds 24.21.2.f1).

That story was "Royal Beatings" (1977), Munro's first in the *New Yorker*, arguably a breakthrough for her, the one destined to open *Who Do You Think You Are?/The Beggar Maid*. Throughout her career Munro has shown antipathy toward writing formal statements addressing just how she writes, making "What Is Real?" a more singular piece for that (see Thacker *Alice* 489–91). In it Munro makes statements which resonate throughout her oeuvre and serve to help define her late style. She treats of "reality"—verifiable fact, autobiography and imagined details—"Yes," she writes, "I use bits of what is real, in the sense of being really there and really happening, in the world, as most people see it, and I transform it into something that is really there and really happening, in my story." Speaking of a key episode in "Royal Beatings," where a batch of town louts administer a beating to man as vigilante punishment for his apprehended deprecations to members of his family, Munro writes that "I put this story at the heart of my story because I need it there and it belongs there. It is the black room at the centre of the house with all the other rooms leading to and away from it." "Who told me to write this story? Who feels any need of it before it is written? I do. I do, so that I might grab off this piece of horrid reality and install it where I see fit." Just after this she comments that "I am not concerned with any methods of selection but my own, which I can't fully explain." Here too, earlier in the essay, Munro asserts that "[e]very final draft, every published story, is still only an attempt, an approach to the story" (*Making* 226, 225).

I have said that, following McMullen, Munro may be seen at what he calls a *caesura* moment in August 2001. Equally, she was at a similar moment when she wrote and sent off "What Is Real?" the day before she traveled to Scotland for the first time in January 1982. Munro was still in the midst of her most fecund period as a writer, one which began with her return to Ontario and Huron County to live, extended through the making of *Who Do You Think You Are?/The Beggar Maid*, saw the writing of and publication of "Working for a Living," and was about to be extended by the publication of *The Moons of Jupiter* in 1982.

"The Ferguson Girls Must Never Marry" is a presence in Munro's oeuvre in that it was published, also in 1982, and while Munro kept working on it throughout the years, it was never included in a collection. It focuses on three Ferguson sisters from a family of Anglicans in Devlin, Ontario, their histories in the town (and that of the town itself), and their relations in the present. It is focalized by the middle sister, Bonnie, and its occasion is the funeral of the oldest sister, Nola, who dies in her early fifties of a heart attack—just as their mother did years before. It involves a revelation: Nola's husband Ted, a Catholic, decides without his wife's stated wishes to have her buried in the Catholic cemetery—an act which shocks her sisters. "'I did it to save her soul,'" he tells Bonnie afterwards, whose focalized thoughts after an extended meditation on the idea of the soul conclude, "What things a man like that must take for granted; what means he must think justified; what monstrous, matter-of-fact presumptions were at home in him" (63, 64). Before the story was published in *Grand Street* it was seen and rejected by the *New Yorker*, *Redbook*, *McCall's*, and *Harper's*. Declining it, Charles McGrath at the *New Yorker* described it as "too large and generous and expansive," "practically Dickensian at times, in the way people and plots seem to multiply." He thinks it is the beginning of a novel (Mary Evans to Munro January 12, 1982; 38.2.63.71; McGrath to Evans October 15, 1981; 38.2.63.63).

I point here to this fugitive story first written amid others which proved salient because it figured in Munro's preliminary work on "What Is Real?". There she begins by writing that there is not "much I can learn in writing one story, that will help me with another. Every story I write is entirely separate. Every story presents me with new problems. There are no general rules regarding form or style which will apply." More than that, Munro writes that after "a year or so has passed since the writing of a story, I forget how it was done." Given this, she presumably had forgotten how the two stories included in *Making It New* were written, so she sets out to describe the three she has written most recently. The first of these is quite clearly "The Ferguson Girls Must Never Marry":

> One of these three stories is quite long, too long to be marketable and maybe too long for its own good. The problem in writing it, a huge problem[,] was that a large number of people and various things that had happened to them over a number of years had to be brought into it, in order to show how something that happened "now"—in the present time of the story—mattered to all of them. That's not a short story at all, some people might say—and probably will say—that's a condensed novel.

Armed with this idea, Munro tried to expand the story—"writing out scenes I had formerly reported or hinted at"—but "[t]hings got worse and worse until I had to admit the expansion wasn't working" (38.12.35.3.f1).

I am taking this prose from a draft that was never published because Munro's comments ring true with regard to "Ferguson Girls" and, more than that, they apply beyond that uncollected and well-worked story to her writing as a whole. In this draft, writing about a second, different, story—one I cannot identify, one which also gave her trouble—Munro writes of it, "I did have to get the voice of the story & and find out what it had to say. There was no way I could figure it out. This sounds very suspicious but it is true." She then returns to "Ferguson Girls," writing of how it had her stymied.

She knows that she had reached a point where "I can't do anything either to repair or re-conceive it" (38.12.35.3.f3-4). Writing still of "Ferguson Girls," earlier in the draft she maintains that at this moment in making story she

> can tinker away with the words and the sentences till Doomsday, and all I'll get is more artifice. I have to back off then and get a revelation. I usually can't admit this. I usually insist to myself that the story is finished and its all right and send it off for the final typing. Then when I think I'm free of it I get a new idea.

She knows that this "is not an efficient way to work, it would be nice to proceed in an orderly way from draft to draft, but I have not found it possible" (38.12.35.3.f2).

"I have to back off then and get a revelation." This process, well described here in an unpublished holograph draft written sometime in 1981 or perhaps January 1982, asserts Munro's organic methods and, written as it was at a *caesura* moment in her career, portends the writing yet to come. The revelations she speaks of—surely a word that Munro would not herself connect to Yeats's "The Second Coming" but others might now, and I most certainly would—are borne out by her methods of story making. Perennially and persistently, she has reshaped her stories and especially their endings, the latter often to the last possible moment in publication. Such revelations are at the recursive center of the long making and shaping of *The View from Castle Rock*, the family book that Munro was also contemplating when she wrote "What Is Real?". They are there too as formative presences in Munro's late style as seen throughout the final three books she produced, each of which she said would be her last. Each volume is thus a testamentary act, a late-style recursion which revisits and reshapes Munro's own particular imaginative materials, her own life and experiences there real, the people she has known and seen remembered, imagined, and extended while placing them, almost always, in her own home place and time. Altogether, these three books are a testamentary finale in fact.

Here follow six chapters and an epilogue. Chapter One, "'*Maybe* I can do something unexpected with it': Imagining *The View from Castle Rock*," sets out the idea of what Munro called her "family book," treating the provenance of the constituent parts of *Castle Rock* and the myriad ways, as seen through archival evidence, by which that book was initially imagined. Chapter Two, "'It is difficult to decide what works in a book of this sort': The Making of *The View from Castle Rock*," presents just how the book came together. Chapter Three, "'It has some real Munrovian Highlights': 'The View from Castle Rock' and *The View from Castle Rock*," treats the submission of what became the first half of *Castle Rock* to the *New Yorker*, its editing and appearance there, and then treats the critical contexts of the book itself. Chapter Four, "'And then another little story comes along and that solves how life has got to be': The Recursions of *Too Much Happiness*," treats the stories in that collection which precede the title story. In the same way, Chapter Five, "'It seemed as if we had gotten time back, as if there was all the time in the world': The Gathering of Stories before the 'Finale' to *Dear Life*," treats the preliminary stories in that book. Chapter Six, "'Simple Truth,'" considers "Too Much Happiness" and the "Finale" to *Dear Life* as extended late-style conclusions to their volumes and to Munro's career. That chapter also treats the "Finale" to *Dear Life* as her final testamentary act, as her ultimate aesthetic recursion, and as her own finale. The epilogue, "'To have got my chance to do it, as well as I could': Alice Munro *Finis*," goes back to the crypt that Munro and Fremlin found near to them in Sullivan Township, Grey County, Ontario, the one at the core of "What Do You Want to Know For?" (1994), the memoir that at one point proclaims, "It's the fact you cherish" (*Castle* 208). The epilogue then calls attention to the 1954 professional photograph used as frontispiece and on the cover here. That photo—of four persons drawn from separate Laidlaw generations, all destined to be characters in Munro's later writing and in this book—seems to catch and capture Munro's methods and materials in her late style.

A final word of introduction: in a once very-well-known essay published in 1953 just as Alice Munro was beginning her career ("a short gallop at full speed": she published her first commercial story that year), the poet John Berryman offered "Shakespeare at Thirty." There, concluding his exegesis of Shakespeare's activities around his thirtieth birthday in 1594, Berryman offers a long list of the plays "to be created in the six years coming" and sends the poet to those tasks (55). So too Alice Munro with *Hateship* and *Runaway* setting up *The View from Castle Rock*: like Shakespeare, she had her six years from that recursive book through *Too Much Happiness* to *Dear Life*.

1

"*Maybe* I Can Do Something Unexpected with It": Imagining *The View from Castle Rock*

> *But it's a wonder how those people had the courage once, to get them over here. They left everything. Turned their backs on everything they knew and came out here. Bad enough to face the North Atlantic, then this country that was all wilderness. The work they did, the things they went through. When your great-grandfather came to the Huron Tract he had his brother with him, and his wife and her mother, and his two little kids. Straightaway his brother was killed by a falling tree. Then the second summer his wife and her mother and the two little boys got the cholera, and the grandmother and both the children died. So he and his wife were left alone, and they went on clearing their farm and started up another family. I think the courage got burnt out of them. Their religion did them in, and their upbringing. How they had to toe the line. Also their pride. Pride was what they had when there was no more gumption.*
>
> (*Moons* 30–1)

In the early 2000s when Alice Munro turned her attentions to the book that became *The View from Castle Rock*, she was consciously finally setting out on a project she had contemplated—and in fact been at work on—for over forty years. She was not, like Shakespeare at thirty as Berryman describes him, a young woman setting out into this period of major work, but analogously she was. An accomplished artist in her early seventies, her recent heart surgery successful and behind her, Munro finally took up her very-long-contemplated subject and, after the work involved in *Runaway*—a collection of stories as tightly imagined and shaped as she had yet produced—she set about the actual making of *Castle Rock*.

In November 2004, when *Runaway* had just been published, Munro was interviewed on the CBC's "Writers and Company" and commented on her ambitions and long-time confidence as a writer during her twenties (1951–61). She knew then that "there *would* be a book," she said remembering. "And it really never occurred to me until much later, when I was around thirty, that I might *not* be able to do this. That confidence lasted for a long time. And then it just went with a big *whoosh*. It was hard when that confidence went away" (Wachtel 277; original emphasis).[1] An indication of this change is in a letter she wrote in December 1959 to Robert Weaver, who produced the CBC's literary programing and who bought and broadcast many of Munro's early stories. There she reports that "I am working again now after a period of considerable depression and uselessness this fall" (December 5, 1959; Robert Weaver Fonds; see Thacker *Alice* 109–14 and *passim*).

Munro was writing here late in the same year her mother, Anne Chamney Laidlaw, had died after an almost twenty-year struggle with Parkinson's disease. When she first published "Dear Life" in 2011, Munro begins the penultimate paragraph in the *New Yorker* version with "I did not go home for my mother's last illness or for her funeral. I had two small children and nobody in Vancouver to leave them with." These sentences become the beginning of the ultimate paragraph in *Dear Life*. In each case in the paragraph before Munro writes about a person then living in Oregon, the daughter of a neighbor, Mrs. Netterfield, had had a letter published in the Wingham paper, one that Munro had discovered there. She writes, again in the *New Yorker*, "The daughter lived not so far away from me, in my adult life. I could have written to her, maybe visited. If I had not been so busy with my own young family and my own invariably-torn up writing, if I had not been so severe, in any case, toward such literary efforts and sentiments as hers" (*New Yorker* 46). In the *Dear Life* version the phrasing becomes "my own invariably unsatisfactory writing" and the last clause about her literary attitudes disappears (*Dear Life* 318).

I shall return to "Dear Life," both versions, in due course. But here it is necessary to see Munro at the end of the 1950s and the beginning of the '60s at another *caesura* moment: she lost confidence then, she wrote to Weaver about being depressed and unable to write, and her mother—whom Munro left in Wingham when she married in 1951—had died in February 1959. During this time Munro wrote, but as she asserts in "Dear Life," what she produced did not satisfy. She was often trying to write the novels people expected rather than the stories she preferred. During this time too she discovered the work of Eudora Welty, most especially her *The Golden Apples* (1949), and the model Welty offered of literary success based on short stories would prove crucial for Munro.[2]

This biographical information sets the context for Munro's composition of "The Peace of Utrecht" (1960), her first story about her mother's illness and death. It was the first story, she has said, "where I first tackled personal material. It was the first story I absolutely had to write." It was her "first really painful autobiographical story … the first story that tore me up" (Struthers interview 21; Metcalf 58; see Thacker, *Reading* 53–61, "This is" 17–18). Put another way, "The Peace of Utrecht" was the first published story where she discovered what should be called her real material. Thus the stories she published during the 1960s, overall, drew upon her own life experiences to a degree not seen previously. Following "Utrecht" two other stories, "Boys and Girls" (1964) and "Red Dress—1946" (1965), indicate this new direction especially, but most of the others published during that decade offer autobiographical materials, leading up to two of the three stories Munro wrote at her editor's behest during 1967–8 to complete her first book, *Dance of the Happy Shades* (1968): "Walker Brothers Cowboy" and "Images."[3] They emphatically do. At the same time, and as shown by the passage from "Chaddeleys and Flemings 2: The Stone in the Field" (1979) offered as an epigraph above, from early in her writing Munro demonstrated willingness to draw upon her family history. The emigration described by the narrator's father there mirrors, with some changes in exact relations, the actual history of the Laidlaws' emigration from Ettrick to Canada in 1818 and then to Huron in the early 1850s. The brother killed by the falling tree is invoked in *Lives of Girls and Women* (1971; see 29); he later becomes a basis for "A Wilderness Station" (1992) and, as himself, James Laidlaw, is killed again in "The Wilds of Morris Township" in *Castle Rock*.

Speaking in June 2003 of her genealogical research, Munro admitted to having done more on the Laidlaw side of her family, even though she had also done "a fair bit on the other side," but "there isn't nearly as much on the Chamney side." And, since she was then at work on the materials that became *Castle Rock*, she continued to tell the whole story of the Laidlaws' emigration to Canada in that interview. The next year, returning to the subject of genealogical work while still at work on it, Munro said, "[I]t's engrossing, it draws you in" (Thacker interviews June 2003, April 2004). Another way of describing what Munro found in Ontario and especially in Huron County when she returned there in the mid-1970s is found, presciently, in a phrase which appeared in "The Peace of Utrecht"; having returned home to Jubilee (an early-career stand-in name for Wingham) to visit her sister after the death of their long-ill mother, the narrator finds one of her own school notebooks in a drawer. Contemplating her own familiar handwriting, she "felt as if my old life was lying around me, waiting to be picked up again" (*Dance* 201).

So Alice Munro returned to Huron: when she abandoned an initial writing project she had undertaken after getting back, "Places at Home," a series of vignettes intended for a book of photographs, Munro apologized to Douglas Gibson, her new editor at MacMillan of Canada, writing, "Sorry I've been slow coming to this recognition but I don't feel the effort to be wasted—in this game, eventually, nothing is wasted" (September 16, 1975; Macmillan 429.4). This comment should be seen as prescient too since, while the book of photographs was never published, many of its vignettes were incorporated into *Who Do You Think You Are?/The Beggar Maid*. And by then too Munro was continuing at discovering, rediscovering, gathering, and working with the local materials of her home place included there. The two-part "Chaddeleys and Flemings" story was intended for it and was among the family-based stories Munro pulled when she reorganized the book at the last minute just before its fall 1978 publication (see Thacker *Alice* 348–50).[4]

Put more pointedly, what I am defining as Munro's late style here was born as an imaginative process begun by her return to Ontario and especially her return to Huron County. So returned, she quite literally found her old life lying around her, "waiting to be picked up again." In that move the initial gestation of *View from Castle Rock* is evident; because of its deep structural recursions, I take it as the beginning of Munro's late style. That book literally revisited previously published memoirs—"Home" and "Working for a Living"—as a way of telling and sequencing her family's history, and her own as well. Doing so, Munro was continuing to reconsider her previous work, something she had long done, but in *Castle Rock* that reconsideration is actually a re-citing and a reshaping, the late-style revisitation that also characterizes the two books that followed it. Something like a footnote. Taken together then, Munro's last three books—each written and assembled after her 2001 heart surgery—display a late style that was accelerating, brought about by an imaginative process that had begun with the return to Ontario and first seen in full form in *Who Do You Think You Are?/The Beggar Maid*. A final fact, salient in all of this, was the death of Munro's father Robert Eric Laidlaw in August 1976. It opened the way for Munro to write "Royal Beatings," the fulcrum story which was her first in the *New Yorker*; to write "Chaddeleys and Flemings," the second part of which, quoted here as epigraph, foresees the materials that became much of *Castle Rock*; and most especially it opened the way for "Working for a Living." In them altogether, the beginnings of Munro's late style emerge.

Of "Home" and "Working for a Living": Alice Munro, Returned to Huron County

"Home," one of the three memoir stories Munro wrote soon after her return to Ontario in 1972–3, is the foundational text of *The View from Castle Rock*. In that book it lends its title to the second section of the gathering and, following the newly written memoir story, "The Ticket," further folds Munro's own life into the Laidlaw legacy which is her overarching subject in *Castle Rock*. Altogether, the autobiographical materials and techniques in these three stories reveal a returned Munro confronting her real material as she settled back into Ontario. While the other two memoir stories complement this process from their places in *Something I've Been Meaning to Tell You*, "Home" is the critical presence: its making, the realities of what Munro finds at home in 1972, the authorial commentaries she includes in its first 1974 version, and its revision in 2001 and 2006 all portend the late style evident in *Castle Rock* and its two successor volumes. Pushing further, "Home" was followed by "Working for a Living," the memoir Munro wrote in the midst of her fecund rediscoveries of Ontario. Like "Home," it is a unique presence in *Castle Rock*, ending the first section, revised and expanded from its first appearance. It began as a straight fiction, was considered and rejected by the *New Yorker* in that form, became a memoir, and was passed over by the magazine in that guise, and was finally first published in the inaugural issue of *Grand Street* (see Thacker *Alice* 87–8, 315–16, 367–70).

Although Struthers respected Munro's request that he pass on a review of *74: New Canadian Stories* in the London *Free Press*, "Home" gleaned some attention when it first appeared. William French, then literary editor at the Toronto *Globe and Mail*, noted that Munro "makes use of a new technique in this story. Every so often she interpolates an italic paragraph or two in which she, as the writer and narrator, criticizes the story so far. It's an effective device." And, in 1979 when he reviewed Robert Laidlaw's historical novel, *The McGregors*, for the same paper, Timothy Findley not only called "Home" "an elegy in prose," he also writes that it reveals that "a daughter deserts her ailing father and his second wife and the scene of her childhood. She abandons all three—even the place—to their integrity and goes away to claim her own" (38.13.14). While at this distance in time it is easy for me to say, there was no abandonment beyond the literal, and even that is doubtful. Rather, in anticipating her father's death and describing his sufferings then, about four years before he died, Munro was claiming an integrity that would persist to the end of her career as a writer.

As French wrote in his review, notice of the "commentary voice"—as Munro called it herself—in "Home" was immediate.[5] The story was begun sometime during late 1973 with the draft title "Notes for a Work." "Home" opens with Munro traveling by three buses (Toronto-Kitchener, Kitchener-Stratford, and Stratford-Wingham) on a Friday for a weekend visit with her father and his second wife in Wingham; she accounts for her travels, describing her fellow passengers and the differences between the buses. And, as noted, as the third bus nears Wingham, she strives to see the landscapes around, "the unremarkable countryside I have always believed would be the last thing I cared to see in my life" (74: New 134).[6] In the first published version the days of her visit are recorded journal fashion, so in the Friday entry she describes in detail the home she grew up in and her father's and stepmother's situations there; after that, Munro then shifts to her commentary voice:

> *Too slow as usual, all that approach with the three buses and then the house, too much house with the wallpaper and plastic chair-cushion kind of thing, hardly anything yet about the people in it. Also the bit about Mother, who probably doesn't belong in this at all but I can't come within reach of her without being invaded by her, then trying to say too much too fast to get her finished with. Even now I am tempted to put in my dream about her.*
>
> (74: New 137; original emphasis)

Later Munro does put her dream about her mother in another commentary, one in which she finds her mother "*on her knees, painting the woodwork yellow. Didn't you know, I said to her that* [her stepmother] *is planning to paint this room mauve? Yes I do know, my mother said, but I thought if I hurried up and got it all done, she would leave it alone.*" She describes her Parkinsonian mother in the same terms she uses in "Winter Wind" and, though at an earlier moment in the progression of the disease, also in "The Ottawa Valley." Munro ends the dream sequence with her mother saying "*I'm dead you know, she said impatiently, painting*" and then steps back to offer an assessment as herself as author: "*I am not able to be the best of witnesses. I can only try to be well-disposed*" (74: New 149, 150; original emphasis). The uncertainty, or anguish, apparent here continues to the end of "Home." Munro accompanied her father to the Wingham hospital to have his heart problems assessed; he was admitted and things are not encouraging, so Munro stayed on into Monday. In a final commentary voice section, she introduces her stepsister who comes to help with the place in Robert Laidlaw's absence, and who tells her to go back to Toronto and to her life. Before she introduces her, Munro writes "*I don't know how to end this*" and then continues to describe "*the first scene I can establish as a true memory in my life*," watching her father milk one of their cows during the winter of 1934–5, an especially harsh one which, in fact, killed that particular cow (74: New 151, 152; original emphasis). Munro then ends "Home":

> *You can see this scene, can't you, you can see it quietly made, that magic and prosaic safety briefly held for us, the camera moving out and out, that spot shrinking, darkness. Yes. That is effective.*

> *I don't want any more effects, I tell you, lying. I don't know what I want. I want to do this honour, if I possibly can.*
>
> (74: *New* 153; original emphasis)

When she revised "Home" for its late 2001 republication, the version which, revised further, was published in *Castle Rock*, Munro was intent on deleting her commentary voice. In the revised versions the direct address to the reader is gone, but the first memory of watching her father milk the doomed cow remains. The last, three-sentence paragraph—an admission of artistic frustration—is gone as well. Yet here in 1974 these paragraphs, and the technique she used through the commentary voice, show Munro enveloped by the imaginative demands of her return to Ontario: "*that magic and prosaic safety briefly held for us ....*" She is seeking something more, and tentatively finds it in this remembered milking scene, but it does not satisfy. The year before Munro had published another story, "Material" (1973), like "Home" a story about how a writer struggles to achieve particular effects, and there she writes of "the marvelous clear jelly that [the writer] has spent all of his life learning how to make" (*Something* 43). That "clear jelly" is equivalent to "*the prosaic safety briefly held for us*" in the penultimate paragraph of the first "Home." Its effects are what Munro rejects, "*lying*," hoping to write, instead, as she said, "*with honour*." Seeking this different element in the newly confronted home material she found in 1972–3, Munro was intent on finding a new aesthetic.

"Winter Wind" is a story that is unique during this time because there is no manuscript material in Munro's papers; asked about this, she was initially perplexed, but then suggested that since its action had happened as described, it was easy to write for *Something* (Thacker interview April 2004). In it, she treats her paternal grandmother and great aunt—both widows living together, two figures who had already appeared in "The Peace of Utrecht" and were to appear again in "The Ticket." Doing so, the commentary voice again emerges:

> And how is anybody to know, I think as I put this down, how am I to know what I claim to know? I have used these people, not all of them, but some of them, before. I have tricked them out and altered them and shaped them any way at all, to suit my purposes. I am not doing that now, I am being as careful as I can, but I stop and wonder, I feel compunction.
>
> (*Something* 201; see *Castle Rock* 273–8)

As in "Home," here Munro points to her presence as the author, writing and wondering, and also by implication she questions the putative distinction between fiction and memoir.[7] The word Munro uses here, "wonder," will prove a frequent presence in her late style, a marker, most especially the last two books.

The end of "The Ottawa Valley," a story based on an actual trip Anne Chamney Laidlaw made with her daughters during summer 1942 to Scotch Corners in eastern Ontario near Carleton Place, where she had grown up, continues these recognitions. There Munro depicts a scene in which she first confronted her mother about Parkinson's. Munro remembers that and closes with a summative paragraph which begins, "If I had been making a proper story out of this, I would have ended it, I think, with my mother not answering and going across the pasture. That would have done" (*Something* 246). The questions Munro's mother did not answer were "'So, are you not going to get sick at all?'" and "'Is your arm going to stop shaking?'" But, as Munro writes in that final paragraph too, "she looms too close, just as she always did" and, continuing to the story's final sentence "[w]hich means she has stuck to me as close as ever and refused to fall away, and I could go on, and on, applying what skills I have, using what tricks I know, and it would always be the same" (*Something* 244, 246; see Thacker *Alice* 51, 72-3 and Ware "Tricks").[8]

These three memoir stories were written in 1973-4—Munro was then putting together *Something* for its spring 1974 publication, where both "Winter Wind" and "The Ottawa Valley" first appeared (see Thacker *Alice* 257-69). "Home," for its part, is dedicated to Munro's friend John Metcalf and dated November 12, 1973, in *74: New Canadian Stories*.[9] Together they are the first bookend to a period between late 1973 and the publication of *The Moons of Jupiter* in fall 1982 during which Munro should be understood sharply transforming her art. Having returned to Ontario and rediscovered her real material there, she probed it thoroughly and deeply, shaping stories that reached entirely new effects. While it is possible to point up several examples of how this happened, "Working for a Living," because of its provenance and its ultimate central presence in *Castle Rock*, is the best single example.

But before Munro got to the version of "Working" published as a memoir in 1981 she first took up and saw through the press as serials a succession of stories which then appeared in *Who Do You Think You Are?/The Beggar Maid*. Prominent among these were "Royal Beatings" and "The Beggar Maid" (1977), her first *New Yorker* stories. In 1976 Munro had hired the Virginia Barber literary agency to represent her and, having received several manuscript stories, Barber set to work placing them (see Thacker *Alice* 317-31, 336-52).[10] Quite apart from the textual details of Munro's publishing history during the late 1970s, the crucial fact then is that, in response to editorial interest that she had never really experienced before, Munro was transforming her work through her visceral response to the home place she had re-found. This response produced an outpouring of narrative: autobiographical fiction, imagined fiction, memoir. Following "Home" and the other 1974 memoir stories, it is clear that some part of this imaginative outpouring was occasioned by her father's death in early August 1976. The sense emerges that Munro was confronting an avalanche of remembrance and, writing it, continually shaping stories based on and in the culture she had herself emerged from. Munro was writing stories that became the material in *Who/Beggar* and, once she had pulled a former version of the book off the press for restructuring in fall 1978, she continued to shape that book in response to American editors as it became *The Beggar Maid*. Once that version of the book was completed and published in fall 1979, she had stories left over which were included in *The Moons of Jupiter*.[11]

"Working for a Living" was in this mix. It began as a fictional Janet story. That is, it appears to have been one of the stories intended for *Who* written by the first-person narrator named Janet who is a writer like Munro herself, with much the same personal history and with some career success. In the first version of *Who*—a version which still exists in a single reviewer's proof copy, a version which was the basis of two published reviews—there was a two-part structure whereby Janet the writer is revealed to have been the author of Rose and her story, made up of much of the material that forms the basis of *Who/Beggar* as eventually published. The two "Chaddeleys and Flemings" stories and "The Moons of Jupiter," autobiographical family stories, the last based on Robert Laidlaw's death, are Janet stories.

Thus one manuscript story version of "Working" begins:

> Janet quit college at the beginning of her final year, after a confrontation with the Bursar. She packed everything she owned into one bulging suitcase—it was the family suitcase, the one Janet's mother had bought for her honeymoon—and took the bus home. The bus left the college town in the late afternoon. A small delegation of Janet's friends came down to the bus depot with her.

"'What are you going to do?,' they said." In reply, Janet says, "Right now I'm going to get a job at the Turkey Barn. I can work there till Thanksgiving" (38.10.38.f1). Thus this version of "Working" bears a relation to "The Turkey Season" (1980; *Moons*).

There are connections too between the story version of "Working" and other Janet stories; she has a boyfriend named Richard whom she eventually marries and who appears in "Chaddeleys and Flemings: 1. Connection." Yet the focus of the story is on the stark contrast between the world of the intellect that Janet has been immersed in at the university and the lower-class, bare bones existence she had come from. Thus in another archival draft Janet ruminates on the effects of what she had just left at the university:

> Every corner of my mind was stuffed with what I had read. When the bus pulled into Dalgleish tonight, I had seen it with an emotion that owed something to Winesburg Ohio and quite a lot to Chekhov, though it was not like a little false-fronted Ohio town and surely less like a Russian village. It was a town of a special type found mostly in Western Ontario—red brick, spaciously and pretentiously built so that it would continue for a long time to look more prosperous than it was, but without either the sternness or grace of the older, eastern towns.
>
> (38.10.36.4.f4)

When she approaches her home after walking six blocks from the bus (and recognized and hooted at from a passing car), she sees her house: "Janet's house was the last one the left hand side; beyond it was a proper field, a corn field with the corn still standing, pale and dry. The house looked so poor, poorer than it had ever looked and more neglected. Everything that had been done to it had been wrong" (38.10.36.2. f1-2). This is Alice Laidlaw Munro's childhood home, the place which appears in numerous guises from her early work to "Dear Life."

When Munro finished "Working" as a story—the first version quoted above appears a clean, submission copy while the others are preliminary—she sent it to Barber who, in keeping with the right-of-first-refusal contract Munro had by then, submitted it to the *New Yorker*. It was rejected on March 28, 1979, McGrath noting that despite the excellent writing, "Janet was never as sympathetic as Alice probably intended her to be"

(*New Yorker* records; 916.17). For her part, Barber sent McGrath's letter on to Munro with the comment, "I'm letting it sit for a while, O.K.? It needs another go-around with you, I think, and as you said" (April 19, 1979; 38.2.63.23).

Throughout her career, and most especially during the late 1970s and into the '80s, Munro's habit was to work on several stories at the same time. Thus it is possible to see connections between the Janet story version of "Working" and "Chaddeleys and Flemings" and, looking forward, also to "The Turkey Season." Equally, it is possible to trace through the archives what Munro did when she turned back to reshape "Working." During the year between its rejection by the *New Yorker* and its resubmission as a memoir (March 27, 1980), Munro was at work on "Wood"—first published in the magazine in November 1980 but not included in a volume until *Too Much Happiness*, rewritten and reconsidered again and again—and she also wrote "Dulse," published there in July 1980.

The continuity between the two versions of "Working" is the narrator's sharp, even caustic, clear-sighted analysis of the life she was born into. In both cases it is analysis shorn of sentiment, especially so in the memoir. First evidence of that version in the archives is a holograph manuscript beginning, "This is the twenty-fourth of October, 1979. A couple of weeks ago my husband and I were driving home from Georgian Bay, through Bruce County. We live in Huron County just south of Bruce; the place where I was born forty-eight years ago almost on the border between the two counties" (38.12.3). This excerpt is found in a notebook in which "Working" is being written along with "Labor Day Dinner" (1982), a story first published in *Moons*, and other items. She continues, "At a crossroads there was a store, a tall narrow building, painted white, its height and narrowness emphasized by store windows with long, old-fashioned panes." Munro describes the place in more detail and then writes:

> As we passed this stand where the gas pumps had been I knew I had seen the store before and I knew when. Just before I knew I felt a chunk of something between my teeth, and a disappointment, a resolution not to be disappointed. The chunk was a chunk of ice, in an ice-cream cone which had more chunks in it; the ice-cream cone was bought in that store on a summer trip to Muskoka with my father, and the year was probably 1943. The reason that we were driving to Muskoka was that my mother was up there, at a summer hotel.
>
> (38.12.3)

These passages, dated and placed, form a central kernel to "Working for a Living," the memoir. Talking to her partner, who wonders why her father would have been so far from the main highway, Munro realizes that it was because their car was in such a sad state of repair that her father, fearing a breakdown, knew he had no business taking that car on the highway.

Quite different from the story version, the memoir "Working for a Living" is a moving tribute to Munro's parents' lives and marriage. In it, she captures her father's lifelong struggle to support his family, initially as a fox farmer; then, after his wife had declined, as a caretaker at the Wingham foundry; and then eventually to his time raising turkeys. When she revised it for *Castle Rock*, Munro added Robert Laidlaw's near-the-end-of-life accomplishments as a writer. And while the memoir has more to say about her father than her mother, Anne Chamney Laidlaw is depicted as largely illness-free and triumphant. An ambitious woman, Munro's mother went to that upscale Muskoka hotel to sell fur wraps and scarves from their farm to American tourists personally, obtaining better profit from them and using her own skills; it was a key moment in her life. For the Laidlaws, she *had* to succeed, for they had so little money they would have had trouble getting home. But she did.

Throughout the narrative too Munro tells much about her family's history. She also features a scene—one shared with the story version of "Working"—when the narrator (Janet or Alice) is sent with a message for her father while he works at the foundry; there, he gives his daughter a tour of the plant, allowing her to contemplate how that work fits into his life. He worked the second shift and, as Munro recounts in an archival typescript, he "also told me that one night not long after he started working at the Foundry he came out at twelve o'clock or so and found a great snowstorm in progress. The roads were full, the snow ploughs would not be out till dawn. He had to leave the car where it was" and "walk home." She continues:

> He felt dragged down, pushing against the storm, and about a quarter of a mile from home he found he wasn't moving. He was standing in the middle of a drift, and he could not move his legs. He could hardly stand against the wind. The storms that come on this country off Lake Huron are momentous productions, they bury the roads and fences, and curl drifts up to the porch eaves, and whip the bare trees around and howl across the open fields; it will rattle and blind you. He was worn out. He thought perhaps his heart was giving out. Then he thought of his death.
>
> (38.10.41.f24-25)

This incident is recounted just before the memoir's final summative paragraph when it was first published in 1981, but in *Castle Rock* the account of Laidlaw's writing was also included. After this passage Laidlaw thinks too of the parlous state of his family, and Munro added something else. Hearing him tell his thoughts in the storm, she wondered if then he had not thought about his own life: "I meant, was his life now something that only other people had a use for?" (*Grand Street* 37).

As it happened, on the same manuscript page just quoted (f25), Munro wrote, "Edith Lewis" and "A Lost Lady," the first the name of Willa Cather's life companion, the second the title of a 1923 novel Cather wrote in part on Grand Manan, New Brunswick, where "Dulse" is set. Each figures there, in a story Munro was also writing then (see Thacker *Reading* 115–31). Receiving and acknowledging both the revised "Working" and "Dulse" from Munro, Virginia Barber wrote to her:

> I sense a new style in this "stuff" you've sent—plainer, bare of metaphor, but with rhythms so strong that I feel safer than I've felt in years. Your sentences always treat the reader so well—no manhandling, no tricks, no dead falls. Not that there is anything placid or safe about the stories. There's that grief in "Dulse" that suddenly springs out and bowls you over. Or "was his life now something that that only

other people had a use for." I hadn't thought about that. I'm not going to go on except to say what fun, and thanks. They're wonderful stories.

(March 27, 1980; 38.2.63.43)[12]

Barber was writing this response—one that is certainly apt, prescient, and holds up—on the same day that she submitted both pieces to the *New Yorker*. Its editors bought "Dulse" and, once again, rejected "Working." Doing so in a letter to Barber, McGrath explains their decision through much the same sentiments he used when they rejected "Chaddeleys and Flemings" (November 1, 1977; 37.2.30.5). His own critique is worth noting:

> Well, I'm afraid that the final decision here has gone against Alice's WORKING FOR A LIVING. This is mostly just a matter of policy, though, and in no way a reflection on what she's done here. As far as I'm concerned, this piece is a considerable achievement: It's lively, touching, and beautifully written. But the trouble—for us, I mean—is that not only is this a memoir, but in tone and form and style it's a kind of <u>classic</u>, or completely traditional, one: exactly the kind of piece, that is, that we did so much of in the past and are now over-compensating for.
>
> Anyway, I'm sorry about this, and I hope you will pass my regret on to Alice. It's some consolation to me—and I hope it will be to her—that we already have DULSE, and I also suspect that you'll be able to sell this in a second somewhere else.
>
> (April 9, 1980; *New Yorker* records 927.17)

After she offered her responses to "Dulse" and "Working" quoted above, Barber then wrote in a separate paragraph: "I hope you'll write more 'memoir.' A book. Have you thought about it?" (March 27, 1980; 38.2.63.43). That was just what Munro was thinking about and, very clearly, "Working for a Living," the memoir, was to be a foundational part of her project.

Although there is no evidence of its submission by Barber to other serials before it got to *Grand Street*, Munro did have an exchange with Robert Weaver as an editor of the *Tamarack Review*—the Canadian literary quarterly Munro had published in since 1957 and was quite loyal to—about it. Evidently Weaver had written to her asking for a submission for its final issue, since the editors had decided to cease publication. Munro responded to his inquiry:

> I'll write to Ginger … and tell her about the offer, also my particular reasons for wanting the story to go to Tamarack. But—I forgot—it is *not really a story*. Its a Memoir & its quite long, so you might well decide not to use it. I think myself its part of a book I'll do after the one I'm on now. Its nice but a bit flat for a story, also the material pretty familiar to my Canadian readers. There are a couple of stories the N.Yer also rejected (that doesn't mean they're not as good, in my view, as the ones they've taken). I could tell her to let you see those too, if she hasn't sold them yet (the Memoir I think she's given up on).
>
> (October 14, 1980; Robert Weaver Fonds M631 D162.12)

Munro was wrong about that last comment, but when Barber got her letter she replied, "O. K., we will send Tamarack Review 'Working for a Living,' but I'm not happy about that. The piece deserves a Universal Showcase, and our failure to sell it has been a real frustration for us" (October 23, 1980; 38.2.63.52). These sentiments notwithstanding, and whether or not Weaver wanted to publish "Working," Barber sold it to *Grand Street* for its inaugural issue. For his part, Weaver published Munro's "Mrs. Cross and Mrs. Kidd" (*Moons*), a story which had been rejected by the *New Yorker* earlier in 1980, as the lead piece in its final issue.

The day before Munro wrote to Weaver about "Working" she had written to Douglas Gibson, her editor at Macmillan of Canada, about the stories she had on hand that could make up her next book. She describes "Accident" and the three stories left over from *Who/Beggar Maid* as being "from olden days"; she also has "the five New Yorker stories"; and two "yet unpublished stories." Throughout, she assesses the length of each story. Continuing, Munro writes:

> [S]o these ten stories quite definitely have enough length for a book. There is also a long Memoir I wrote about my father, which I think is pretty good, but I think it should be kept out for a kind of family book I want to do someday—maybe about the Laidlaws in Huron County and in Ettrick & James Hogg whose mother was a Laidlaw. There's a whole lot of interesting stuff about the family, who seem to have been story-tellers since the Middle Ages. I know people going on about their families can be very tiresome but *maybe* I can do something unexpected with it.
>
> (October 13, 1980; Macmillan 429.4)

Gibson, who is from Scotland and who was the person to whom she dedicated that book, was understandably drawn to the idea. In his reply to Munro's letter he is evidently quite interested in it, ending, "And please don't feel apologetic about it; the process you describe as 'people going on about their families' has produced some of the world's greatest books" (October 31, 1980; Macmillan 429.4).

The notebook draft of "Working for a Living" which began on the 24th of October 1979 continues beyond Munro's recognition of the store where her father bought her an unsatisfactory ice-cream cone on their way to pick up her mother at a hotel in Port Carling (she names that place too); it treats their fox-farming business in Wingham begun after their marriage and, significantly here, it retells the Laidlaw family's emigration from Scotland to Ontario and Huron County—the same story summarized in "Chaddeleys and Flemings: 2. The Stone in the Field." It then continues to detail her paternal grandparents' marriage and life and then gets to her father himself, why he was as he was. Most of this is included in the memoir "Working," though not much of the detail from the 1818 immigration voyage is there.

In that same notebook draft there is a holograph page—two paragraphs in all—immediately following the material I have just described. Munro may have seen it as continuing what she had written there or, equally plausibly, it may be a new section beginning within "Working" or the start of an altogether new piece. In any case, these paragraphs, probably written in late 1979, point clearly to the imaginative direction that Munro would ultimately pursue in *The View from Castle Rock* and its successor volumes. Here is what is on that holograph page:

> Most people from ordinary families can't go back beyond a few generations, can't even claim a place, though usually they know the country, where their people would be living in, say, the sixteenth century. Its easier for me to say people than ancestors; ancestors is too heavy a word; it means men and women who had themselves photographed or even painted, wrote letters, diaries, homilies, are settled under tombstones. No picture was ever made of these people and I have evidence that those in the direct line were not used to reading and writing. Some could do it, some couldn't. The reason I know anything at all about them is that one of them, William Laidlaw, could read and write well enough to make that his profession; that is, he became a secretary. He worked for Sir Walter Scott. Kenilworth is dedicated to him.
> There is a good deal about William Laidlaw and his family in Lockharts Life of Scott. Lockhart was Scott's son in law, he wrote his *Life* in
>
> (38.12.3)

The passage breaks off here. Ending it, Munro points to the researches she would take up that led her toward *Castle Rock* over the next twenty-five years.

"Its Hard to Know What I Expected to Find in Scotland": "Hold Me Fast, Don't Let Me Pass" (1988)

When *Castle Rock* was published, and subsequently looking back on that book as they took up Munro's final volumes, reviewers offered phrasings that sharply assert her methods within it. In *The Atlantic*, Deborah Eisenberg reacted by writing that "this amalgam of history, fiction, and memoir is unlike any historical fiction or autobiographical fiction that I have ever encountered," and continued observing that this "book looks simultaneously back and forward, even beyond the confines of its own end, seeking to divine the place and internal experience of certain individuals, including the author herself, within history and passing time." Tessa Hadley, in the *London Review of Books*, strikes the same note when she writes of Munro, "Without ever losing her focus on these other, past lives, she also seems to be giving us a magical account of her own life in writing, tracing a history for her imagination." Also continuing and better yet, Hadley writes that, for Munro, Scotland's Ettrick Valley, down along the border land where Munro's "people" came from,

> begins to seem one of those uncanny spots where the skin between ordinary life and story is more than usually permeable. Through being imagined intensely enough, it becomes a signifying somewhere, a fitting place for a writer of Munro's stature and provenance to project her beginning, connecting herself with a long tradition of gifts that have sprung up fresh at the margins of organised, urbanized cultural life.
>
> (17)

And three years later while beginning a review of *Too Much Happiness* in the *Times Literary Supplement*, Michael Gorra comments in passing, "I suspect that with time *The View from Castle Rock* will stand as something like her *Enigma of Arrival*" ("Mortal" 3). Gorra is aptly comparing Munro's book to V. S. Naipaul's 1987 novel of that title. This sharp and prescient comment echoes another Gorra made about a decade before, relevant here, when he was reviewing Munro's *The Love of a Good Woman* (1998): "[N]ever before has she seemed so autumnal, so concerned with mediating between the way we live now and the way we lived then" ("Crossing" 6).

A signifying somewhere, Scotland's Ettrick Valley. Her *Enigma of Arrival*, her book *The View from Castle Rock*. *Never before has she seemed so autumnal*. Though written for other contexts, these phrasings nevertheless direct us from the outpourings of singular writing that included and followed *Who Do You Think You Are?/The Beggar Maid*, most especially the shaping of both versions of "Working for a Living," toward the making of *Castle Rock* and to the shaping of her late style as primary consequence of that book's structuring and effect.

In 1979, having received for the second time the Canada-Australia Literary Award, and having traveled there under its auspices, Munro told an Australian journalist, "I want to see Europe" (Riddell). Her first chance to do so came in January–February 1982 when she went first to Scotland and England on her own and then, joined by Fremlin, toured Norway, Sweden, and Denmark in connection with the publication of the Norwegian translation of *The Beggar Maid*. In Scotland Munro gave a memorable reading in Dundee—memorable because the Scots, her "kind of people," she wrote wryly to a friend the day after, refused to laugh when she expected them to (Munro to Robert Kroetsch January 29, 1982; 591.96.6.9.46). The next day she read the same story in Leeds and there, she recalled over twenty years later, the audience laughed at the same point. "'The English were enjoying it. What's wrong with the Scots?,' she asked" as she recounted the occasion to a journalist (Ross R1). Telling me the same story in August 2001, Munro commented that the Scots in Dundee "just reminded me so much of home, because I'm of Scottish stock, and it's the way we behave. You're not going to make me laugh, I don't think that's funny" (Thacker interview).

During that trip too Munro made her way to Selkirk in the Ettrick Valley to see the place her people came from and, doing so, she was embarked on the direct investigations which would produce *Castle Rock*. Given Munro's working methods, with story following upon story, there is an archival trail to follow. Ironically that trail begins in Ireland, not Scotland, for in the midst of her late 1970s outpouring Munro researched and produced a television script depicting Irish emigration to Canada, *1847: The Irish*, broadcast as part of a series called *The Newcomers/Les arrivants* on CBC television in January 1978; it was published as a story in the volume associated with the series (see Thacker *Alice* 304; *Reading* 217–26). Each version anticipates the historical material which forms the basis of *Castle Rock*, but Munro then had yet to discover that material through her investigations of the Scottish Laidlaw side of her family. While well aware of it as a living inheritance in Huron County, as she had said and written, the historical detail of that inheritance lay largely inchoate when she arrived in Selkirk in the Ettrick Valley for her first visit at the end of January or in early February 1982.

Two stories Munro published in *Friend of My Youth* are key: "Hold Me Fast, Don't Let Me Pass" and "Friend of My Youth" (1990). In quite fundamental ways, each defines and points toward the making of *Castle Rock*. In 1974 or earlier, as Magdalene Redekop first noted in 1998 in the best early treatment of Munro's Scots connections, Munro makes a reference in "Something I've Been Meaning to Tell You" to a "Scottish ballad singer" who was performing at a resort hotel along Lake Huron (*Something* 9). Key to "Hold Me Fast, Don't Let Me Pass" is the ballad "Tam Lin," which is recited in its entirety by one character in the story and, later, reprised by another. When Munro arrived in Selkirk in 1982, it is reasonable to surmise that she was very much like her protagonist, Hazel, in that she checked into her hotel and immediately embarked on a "couple of hours' walk," returning to write her impressions in a notebook just as Hazel does at the outset of the story. They read in part, beginning:

> *Ruins of 'Kirk of the Forest.' Old graveyard, William Wallace declared Guardian of Scotland here, 1298.*
> *Courthouse where Sir Walter Scott dispensed judgment, 1799–1832. Philiphaugh? 1645.*
> *Gray town. Some old gray stone like Edinburgh. Also grayish brown stucco, not so old. Library once the jail (gaol).*
>
> (*Friend* 75, 74; original emphasis)

Munro completes the notes and then turns to Hazel who, she writes,

> was a widow. She was in her fifties, and she taught biology in the high school in Walley, Ontario. This year she was on a leave of absence. She was a person you would not be surprised to find sitting by herself in a corner of the world where she didn't belong, writing things in a notebook to prevent the rise of panic.
>
> (*Friend* 75)

Hazel has traveled to Ettrick to see it and perhaps connect with Margaret Dobie, an elderly cousin of her husband's whom he visited when he was a bomber pilot during the war. She does not know if Dobie is still alive but wants nevertheless to visit the place Jack spoke so much about. He had no desire to return after the war. Ironically, the first person Hazel meets after stepping into the Royal Hotel there was Antoinette, its owner, who had been Jack's girlfriend years ago.

Leaving the story to one side momentarily, I want to return briefly to its beginnings. When Munro visited Selkirk in 1982, she has said, "the innkeeper did take me out to visit this old lady" who recited "Tam Lin" to her: "[T]he poem is one that was really recited to me. It's a fairly well-known ballad" (Thacker interview April 2004). Although Hazel is in some respects similar to Munro herself—given her age and the fact that Fremlin was a bomb aimer in the Royal Canadian Air Force stationed in England, 1942–5, and flew thirty-seven operations—she is essentially a fictional character. As is Margaret Dobie, the old woman in the story who recites the whole of "Tam Lin" (see Martin and Ober "'Tam Lin'").

Archival evidence reveals that this story began differently than it was concluded. Instead of a quest connected to a dead husband, in a notebook draft Munro wrote during the 1980s—there are connections to "White Dump" and other stories included in *The Progress of Love*—the initial narrator is a Canadian teacher who visits Ettrick after spending time in Stockholm and Edinburgh with a lover, a married man who goes off to London to meet his family while she takes "a one o'clock bus for a Bordertown," to "a place in Selkirk." There she is seeking information on James McMurchie, a Canadian poet and novelist who was born in Scotland, came to Canada at twenty-five and died in the Spanish Flu pandemic in 1918. The narrator writes that she "was going down to the Borders to try to see an old woman, the sister of a writer I am working on." The woman, never married and ninety-four years old, had not replied to the narrator's letters. Munro sketches out a plausible literary career for McMurchie and, most particularly, describes the narrator's motives and her curiosity over his life, in both Scotland and Canada.

"Its hard to know what I expected to find in Scotland," she writes amid these explanations. Elaborating, the narrator imagines finding "[a]n early diary, heaps of letters home, the story of a love-affair that sent him packing in the first place. As is usual in treasure hunts, I hoped for something that couldn't really be expected, or even put into words" (Green Coil Notebook, 396/87.3: 6.6).[13] Having arrived on the Borders, the narrator goes to the local library where she sketches the location of Catherine McMurchie's house seven miles away and reads "about the history of the town and the county." Continuing, Munro elaborates her characters', and her own, position as she discovers the history of the Borders:

> The events I read about were bloody and desperate. I come from a part of Canada where local history means the date of the establishment of the flour mill and names of the first members of the Anglican Ladies Guild. I knew that the history of the Borders was quite another matter but it was still surprising to read, for instance, how the citizens of this town had ripped the thatch from their houses, thrown it into the streets and set it ablaze, one day in the 1300's when they were being besieged by the English, or—at another skirmish—a headless English Captain's body was borne by his horse through the Scottish ranks, scaring them into flight. Ballad verses kept cropping up, most of them dolorous but some fairly ecstatic about various killings. Love was just about always consummated by the joining of the streams of life blood from the brave true breast of the lovers or by their dust mingling in the one grave.
>
> (Yellow Coil Notebook, 396/87.3: 6.4)

"Its hard to know what I expected to find in Scotland," Munro wrote: this distant history is part of her attraction, judging by the trajectory she embarked upon here in the early 1980s and of which this story, "Hold Me Fast, Don't Me Pass," is the first concrete manifestation. But there is more to her search than narrative history. Ultimately in the published story the first-person narrator seeking information on a dead writer drops away, as does the affair. These are replaced by the visiting Hazel seeking to discover

Ettrick and to understand better the circumstances then of her husband Jack, who told Hazel of his wartime visits there and of his girlfriend Antoinette. That person lives on but denies any knowledge of that relation through venality, for she claims to have been a little girl during the war. Antoinette is now in the present of the story, herself, and has been in a long-term relationship with Dudley Brown, a solicitor. Spending a week in Selkirk and near Carterhaugh, at the junction of the Ettrick and Yarrow rivers, Hazel discovers a love triangle involving Antoinette and Dudley and Judy Armstrong, a young woman whose illegitimate daughter Dudley fathered. Yet at the core of "Hold Me Fast, Don't Let Me Pass" are Hazel's own reasons for traveling to Ettrick and, even more, Margaret Dobie's recitation of the whole of "Tam Lin" within the story and, afterward, Dudley's own repetition of the ballad itself for Hazel alone after she had heard Dobie's recitation that day.

As W. R. Martin and Warren U. Ober comment, "Though Jack was largely responsible for the lack of fulfillment in their marriage, Hazel herself appears to be aware of a shade of guilt for failing to hold him fast, and her trip to Scotland seems to be a kind of homage, a sort of restitution". Both in "Tam Lin" and in Munro's story, they assert, the characters "are divided between two worlds, the one vital and alive, the other unfulfilling and sterile," yet in her version she creates "a striking ironic reversal in which Munro turns the ballad upside down" ("Hold" 47, 45). This is what is found in Dobie's recitation and in Dudley's reprise, and it is part of what Munro found in Scotland that first time she visited when someone there recited "Tam Lin" to her.

The day's visit over, Hazel meets Dudley in the hotel's lounge and explains Antoinette's absence. Antoinette effected the visit so that Dudley, who had at first volunteered to take Hazel, did not go—either because she was preventing his visit on her own or because of their relation, with his acquiescence, so that he did not see Judy, who evidently expected him by her dress and manner during the visit. When Dudley asked how Miss Dobie had entertained them, Hazel replies, "'She recited a long poem,'" and he corrects, "'Ballads, they're rightly called, not poems,'" and asks which one. Hazel considers mentioning those lines she remembers "concerning the maidenhead" but rejects them "as too crudely malicious" and finds others. He recognizes "Tam Lin" and responds, "'But hold me fast, don't let me pass,' Dudley cried, very pleased. 'I'll be your bairn's father!'" (*Friend* 100). The scene continues:

> Indeed, he threw himself back in his chair, looking released, and lifted his head and started reciting—the same poem that Miss Dobie had recited, but spoken with calm relish now, and with style, in a warm, sad, splendid male voice. His accent broadened, but, having absorbed a good deal of the poem once already, almost against her will, Hazel was able to make out every word. The boy captured by fairies, living a life of adventures and advantages—not able to feel pain, for one thing—but growing wary as he grows older, scared of 'paying the teint to hell,' and longing for a human climate, so seducing a bold girl and instructing her how she can get him free. She has to do it by holding on to him, holding on no matter what horror the fairies can change him into, holding on until all their tricks are exhausted, and they let him go. Of course Dudley's style was old-fashioned, of

course he mocked himself, a little. But that was only on the surface. This reciting was like singing. You could parade your longing without fear of making a fool of yourself.

"*They shaped him in her arms at last,*
A mother-naked man;
She wrapt him in her green mantle,
And so her true love wan!"
You and Miss Dobie, you are a pair.

(*Friend* 100–1; original emphasis)

Just after this there is a moment of real sexual attraction between these two that she acknowledges: "Hazel could feel something, as if a cat jumped into her lap. Sex." But "all that was beyond them at present. They would let the attraction wash over them and ebb away" (*Friend* 102).

Yet there is more in the imaginative explosion that is "Hold Me Fast." Just as Munro knew when she was writing "Working for a Living" that one of her ancestors, William Laidlaw, worked for Sir Walter Scott as secretary and steward, she also knew that another one, James Hogg, the "Ettrick Shepherd" also assisted Scott with the gathering and in the transcriptions of oral ballads in *The Minstrelsy of the Scottish Border* (1802), the version Munro relies on for her quotations from "Tam Lin" in "Hold Me Fast." Hogg figures too in *Castle Rock*, where his mother "Margaret Laidlaw made a great fuss when she saw the book Scott produced in 1802 with her contributions in it," as Munro writes. "'They were made for singin and no for prentin,' she is supposed to have said. 'And noo they'll never be sung mair'" (*Castle Rock* 22).

Magdalene Redekop, treating "Hold Me Fast" with clarity, argues that Hazel's visit of homage or restitution (as Martin and Ober write) "stages" what she calls "the Scottish nostalgic grotesque as a tourist destination. In an astonishingly bold gesture, Munro reinstates the figure of the ballad transmitter eliminated by the ballad collectors. The effect, for me at least, is a kind of extratextual scene of recognition." By this insight Redekop gets right at what Munro was doing with her first Scots story: a writer never sentimental in her treatment of biographical or historical information, Munro created Margaret Dobie and her recitation of "Tam Lin" as a way of reinstating the presence of Margaret Laidlaw: "As the story moves around the central figure [of Dobie] … there is a gradual recognition of the importance of the figure" (35; see also Ventura "Female Bard").

This is so and, altogether, it is what Hazel discovers through her experiences in Selkirk. Having realized the facts of the Antoinette-Dudley-Judy triangle, having heard both Margaret Dobie's recitation of "Tam Lin" and Dudley's full-throated reprise of it, one he knows applies to his own circumstances, Hazel could see that "the ballad had stirred and eased his heart." "'What am I to do?' Dudley asks, 'I can't make two women happy.' A statement that might have been thought fatuous, conceited, evasive. Yet it was true. Hazel was stopped. It was true." Judy had a claim, but so did Antoinette, she realizes. "So had Antoinette foiled him today for his own good? That was the way she must see it—the way he might see it, too, after a little while. Even now, perhaps—now that the ballad had stirred and eased his heart" (*Friend* 103).

The story ends with Hazel recalling a moment when, years ago, driving by Jack's place of business she happened to see him "looking out the front window of the appliance store. He wasn't looking in her direction, he didn't see the car." "She noticed Jack—how slim and youthful he looked, in his slacks and pullover—how gray and insubstantial." Munro details things about him that Hazel didn't notice then but, recalling this moment, sees now from Scotland.

> A life of chores, routines, seasons, pleasantries. All she saw was the stillness about him, a look you could have called ghostly. She saw that his handsomeness—a particular Second World War handsomeness, she felt, with a wisecracking edge to it and a proud passivity—was still intact but drained of power. A ghostly sweetness was what she showed her, through the glass.

Munro then starts a new paragraph, writing "she could be striving toward him, now as much as then" (*Friend* 104).

"Hold Me Fast, Don't Let Me Pass" does not end with these words; the paragraph continues to describe Hazel's musings in Scotland, thinking of herself as she was then, against as she is now. Thinking more like this "would be like testing the pain in a lost limb. A quick test, a twinge that brings the whole shape into the air. That would be enough" (*Friend* 104). Even then, Munro is not done, for Hazel thinks that she might say to Dudley "that perhaps he *was* making those two women happy" "giving them something to concentrate on," "that sort of thing will make you pay attention, even when you've taught yourself not to. Could it be said to make you happy?" (*Friend* 104–5; original emphasis). This question is asked rhetorically, by Hazel certainly, but also by Munro, who ends the story with a whimsical joke attributable to both women, wondering "what makes a man happy?": "It must be something quite different" (*Friend* 105). Mary Jo Salter, reviewing *Friend of My Youth*, singles out this question and calls it "a door boldly opened into another room" while pronouncing "Hold Me Fast" an "intricately designed mansion of a story" (53).

By the time the completed "Hold Me Fast" was submitted to the *New Yorker* in January 1988, Munro had become one of its regulars and was, pretty clearly then, on a tear. Eight of the ten stories in *Friend of My Youth* first appeared in the *New Yorker* while the other two, having been seen and rejected there, were taken by the *Atlantic Monthly*. One of the latter was "Hold Me Fast, Don't Let Me Pass." As it happened, this was the first story handled by Munro's new editor at the *New Yorker*, Daniel Menaker, who wrote to her on January 18, 1988, expressing delight at the assignment, making some comments, mostly positive but not entirely so, on another story they had just bought, and delivering the bad news regarding "Hold Me Fast." Summarizing the editors' assessment of the story, Menaker wrote that "it seemed to us a little contrived, in part because we weren't sure what Helen [an earlier name] was after on this mission back into her husband's past." Because of that uncertainty, "the triangle she uncovers also seemed a little artificial. And the business about the ballad may be a little protracted, for the story's length, and the coincidence between the verse's content and the matter of the story may be a little too happy." But he then offers a chance that the *New Yorker* seldom does: "If you'd like to have another go at HOLD ME FAST … we would of course be more than pleased to see it again" (original ellipsis).[14] Munro did revise the story, since Barber resubmitted it on March 25, 1988, but on April 5 Menaker wrote to Barber telling her that "our decision has gone against Alice Munro's HOLD ME FAST once again. I'm very sorry—we felt that she had solved some of the difficulties we had with the piece but that it remained plotty and over-complicated" (752/04.3:1.8; see Thacker *Alice* 319–21, 444–51).[15]

That everything Hazel experiences in Scotland leads her back to Jack, and to her now gone life with him in Walley while she was married to him after he had come back from the war, points to Munro's recursions and to ways she ends her stories. Hazel's memory of her moment seeing Jack staring out the appliance-store window while she was busy with her college studies on her way to becoming a teacher in midlife represents something of an epiphany, and certainly that scene is also a fulcrum point. Earlier Hazel, sizing up the Antoinette she finds in Scotland and comparing her to the memories of his young girlfriend, "a cozy bundle," whom Jack had told her about, thinks "But how much would you find in Hazel," she wonders, "of the girl Jack had taken home from the dance?" (*Friend* 82) when they first met. Thinking back to the life she then led with him, to the person who knew—as it had been made clear with the notes she took as the story opens—that "panic was a problem at dusk" (*Friend* 75). Focalizing Hazel's thoughts, Munro details another revelatory moment years before, while Jack was still living and when, having taken to her bed with a breakdown, Hazel "broke open the shell of her increasingly doubtful and expensive prettiness; she got out." She "took hold of her life"; "having her breakdown," Hazel "knew that when she had got out of bed (this is what she doesn't say), she was leaving some part of herself behind. She suspected that this was a part that had to do with Jack" (*Friend* 82, 83). She then transformed herself from wife and mother to first a student and then a biology teacher. Her life with Jack was, Munro makes clear with Hazel's years-later recollection of him staring out of that window, recalled in the story's present in Scotland as the story ends, obviated. Yet, thinking of that Jack now, "[a]ll she saw was the stillness about him, a look you could have called ghostly" (*Friend* 104). This moment is Hazel's final fulcrum: "Hold Me Fast, Don't Let Me Pass" effectively ends with it and it shapes everything that a reader knows.

I have gone into some detail regarding "Hold Me Fast" here because the very things that Menaker and the other editors at the *New Yorker* were troubled by were also, however well taken for their own editorial purposes, just what most interested Munro and were most clearly defining the path she was then taking. There Ettrick specifically and Scotland more broadly were together "a signifying somewhere," an "enigma" to be solved. What is more, however "plotty and over-complicated" "Hold Me Fast" remained, the process of its writing and revision moved Munro along within the Scottish materials she was discovering. Retrospectively seen, Munro was creating a new level of complexity that would prove to be, once that Scots material was distilled, the basis of *Castle Rock* and of her late style. The next story, "Friend of My Youth," one the *New Yorker* accepted with alacrity and enthusiasm, both continued her Scottish elaborations and brought them home to Ontario's Ottawa Valley and to Huron County.

"Friend of My Youth," the Cameronians in Ontario, and a Return to the Borders

"Friend of My Youth" is very much part of Munro's progression of stories about her mother which began with "The Peace of Utrecht." In crucial ways, it also extends Munro's deepening understanding of her own Scots connections following as it does right after "Hold Me Fast." Arguably, a key connection between the two stories is evident in the reading that the draft "Hold Me Fast" narrator does in the local library in which the "events ... read about were bloody and desperate," a place and time when "Ballad verses kept cropping up, most of them dolorous but some fairly ecstatic about various killings."

"Friend of My Youth" depicts a narrator who, in her recollections, looks very much like the young Alice Laidlaw still living at home and, as the eldest daughter in the family, dealing daily with her mother's precipitate illness. Its substance focuses on what Eric Reeves has called the "competing, dueling narratives of mother and daughter concerning Flora," the titular friend of the mother's youth, a person she boarded with and learned the history of in the Ottawa Valley years before when she was a teacher there and was about to be married. Of especial interest is that Flora and her family belonged to a Scots Protestant sect called the Cameronians (Reformed Presbyterians), and the story deals with their beliefs and practices.

Two aspects are particularly significant here: its dedication and its ending. When it was published in *Friend of My Youth* in 1990 the story was dedicated "With thanks to R.J.T.," and in every version of it that I have seen—admittedly just the typescript submission that went to the *New Yorker* dated February 26, 1989, followed by magazine proof versions (752/04.3.3.2)—it ends with this paragraph after a white-space break:

> The Cameronians, I have discovered, are or were an uncompromising remnant of the Covenanters—those Scots who in the seventeenth century bound themselves, with God, to resist prayer books, bishops, any taint of popery or interference by the King. Their name comes from Richard Cameron, an outlawed, or 'field' preacher, soon cut down. The Cameronians—for a long time they have preferred to be called the Reformed Presbyterians—went into battle singing the seventy-fourth and the seventy-eighth Psalms. They hacked the haughty Bishop of St. Andrews to death on the highway and rode their horses over his body. One of their ministers, in a mood of firm rejoicing at his own hanging, excommunicated all the other preachers in the world.
>
> (*Friend* 26)[16]

Such historical details motivated by religion echo those the draft narrator of "Hold Me Fast" learns and, as well, remind readers that the Ettrick place Hazel visits was the site of equally horrific scenes. Thus she writes in the notes that open the story, "*Philiphaugh? 1645.*" During the Wars of the Three Kingdoms on September 13, 1645, the Covenanters won a decisive battle over the Royalists at Philiphaugh near Selkirk and, afterwards, as Munro recounts it in "Hold Me Fast" through Dudley speaking to Hazel after her visit to Margaret Dobie,

> The Covenanters hanged all their prisoners. Right out there in the town square, under the dining-room windows. Then they butchered the women and children on the field. A lot of families traveled with [the Royalist] Montrose's army, because so many were Irish mercenaries. Catholics, of course. No—they didn't butcher all of them. Some they marched up toward Edinburgh. But on the way they decided to march them off a bridge.
>
> (*Friend* 86)

Yet rather than taking a character off to Scotland in "Friend of My Youth," Munro brought the Cameronians and their beliefs, and so Scots history, into her story, and into her mother's story too. Thus the dedication and thanks to R. J. T.—Reg Thompson, a long-time friend of both Munro and Fremlin, a librarian in Goderich with a deep interest in local history and, most significant here, a person with roots in Lanark County, near Almonte, in eastern Ontario. Munro's mother came from Scotch Corners in Beckwith Township there, she taught at the James school away from home (1919-21), and during that time befriended Thompson's Aunt Alice and began a lifelong friendship with her. In fact, Alice Ann Laidlaw was named after Alice Mary Thompson.

That woman's nephew recalls telling Munro of a reception his parents gave once "to acknowledge the marriage of a well-known man in the community, who had suddenly in middle age wed and brought his bride into the neighbourhood. This was a surprising event. The couple were both mature folks." Continuing, Thompson explains the contexts further, just as he explained them to Munro and Fremlin: "The man was the only son of an old family, which consisted of him and three sisters." "These people were members of the Reformed Presbyterian church. A congregation was based in Almonte, about two miles from the 7th Line of Ramsay, where [this family] were our closest neighbours, next farm to ours. We knew them well. They preferred to call themselves Reformed Presbyterians. Everybody else called them the Cameronians." They were "strict in their activities. No work on Sunday (other than a necessity such as feeding and milking the cows). No dancing. No card playing." Because the guest of honor would not play cards, Thompson's parents arranged for crokinole, a game Munro mentions in the story. Thompson also told some history of the Cameronians and

> [t]alking to Alice and Gerry about the party and the … family personalities and events, I went on rambling about another marriage, one of the sisters. Some years earlier. A fellow had come to be a live-in hired man. He was supposed to be the fiancé of one sister, but then got the elder sister pregnant, so he had to marry her instead.

While these people did not continue to live in that same house—as in the story—they did have "one daughter, and several miscarriages" with no further surviving children

(Thompson). Other details in the story—the dividing of the house, its improvement once Audrey Atkinson married Robert and supplanted Flora's hopes after Ellie finally dies, "a poor botched body, a failed childbearer" (*Friend* 22)—Munro gleaned from other stories Thompson and others had told her about life in the Ottawa Valley.[17] Imagining and adapting her own connections from the stories she had been told, Munro shaped them into her own version.

But what "Friend of My Youth" is really about is what Reeves calls the "competing, dueling narratives of mother and daughter concerning Flora," the twice-supplanted sister. Because Flora is her mother's friend of her youth, the narrator depends on her mother's recollections for the details of Flora's circumstances years ago and so, herself, is seen wondering throughout the narrative as to just what motivated these particular Cameronians. She thinks about Flora especially amid Ellie's decline to death. Flora helped the hired man Robert divide the house into two living sections after the rushed wedding was held at the manse when it became clear that he had impregnated Ellie, although he was betrothed to Flora. That division was in anticipation of live children who never arrived, a stillbirth and succession of miscarriages the only fruit of that marriage, this to no one's surprise: "God dealt out punishment for hurry-up marriages—not just Presbyterians but almost everybody else believed that," the narrator asserts. "God rewarded lust with dead babies, idiots, harelips and withered limbs and clubfeet" (*Friend* 11).

The narrator then imagines Flora sailing through all this: "[A]fter she came in from helping Robert with the barn chores, Flora would wash and change her clothes and go next door and read Ellie to sleep. My mother might invite herself along, taking whatever sewing she was doing, on some item of her trousseau" (*Friend* 11-12). Still thinking about this repeated scene, the narrator asks "What did Flora read?" and answers herself:

> Stories about Scottish life—not classics. Stories about urchins and comic grandmothers. The only title my mother could remember was *Wee Macgregor*. She could not follow the stories very well, or laugh when Flora laughed and Ellie gave a whimper, because so much was Scots dialect or read with that thick accent. She was surprised that Flora could do it—it wasn't the way Flora ordinarily talked, at all.
>
> (12)[18]

Here the narrator's wonderings are intertwined with what her mother had told her years later, lying in bed and ill herself. They continue and deepen by shifting to Robert, who came directly from Scotland, in a paragraph-long parenthesis:

> (But wouldn't it be the way Robert talked? Perhaps that is why my mother never reports anything that Robert said, never has him contributing to the scene. He must have been there, he must have been sitting there in the room. They would only heat the main room of the house. I see him black-haired, heavy-shouldered, with the strength of a plow horse, and the same kind of sombre, shackled beauty.)
>
> (*Friend* 11-12)

This paragraph, and especially its last sentence, reveals the narrator's imaginings which point to the story she herself wishes to tell about these people, and about how her mother saw them. "Then Flora would say, 'That's all of that for tonight.' She would pick up another book, an old book written by some preacher of their faith. There was in it such stuff as my mother had never heard. What stuff? She couldn't say. All the stuff that was in their monstrous old religion" (12). Continuing to consider what was being read and of what her mother thought about it, the narrator writes:

> All the configuration of the elect and the damned, my mother must have meant—all the arguments about the illusion and necessity of free will. Doom and slippery redemption. The torturing, defeating, but for some minds irresistible pileup of interlocking and contradictory notions. My mother could resist it. Her faith was easy, her spirits at that time robust. Ideas were not what she was curious about, ever.
>
> But what sort of thing was that, she asked (silently), to read to a dying woman? This was the nearest she got to criticizing Flora.
>
> The answer—that it was the only thing, if you believed it—never seemed to have occurred to her.
>
> (*Friend* 12-13)

It was the only thing, if you believed it. Beyond the narrator's wonderings and back to Munro, the artist who shaped the materials she had variously discovered into "Friend of My Youth," the titular story in her seventh book, these passages contribute to and further point to the story's coda ending on the history of Cameronians. Beyond that further, on the path she was on which would ultimately produce *The View from Castle Rock*, Munro may be seen probing the Scots religious beliefs and cultural attitudes which she knew and had inherited. This writing, which culminated in her last three books, constitutes her late style.

The wondering narrator in "Friend of My Youth" may be seen, retrospectively, as a bellwether to this trajectory. She continues on through the drama of Flora's story, the arrival of nurse Audrey Atkinson to tend to the dying Ellie (a figure Munro had used before and would use again)—Atkinson's marriage to Robert and Flora's decision to leave the farm to work in town, her mother's diminished contacts with the friend of her youth. Throughout, the young Munro is there in the wondering narrator nursing her mother who, "[i]n later years, when she sometimes talked about the things she might have been, or done, she would say, 'If I could have been a writer ... then I would have written the story of Flora's life. And do you know what I would have called it? 'The Maiden Lady'" (*Friend* 19). The narrator "had no use for" her mother's sentimental construction of Flora's story then, knowing now as she writes, an older person than her mother ever was, her mother and Flora both years dead, that she "was no comfort and poor company to her when she had almost nowhere else to turn." Yet, she continues, "I had my own ideas about Flora's story. I didn't think that I could have written a novel but that I would write one. I would take a different tack. I saw through my mother's story and put in what she left out. My Flora would be as black as hers was white" (*Friend* 20).

Just before she died the narrator's mother "got a letter from the real Flora," one which acknowledged her illness and wished her well. This circumstance allows the narrator to imagine and detail the balance of Flora's life based on its information and, in a dream, she imagines approaching her in the store and sizing her up then. Doing this, she "would have wanted to tell her that I knew, I knew her story, though we had never met" (*Friend* 23, 25). But with that, after a paragraph break, the narrator returns to the beginning of this story ("I used to dream about my mother" [*Friend* 3]) and dispels the dream of Flora later in life by writing, "Of course it's my mother I'm thinking of, my mother as she was in those dreams, saying, It's nothing, just this little tremor; saying with such astonishing lighthearted forgiveness, Oh, I knew you'd come someday." Hearing this, the narrator feels "[o]ffended, tricked, cheated, by this welcome turnaround" (26) in this penultimate paragraph reminiscent of its predecessor in the ultimate paragraph of "The Ottawa Valley." She continues describing her "mother moving rather carelessly out of her old prison," then pointedly asserts a deep personal truth: "She changes the bitter lump of love I have carried all this time into a phantom—something useless and uncalled for, like a phantom pregnancy" (*Friend* 26). After a white-space break, there follows the paragraph about the Cameronians.

Commenting on this ending Reeves writes that "a story ending with" "a phantom pregnancy"

> would be unimaginable, but what closure resources are available to Munro in completing the story? She can't "intervene" in ways possible in a third-person narrative—but she can have the narrator's eventual discovery of who the Cameronians were. And the austerity and harsh convictions that define Flora, so often appearing as acts of gentleness and charity in the story, are suddenly given all the ferocity and hatred of the world outside Cameronian belief: "One of their ministers, in a mood of *firm rejoicing* at his own hanging, excommunicated all the other preachers in the world."

What this action suggests, Reeves also writes, is that "the primary closure strategy in most of her stories involves a kind of recursion—an obliging to re-consider/re-read/re-think the story in light of how it ends" (Reeves; original emphasis).[19] Reeves foresees Munro's emerging late style.

There readers are yet again wondering with Alice Munro, just as her narrator wonders over the dueling versions of Flora in "Friend of My Youth" and after Hazel thought about Jack's life and about her failure to "hold him fast." The final paragraph on the Cameronians concludes the story by offering a final mystery about Flora and especially about the narrator's mother forcing readers to return and revaluate what we have just read. These are mysteries, closing the story, which are to be both wondered over and carried forward, and with regard to the mother what is being carried over is, in one of Munro's most redolent and personally evocative phrases, a "bitter lump of love" (26). Each woman here, remembered and wondered over, is like Mr. Black in "Chaddeleys and Flemings: 2. The Stone in the Field" whom Munro describes in the fictionalized obituary there as "taking the mystery of his life with him" (*Moons* 33).

"I Looked around the Cemeteries, and This Man Does Not Have a Grave Anywhere": Imagining *The View from Castle Rock*, 1990–7

By the time "Friend of My Youth" was first published in the January 22, 1990, issue of the *New Yorker*, Alice Munro was back in Scotland. Having left Canada on New Year's Day, she and Fremlin spent the first three months of 1990 living in Melrose, a town just under ten miles from Selkirk and near to the Ettrick Valley in the Border Country. Sometime in that January Munro sent Barber a postcard picturing Dryburgh Abbey on the Tweed near Melrose (where Sir Walter Scott is buried) and wrote that it is "wonderful here, *thick* with grim ghastly history. We will steep you in it mercilessly" (883/11.5.1.1). On February 2nd she sent another to her editor Menaker, this one picturing Melrose Abbey which, she wrote, "is what you see across from the green-grocer's. The other way is the Eldon Hills where King Arthur & Co. are waiting a good enough reason to come out." Over there too, Munro was in touch with her British editor, Carmen Callil at Chatto & Windus, who passed her phone number in Melrose on to Barber and also reports on her health, saying that "she felt exhausted so thinks she's been doing too much gallivanting over battle fields" (January 19, 1990; 883/11.5.1.1). While she was away in Scotland *Friend of My Youth* was published in Canada and the United States, so she returned to North America in late March for the launch and other promotional events (see Thacker *Alice* 436–7).

Beyond battlefields, Munro spent time researching the Laidlaws, her "people." She and Fremlin "drove up the Ettrick Valley—we went for walks there when the bloody wind was enough to permit us—the most desolate place," she recalled in April 2004. "And we actually found the bothy—a bothy is a sort of primitive shelter, stone built, which may have been—it's a sheep shelter now, but may have been, I think, where Will O'Phaup [William Laidlaw, father to Margaret Laidlaw Hogg] lived. I think it is because—we couldn't go inside it because the sheep shit is about that deep, but there was a fireplace in one corner, so obviously it had not always been an animal shelter. And it was certainly the place where Will O'Phaup lived. I did research there in the library in Galashiels" (Thacker interview April 2004).

In May 1992 Munro was interviewed by Christopher Gittings—the result was published in *Scotlands* as "The Scottish Ancestor"; its timing is especially resonant here. Munro makes various comments and observations which reveal her thinking and knowledge then and, as well, are suggestive of the trajectory that ultimately became *Castle Rock*. She confirms her 1982 visit to the Borders and her desire "to come back and live there for a while" (85). Throughout the interview she makes numerous comments regarding the materials and the writing of both "Hold Me Fast" and "Friend of My Youth" and, regarding the latter story, she confirms that she got the Cameronian material from another person. Reiterating her reasons for going back to Scotland and the Borders, Munro said, "[I]t all did begin to interest me a lot, the whole history of the Covenanters." Once there, she discovered that "the Presbyterian Church in Canada doesn't arrive from the … established Presbyterian church in Scotland," that it came from "a radical fundamentalist wing," which she names the Glasgow Mission of the eighteenth century, "and so what took over in Canada was really a kind of fundamentalist Presbyterianism, very narrow and tough," "a more difficult strain" than Scots Presbyterianism (85).

This fundamentalist Presbyterianism that came to Canada, to Ontario, and especially to her own people in Huron County provided "an enormous drama, though a difficult one, to your life," she said (86).[20] She also makes it clear throughout that she has inherited letters and other materials that are moving her toward the family book she envisioned; when Gittings asked her specifically about that project, she replied, "I've found it's difficult because if you're used to writing fiction keeping oneself within the bounds of fact instead of taking that fictional germ and doing something with it is very difficult. So I still haven't hit on the form for the book—I keep coming closer to it all the time" (87). She then mentions her most recent story in the *New Yorker*, "A Wilderness Station" (April 27, 1992), saying "it takes off from my ancestors coming up to Huron county, except that I have completely invented a dreadful macabre incident that takes place, and I have no justification for this at all" (87). Writing to Gittings after their interview, Munro expressed pleasure that he liked "A Wilderness Station," "which is an important story for me" (November 16, 1992).

When *Open Secrets* was published in the fall of 1994, it contained "A Wilderness Station" along with seven other new stories. Speaking to a reporter from *MacLean's* about that story's point-of-departure, "her great-great-uncle, who was killed by a falling tree" in the 1850s, Munro remarked, "'I looked around the cemeteries, and this man does not have a grave anywhere. All my other ancestors do, going back to the 1850s.'" This absence likely means that "they buried him on the farm," she continues, but then she explained how she connected an imagined fictional plot to this "kernel" of truth to make the story (Turbide 49).

So saying in 1994, Munro offered a motif—"'I looked around the cemeteries'"—which would become crucial to *Castle Rock* and indicative of her recursive late style. There, describing a visit to the graveyard of Ettrick Church in the first section of the "No Advantages," the book's outset, Munro wrote, "I felt conspicuous, out of place, and cold. I huddled by the wall till the rain let up for a bit, and then I explored the churchyard, with the long wet grass soaking my legs" (6). She finds the grave markers of her people, tells about some of them (and of another, not a relative, the reverend Thomas Boston), and ends with "Robert Laidlaw, who died at Hopehouse on January 29th 1800 aged seventy-two years." Then a single-sentence paragraph: "My great-great-great-great-grandfather" (*Castle Rock* 6).

In the epilogue as *Castle Rock* closes, Munro has herself in two separate cemeteries, looking about, wondering, offering what she was doing and what she has discovered or, in the first case, *not* discovered. The epilogue is titled "Messenger"—in the last paragraph she focuses on "a big mother-of-pearl seashell," one "that I recognized as a messenger from near and far, because I could hold it to my ear" (*Castle Rock* 349). For most of the time Munro was working on the book this section was called "Remnants." As published, "Messenger" begins with a description of changes in farming and in the land in Huron County over time and, after a break, Munro writes in her own voice: "In the summer of 2004 I visited Joliet [Illinois], looking for some trace of the life of William Laidlaw, my great-great-grandfather, who died there" (*Castle Rock* 344). Researching graves in a local library, Munro describes herself a person

> Looking for a grave, a memory. There is only one listing that gets my attention. *Unknown Cemetery*.
> In a certain corner of Homer Township, a burial ground in which only two stones have been found, but in which as many as twenty were said to have existed at one time. The two stones remaining, according to the lists, bear the names of people who died in the year 1837. There is speculation that some of the others might have been soldiers who died in the Black Hawk war.
> This means that there was a graveyard in existence before Will died.
> (*Castle Rock* 346; original emphasis)

I will return to this scene once I have treated the whole of *The View from Castle Rock*, but for now suffice it to say that Munro finds this place, describes its location and appearance in 2004, and, as she writes, "I clamber into it, brushing aside the vigorous poison ivy" (*Castle Rock* 346). "I do not see any leaning or fallen or broken gravestones, or any plants growing—rose bushes, for instance—that might be a sign that graves had once been here. It is useless. I become apprehensive about the poison ivy. I grope my way out" (*Castle Rock* 346–7).[21] She meditates on this experience some, but then shifts to "Another cemetery, in Blyth" (*Castle Rock* 347), another scene I will return to in due course. This is the cemetery in Blyth, Ontario where Munro and Fremlin bought a plot and where, after his death in April 2013, he was buried. So too are many of the Laidlaw relatives. Even James Laidlaw, the great-great uncle, killed by a falling tree, whose grave Munro looked for and did not find, the search she mentioned to Turbide in 1994 in connection with "A Wilderness Station." It is the cemetery, she writes as she begins the final section of "Messenger,"

> [w]here the body of James was moved for burial, decades after he had been killed by the falling tree. And here is where Mary Scott is buried. Mary who wrote the letter from Ettrick to lure the man she wanted to come and marry her. On her stone is the name of that man, *William Laidlaw. Died in Illinois*. And buried God knows where.
> (*Castle Rock* 347; original emphasis)

Taken together, these cemetery scenes are synecdoche for Alice Munro in the 1990s, a second period in her career at which she may be seen most fecund. After *Friend of My Youth* in 1990, she produced *Open Secrets*, her first *Selected Stories* (1996), and *The Love of a Good Woman* (1998). There would be two more books, *Hateship, Friendship, Courtship, Loveship, Marriage* (2001) and *Runaway* (2004) before Munro in 2006 finally produced the family book she had so long imagined. Yet throughout the 1990s, most especially in a memoir, "What Do You Want to Know For?" (1994), which would ultimately be included in *Castle Rock*, and in a historical sketch treating the emigration of the Laidlaws from Scotland in 1818, "Changing Places" (1997), which would not, Munro was imagining that book and, as she told Gittings, trying to find its form. The latter sketch became the basis for "The View from Castle Rock" (2005), first a *New Yorker* piece and ultimately in its extended submitted form most of the "No Advantages" section of *Castle Rock* but for its last, "Working for a Living." That memoir found a permanent place at the end of the section "No Advantages" after its peripatetic provenance, moving from a story intended for the first *Who*, considered and rejected by the *New Yorker* in that form, reshaped into a memoir, and rejected by that magazine again before it found its way to *Grand Street*. Shaped further and added to, it reached its place in *Castle Rock*. Given this, "Working" truly was "grafted on from some other reality," as Munro had written in "Material" in 1973 (*Something* 42). The wondering and imagining Munro was doing throughout all these years led her finally to the making of *The View from Castle Rock*, a larger recursive shaping that required considered reality grafting itself.

2

"It Is Difficult to Decide What Works in a Book of This Sort": The Making of *The View from Castle Rock*

> On one of those cloudy summer days that are commoner than anybody remembers, I was riding a slow train, that takes you north from Toronto to the Muskoka Lakes, to Perry Sound, and then along the shores of Georgian Bay. I had a one-way ticket to Baie aux Pins, a resort village north of Parry Sound. I was happy because I had a whole day free, and because I was going where I had never been. In my lap I had a package of cigarettes, unopened, a couple of chocolate bars and a copy of Seven Gothic Tales.
>
> (37.19.16.3)

Writing to Douglas Gibson in November 2005, Munro tells him she has decided that "the whole of 'What Do You Want to Know For?' [1994] could and should be included" to replace "Wenlock Edge" (2005) in the manuscript of *The View from Castle Rock*. Her letter is attached to a typescript of the former, signed and dated November 10, 2005. She apologizes, since the substitution is one she had been mulling for some time, writing that she "is sorry to have come late to this conclusion but it is difficult to decide what works in a book of this sort" (M&S Z106.f1). Munro had expressed this same uncertainty to Christopher Gittings in May 1992 (87). After the stories using Scots material in *Friend of My Youth*, she clearly began focusing on stories which would ultimately be included in her long-contemplated family book. What this suggests too is that as Munro was writing the stories she produced and published in the late 1980s, throughout the 1990s, and into the 2000s, the imaginative and formal demands of *The View from Castle Rock* were always with her and were becoming more urgent.

This was nothing new. The passage just offered as epigraph here, a verbatim fragment on a single typed sheet, not really even a paragraph, is one of hundreds dating from before 1970 to be found in the Alice Munro Fonds. Just as the epigraph passage offered in the introduction of this book reveals a narrator on a train, looking out, and points toward subsequent later stories, so this one too. But here the fragment points to a specific story: "Hired Girl" (1994), one of the "special set of stories" Munro mentions in her foreword to *Castle Rock*, "not memoirs but they were closer to my own life than the other stories I had written" [x]. It is included there after being kept out of four collections over a dozen years. The fragment narrator's circumstances on the train, her destination, and most especially the copy of Isak Dinesen's *Seven Gothic Tales* (1934)—it is quoted from twice in both published versions of the story—confirm the relation.

"Hired Girl" was first published in the April 11, 1994, issue of the *New Yorker* while "What Do You Want to Know For?" first appeared at about the same time in a PEN Canada fundraising anthology, *Writing Away*. This coincidence may be no more than that—coincidence—but it nevertheless defines an imaginative pairing that leads directly to the shaping of *Castle Rock*, since each ultimately appeared in book form there. About a year before those publications Munro sent Barber a finished story, commenting jocularly, "another *signed* story!," continuing "But—I have doubts as to whether its a story really, just a kind of straight memory piece which kept me occupied while I eased myself into the real hard story I'm doing now" (March 11, 1993; 883/11.5.1.4). The record does not confirm which story Munro sent, but the phrase "straight memory piece" and the timing suggest that it was either "Hired Girl" or "What Do You Want to Know For?." Though more overtly fictional than the memoir, "Hired Girl" is based on the summer job Munro had in 1948 when she was seventeen—it took her to a cottage on an island in Georgian Bay near Pointe au Baril, Ontario (see Thacker *Alice* 81–2; Carrington "Other Room"). The "real hard story" Munro was easing herself into was one of those which would appear in her next book, *Open Secrets*, likely "The Albanian Virgin" (1994).

Munro's differentiation between this finished "straight memory piece" and the "real hard story" defines my method here analyzing the making of *Castle Rock*. Working through the archival and published provenance surrounding the book chronologically is a demonstration of Munro's recursive late style. And much of the same history was replicated in making the two books which followed it. Resting upon Munro's longstanding intention and the beginnings of a family book—"Home," "Working for a Living," and the Scots stories in *Friend of My Youth*—this chapter begins with her methods evident in the coincident "Hired Girl" and "What Do Want to Know For?" and then analyzes the actual making of *Castle Rock*.

"Wooing Distant Parts of Myself": The Recursive "Hired Girl," "Straight Memory" in "What Do You Want to Know For?"

Writing during the 1980s in a patently autobiographical story, "Miles City, Montana" (1985), Munro has her narrator comment that in her home in Vancouver with her husband and two young daughters, she "seemed to be often looking for a place to hide …," and she continues, "I wanted to hide so that I could get busy with my real work, which was a sort of wooing of distant parts of myself" (*Progress* 88; see Thacker *Alice* 126, 171–2). This is a coda to Munro's work, one that most certainly obtains in the "straight memory" pieces found in *Castle Rock*; these are not so much focused on a narrator wooing herself as they are on the place and people in her family who raised her, Munro the narrator there remembering, wondering, and evaluating, seeing that place and those people now, years later, with the understanding and perspective of the older person she became.

There is a numbered handwritten note in Barber's papers in Calgary in which she asks Munro questions after, apparently, having read the manuscript of *Castle Rock* as it was on May 2, 2005. It was a version which still included "Wenlock Edge" and, rather than the two-part structure of the published version, it alternated stories from the "No Advantages" section with ones from the "Home" section.[1] That is, more historical pieces were interleaved with more fictional ones. These questions were probably put in May or June since Munro sent Barber her draft foreword, dated June 30, 2005, likely in response. Barber first asks, "Why hadn't you collected 'Hired Girl' before?" and continues with a crucial question about "the semi-autobiographical stories": "How can we characterize these stories so that they seem like a group? 'Wenlock Edge,' how does it belong here?—Is 'Lying Under the Apple Tree' you?" Barber then asks about "the problem of 'Nature'" and ends, "Did you fix the end of Wenlock Edge? Problem of *time*" (2015.062.1.1).[2] In response, Munro sent Barber what she characterized as a "leaner, meaner 'Wenlock' though I still think it probably should not be included. And a new slightly more story-ish 'What … For.' What do you think? *I* think it could replace 'Wenlock'" (August 2, 2005; original emphasis; 2015.062.1). During this time too Munro was following her usual practice of revising endings—a new two-paged one for "The Ticket" dated July 25, 2005 (2015.062.2) came in and, in early September, another unnamed revision appeared (September 26, 2005; 2015.062.1).

Taking up "Hired Girl" in the midst, Barber's question about it is salient toward the making of *Castle Rock*, just as is the discussion surrounding "Wenlock Edge" versus "What Do You Want to Know For?" The "special set of stories" Munro writes of in her foreword, began *with* "Hired Girl" which, based as it is on autobiographical experience, is certainly "closer to [her] own life than the other stories [she] had written" (*Caste Rock* [x]).

In the best published critical analysis of "Hired Girl," Ildikó de Papp Carrington sees it as a sequel to Munro's 1957 story, "Sunday Afternoon," one of the stories collected in *Dance of the Happy Shades* and one based on the same 1948 job. That story is set at the employers' home in Toronto, the same people who own the summer place on the island in Georgian Bay, and includes much of the same emphasis on class-based differences found in "Hired Girl." That third-person story ends with Alva, the poor girl working there thinking, after one of the guests made a pass at her, about what is ahead for her with a vagueness which characterized Munro's endings then: "This stranger's touch had eased her; her body was simply grateful and expectant, and she felt a lightness and confidence she had not known in this house." "She would not mind thinking of the Island now, the bare sunny rocks and the black little pine trees. She saw it differently now; it was even possible that she wanted to go there. But things always came together; there was something she would not explore yet—a tender spot, a new and mysterious humiliation" (*Dance* 170–1).

Comparing the two stories, Carrington argues that in "Hired Girl" "Munro develops and resolves this open-ended situation"—the ending just quoted—"by assigning literature, reading, and storytelling much more significant functions than they have" in the first version ("Other Rooms" 4). Among many other things about the two versions Carrington analyzes, she cites a comment Munro made in a published 1983 interview just after she had discussed Welty's return to the same material: "It may be that you have to go back over and over again and mine the same material and look at it in different ways, or in the same way, and sometimes you get to it and sometimes you don't" (Struthers interview 12). While Munro was not speaking directly to "Hired Girl," a story yet a decade off, her comment is crucial here by its recursive cast. The changes reveal an author revisiting her young self, delving deeper. This action is, certainly, what Munro has done. Alva in "Sunday Afternoon" is treated from the outside by a third-person narrator, while in "Hired Girl" she is renamed Elsa and made the first-person narrator. Core literary presences in "Hired Girl" are Nausicaä from the *Odyssey* transformed by James Joyce in *Ulysses* and, more explicitly, two of Isak Dinesen's *Seven Gothic Tales*, each of which is quoted from directly.

As Carrington holds, literature, reading, and storytelling are of far greater significance in "Hired Girl" than in "Sunday Afternoon." From the moment in the *New Yorker* version of the story, while arriving by boat after having been met at the train in Pointe au Baril by Mrs. Montjoy, her employer, Elsa sees that the "island that was our destination had a name—Nausicaä," the literary is never far distant. Weighing this, she then thinks "This name seemed to me a good sign, and I said it aloud as I clambered out of the boat. I was anxious to appear appreciative and at ease." "'Oh, yes,' Mrs. Montjoy said. 'That was its name when Daddy bought it. It's after some character in Shakespeare.'" Having already begun the story with details of class distinction between Elsa and Mrs. Montjoy, a superficial, athletic, upper-class woman whose "commonest expression seemed to be one of impatience held decently in check," Munro has the lower-class Elsa dwell on her superior knowledge. After Mrs. Montjoy's remark, she then "opened" her "mouth to say no, no, not Shakespeare, and to explain all about Nausicaä being the girl on the beach—the princess playing ball with her friends—whom Ulysses surprised when he awoke from his sleep." Weighing further in this her first real exchange with her new employer Elsa notes "some briskness in Mrs. Montjoy's tone [that] warned me off, this time. My superior knowledge gave me a familiar feeling, of satisfaction and misgiving" (*New Yorker* 82). When Munro took up this passage for *Castle Rock*, the scene and descriptions are substantially the same, but years later Munro achieves further depth as she offers this revised and more expansive final sentence to the paragraph: "Just in time I recognized the briskness of Mrs. Montjoy's tone when she said 'some character in Shakespeare'—the suggestion that Nausicaa, and Shakespeare, as any observations of mine, were things she could reasonably do without" (*Castle Rock* 230).[3]

As with her previous story remembering and reexamining the details of her 1948 summer job—Munro was then "a country girl, used to doing housework," as she writes—much of "Hired Girl" is taken up with her employers, their ways of living, and the differences the narrator first discovers and then comes to understand between their lives and her own. As she writes after accounting for just how she got the job, the woman whom Mrs. Montjoy consulted "thought that it would be the very thing for me. I thought so too—I was eager to see more of the world" (*Castle Rock* 228-9).

And see more of the world and the ways of wealthy people Elsa (who becomes an unnamed narrator in *Castle Rock*) does. She sleeps in the boat house with the

Montjoy's ten-year-old daughter Mary Anne, who informs Elsa of the family dynamics: her mother; the Foleys, her grandparents with the elderly grandmother who "'gets her wires crossed occasionally'" (*New Yorker* 84); an immigrant caretaker couple; and most centrally her dead sister Jane, a three-year-old infant killed years before in an accident. A piece of furniture toppled on to her. In the first version Mrs. Montjoy was looking for something behind it, in the second it was Mr. Montjoy. At one point Mary Anne is evaluating the appearances of people she knows—"'Mother isn't pretty and Daddy is really ugly .... Nana used to be pretty, but she's old'"—and turns to Elsa, "You are sort of pretty, but it isn't the same thing, because you're a maid. Does it hurt your feelings when I say that?' I said no. 'I'm only a maid when I'm here'" (*New Yorker* 83; *Castle Rock* 233).

That articulated crux is the key to "Hired Girl," since wherever Elsa looks she is evaluating the lives around her in light of the poorer life she has herself known. "When Mr. Montjoy came to the island on the weekends, there was always a great deal of noise and activity." One morning Mr. Montjoy looks for a misplaced book; "'That Book-of-the-Month Club book?'" Mrs. Montjoy replies when he asked about it. "'I think you left it in the living room.'" Elsa continues:

> She was right. I was vacuuming the living-room floor, and I had found a book pushed partway under the sofa. Its title was 'Seven Gothic Tales.' That made me want to see what it was about, so I opened it, and even as I listened to this conversation on the deck I was reading, holding the book open in one hand and guiding the vacuum cleaner with the other: 'Nay, I speak from my heart,' said Mira.
> (*New Yorker* 85)

This quotation continues briefly and is from "The Dreamers" in that book, one that took America by storm when it was a first selection of the Book-of-the-Month Club in 1934.[4]

While Nausicaä in the *Odyssey* and Joyce's use of that story are subtext here as well, Munro's two quotations from Dinesen are more overt and central to the story, much more directly related to her hired girl's real character. "He must have seen me reading it. He said, 'It's a queer kind of book, but sometimes you want to read a book that isn't like all the others.'" This exchange is a key moment, and Mr. Montjoy's comment is immediately followed by his wife's: "'I couldn't make heads or tails of it' ... 'We'll have to get out of the way here and let her get on with the vacuuming'" (*Castle Rock* 242). As Munro makes clear in both versions of her story—her edits for book publication are slight smoothings, not substantial changes—Mrs. Montjoy has no time for imaginative literary speculations. Yet her husband is drawn to them, and Elsa certainly is.

"The Dreamers" is a long tale about storytelling reminiscent of Scheherazade's *One Thousand and One Nights* or Boccaccio's *Decameron* and, although the passage Munro quotes is offered as Elsa's random selection, in fact it is the story's climax and key revelation as it ends. So here early in "Hired Girl" this quotation reveals Elsa's character and imaginative direction. Throughout—the family's histories and interactions, what she sees and does, how she understands her own social position among the Montjoys and their ilk—Elsa observes and gauges. When she is sent to "help Corrie"—one of the immigrant caretaker couple—she observes closely: "She never just wiped the kitchen counters—she scoured them." "When she wrung out a cleaning rag she might have been wringing the neck of a chicken" (*Castle Rock* 234). Elsa tries to get this Dutch woman to talk about the war to no avail. Telling her own story as the narrator, Elsa collects those of others.

While she sees and gauges the people around her and imagines an attraction to one of the Montjoy's guests at a cocktail party they host in his honor, the central acts in "Hired Girl" are between Elsa and each of the Montjoys. Even though Mary Anne told her what happened to her sister, Elsa feigns ignorance and uses a question grandmother asked her about Jane to inquire of Mrs. Montjoy about the accident, just so she could hear the woman's explanation. After telling what happened, and quite true to the superficial character she displays throughout, Mrs. Montjoy concludes with a cliché in both versions: "'It was just one of those things'" (*New Yorker* 88; *Castle Rock* 252). In the *New Yorker* version, Munro then writes:

> At that time I didn't recognize brutality in myself, or boorishness, I thought I had the right—the right to barge in, stir up feelings, demand intimacy, or at least attention. I thought myself blameless, beyond judgment, in my dealings with Mrs. Montjoy. Because I was young and I knew about Nausicaä. I didn't have the grace or the fortitude to be a servant.
>
> (88)

Revising this paragraph for *Castle Rock* Munro expands these feelings and offers more precise detail. After Mrs. Montjoy says "'It was just one of those things,'" she continues:

> My deception made me feel queasy. I dropped a fork on the floor.
> Mrs. Montjoy picked it up.
> Remember to wash this again.
> How strange that I did not question my right to pry, to barge in and bring this to the surface. Part of the reason must have been that in the society I came from, things like that were never buried for good, but ritualistically resurrected, and that such horrors were like a badge people wore—or, mostly, that women wore—throughout their lives.
> Also it may have been because I would never quite give up when it came to demanding intimacy, or at least some kind of equality, even with a person I did not like.
> Cruelty was a thing I could not recognize in myself. I thought I was blameless here, and in any dealings with this family. All because of being young, and poor, and knowing about Nausicaa.
>
> (*Castle Rock* 252)

Paired together, these two versions of the same passage are a clear indication of Munro's developing late style as she set about *Castle Rock*. While in the 1994 version Elsa offers some perspective on her actions, in the revision about ten years later Munro deepens that perspective, adds detail as a greater basis for it, and creates through the clipped paragraphing the effect of the older narrator thinking about her own actions and evaluating them. Reading these together, I see Munro shaping her own memories of her younger self ("brutality" becomes "cruelty," the latter a motive which figures often in her late style) and most especially her understanding of her younger self. And of what she has written of such things before. Thus with the parenthetical that Munro adds ("or, mostly, that women wore") I note that this is an author who early on wrote a story about the reactions of a mother whose youngest child is scalded to death ("The Time of Death" [1956]), a writer who has long meditated on cruelty and, here, returns to it again.[5]

With Mr. Montjoy, conversely, Elsa receives a beneficence. Having seen her reading his copy of *Seven Gothic Tales*, Mr. Montjoy seeks her out at the story's end to present his copy to her. Here again the two versions of the story reveal Munro's methods in revision. Each turns on another quotation from Dinesen—this one from another climatic passage, in this case from "The Supper at Elsinore" in which two sisters, old maids despite wealth and charm, share supper with their long-lost brother, a ghost and hanged pirate who visits them from hell to reconnect and tell them the details of his life which they never knew. Here the matter is not storytelling and wisdom, as in "The Dreamers," but ultimate destiny. Following its quotation, the *New Yorker* version ends: "Reading this, I felt as if I had just been rescued from my life. Words could become a burning-glass for me in those days, and no shame of my nature or condition could hold out among the flares of pleasure" (88). The story ends.

In *Castle Rock*, Munro again expands the scene, this time to set up the Dinesen quotation, which is offered just before a brief final paragraph. Whereas the *New Yorker* version includes some details of Mr. Montjoy's childhood Munro drops them in favor of the narrator's wonderings about why he decided to give her the book, writing in her narrator's voice,

> I see him now as pure of motive, leaning against the boathouse wall. A person who could think me worthy of this gift. Of this book.
>   At the moment, though, I didn't feel particularly pleased, or grateful, in spite of my repeated thank-yous. I was too startled, and in some way embarrassed. The thought of having a little corner of myself come to light, and be truly understood, stirred up alarm, just as much as being taken no notice of stirred up resentment. And Mr. Montjoy was probably the person who interested me least, whose regard meant the least to me, of all the people I met that summer.[6]

After he left, she "opened the book just anywhere, as I had done the first time, and began to read. 'The walls of the room had once been painted crimson ....'" Implicitly, she luxuriated in Dinesen's description as it is quoted, and concludes, "I forgot Mr. Montjoy almost immediately. In hardly any time at all I came to believe that this gift had always belonged to me" (*Castle Rock* 254).

Given Munro's methods of composition, this paragraph should be seen as her final version. That said, the archives and the *New Yorker* reveal other endings. As she worked toward an ending, which was written sometime after late August 1993, Munro sent Barber two other final paragraphs that are comments after the second Dinesen quotation. The first, dated by Barber August 21, 1993, reads "As she had expected, radiance seeped irresistibly into the world, and for some time she was painfully happy." Then, just after, Barber got another final page, this one dated in Munro's hand August 27, 1993. After the quotation from "Supper at Elsinore" there is this final paragraph: "Like a queen bee then, growing sleek and full, lapping up the providential nourishment" (883/11.5.1.4). Working perpetually on endings, striving ever and always to get the language and description just right, just as she envisioned, just as she thought the story demanded, Munro was sharply focused in "Hired Girl." As Carrington argued, Munro was consciously returning to the material of "Sunday Afternoon" in the story, but when she selected it as one of her "special stories" to be revised for *Castle Rock*, Munro was taking a yet further recursive step. It, along with "Fathers" (2002), "Lying Under the Apple Tree" (2002), and "The Ticket" (2006), returned to revisit the girl and teenager, the young woman she was as she became Alice Munro. Thus the clear subject of "Hired Girl" is first who she was on that island in Georgian Bay in 1948 and how she then understood herself and, years later, as she judged herself then, at first brutal and then cruel.

Of these two pieces first published in 1994, "What Do You Want to Know For?" is more likely the "straight memory piece" Munro sent to Barber in March 1993. That is what it is, a memoir story. It was written to order for *Writing Away*, a fundraising volume with contributions by invited Canadian writers published in the spring. As Munro said about it in a 2004 interview when she was thinking out loud about the shape of *Castle Rock*, "I just wrote it for the book, they asked us to do something about travel." Commenting then too, she also expressed doubt as to whether or not "What" belonged in the family book she was then putting together, saying that it "doesn't begin like a story. It's more thoroughly memorial" (Thacker interview April 2004).

That is literally so, since the 1994 "What" begins:

> I saw the crypt first, though it was in a cemetery to the left of the road, on my husband's side of the car.
>
> "What was that?" I said. "Something strange."
>
> I had seen a big mound, an unnatural lump, blanketed with smooth grass.
>
> We turned back, though we hadn't much time. We were going to visit friends who live on Georgian Bay.
>
> There it was, set in the middle of the little country cemetery. Like a woolly animal—huge and somnolent, prehistoric. We climbed a bank and unhooked a gate and went around and looked at the front end of this thing. A stone wall between an upper and a lower stone arch, and a wall of bricks within the lower arch. No names, no dates, just a cross roughly carved into the keystone of the upper arch. At the other end earth and grass covered the wall. Some stones protruded—they were probably set there to hold the earth in place. No markings on them, either, no clues as to what might be inside.
>
> (*Writing* 203)

When she revised this opening for *Castle Rock*, Munro did some smoothing but largely kept her original detail and language—save for three notable points: the crypt is "Like a

Figure 1 Mannerow Cemetery (Cedardale), McCullough Lake Road, Chatsworth, Sullivan Township, Grey County, Ontario. Author photograph.

woolly animal—like some giant wombat, lolling around in a prehistoric landscape." Just before this description too, she adds a revelatory sentence: "But we are possessive about this country, and try not to let anything get by us" And the phrasing to end the last sentence above is changed too: "as to who or what might be hidden inside" (*Castle Rock* 316).

As Munro said in 2004, "What" "is more thoroughly memorial." Having discovered this crypt (Figure 1), Munro and Fremlin subsequently set about investigating it, most likely around 1992: "I got it into my head that I would like to see the crypt again and find out something about it." Before they did, Munro explains the circumstances surrounding a mammogram she had just had, one that revealed "a lump deep in my left breast, which neither my doctor nor I had been able to feel. We still couldn't feel it" (*Writing* 204). Revising these descriptions years later, Munro again retains most of what was originally there but again adds, as she did at key points in "Hired Girl," phrasings which create longer perspective. Telling readers how she spent her time during the ten days she had to wait before going for a biopsy, Munro adds:

> It was a surprise to me that I was busying myself in this way instead of thinking about what you might call deeper matters. I didn't do any serious reading or listening to music and I didn't go into a muddled trance as I so often do, looking out the big window in the early morning as the sunlight creeps into the cedars.
> (*Castle Rock* 317)[7]

Two retained sentences establish the threat Munro felt. When, after hearing what her doctor had to say and what the plan was, she writes: "As I was leaving he touched my shoulder. He is a friend, and I knew that his first wife's death had begun in just this way" (*Writing* 204; see *Castle Rock* 317).

Thus two mysteries are established at the beginning of "What Do You Want to Know For?": the provenance of the crypt and the implications of a just-discovered health threat—and Munro follows their parallel tracks throughout. When they went looking for the crypt a second time they could not find it, but they persisted, looking for information. They finally found it through the agency of their friend Reg Thompson, whom they had told about it when they first discovered it, knowing of his interest in rural cemeteries.[8] When they did he had written notes which, hearing of Munro's searches, he found again. "Farther north than we had thought—just beyond the boundary of the territory we had been so doggedly covering," Munro writes, noting that when they got back there "we had lots of time to look around."

> We saw that all the old stones in one section had been collected and set in concrete, in the form of a cross. Most of these were the tombstones of children. In any of these old country cemeteries the earliest burials were likely to be those of children, and young women dead in childbirth, and a few young men who had drowned or been killed in the sort of accidents that happen when trees are being cut down, barns put up. There were hardly any old people around to die, in the early days.
>
> (*Writing* 209)

Returning to this passage for *Castle Rock*, Munro recast the penultimate sentence in a revelatory way: "In any of these old cemeteries the earliest dates were apt to be those of children, or young mothers lost in childbirth, or young men who had died accidentally—drowned, or hit by a falling tree, killed by a wild horse, or involved in an accident during the raising of a barn" (*Castle Rock* 323–4). Composing the 1994 version of "What," having just written and published "A Wilderness Station" based in part on her ancestor's death from a falling tree, James Laidlaw's death in the bush is implied in the first version of the passage. But because he is a character earlier in *Castle Rock*, Munro's reference to the accident which killed him is more explicit in the revision. More than that, she refers to his reburial in the Blyth cemetery in that book's epilogue, "Messenger" (*Castle Rock* 347).

But if sudden death at an early age is important here—it certainly is, since as they discover the origins of the crypt she learns that it was built to hold a three-year-old's body—anticipating her own death is evident too in the parallel story. She discovers that, though she "thought that the appointment I had was for a biopsy," "it turned out not to be. It was an appointment to let the city doctor decide whether he would do a biopsy, and after examining my breast and the results of the mammogram, he decided that he would." A date was set "two weeks ahead" but, hearing this, Munro commented "that two weeks seemed like quite a while to wait." This doctor replied that "at this stage of the game" "two weeks was immaterial." But

> That was not what I had been led to believe. But I did not complain—not after a look at some of the people in the waiting room. I am over sixty. My death would

not be a disaster. Not in comparison with the death of a young mother, a family wage-earner, a child. It would not be *apparent* as a disaster.

(*Castle Rock*, 322–3; original emphasis)

In the 1994 version, the word used is "calamity," not "disaster," and the description ends without the final sentence with its emphasis on "apparent." There is a white-space break in the text just after this meditation on death in both versions. After it, in *Writing Away* she tells us that they "were becoming absurdly stubborn about finding the crypt." In *Castle Rock*, it becomes "It bothered us that we could not find the crypt" (323).

Most of "What Do You Want to Know For?" focuses on their search for the crypt that second time and what they found as they had figured it out. "We spent three or four afternoons looking for it and were puzzled and disappointed. But it was a pleasure, as always, to be together in this part of the world looking at the countryside that we think we know so well that is always springing some surprise on us" (*Writing* 204). With this, Munro turns to an extended analysis—something of a small lecture, really, quite specific, and knowledgeable—on the geological history of her region of Ontario, citing by title *The Physiography of Southern Ontario* by Lyman Chapman and Donald Putnam (1951). They carried a copy with them, referring to the geological maps it includes, Munro offering specific information taken from the maps and also writing that they refer to the authors "familiarly but somewhat reverently, as Put and Chap" (*Writing* 205; *Castle* 319). She details the features of the glaciated landscape they see—running through and describing the making and present appearances of eskers, moraines, drumlins, till, and the remnant gravel the glaciers left.[9] While the 1994 version is thorough and precise, Munro transformed it considerably in its revision for *Castle Rock*. The prose is livelier, with added detail and more textures, more specifics, ending with this paragraph:

> My favorite of all the kinds of country is the one I've left till last. This is kame, or kame moraine, which is a chocolate burgundy color on the map and is generally in blobs, not ribbons. A big blob here, a little one there. Kame moraines show where a heap of dead ice sat, cut off from the rest of the moving glacier, earth-stuff pouring through all its holes and crevices. Or sometimes it shows where two lobes of ice pulled apart, and the crevice filled in. End moraines are hilly in what seems a reasonable way, not as smooth as drumlins, but still harmonious, rhythmical, while kame moraines are all wild and bumpy, unpredictable, with a look of chance and secrets.

(*Castle Rock* 321)

This paragraph winds down the geological history and, after a white-space break, Munro writes, "I didn't learn any of this at school. I think there was some nervousness then, about being at loggerheads with the Bible in the matter of the creation of the Earth." For *Castle Rock*, Munro added that last phrase after "Bible" and then also asserted her own history by adding "I learned it when I came to live here with my second husband, a geographer. When I came back to where I never expected to be, in the countryside where I had grown up." A "look of chance and secrets," peering out the window of that bus in 1972 in "Home," comes back—as Munro wrote in 1994 and, in this her family book in 2006 most emphatically—to stay. She continues here: "So my knowledge is untainted, fresh. I get a naïve and particular pleasure from matching what I see on the map with what I can see from the car window. Also from trying to figure out what bit of landscape we're in, before I look at the map, and being right a good deal of the time" (*Castle Rock* 321). Ending her meditation on geology, Munro revises a paragraph from the 1994 version which led in its final sentence to what is a coda to "What Do Want to Know For?" and, as will be yet seen, the whole of *The View from Castle Rock*:

> But there is always more than just the keen pleasure of identification. There's the fact of these separate domains, each with its own history and reason, its favorite crops and trees and weeds—oaks and pines, for instance, growing on sand, and cedars and strayed lilacs on limestone—each with its special expression, its pull on the imagination. The fact of these little countries lying snug and unsuspected, like and unlike as siblings can be, in a landscape that's usually disregarded, or dismissed as drab agricultural counterpane. It's the fact you cherish.
> (*Castle Rock* 321–2)

Revising this passage, Munro added the repetition of "fact" leading up to its final sentence, which was not there in 1994, and when the book was in proof she added the parenthetical details regarding trees and soil (MsC 323.1.2).

While, as Munro said, "What Do You Want to Know For?" is "more thoroughly memorial," a memoir, at its core, it is this assertion which resonates throughout its geological concerns and, more precisely, throughout the quest Munro and Fremlin were on in 1992 to rediscover the crypt they had come across by happenstance. Once re-found, learning its provenance and history became an overriding concern, one that took on its own "particular pleasure" for them in its mysteries. Alongside too, there was the concurrent and personal mystery of the implications of the lump in Munro's breast. Together, these two strands of inquiry drive this memoir and together define the trajectory of every human's life, including Munro's—"thoroughly memorial" in fact. It *is* "the fact you cherish," and at the center of each story included in *Castle Rock* there is some fact or set of facts key to its provenance, as has already been shown with some and will yet be with others. Here too, in "What Do You Want to Know For?" there is a geological sensibility. one which is especially evident in her late style but was also apparent early. Munro had shown an awareness of geological time—in "Walker Brothers Cowboy" (1968), the story which opens her first book, the narrator, when listening to her father's explanation of the formation of the Great Lakes, writes that the "tiny share we have of time appalls me, though my father seems to regard it with tranquillity" (*Dance* 3). As Munro says in "What Do You Want to Know For?," much of the specificity of her knowledge occasioned from her relationship with Fremlin, but it had been a factual interest for some time. It continues into *Dear Life* which was to include the geologically focused "Axis" (2011) until Munro decided against its inclusion there.

When "What Do You Want to Know For?" was first published it included, in the midst of Munro's explanations of her region's glaciated landscape, a black-and-white photograph by David Goldie Kilgour of the east end of the crypt (*Writing* 207). Kilgour was a retired lawyer who lived in Huron County near Goderich; he and wife Elizabeth were friends. Presumably at some point Munro and Fremlin told him about the crypt and of their investigations. He took the photo and Munro submitted it to the publisher along with her memoir (Thacker interview September 6, 2013). Its presence in *Writing Away* complements Munro's memorial story, their quest to discover and understand the crypt's meaning—that is, it vivifies it.

Having finally re-found the crypt again and having spent time examining the tombstones in the cemetery, the two puzzle them out. "The names were nearly all German ones, and many of the inscriptions were in German." Various descriptive phrases on the stones, "then *Gestorben*, with a date in the seventies or the eighties of the last century. *Gestorben*—here, in Sullivan township in Grey County in a colony of England in the middle of the bush."[10] Munro then quotes four lines from a tombstone in German, telling of her translation of it. In English it reads: "The poor heart here now / Moved by many a storm / Obtained pure peace / Only when it stops beating" (my translation). "It's odd how you think you can read German, even when you can't," she remarks, and then asserts its clear meaning: *"Better off dead"* (*Writing* 209, 210; original emphasis). That said, "Not a word on the crypt, though we searched far more thoroughly than we had done before" (*Castle Rock* 325).

In the revision there is a break in the text here and Munro sets to describing the research she then undertook in London at the university "to read some books about Grey County and find out whatever I could about Sullivan Township." She offers some detail from what she read and, wondering about something there, comments in the same vein as the cherished fact, "There are always puzzles" (*Castle Rock* 325). Further describing her research, Munro reveals her own cultural inheritances, her Scots-Presbyterian self-consciousness, when she writes that she is hesitant: it "is difficult to make such requests in reference libraries because you will often be asked what it is, exactly, that you want to know, and what do you want to know it for?" (*Castle Rock* 325, 326).

Reading this memoir now, one wonders just why Munro doubted including it in *Castle Rock*. Throughout its factual memorial a reader sees and feels the motives and desires behind that book. Just as the memoir is a synecdoche to the book, so too is *Castle Rock* one to Munro's writing career. Thus after she tells of her researches in London and what she's discovered there, most especially a church that may be connected to the cemetery, Munro revises the order of her descriptions of changes in the land before she continues with her story of the crypt. She describes new things people try as farming has faded, and then accounts for their visit to St. Peter's Lutheran church of a Sunday, where they eventually find a woman who knows about cemeteries in the area. They visit her home and are invited in—the woman does not seem surprised by their interest, she produces a history of the township, and in

> a short time she and I are reading together a section on the Mannerow Cemetery, 'famous for its two vaults.' There is a grainy photograph of the larger

crypt. It is said to have been built in 1895 to receive the body of a three-year-old boy. A son of the Mannerow family. Other members of the family were placed there in the years that followed. One Mannerow husband and wife were put into the smaller crypt in the corner of the cemetery. What was originally a family graveyard later became public and the name of it was changed, from Mannerow to Cedardale.

(*Castle Rock* 329)[11]

Overhearing the conversation between Fremlin and the woman's husband, an immigrant from Holland of some years who had just been recounting his work history, Munro asks him if he had been at the Wallace Turkey Farm. That was right, so she asked him if he knew Bob Laidlaw. He did, though he associated him with Wingham, not Blyth where the Wallace farm was located. Munro tells him that Bob grew up near Blyth.

He takes a closer look at me, and laughs.
'You're not telling me he was your dad, are you? You're not Sheila?'
'Sheila's my sister. I'm the older one.'
'I didn't know there was an older one,' he says. 'I didn't know that. But Bill and Sheila. I knew them. They used to be down working at the turkeys with us, before Christmas. You never were there?'
'I was away from home by then.'

(*Castle Rock* 330–1)

Detailing this exchange, Munro writes that

We explore the connection as far as it will go, and soon find that there is not much to be got out of it. But we are both happy. He is happy to be reminded of himself as a young man, fresh in the country and able to turn himself to any work that was offered, with confidence in what lay ahead of him.

(*Castle Rock* 331)

Turning to herself and to her own happiness at this moment, she writes, "And I am happy to find somebody who can see me still as part of my family, who can remember my father and the place where my parents worked and lived for all their married lives, first in hope and then in honorable persistence" (*Castle Rock* 332). Here Munro enters the text for the *Castle Rock* version and changes the direction of the narrative, bringing it back to herself: "A place that I seldom drive past and can hardly relate to the life I live now, though it is not much more than twenty miles away." She then overlays her specific memories of the Laidlaw fur farm where she grew up with the changes that have come since: "it has changed utterly, becoming a car-wrecking operation." "But that is not the only thing that deprives it of meaning for me. No. It is the fact that it *is* only twenty miles away that I could see it every day if I wanted to. The past needs to be approached from a distance" (*Castle Rock* 331, 332; original emphasis). This last sentence should also be seen as a coda to *Castle Rock*.[12]

Munro and Fremlin then go with the woman to look inside the church, where there is evidence on its walls of German texts having been painted over—probably during the First World War in response to anti-German sentiment—and then she tells that they made another trip to nearby Scone where they talk to the wife of the last living Mannerow about the family history of the crypt. In between the two visits, Munro then hears from the city hospital cancelling her biopsy. "I am to keep the appointment anyway, to have a talk with the radiologist, but I do not need to fast in preparation for surgery." Munro also mentions a friend who had gone in to have what seemed a minor growth removed, one that he had made light of, which turned out to be a cancer that killed him.

When they talk in Scone to the wife of the last Mannerow she recalls the final funeral involving the crypt:

> It was for Mrs. Lempke, who had been born a Mannerow. There was just room for one more and she was the one. Then there was no room for anybody else. They dug down at the end and opened up the bricks and then you could see some of the inside, before they got her coffin in. You could see there were coffins in there before her, along either side. Put in nobody knows how long a time ago. "It gave me a strange feeling," she says, "it did so".
>
> (Castle Rock 338)

Looking into the opened crypt, she saw:

> a little table at the far end. A table with a Bible opened up on it.
>   And beside the Bible, a lamp.
> It was just an ordinary old-fashioned lamp, the kind they used to burn coal oil in.
>   Sitting there the same today, all sealed up and nobody going to see it ever again.
>   "Nobody knows why they did it. They just did."
>
> (Castle Rock 338–9)

In the 1994 version, Munro's talk with the radiologist in the city precedes this visit to Scone, but in *Castle Rock* it follows. Having received the mammograms from 1990 and '91, the doctor saw that that lump had been present in them then and that it had not changed. She advises Munro to wait and watch without having the invasive biopsy done. When Munro asks why it hadn't been spotted when it first appeared, the doctor responds that presumably they didn't see it. "So this is the first time," Munro thinks after a white-space break. "Such frights will come and go. Then there'll be one that won't. One that won't go" (*Castle Rock* 339). Writing this likely some time in late 2005 or early 2006—when she was about seventy-five and had had other such scares herself—Munro looks back to herself hearing this news in 1992, when she was about sixty-one. She reshapes the ending quite explicitly to create this sense of time passed and physical threat, well aware that she, and all of us, is heading inevitably toward our end. The last surviving Mannerow, the husband, could not talk because he was hard of hearing and had just emerged from the hospital, but Munro adds her friend who dies from cancer to *Castle Rock*. With the rearranged ending, she shifts after "One that won't go" to the following paragraph, a revised and expanded version of the paragraph that ends the first version:

> But for now, the corn in tassel, the height of summer passing, time opening out with room again for tiffs and trivialities. No more hard edges on the days, no sense of fate buzzing around in your veins like a swarm of tiny and relentless insects. Back to where no great change seems to be promised beyond the change of seasons. Some raggedness, carelessness, even a casual possibility of boredom again in the reaches of earth and sky.

The 1994 memorial ends with "Back where nothing seems to be happening, beyond the change of the seasons" and just before that Munro, while they were driving back from Scone, asked Fremlin, "'Do you think they put any oil in that lamp?'" He replies that "he had been wondering the same thing" (*Writing* 220). This exchange is in *Castle Rock* to end the memoir, but they are driving home "from the city hospital" (*Castle Rock* 340).

Placed in *Castle Rock* over "Wenlock Edge" and ending in this way just before Munro turns to two more cemeteries in the book's epilogue, "Messenger," "What Do You Want to Know For?" looks both to the past and, in perhaps a strange way, to the future. The exchange Munro had with the man who knew her father and knew her siblings too as they worked at the Wallace Turkey Farm, points over ten years back to the materials of her "The Turkey Season" (1980) and, also, to a brief scene in "Miles City, Montana" when the narrator recalls helping her father with his turkeys threatened by a rainstorm (*Progress* 93–4). When Munro meditates on the state of the Laidlaw place as it was in 1992, she is pointing directly to "Home" and "Working for a Living." And when she ends both versions of "What Do You Want to Know For?" with references to "tiffs and trivialities," she pointed—perhaps unknowingly, though likely not—to stories to come in her final two books. Tiffs and trivialities figure in "Too Much Happiness" and "Dolly," the latter serving as a bridge in its book, offering another older couple who look much like Munro and Fremlin looking into the crypt they had run across, just before she finally turns back to herself as a child amid her family in Wingham in her "Finale" in *Dear Life*. When *Castle Rock* was published a review by Alison Lurie caught the essences of Munro's art and of that book by focusing attention on "What Do You Want to Know For?"—its title was "The Lamp in the Mausoleum." In view of all this, it is difficult to imagine *Castle Rock* without "What Do You Want to Know For?": in so many ways, it points directly to the accomplishment of that book as both harbinger and fruition of Munro's late style.

"The Past Needs to be Approached from a Distance": "Changing Places" and "Memoirish" Stories, 1997–2002

When Munro spoke about the emerging structure of *The View from Castle Rock* in April 2004, she was still undecided as to whether "What Do You Want to Know For?" belonged there. I commented favorably on it and she interjected, "It's just factual story. All that just happened, and I haven't changed the names of the people, or anything, so I don't know." Just before, Munro told me that she would not include "Changing Places" (1997) in it "because I'm using that in the big story. The big story at the beginning of the new book," *Castle Rock* (Thacker interview April 2004). That big story Munro was at work on then, and had been at work on for a while, was "The View from Castle Rock"; when it was submitted to the *New Yorker* in March 2005 the manuscript was 140 double-spaced pages long, containing most of what later appeared as the "No Advantages" first section of *Castle Rock* plus the epilogue. While I will take up just what the editors did with this submission below, two contemporary comments by Munro help define her process of composition. Sending this big story to Barber in June 2003, Munro wrote that "you must be sick of seeing this but I do think I've *finally* got it into the right shape—a *kind* of a story." In a postscript, she offers another wry comment about her perennial hesitations, "Note assertive signing of *name*" (June 18, 2003; original emphasis; 947/14.12.1, file Correspondence 2001–3, 1 of 4).[13]

While in the last chapter I considered some of the research Munro did in Scotland and with Scottish materials in the two stories considered there, the point needs emphasizing that Munro had been doing the sort of traditional research seen there—and seen in "What Do You Want to Know For?" as well—for some time. After she returned to Huron County to live in the fall of 1975, she wrote a script on Irish emigration to Canada for the CBC. These various contexts underlie "Changing Places." Munro's researches just after she returned to Huron County bears relation to the narrator in "Meneseteung"; it was followed by the work she did in Ettrick in early 1990, and it continued as she turned to her own pioneering ancestors in Morris Township in "A Wilderness Station" (see Thacker *Reading* 217–26, 282). With "Changing Places," though, Munro turns explicitly to the exact details of her own people's emigration from the Ettrick Valley to North America in 1818.

"Changing Places" appeared in another volume published as a fundraiser for PEN Canada, this one entitled *Writing Home*. It begins abruptly with an unexplained extended block quotation running two pages of text:

> We sailed from the Harbour of Leith on the 4th June into the Leith Roads. There we lay the 5th, 6th, 7th and 8th getting the ship cleared out till the afternoon of the 9th when we set sail the 10th. We passed the corner of Fifeshire all well nothing occurred worth mentioning till the 13th in the morning we were awakened with the cry of 'John o'Groat's House' but we had a fine sail across Pentland Firth having both wind and tide with us and no way dangerous as reported but it came on such a breeze of wind in the afternoon from the Northward that set the ship a trembling and almost every passenger in the ship was spueing but I never got sick nor none of our family that I remember of, 14th was a calm day and we all well again but could take little meat and that night we lost sight of Scotland.
>
> (190)

The account of this trip continues in the letter, beginning on the east coast of Scotland, sailing north and west over the top of Britain and south of the Orkney Islands, across the Atlantic around Newfoundland and past Nova Scotia into the St. Lawrence River, arriving in Quebec City on 2 August. "We are to sail for Montreal tomorrow in a steamboat" (192).

This long quotation done, Munro steps into the text in her own voice:

> This letter, posted from Quebec on August 3, 1818, was addressed to William Laidlaw, Wolfhope, Parish of Ettrick, County of Selkirk, Scotland. The person who signed it was his father, James Laidlaw, but it was obviously written by his brothers Walter and Andrew. Nineteen-year-old Walter writes with a quick appreciation of himself and his adventure, Andrew more cautiously and circumspectly and with a hint of dry amused reproach. These different ways of responding to experience seem to me not reconciled in my family to this day.
>
> (192)

Introducing her people here, Munro begins with the recipient of this letter, William Laidlaw, one of the other sons who remained in Scotland and, as it happened and as she later explains, would become her own great-great-grandfather. In the long quoted passage it is reported that Andrew's wife Agnes bore a baby girl at sea and that, as well, they have a two-year-old son, James, with them on the ship. Here, Munro identifies the relations and comments on the group, "They may have all been well when they landed, but little James was dead before the end of the month. The baby Isabella had six children and lived to be an old woman. On her tombstone is written *Born at Sea*" (192).

Just what killed James is never discovered, neither in "Changes Places" nor in either of the two guises of "The View from Castle Rock," where he is a well-developed character on this same voyage across the Atlantic. According to a family marker in the Boston Presbyterian Church Cemetery in Halton, Ontario, where many of these Laidlaws are buried, he died August 29, 1818, but is not buried there. "There are always puzzles," as Munro wrote. And the baby Isabella's tombstone there does not say "Born at Sea." Munro does not appear to have known that when she wrote "Changing Places," but she apparently discovered that fact between it and "The View from Castle Rock" in the *New Yorker* since the claim of its presence on the tombstone has disappeared—though not the redolent phrase itself. After all, Isabella *was* born at sea (*New Yorker* 77; *Castle Rock* 87).[14]

I point to these facts to get at the singularity of "Changing Places" as a document revealing Munro's past and ongoing researches in the process which led to *Castle Rock* and, most especially, its first section. "Changing Places" is a first-person historical essay based on a mélange of documents, some researched but mostly inherited. Read now, it makes the path Munro was embarked on quite clear. Her researches are evident, for in the paragraph which follows that ending, "*Born at Sea*," just quoted, Munro offers speculative comments about family history: "it seems that they may have come north in some big pre-feudal migration, reached a part of Scotland that was maybe not Scotland then but Northumbria, settled down, and stayed put." Having discovered these early Laidlaws, she gets down to specifics: "I have found the name on court rolls for the fifteenth century—Laidlaws brought up more than once for 'theftuously removing' wood from Ettrick Forest when it belonged to the Kings of Scotland." So too she cites the mentions made of the elder James Laidlaw (1763–1829) by James Hogg, a cousin, in *Blackwood's Magazine*, including the publication of a letter by him to his son Robert written from York (Toronto) which appeared in the March 1820 number (see Thacker *Alice* 15–17).

As she describes the elder James, her great-great-great grandfather, Munro quotes Hogg on his cousin James Laidlaw in *Blackwood's*; he

> 'talked and read about America until he grew perfectly unhappy, and when approaching his sixtieth year actually set out to find a temporary home and a grave in the new world.' When Laidlaw first began to hear about America, Hogg adds, 'He would not believe that Fife was not in it, or that he could not see it from the top of Castle Hill in Edinburgh.'
>
> (193)

This last observation would prove to be, as discussed below, Munro's point of departure for "The View from Castle Rock" in the *New Yorker* and in the book. Using more of Hogg's descriptions of Laidlaw as well, Munro quotes at some length from the letter—about two pages' worth—to Robert, which treats mainly of the conditions in Upper Canada and signs off with the "'wish that the god of Jacob may be your god and may he be your gide for Ever and Ever is the Sincer prayer of your Loving Father till Death'" (196).

In the midst of this letter James encourages Robert to "'take it over to Wolfhope and Let William see it …'" (195) and, after more quotation about the living conditions in Upper Canada this points Munro toward her great-great-grandfather William, working in the Highlands for a sheep farmer. She has no letter from him (these letters have come down through the family), but she has one from Mary Scott, "a girl in Ettrick" whom William was courting, in answer to a lost letter from him.[15] Here Munro quotes the whole letter, which offers him local news from Ettrick and, as well, news from his father and family in Upper Canada from a mutual friend who visited them there; he reports that "'they were doing verry well your Father says he would not change with any farm in Ettrick.'" Mary Scott also mentions a local engagement which was "'stoped … becaus he is poor and perhaps he is not a Cameroning'" as well as other local weddings. Throughout, Munro sees, Mary Scott is being coy; she writes that she "'will be lik the old Almaniks that no person will by,'" but he has written of her about "'comming to you'" and that he "'may come some moonlight night and see me …'" (197). The subtext of this letter is literal wooing and, after concluding the quotation, Munro comments first that "By Cameroning she must mean a Cameronian" and then: "This letter was written in January of 1825 and within the year William and Mary were married" (198). Though still in Scotland, they too would emigrate to America—though to Illinois rather than Upper Canada without, apparently, visiting any family there—and through their youngest son Thomas, a baby when they emigrated, become Munro's great-great-grandparents.

After this letter Munro turns to another one written by James Laidlaw in 1827 and published in the *Colonial Advocate*, William Lyon Mackenzie's paper in York (Toronto) and very much a part of the political ferment then ongoing in Upper Canada—there would be a rebellion in 1837. The letter is wide ranging, Munro commenting that Laidlaw "is an old man taking a whack in every direction" (201). After the letter is published Laidlaw writes another complaining of its having been. There follows the full quotation of a May 1831 letter by Andrew to his brother William in Inverness-Shire in the Highlands, telling him of the family's circumstances, of the unanswered letters he had written to their aunts, and of the death of their father on February 13, 1829. As with the others, Munro glosses this letter, and then moves on to the circumstances of William and Mary's emigration to America in 1836. By then they had lost an infant daughter and had four sons, including her great-grandfather Thomas, and the "family settled in Will County, about thirty miles from Chicago." She takes up a memoir by the second son, John, written "when he was an old man, [recording] everything he could recall about their time there." "The eldest son James had at that time been dead for fifty years so John was the only source" (203). James was killed by falling tree in 1853, the son who figures in "A Wilderness Station" and "The Wilds of Morris Township." There John makes a reference to "'in the direction of Father's grave'": William caught cholera and "died on the 5th of January 1839." "He was forty years old. On the same day, no doubt in the same sod house, his daughter Jane was born, the first girl in the family since the baby Ellen had died in Inverness" (204). Munro continues, "Mary had her husband buried where nobody could find him today, and her daughter christened, and she wrote to her brothers-in-law, and when the winter was over and the roads were dry either Walter or Andrew came to Illinois with an ox-cart" (203). As Munro later learned, it was Andrew.

Telling this family history in "Changing Places," Munro is accounting for herself in many ways, and for some of the stories she had already written. Back then these Laidlaws "came to Upper Canada, to Esquising in Halton County, bound to the family after all, and not to become Yankees as their father must have wished." Munro acknowledges that these children were treated well, "but there was no land for them, and as soon as they were old enough the boys struck out for a new wilderness, for Morris Township in Huron County. When they had a shack built, their mother and young sister came to join them." Shifting then from this history to the Blyth Union Cemetery in Morris Township, Munro focuses on Mary Scott Laidlaw, tabulating her deaths. James's body was moved there but the grave is unmarked; Jane, the baby girl born the day of William's death in Illinois, died herself in childbirth at twenty-six; two of Mary's grandchildren, a girl thirteen and a boy one, also dead from cholera in 1868; and Mary herself, from cholera too, supposedly at the same time in family lore. Munro writes that she "had heard all my life, it seemed, the story of the two children and the grandmother who died all at the same time, of cholera, in the hot weather, and how in the haste to bury them, the lace curtains in the house were taken down and used for shrouds." Puzzling out this story for herself, Munro "saw that the girl had died in July and the boy in August and their grandmother Mary in October, so the story falls apart" (205, 206).

Yet even though the family story of the deaths and burials is not factual, Munro returns to Mary's life and accounts for it—adopting the long perspective toward it which is in many ways her hallmark: "A husband, a son, a baby daughter and a grown daughter, two grandchildren—this may not be so high a count of losses, for somebody born in 1800 who lived sixty-eight years. And Mary, like old James, was a person who had got her heart's desire" (206). These are the final words in "Changing Places." Mary wooed William into marriage, James finally got to America.

When Munro ended her story of Irish emigration, "A Better Place than Home," she had another widowed Mary—that name likely not coincident—about to be wooed by another man, slip off her wedding ring and put it "into her apron pocket." She continues, imagining her future and thinking of her letters from her dead husband:

> Her name would be Mary Norris. She would stay here, she would die here. She would change from the person she was into someone she could not imagine, another man's wife, and she would put those letters away where she could not look at them until she was old, so old they could not trouble her, and with so much life between her and them she would read them like a story.
>
> (124)

Another story written about that time, "Accident" (1977), ends with much the same sentiment (*Moons* 109). And here, in "Changing Places," Munro takes this long view again. But here her characters are not imagined; they lived, breathed, and died. They were her people, ancestors she knows a good deal about and sought to know more. Given this, "Changing Places," with its gatherings of letters, Munro's commentary, and that of others is an historical essay which should be seen as an outline, a schema, of *The View of Castle Rock* yet to come. In 1997 Munro was accelerating into that long-imagined family book.

Among Virginia Barber's papers is an undated single sheet written in her hand, headed "Alice Munro revised, earlier stories." It is clearly connected with the shaping of *Castle Rock*. One group of five stories is designated "memorish"; it is followed by line and two more titles, each published but not yet collected, "Wood" (1980) and "The Ferguson Girls Must Never Marry" (1982); then there is another line and two more titles, "Home" and "What Do You Want to Know For?." These are designated "memorial." While it is hard to say absolutely, this list is likely the result of a telephone conversation had by Barber and Munro, probably during 2002 since two of the "memorish" stories, "Fathers" and "Lying Under the Apple Tree," are the latest published stories listed. "The View from Castle Rock" is listed there as unpublished (947/14.12.1; Correspondence 2001–3, one of four). This sheet suggests that in conversation Munro was then differentiating between the two types of stories that would comprise *Castle Rock*, those that are "memorials" and those that are "memorirish."[16]

"Fathers" and "Lying Under the Apple Tree" are a critical pair here. They were written at about the same time—in 2001when Munro was revising "Home" and other fugitive pieces while awaiting heart surgery that fall—and they each appeared in the *New Yorker* within weeks of one another during the summer of 2002. As consequence, the two went through production concurrently—her editor at the magazine, Deborah Treisman, wrote Munro with proofs of "Fathers" on April 29 and then wrote about "Lying Under the Apple Tree" on the 16th and 30th of May. Ironically, in view of the "memorish" / "memorial" differentiation, "Lying Under the Apple Tree" appeared there as a memoir even though, as the fact checkers and editors saw it through production, they discovered a good deal of invention in the story which they addressed by writing a disclaimer themselves. They also considered accompanying the "memoir" with a family photo of the young Alice at about fifteen with her younger sister Sheila along the Maitland River in Lower Town Wingham (see Thacker *Alice* 17, 511–12).[17]

The manuscript version of "Fathers" Munro sent to Barber was received in September 2001. By April 19, 2002, the story had been accepted and, evidently, either the editors had suggested revisions or Munro had decided to revise herself, since she rewrote the last eight pages and faxed them to New York. When Treisman sent edited proofs on the 29th, she commented that the story "seems to pull together much more cohesively now, thanks to your wonderful additions" (*New Yorker* files).[18] The submitted manuscript of "Fathers" begins with an image of the circumstances of farmers during the spring of 1945, just at the end of the Second World War in Europe:

> All over the countryside, in spring, there was a sound that was soon to disappear. Perhaps it would have disappeared already, if it were not for the war. The war meant that the people who had the money to buy tractors could not find any to buy, and the few who had tractors already could not always get the fuel to run them. So the farmers were out on the land with their horses for the spring ploughing, and from time to time, near and far, you could hear them calling their commands, in which there would be degrees of encouragement, or impatience, or warning. You couldn't hear the exact words, any more than you could make out what the seagulls on their inland flights were saying, or decipher the arguments of crows. From the tone of voice, though, you could probably tell which words were swearing.
>
> (*New Yorker* files; *Castle Rock* 173)

But for one word and an added comma, this paragraph-long opening image is exactly the same as that found in *Castle Rock* (173). In between, there were a few small changes to this paragraph in the *New Yorker* version that Munro elected to leave out of *Castle Rock* and, as well, a very big change, for there this paragraph does not open the story, it follows the text of a newspaper announcement beginning, "On Friday morning last Harvey Ryan Newcombe, a well-known farmer of Shelby Township, lost his life due to electrocution." The putative newspaper text is followed with this sentence: "Dahlia Newcombe could not possibly have had anything to do with her father's accident" (*New Yorker* 64; *Castle Rock* 196). Submitting the story through her agent, Munro has "Fathers" begin with this image of farmers forced to use their horses for ploughing in spring 1945, an image that captures that historical moment's particularities as well as the conversations of birds, before she begins the second paragraph with this sentence: "With one man it was all swearing" (*New Yorker* files; *Castle Rock* 173). That man is Bunt Newcombe, one of the titular fathers and the man whose death by electrocution is described at the end of the submitted and *Castle Rock* versions of the story and, owing to its demands, at the beginning of the *New Yorker* first-published version. This electrocution, as well, has a basis in fact: such an accident nearly befell Munro's own father.[19]

When she wrote Munro with the magazine's edited proofs on April 29, 2002, Treisman suggested that Munro end the story with "Mysterious, uncomforting, unaccusing" as comment on her elders' saying that what "molds or warps" a child, "if it's not one thing it will be another" (*New Yorker* 71, *Castle Rock* 196). She writes that Newcombe's electrocution "feels like a postscript, and somehow draws the attention away from the real focus of the story—the narrator's synthesis of the fathers she's observed with her own father," so she asks if the death notice might "come a little earlier in the story and thus carry less emphasis?" Munro conceded, her imagined ending was moved to the beginning of the story before her imagined beginning and the *New Yorker* version ends with the phrase Treisman cites. But in *Castle Rock* she returned to the beginning and the ending she first wanted, typically adding a bit to the latter, since there in the last paragraph she extends two sentences connected to the circumstances of Newcombe's electrocution to: "He had taken one of his cows there to visit the bull," which is in the submission and the *New Yorker*, but she adds "and he was arguing at that moment about the fee," and to the absent rubber boots she adds "which everybody said might have saved his life" (*Castle Rock* 196).

Treisman is right to assert "the narrator's synthesis of fathers" as the focus of "Fathers," but it is more than that. The narrator's interiority, that is, her long retrospective recreation of herself at two key moments during her adolescence and childhood—just starting high school in the Newcombe instance, just starting grade five in the Wainwright connection—seen and recreated from years and a life later, is the story's essential point. How she saw and reacted to the two other fathers she learned of and saw, understood in comparison with her own father and his actions, is the point of "Fathers." Beginning it as Munro does, with the image of farmers ploughing with horses, cajoling them and swearing at them, their interactions heard from distance like disputing birds during the spring of 1945 (when she was herself in her first high-school year) is a means of introducing Bunt Newcombe as the horrid soul he was, and placing him in time and space. It also places the narrator, first remembering herself in 1945 and then, after she moves to Frances and her parents the Wainwrights, as a ten-year-old beginning grade five.

For their part, the Newcombes' family tale of a father's maltreatment of each of them, seen through Dahlia's desire to kill her father, frames the story as a whole. For that reason, the account of Bunt Newcombe's electrocution, a somewhat comic (he was "arguing about the fee") instance of *schadenfreude*, needs to be at the story's end, not its beginning. Equally, "Fathers" needs to begin with the image of ploughing with horses in 1945 amid distant cajoling and swearing.

Beyond capturing an autobiographical moment and the historic circumstances of that spring, "Fathers" also recursively visits circumstances seen previously in at least three of Munro's earlier stories. I say "at least" because echoes abound throughout. In much the same way as the story's opening, when Munro shifts from her high-school connections with Dahlia there is a space break and the narrator continues:

> On our road there had been at one time perhaps a dozen houses. Most were small cheap rental houses—until you got to our house, which was more of an ordinary farmhouse on a small farm. Some of those houses were on the floodplain of the river, but a few years ago, during the Depression, they had all sorts of people living in them.

Imaginatively there is a telescoping here: while Munro had already detailed something of her narrator's route along this road to high school, readers will recognize it in its various guises throughout Munro's early stories, stories like "Walker Brothers Cowboy" in *Dance*, the opening "The Flats Road" section of *Lives of Girls and Women* and, when later in this paragraph there is mention of "the old couple who used to have a grocery store and still had an Orange Crush sign in the front window, Munro has returned to Flo's store in *Who Do You Think You Are? / The Beggar Maid*.[20] She details three eccentric "old women left on their own," the like of which have been seen before and will appear again in Munro's final piece in her final book, "Dear Life." These descriptions and characters are by way of introduction to the second major father along that road, as the putative narrator writing in 1945 explains: "For a short while, years ago—that is, four or five years before I ever met Dahlia, a long time in my life—some people named Wainwright had lived in that house" (*Castle Rock* 182–3).

Introducing the Wainwrights and their daughter Frances, with whom the grade-five narrator walks back and forth to school, Munro returns explicitly to the circumstances of a very early story, "Good-By, Myra" (1956) which, revised, was included in *Dance* as "Day of the Butterfly." There the young narrator befriends a younger girl and walks back and forth to and from school with her, feeling ambivalent about the association owing to its possible effects on her own status among her peers. Ultimately such possible difficulties are resolved when the other girl, Myra, falls ill, is hospitalized, and declines toward her death. In "Fathers" some of this is retained, but Munro shifts the primary focus to the narrator's observations of Frances' family life and to her parents in particular—their former family life in Chicago, Frances' movie magazines which the narrator relishes, the parents' involvement there in the Light Opera Society and *The Pirates of Penzance*. The narrator takes it all in, recognizing her own participation in cruel treatment of Frances at school; looking back, she sees her own culpability: "Living out at the end of that road as I did, and being easily embarrassed, yet a show-off as I improbably was, I could never stand up for anybody who was being humiliated. I could never rise above a feeling of relief that it was not me" (*Castle Rock* 184).

As in "Day of the Butterfly," the cruelty at school the narrator participates in is left behind when Frances and her family move away, but before they do she is invited to a special dinner, one where the mother cooks and the father serves as fawning waiter. This is disquieting for the narrator, but then during the dinner there is a "near disaster" when the stove pipe catches fire and is initially ineptly dealt with by the parents. During this episode, the narrator witnesses parental behavior of a sort she had never before seen. She does not later tell any of this experience at home, for "there were other things I could not describe and that made me feel off-balance, slightly sick, so that I did not like to mention any of it." The narrator then details the behaviors that most upset her, that she now sees as a "menace," such as the "the charade of Mr. Wainwright as the waiter, his thick soapy-white hands and pale face and wings of fine glistening light-brown hair. The insistence—the too-closeness—of his soft footsteps in fat plaid slippers." "There was a creepy menace about all of this, starting with the falsity of corralling me to play the role of little friend—both of them had called me that—when

I was nothing of the kind. To treat me as good and guileless, when I was not that either" (*Castle Rock* 192–3).

What is most striking about this narrator and the story she tells throughout "Fathers" is the surety of Munro's control. Namely, as I have long argued and has been established in criticism since the early 1980s, Munro is using a sure-handed first-person retrospective technique in which a real focus is the narrator's assessment and understanding in the present of the person she was then, how she reacted to the action, how she sees it now (see Thacker *Reading* 23–44). Recursively returning to the circumstances found in "Day of the Butterfly" in "Fathers"—the Wainwright episode is the same story, essentially—Munro probes much deeper, wondering still, trying yet to see and articulate just who she was herself then in its narrative. Thus just after this last quotation, she asks in a paragraph that captures her surety and late-style control as it digs deeper:

> What was this menace? Was it just that of love, or of lovingness? If that was what it was, then you have to say that I had made its acquaintance too late. Such slopping-over of attention made me feel cornered and humiliated almost as if somebody had taken a peep into my pants. Even the wonderful unfamiliar food was suspect in my memory. The movie magazines alone escaped the taint.
>
> (*Castle Rock* 193)[21]

After accounting for the Wainwrights' departure from their house, the narrator shifts back to Dahlia whom she did tell her family about. "In my early teens I had become the entertainer around home." "I had mastered a deadpan, even demure style that could make people laugh even when they thought they shouldn't and that made it hard to tell whether I was innocent or malicious." That was how she told of Dahlia and her father years before, "the spying, the threats, the melodrama." In the midst of this discussion, Munro returns to the exact circumstances of "Royal Beatings," her first story in the *New Yorker*. The narrator and her parents had their "conversation" about Dahlia and her father "so easily, without its seeming ever to enter our heads that my father had beaten me, at times, and that I had screamed out not that I wanted to kill him, but that I wanted to die." This "had happened not so long ago," "in between my knowing Frances and my knowing Dahlia." These beatings were caused by "some falling out with my mother": she "would fetch my father from his outside work to deal with me, and I would await his arrival, first in balked fury, and then in a sickening despair" (*Castle Rock* 193–4).

This comment is followed by another salient one: "I felt as if it must be my very self that they were after, and in a way I think it was," and Munro then details the beatings: her father's belt, her own protestations, and more wondering. "How could I not find myself howling at such perversion in nature," she asks, and one word there, "howling," is especially notable in Munro's late style. Just as these beatings are alluded to in the "Finale" to *Dear Life*, the narrator of "Dolly," the story which just precedes the "Finale," also finds herself howling at a critical moment in her story, a story which through the age of the principals also echoes "What Do You Want to Know For?" (*Dear Life* 306, 252). The narrator continues to muse about what her father would say now, were he still alive, about these beatings. She knew too that she had changed and that she "never once thought to compare my situation with" Dahlia's, explaining,

> My father did not swear. He was a man of honor and competence and humor, and he was the parent I sorely wanted to please. I did not hate him, could not consider hating him. Instead, I saw what he hated in me. A shaky arrogance in my nature, something brazen yet cowardly, that woke in him this fury.
> Shame. The shame of being beaten, and the shame of cringing from the beating. Perpetual shame. Exposure. And something connects this, as I feel it now, with the shame, the queasiness, that crept up on me when I heard the padding of Mr. Wainwright's slippered feet, and his breathing.
> (*Castle Rock* 195–6)[22]

With this, Munro's three fathers are connected, and synthesized, in their shared implications toward this narrator as Munro has recreated them in "Fathers." Realizing now their shared implications, the narrator continues: "There were demands that seemed indecent, there were horrid invasions, both sneaky and straightforward. Some that I could tighten my skin against, others that left it raw. All in the hazards of life as a child." Munro refers to elders' saying and then ends the next paragraph with the words "Mysterious, uncomforting, unaccusing" before offering the expanded newspaper account of Bunt Newcombe's electrocution (*Castle Rock* 196).

Opening the second part of *The View from Castle Rock*, immediately following the revised and expanded "Working for a Living" which ends with an account of her father's late-life career as a writer and an extended quotation from a published memoir of his, "Grandfathers"—a quotation rather like those she offers in "Changing Places"— Munro is making a recursive return in "Fathers" both to earlier attempts to probe her own life and to probe her relation to her father at a fraught time. Munro knows that Bob Laidlaw's rubber boots "saved his life" from electrocution in 1943 just as she knows that the beatings he administered, the fury his daughter knows he felt, led her to "Royal Beatings" in the *New Yorker*. "Fathers" reprises her lifelong subject of growing up at the end of West Street, that rural road, in Lower Town Wingham. Doing so in this story that is "closer to [her] own life" than other stories she has written, she begins the second section of *Castle Rock* and effectively leaves the story of her "people"—her immigrant and pioneer ancestors as well as her immediate predecessors, relatives she knew— behind. They are the focus of the first part of *Castle Rock*, "No Advantages." "Fathers," opening the second part, "Home," shifts the focus to assert Munro's own presence, born and growing up there in Lower Town Wingham, in Huron County Ontario, in her home place. The primary site, ever and always, of Munro's own "Dear Life."

Continuing this process, the second story, "Lying Under the Apple Tree," joins with "Fathers" to extend the intentions at the core of *Castle Rock*. Here again the first-person narrator is thirteen and in her first year of high school, though the action takes place during the spring and summer preceding "Fathers," 1944. Its primary focus is the narrator's first infatuation.

In each of these stories the most urgent matter is less putative factuality than its imaginative directions, and the ways by which Munro, looking back to 1944–5, recreates her own feelings then and describes their shaping as she experienced new circumstances and matured. Doing that within the circumstances of her life then, who she was as an adolescent, who her parents were (her mother sick with a progressively worsening disease, her hardworking father dealing with his wife's illness and the collapse of the family's fox farm) and, more especially in "Fathers" and in "Lying Under the Apple Tree," how she understood and defined her own trajectory as a person as she grew up. Because of this, each story is key to the structure of *Castle Rock*.

After introducing Miriam McAlpin, a woman "who kept horses" on the other side of town and who figures in the story's action, Munro tells of three apple trees that the narrator noticed on the horse farm as she rode her bicycle about the town, "apple blossoms hanging on everywhere, so that the branches looked from a little way off to be absolutely clotted with snow" (*Castle Rock* 197).[23] Like the ploughing scene which opens "Fathers," Munro here opts to begin with a central image: the blossoming apple tree. She tells of the narrator riding about on a bike, a dangerous thing for the social standing of a thirteen-year-old girl, the narrator's younger sister reminds her. "'Not to school,' I said" (*Castle Rock* 198). As she explains these rides, Munro brings the image of the apple trees into central focus for the narrator and for the story:

> But I did start making use of the bike, riding it out into the country along the back roads on Sunday afternoons. There was hardly a chance then of meeting anybody I knew, and sometimes I met nobody at all.
>
> I liked to do this because I was secretly devoted to Nature. The feeling came from books, at first. It came from the girls' stories by the writer L. M. Montgomery, who often inserted some sentences describing a snowy field in moonlight or a pine forest or a still pond mirroring the evening sky. Then it had merged with another private passion I had, which was for lines of poetry. I went rampaging through my school texts to uncover them before they could be read and despised in class.
>
> To betray either of these addictions, at home or at school, would have put me into a condition of permanent vulnerability. Which I felt that I was in already, to some extent. All someone had to say, in a certain voice, was *you would*, or *how like you*, and I felt the taunt, the chastening air, the lines drawn.
>
> (*Castle Rock* 198–9; original emphasis)[24]

The narrator's aesthetics set her apart, drawing her in directions of desire and want, as she continues explicitly,

> But now that I had the bike, I could ride on Sunday afternoons into territory that seemed waiting for the kind of homage I ached to offer. Here were the sheets of water from the flooded creeks flashing over the land, and here were the banks of trillium under the red-budded trees. And the chokecherries, the pin cherries, in the fencerows, breaking into tender bits of bloom before there was a leaf on them.
>
> (*Castle Rock* 199)

As mentioned, during editing at the *New Yorker* the fact checker turned up indications that details in "Lying" were imagined, so that on May 30, 2002, Deborah

Treisman wrote Munro that they "think that so long as we put in a disclaimer stating that information has been changed, the piece will be fine running as nonfiction." She had already written one and put it at the end of the first paragraph, and she also writes, "It feels better that way, given the tone and voice, which is so much more memoirish than fictional" (*New Yorker* files).

This is actually true of both this story and "Fathers," for the passage just quoted reveals a narrator, Munro herself, recalling and assessing herself at thirteen in the midst of her own blossoming—the analogy is unavoidable; ever drawn to books, Munro in "Lying Under the Apple Tree" accounts for her secret interests and desires as she also experiences her first romantic attraction to Russell Craik, a probably seventeen-year-old boy who pursues her and whom she secretly meets Sunday afternoons during her bike rides in the country. In nature they meet, share time, looking about at its munificence and at evidences of others who have been down the same road, and end their visit with a petting session. When, early in the story, Miriam McAlpin questions the narrator as to why she was seen lying beneath one of the blossoming apple trees on McAlpin's property, the narrator does in fact lie about her real aesthetic motivation. Pressing her, McAlpin tells her to stay away and, after she "looked me up and down," she "said what she'd been wanting to say all along. 'You're starting early, aren't you?'" (*Castle Rock* 201). She was doing just that, and it is one of the main considerations in "Lying Under the Apple Tree," but first teen-aged heterosexual attraction is the lesser part. That plays out, Russell goes off to the army before coming back to marry another, but the narrator's aesthetic desire remains, her attraction to nature, with its poetry, and ultimately to the plots of fiction.[25]

Munro's own fictional plot moves from the incident under the apple tree to an account of the narrator's family's social position in the town seen through her activities on Saturday nights, when everyone was out for shopping and socializing. She tells of her friends, who "were not out of the top drawer," a fact that made her mother sorry, but "it was all right with me. This way, I could be a ringleader and a loudmouth. If that was a disguise it was one I managed easily." They would go to "Neddy's Night Owl," a dance hall where dances cost ten cents but the narrator and her friends weren't asked to dance—such a place was one Munro had used before and would use again in her "Finale" in "The Eye" (2012). Just after explaining her role and "disguise," the narrator continues describing the Saturday night scene, focusing on a Salvation Army band.

The girls and others paused to watch the performance, "waiting for something to laugh at." Looking on, the narrator realizes that

> the boy who lifted the trombone was the same stable boy who had stood in the yard while Miriam McAlpin was giving me the dressing-down. He smiled at me with his eyes as he began to play and he seemed to be smiling not to recall my humiliation but with irrepressible pleasure, as if the sight of me woke the memory of something quite different from the scene, a natural happiness.
>
> "There is Power, Power, Power, Power, Power, Power in the Blood," sang the choir. The tambourines were waved above the players' heads. Joy and lustiness infected the bystanders, so most people began to sing along with a jolly irony. And we permitted ourselves to sing with the others.
>
> (Castle Rock 205)

This is quite a scene, one in which the narrator's social position is asserted, one which sparks her relation with Russell Craik, the trombone-playing stable boy, and one about which it is worth noting that for a time *Power in the Blood* was expected to be the title of *The View from Castle Rock*.[26]

The two begin their relationship with their Sunday afternoon meetings in nature and, as it develops, Russell shows himself keen to deepen it. The narrator is invited to dinner at the Craik's and, in a scene reminiscent of one Munro had written and published in *Lives of Girls and Women* (219–24), there she meets his family and sees where he is from. Knowing her mother's views on class—these people are emphatically not "from the top drawer"—she also lies to her about where she is going to dinner. Whereas the previous dinner scene in "Baptizing" in *Lives* was infused with sexual tension—Del Jordan and Garnet French have their first sexual experience that night—in "Lying Under the Apple Tree" there is a serenity as the narrator recalls what was happening at the dinner at the Craik's home. She explains,

> It never crossed my mind that a young couple in our situation did indeed belong right here, that we had entered on the first stage of a life that would turn us, soon enough, into the Father and the Mother. Russell's parents probably knew this, and may have been privately dismayed, but decently hopeful, or resigned. Russell was already a force in the family whom they did not control. And Russell knew it, if he was capable at the moment of thinking that far ahead. He hardly looked at me, but when he did it was a steady look, laying claim, and it hit me and resonated as if I'd been a drum.
>
> (*Castle Rock* 218–19)

And here, though Russell clearly expects to have sex when he takes her to the horse barn, his plans are put awry when McAlpin thinks them intruders and fires a shotgun in the barn. Munro had already stymied a planned sexual liaison between Del Jordan and Jerry Storey in *Lives*, also in "Baptizing" (199–203), and would do so again in "Axis," her last published but uncollected story.

Ending this one, Munro breaks the text just after the narrator flees the barn, leaving Russell consoling Miriam over the shotgun blast, and heads home. But before she gets there Munro telescopes time, reporting that the narrator "didn't see Russell again" and tells of her subsequent knowledge of him and of his history. Arriving home, she again lies to her mother about what she had for dessert, thinking "I thought that if I said any part of the truth, if I said 'pie,' I would immediately betray myself. She did not care, she only wanted a bit of conversation, but I was not able to supply it" (*Castle Rock* 225–6). Leaving her mother, whose infirmities keep her in bed, she continues saying that she "went downstairs and into the living room, where I sat on a low stool in front of the bookcase and took out a book." She accounts for the scene and for her posture, reading, "filling my mind with one sentence after another, slamming them into my head just so I would not have to think about what had happened" (*Castle Rock* 225–6). In the *New Yorker* this description is not a "slamming," it remains a "filling," and it continues "just to get away from what had happened, the distortion that had appeared in my life" (*New Yorker* 114). This last phrase is deleted in *Castle Rock*, but clearly Munro is getting at this moment as a fulcrum point, a shift, perhaps an epiphany. Both versions then offer an account of the titles in that bookcase, and among other well-known novels, all of which the narrator has already read, there are *Wuthering Heights* and *Gone with the Wind*, both of which are apt. More than that, Emily Brontë's is a central text of Munro's adolescence. And while it is impossible to really say, I certainly think that this list is an accurate remembrance of what was actually there. Both versions, with some small edits, then offer this paragraph:

> It must have meant something, though, that at this turn of my life I grabbed up a book. Because it was in books that I would find, for the next few years, my lovers. They were men, not boys. They were self-possessed and sardonic, with a ferocious streak in them, reserves of gloom. Not Edgar Linton, not Ashley Wilkes. Not one of them companionable or kind.
>
> (*Castle Rock* 226)

The *New Yorker* version then ends the story with this paragraph: "But steadfast, as they had to be. Not allowed to transform themselves, slip away, turning a stranger's solid back to me" (114). This was quite close to the original ending to the submitted story—in the original "stranger's" was "strange," Treisman having suggested the change to possessive (*New Yorker* proof, 23; May 15, 2002)—but returning to the story for *Castle Rock* Munro deleted that paragraph and added this one:

> It was not as if I had given up on passion. Passion, indeed, wholehearted, even destructive passion, was what I was after. Demand and submission. I did not exclude a certain kind of brutality. But no confusion, no double-dealing, or sleazy sort of surprise or humiliation. I could wait, and my all due would come to me, I thought, when I was full blown.
>
> (*Castle Rock* 225)

When Munro published her first book, *Dance of the Happy Shades* in 1968, one her publishers at Ryerson had to work hard to convince her to bring out, most of its strongest stories were first-person retrospective dealings with childhood experience. With "Fathers" and "Lying Under the Apple Tree" as presences in *Castle Rock* Munro shows herself still engaged in the same retrospection but, here in her seventies, at a longer distance and, quite certainly, with sharper perspective. Both stories' endings in *Castle Rock* show this, that of "Fathers" reasserted after the *New Yorker* reshaping to make "might have saved his life" its last words, and the new paragraph added to "Lying Under the Apple Tree" for its ending has Munro looking back and, caustically, forward: the "destructive" passion she sought was just what she got. "Demand and submission" in fact. These personal fictions, shaped as they were in *Castle Rock* are integral to *its* retrospective cast. Memoirs, "memoirish" stories, family history: *The View from Castle Rock*, a book Munro had to do, and she said, one she did for herself.

3

"It Has Some Real Munrovian Highlights": "The View from Castle Rock" and *The View from Castle Rock*

> When I was a teenager I did discover that my grandmother had all these letters. She told me [about them] and she read them to me. They were a wonderful collection to have because there was a description of early Toronto, a description of early Vancouver, and a description of the voyage over. These are remarkable letters. The one Walter wrote is really very good and James's letter from Toronto is just fantastic. His is more idiosyncratic, Walter's a more observant, a very intelligent young man. But James is that of a character who finds a lot to complain about but describes it in a very funny way. How are these things passed down?

This quotation is from an interview Munro did with her daughter Sheila in March 1997, an interview full of family history, one that reveals the ongoing imaginative process which had then produced "Changing Places" and would ultimately produce *The View from Castle Rock*. Walter Laidlaw (1799–1873) was the youngest of two sons James Laidlaw brought with him when he emigrated to Canada from Ettrick in summer 1818 with a part of his family. Another passage from that interview:

> My grandma had some letters and I don't know how she came by them, letters about the voyage and the letter of Mary [Scott Laidlaw, 1800–68], in which she wooed her husband, were in that collection. The letter from old James home to Scotland describing Toronto was published in Blackwood's Magazine. He professed great indignation but was probably secretly satisfied. [James Hogg, his cousin the Ettrick Shepherd, 1770–1835] was the one who put it into Blackwood's Magazine along with a character sketch of cousin James and telling various stories about him which was my material for finding out what James was like. He was also a great flat-earther. I don't know how much education any of these people had. They were always poor, they were *always* at the bottom of the heap even after they came to Morris Township. They never seemed to make much money.

Here, being interviewed by Sheila—who was then at work on her own book, *Lives of Mothers and Daughters* (2001)—Munro details facts that she had already begun using in "Changing Places" and, continuing further, would go on to shape into *Castle Rock*. As its facts fermented and were shaped in Munro's imagination during the 1990s and into the 2000s, she was prolifically engaged in fiction since that period saw a succession of four new collections from *Open Secrets* in 1994 through *Runaway* in 2004, numerous first serials in the *New Yorker* and elsewhere, plus her first volume of *Selected Stories* in 1996. And when Munro came to produce *Castle Rock* as a book, she had contracted to do it in tandem with *Runaway*, a fictional collection without explicit autobiographical cast.[1]

When Michael Gorra likened *Castle Rock* to Naipaul's *The Enigma of Arrival* in his review of *Too Much Happiness*, he was intimating the personal singularity of that book for Munro herself.[2] Detailing its methods, William Butt writes aptly that in it readers "are favoured with almost exhibitionistic research" and he continues to assert, also aptly, that *Castle Rock* "is explicitly intertextual, a gabble of authors and passages quoted from and referred to" which he then goes on to specify (347, 353). Concerned primarily with intertextual references published there, Butt has little to say about Munro's use of her own family history beyond that offered in her text.[3] Yet early in my *Alice Munro: Writing Her Lives*—before she had published her "enigma of arrival," what she saw as her last book, though not before I had seen a different preliminary version of the manuscript of *Castle Rock*—I made this observation: "the presence of her ancestors in the writing that has made her reputation needs to be both acknowledged and specified. What Munro offers by her namings—by using the facts of her families' histories to pose the human mysteries she probes in her fiction—is persistent tribute to what her ancestors were, what they believed, what they did" (Thacker *Alice* 29). While she had been doing this throughout the whole of her writings, at times more specifically factual than at other times, Munro most emphatically demonstrates something Leon Edel wrote of Henry James in a foreword to a volume of his biography: "A writer of novels and tales, in particular, in the act of creating universal works is at the same time telling us personal parables about himself. 'Poetry,' said Thoreau in a moment of great insight, 'is a piece of very private history, which unostentatiously lets us into the secret of a man's life'" (17).[4] The enigmatic qualities found in *Castle Rock*—the family history, the "exhibitionist research" and intertextuality, the fictionalized autobiography—combine, just as Thoreau maintained and Edel notes, into poetic narrative. One Alice Munro had been contemplating by the time she made her book for more than twenty-five years. *Castle Rock* was like no other book she had before made, certainly not in any way like the other collection also then being gathered, *Runaway*; yet in its factual bases, its acknowledgments of her historical connections to the people of the Ettrick Valley, to their culture and to their Presbyterian rigidities, and to the continuities of that culture borne out in Huron County, the book displays this poetic authorial secret in ways personal to Munro, and to her own being. As Deborah Eisenburg asserted in her review, *Castle Rock* is "a work of dizzying originality," "an entirely new category of book into which only it can fall." The two previous chapters have examined the book's imaginative underpinnings chronologically, so it remains here to drill down into the making and reception of the *Castle Rock* itself as poetic harbinger of Munro's late style.

The earliest mention of "The View from Castle Rock" as a story nearing completion is found in a letter Munro wrote to Barber in June 2003; there Munro sends her the manuscript, writing "You must be sick of seeing this but I do think I've *finally* got it into the right shape—a kind of a story." She tells her to "pitch" the previous versions she has "and let this sit until we are inspired to put it in a book (?)" (received June 18, 2003; original emphasis; 947/14.12.1: Correspondence 2002–3, 1 of 4). The parenthetical question mark which ends the note is indication of Munro's perpetual hesitations about her work, but in this case it should also be seen as indicating an especial uncertainty about this particular book, whether it would emerge at all, given its demands.

When Munro spoke to me in April 2004 about the two books she was making just then, she said that she had written "a long story—I think it's a seven-part story—about the Laidlaw family coming out on the boat" (Thacker interview). That story may have been the one Munro sent to Barber the year before, or it may have been a more extended treatment reflecting further work. In any case on March 7, 2005, Barber's successor as Munro's agent, Jennifer Rudolph Walsh, wrote Deborah Treisman at the *New Yorker*, saying "I'm happy to (finally) send you Alice Munro's story 'The View from Castle Rock,'" commenting, "it's totally autobiographical" (*New Yorker* files). The parenthetical "finally" probably indicates that some time had passed since Walsh had first told Treisman to expect the story, but what she enclosed was a 140-page manuscript entitled "Laidlaws II: The View From Castle Rock" made up of six subtitled parts: "Singular Characters," "Men of Ettrick," "Illinois," "The Wilds of Morris Township," "Working for a Living," and "Remnants." Most every page of the manuscript is dated in Munro's hand—February 7, 2005—with three revised pages dated February 28, 2005 (66, 138–9—containing factual changes connected with Munro's great-great-grandfather, William Laidlaw) (*New Yorker* files). While other revisions would be made as the manuscript was edited at the *New Yorker* and then later shaped into the book, what was here in this submission was essentially the first section of the published *Castle Rock*, "No Advantages," plus the epilogue.[5]

Treisman and her fellow editors at the magazine were attracted by the submission, but they knew it would need to be cut considerably. Offering a reading, Carin Besser writes that she "could imagine a piece centered around the boat trip, starting with what she has on p. 11—a very brief intro to James Hogg and the reading habits of his circle, including the mention of Blackwood's magazine and Wuthering Heights"; she also said "I like all the stuff about reading and recording, and the sense of Munro trying to fill in and reanimate these things." Besser concedes that Munro may not want to revise as she imagines, but "the way this telescopes out [when Munro describes the characters' lives after the voyage], catching up with their individual aspirations, reducing them to their letters, is really great" (Besser to Treisman March 16, 2005; *New Yorker* files). Another fiction editor, Cressida Leyshon, suggests that their excerpt begin with "Men of Ettrick," leaving out much historical background, and so start as the Laidlaws step onto the ship, and "finish on the death of young James" (Leyshon to Treisman March 24, 2005; *New Yorker* files). Treisman combined these two sets of suggestions and, writing on the same day she received Leyshon's reading, sent a forty-four-page excerpt to David Remnick, the chief editor. Describing it as "a very rough cut" from Munro's long "combination of family history and fiction (the characters' names and details are all true—the happenings on the boat imagined)," she summarizes some cuts she intends and concludes, "But I think it could be made to work, and it has some real Munrovian highlights, which cutting would only accentuate" (Treisman to Remnick March 24, 2005; *New Yorker* files).

Remnick accepted this recommendation, "The View from Castle Rock" was bought, scheduled, edited, and published as fiction in the August 29, 2005, issue of the magazine with an historical photograph, "Emigrants Coming to the 'Land of Promise'" as a frontispiece.[6] A pause here to comment on the typically thorough editing the story received. On April 15, 2005, Munro faxed a new opening to "The View from Castle Rock" with the title written in her hand, so she had dropped "Laidlaws II"; though edited, it is what appears in the magazine before the first text break (68). Presumably Treisman requested this. Along with it, Munro also sent new material describing old James telling young James about his own grandfather, Will O'Phaup, meeting with fairies (73–4). The full copy of the proofs of "Munro Fiction Castle, Revision 9: Thursday, August 4, 2005" is tightly edited, with Treisman making numerous suggestions sentence by sentence—syntactical rephrasings, transpositions, tense changes, noted repetition, and deletions—but with no major reshaping. Almost all of these suggestions were incorporated into the *New Yorker* text but some, x'ed out throughout, were not accepted by Munro. This process had been the magazine's practice from her first story in 1977, certainly, but I mention it here because these proofs also show something else: while Munro accepted Treisman's edits by and large for the magazine's excerpted text, she returned in *Castle Rock* to her own submitted version—that is, the exact wordings and phrasings she submitted and preferred (August 4, 2005 proof; *New Yorker* files). Finally, Barber commented to me that the

> August 29th New Yorker has some of "The View from Castle Rock," published as if it were pure fiction when much of the piece was based on her research. True, the section they use, the voyage, is chiefly dramatized, and thus, becomes fiction although she had letters and journals to guide her. I wonder what readers will make of the story.
>
> (email August 24, 2005)

Taking up the version of this story in the contexts of *Castle Rock*, Dennis Duffy writes that Munro "seems at play in the opening five historical stories in *The View from Castle Rock*. After masking herself as the familiar omniscient narrator for fifty-seven of the title story's sixty-one pages, she insouciantly breaks character with the announcement that she 'can look it up' in a letter that she has in her possession today." Duffy then harkens back to an instance in the narrative of Charlotte Brontë's *Jane Erye* before contrasting it with *Castle Rock* where, he argues, the reader "is faced with a collection of family lore, of recollected and transmitted experience, subject to all the alterations that time, distance, and shifts in narrators compel. We are reading what we might call a background to objective autobiography, 'something closer to what a memoir does,' according to the author" (376).

Shaping *The View from Castle Rock*

Each of the critics I have cited here—Gorra, Butt, and Duffy—points toward the "dizzying originality" that Eisenburg saw in *The View from Castle Rock* when it was published. Each is focused on what might be called the disaffecting quality of the reading experience, and each complements the other. Gorra's phrasing from Naipaul's title, *Enigma of Arrival*, catches the way *Castle Rock* creates in its reader the sense of its long, deep provenance. That is, it creates the wonderings that readers feel, and Munro senses herself, through its assembling from pieces, some new but others some time since written and published. Butt's notice of the book's wide ranging and explicit intertextuality (after its foreword the book's first text is a quotation from the 1799 *Statistical Account of Scotland*), well taken as it is, might also have proceeded from the fact that, in the first stories of her career, Munro avoided any explicit literary allusion almost altogether. And Duffy, with his comment that Munro "insouciantly breaks character," points toward the same enigmatic intertextuality of *Castle Rock* and of Munro's late style in its affects *and* its effects.

Mostly "The View from Castle Rock" in the *New Yorker* reads like fiction though, given its clear use of historical documents, Barber's questioning of that presentation was well considered. Though bookended by Andrew Laidlaw's boyhood visit to Edinburgh with its highlighted gaze from Castle Rock across Blackness Bay to Fife at its beginning and, at its end, the narrator's summative visit to "the graveyard of Boston Church, in Esquesing, in Halton County, Ontario" (77), the narrative of the voyage, the personal qualities and intentions of the characters, the occurrences during it that Munro imagines and ponders—all tell that version of the tale. Yet when the narrative reaches that graveyard, as the narrator details the presences there, and as Besser wrote upon first reading the story, the story does in fact "telescope out," "catching up with their individual aspirations, reducing them to their letters" and finishes with the fact of young James's death "within a month of the family's landing in Quebec." And also his body's absence in that graveyard, for he was "Dead of some mishap in the busy streets, or of a fever, or dysentery, or any of the ailments, the accidents, that were the common destroyers of little children in his time" (*New Yorker* 77). Though edited slightly for the book, a version of these words ends the story.

In *The View from Castle Rock* that graveyard is one of four Munro highlights to tell her family's history: Ettrick Kirk; an unknown cemetery in Illinois perhaps holding the body of William Laidlaw; this Boston Church graveyard; and Blyth Union Cemetery in Huron County where she expects to lie herself. These places represent the bases of the family history Munro had long been intent on discovering herself, wondering over, and telling in *Castle Rock*. She had begun this work in some of her earliest stories. But the imaginative trajectory which led to that book really began in 1972 when she returned to Ontario from British Columbia and took those three buses from Toronto to Wingham to visit her father still on the family farm. Then she wrote and published "Home."

The passages Duffy points to when Munro "insouciantly breaks character" are not in the *New Yorker* version of the story. There, the ship arrives in Quebec and Munro quotes first from Walter's journal description and then, without comment, shifts to the text of a letter Walter and Andrew wrote to their brother William in Scotland, had signed by their father, and "posted from Quebec on August 3, 1818." She quoted most of that letter to begin "Changing Places" (192, 190–2). After these quotations there is a section treating of the travelers' aspirations now that they have arrived, ending "Old James has sensed defection" among his family fellow travelers "and begins to lament openly, 'How shall we sing the Lord's song in a strange land?'" (*New Yorker* 77). In the book's version, there is a break after this and Munro quotes excerpts from a letter James Laidlaw wrote to his eldest son Robert in Scotland from York (Toronto) on September 19, 1819. This quotation is followed by the passage Duffy alludes to: "There is more—the whole letter passed on by Hogg's connivance and printed in *Blackwood's Magazine*, where I can look it up today" (*Castle Rock* 82–3). Munro follows this with another long quotation from a letter by James to William Lyon Mackenzie, the editor of the *Colonial Advocate*—it was published in that newspaper on January 18, 1827—where, among other subjects, Laidlaw complains of Hogg's putting his letter to Robert "in Blackwood's Magazine and had me all through North America before I knew my letter had gone Home … [.]" After the ellipsis she continues:

> Hogg poor man has spent his most of his life conning Lies and if I read the Bible right I think it says that all Liares is to have there pairt that Burns with Fire and Brimstone but I supose they find it a Loquarative trade for I believe that Hogg and Walter Scott has got more money for Lying than old Boston and the Erskins got for all the Sermons ever they Wrote …[7]

Ending the quotation here, Munro starts a new paragraph and comments in the same vein as Duffy notes, "And I am surely one of the liars the old man talks about, in what I have written about the voyage. Except for Walter's journal, and the letters, the story is full of my invention." Another paragraph break, then "The sighting of Fife from Castle Rock is related by Hogg, so it must be true" (*Castle Rock* 84; original ellipses). So it is, for in the March 1820 *Blackwood's* Hogg writes of Laidlaw, "When he first began to hear tell of North America, about twenty ears ago, he would not believe me that Fife was not it; and that he saw it from the Castle Hill of Edinburgh" ("Letter" 630).

"And I am surely one of the liars the old man talks about …," Munro adds to the book after the *New Yorker* account of the voyage from Leith to Quebec. "It's the fact you cherish," she wrote also in "What Do You Want to Know For?," just as she was imaginatively finding her way through "A Wilderness Station" more deeply into her family history, and through "Hired Girl" more deeply into her own, and so both moving her toward *Castle Rock*. That is certainly so, but the facts used there, the breaking of the narrator's character that Duffy notes, the self-conscious admission to being a "liar," was also taking Munro in a different direction than her readers expected. And most especially just after *Runaway*. Some 2006 reviewers showed the discomfort. When *Castle Rock* was published, Alex Good asserted that it "is obviously a lot more than a conventional Ontario family history / memoir. But it is also a lot less than Munro's best work." He continues, "But the usual music of her language is only playing faintly in the background here, dominated by easy notes of local colour and sentimental charm. Strong evidence that Munro's great mythic ground—perhaps the greatest in all our literature—may finally be written out" (see also Henighan). At the point Good was writing his review during late 2006 Munro had announced that it would be her last book, so perhaps this ruminative sense of a long career ending was warranted. But his notion of "easy notes and sentimental charm" not only misses what *Castle Rock* actually does, it fundamentally misreads its actual and most telling effect, which is to place Munro herself—writing and reshaping its pieces—sharply and precisely within time. Tessa Hadley's review of *Castle Rock*, in which she sees the Ettrick Valley in the book as "a signifying elsewhere," also offers an account of the effects this book creates which both define its importance within Munro's oeuvre and also confirm it though its authorial technique as the beginning of her recursive late style. "Without ever losing her focus on these other, past lives," Hadley writes of Munro's use of historical figures, "she also seems to be giving us a magical account of her own life in writing, tracing a history for her imagination" (17). That is just right.

Or Karl Miller, himself a biographer of James Hogg, who writes of *Castle Rock* that it

is a rare and fascinating work, in which the past makes sense of the present and the present makes sense of the past, and the two are both a continuum and a divorce. It is very much a memoir, as well as a set of fictions. But then the whole corpus of her stories is a memoir, the novel of her life.

(21; see Thacker *Alice* 548–9)[8]

Miller ends the paragraph in which this passage appears with this aside from "Working for a Living," "'When you write about real people you are always up against contradictions,'" an added amplification Munro made to the revised version of that memoir of another she makes in the book's first section, "No Advantages": "The past is full of contradictions and complications, perhaps equal to those of the present, though we do not usually think so" (*Castle Rock* 136, 17).

My friend Tracy Ware, a sharp student of Munro, once commented "she's a brilliant historian." That is a fact, one that might be asserted and traced throughout her work wherever one looks; to some extent, it has been (see John Weaver for example). Munro's draft foreword to *Castle Rock* dated June 30, 2005, includes this sentence in the final paragraph: "And the part of this book that might be called non-fiction, or family history, has in some places expanded into fiction, but always within the outline of a true narrative." Published, the reference to non-fiction is gone, as is "in some places," but the final phrase remains. As does the final draft sentence, but for one small edit: "With these developments the two streams came close enough together that it seemed to me that they were meant to flow in one channel, as they do in this book" (Draft Foreword June 30, 2005, 2015.062.1.1; *Castle Rock* [x]). Munro's notion of "true narrative" here is one that, just as she intended, permeates *Castle Rock*—it does so through the book's long provenance and its myriad difficulties for her in its making, and it does so especially in its creation of the very historical and imaginative qualities which Hadley and Miller understood and Good, Henighan, and other reviewers of *Castle Rock* did not.[9]

Given both Douglas Gibson's own Scottish background and his long association with Munro as her Canadian editor, his involvement in the editing of *Castle Rock* appears to have been more active than it had been with her immediately foregoing volumes, the five published in 1990 and after.[10] In early July 2005 Gibson reports that the previous Sunday he and his wife Jane drove out to inspect the Boston Church cemetery and saw the Laidlaw graves there (Gibson to Munro July 5, 2005; M&S Z116.5). Owing to a personal trip to Scotland just after, he did some Munro connected research of his own and also visited Ettrick Kirk cemetery. He returned and made some editorial suggestions focused on the first chapter—then probably still the thirteen-page "Singular Characters" section from the February 7, 2005, version submitted to the *New Yorker*. He tells Munro that he likes "What Do You Want to Know For?," which he has apparently just read for the first time, and he suggests that his "inclination is to put it as the second last story, just before the improved 'Messenger.'" He had told her that he "was thinking about the opening chapter and the last one. You've done a lot with the last one, and it's fine." He continues,

> As for the first one, armed with all sorts of exciting new information from Phaup [Far Hope] and Ettrick Churchyard (and even a peek at Thomas Boston's bestseller, "15th edition"), I have a reorganizing suggestion, my only one. I propose that you should follow the gloomy opening quote about the parish not with the second quote but with more information about Ettrick, leading to the location of Phaup and then, of course, to your treatment of Will O'Phaup. (I've dared to put down the sort of geographic fixing of the setting that I have in mind).

Gibson includes his draft factual historical overview of Ettrick of about 350 words, some of which Munro ultimately uses, though by no means all, but she also adopts his suggestion about the nature of the first chapter, "No Advantages." Following his suggestion too she also moved what was the second epigraph, Hogg's description of James Laidlaw from the March 1820 *Blackwood's*, moving it to head Laidlaw's section in "Men of Ettrick" (*Castle Rock* 19). Toward the end of his letter, Gibson also writes "This is going to be a very good book; with your foreword's encouragement I'm going to list it as fiction, noting it is heavily based on historical fact." He also drafted flap copy, noting "Alice Munro turning real life into fiction and honourably and honestly explaining what she has done" (Gibson to Munro August 15, 2005, M&S Z116.5; Undated Flap Copy, M&S Z106.7).

Following these editorial shapings, *The View from Castle Rock* begins after Munro's foreword with "No Advantages." As Pilar Somacarrera notes in her far-reaching analysis of the ways Scots-Presbyterianism infuses Munro's writing, it situates the reader by providing "the background information needed to understand the rest of the stories in the collection. Resembling an essay, the text is divided into four sections, each of which is preceded by an epigraph" (99 and *passim*). That is, "No Advantages," a contextualizing essay, establishes what Katie Trumpener calls "the relationship between Munro's mode of historical fiction and early nineteenth-century Scottish experimental novels, including those of Hogg." Calling *Castle Rock* "a speculative, fictionalised family memoir," she sees Munro "pondering the accidents which established Munro's eventual line of descent, the nature of family memory." Trumpener continues in a passage that aptly situates the trajectory of Munro's whole book, citing the drives about Huron County in "What Do You Want to Know For?" that she takes with Fremlin. She also links what Munro is doing here in her last "story"—actually a memoir—through her learned explanations of her region's geology to "Romantic-era British naturalists" who "developed a new sense of 'locale,' a symbiotic biotope fostering specific plants and animals" (54).

Introducing a 2016 volume of critical essays by various hands focused on three of Munro's late books, I wrote about a "deepening geological sensibility" in "Axis" (2011) (Thacker Introduction 12-19). I shall return to that story, but Trumpener's comments get to the essence of "No Advantages" at the outset of *Castle Rock* and to the whole book. Beginning with what Gibson called the "gloomy opening quote" from 1799 about Ettrick ("'This parish possesses no advantages'" [3]), Munro outlines its history, its specific characteristics, and her own connections to it. Detailing its qualities, Munro is precise—with geographic, historic, linguistic, cultural detail—and takes a reader back to her own first sight of it. Her own presence is evident on the page even before she shifts from description to personal writing; for example, she writes that "William Wallace, the guerrilla hero of the Scots, is said to have hidden out here from the English, and there is a story of Merlin—*Merlin*—being hunted down and murdered, in the old forest, by Ettrick shepherds" (5; original emphasis). That probing voice, wondering over all it finds, a voice which repeats "Merlin" with emphasis, is the same Munro whom Duffy notes.

She then continues in a passage that connects what she first saw with the contextual materials she had read, stepping herself into Ettrick as a visible place being understood through her own eyes, observations, and assumptions. Writing these paragraphs, Munro is recreating a locale she first visited and discovered in 1982:

> Nevertheless the valley disappointed me the first time I saw it. Places are apt to do that when you've set them up in your imagination. The time of year was very early spring, and the hills were brown, or a kind of lilac brown, reminding me of the hills around Calgary. Ettrick Water was running fast and clear, but it was hardly as wide as the Maitland River, which flows past the farm where I grew up, in Ontario. The circles of stones which I had first taken to be interesting remnants of Celtic worship were too numerous and well kept up to be anything but handy sheep pens.
> ....
> After a while the postman came along and I rode with him to Ettrick Church. By that time it had begun to rain, hard. The church was locked. It disappointed me, too. Having been built in 1824, it did not compare, in historic appearance, or grim character, to the churches I had already seen in Scotland. I felt conspicuous, out of place, and cold. I huddled by the wall till the rain let up for a bit, and then I explored the churchyard, with the long grass soaking my legs.
>
> (*Castle Rock* 5-6)[11]

This takes Munro into the first of her four graveyards. The first important gravestone she discovers was that of William Laidlaw,

> my direct ancestor, born at the end of the seventeenth century, and known locally as Will O'Phaup. This was a man who took on, at least locally, something of the radiance of myth, and he managed that at the very last time in history—that is, in the history of the people of the British Isles—when a man could do so.
>
> (*Castle Rock* 6)

On that same stone she finds "the names of his daughter, Margaret Laidlaw Hogg, who upbraided Sir Walter Scott, and of Robert Hogg, her husband, the tenant of Ettrickhall," and next to it that of "the writer James Hogg, who was their son and Will O'Phaup's grandson. He was known as the Ettrick Shepherd." Then that of "the Reverend Thomas Boston" who figures in her story and for Munro is the embodiment of the cultural press of the harsh Canadian Scots Presbyterianism she was born to. He was, as well, the cleric whose name memorializes the church in Halton's Scotch Block where so many of the Laidlaws seen in "The View from Castle Rock" are buried. Finally, there at Ettrick Kirk she finds "a stone bearing the name of Robert Laidlaw, who died at Hopehouse on January 29th, 1800, aged seventy-two years. Son of Will, brother of Margaret, uncle of James, who probably never knew that he would be remembered by his link to these others, any more than he would know the date of his own death." Munro ends the paragraph here and then offers in a single fragment paragraph, "My great-great-great-great-grandfather" (*Castle Rock* 6).

Each "great" and the final "grandfather" signifies a person Munro is about to write about here. With their repeated first names in the Scots manner, these implied yet invoked ancestors form a progress through the generations: Robert, lying here in Ettrick Kirk, with James, William, Thomas, William, and Robert Laidlaw lying elsewhere in North American graves. Their line leads ultimately to Munro herself, and each of these men is about to be described, wondered over, acknowledged here in the long-imagined book Munro was then finally writing, *The View from Castle Rock*. Turning back to herself in that graveyard after these examinations there, Munro ends the initial section of "No Advantages" with two sentences that should be taken as a coda for the whole of *Castle Rock* and for her late style as seen in her last three books, certainly, but also for the whole of her work: "I was a naïve North American, in spite of my stored knowledge. Past and present lumped together here made a reality that was commonplace and *yet disturbing beyond anything I had imagined*" (*Castle Rock* 6–7; my emphasis).

Her imaginative position established, Munro turns to her "Men of Ettrick," beginning with Will O'Phaup and quoting from the epitaph James Hogg wrote for "his tombstone in Ettrick Kirkyard."[12] He

> was said to be "one of the old Laidlaws of Craik"—about whom I have not been able to discover anything at all, except that Craik is an almost disappeared village

on a completely disappeared Roman road, in a nearby valley to the south of Ettrick.
He must have walked over the hills, a lad in his teens, looking for work.

(*Castle Rock* 7, 8)

Munro's use of quotation marks here points readers to her main source regarding Will O'Phaup, James Hogg's "The Shepherd's Calendar" in *Blackwood's Magazine* in the April 1827 number. There under the heading of "Odd Characters," he treats Will O'Phaup, whom he characterizes as "one of the genuine Laidlaws of Craik, where he was born in 1691. He was a shepherd in Phaup for fifty-five years. For feats of frolic, strength, and agility, he had no equal in his day" (Hogg 440). Munro quotes that last sentence from O'Phaup's tombstone and she likely substituted "old" for the "genuine" of Hogg's first sentence here. Noting the adaptations she makes, it is worth mentioning here too that "Craik" is the last name she gives to Russell in "Lying under the Apple Tree."

Such shaping is what Munro undertakes with her "Men of Ettrick." Adapting from Hogg's version of Will O'Phaup, Munro tells of his feats of running and leaping, and of two of his meetings with fairies, in the second instance writing, after she has just told of his flight from them, that his "fear is different from the fear he felt the other time, but just as cold, because of the notion he has that they are ghosts of humans bewitched into fairies." She pondered such beliefs and contextualizes them, admitting from the history of the early eighteenth century that "they belonged to times of bad powers and evil confusion, and their attentions were oftener than not malicious, or even deadly" (*Castle Rock* 13). Turning then to her second "Man of Ettrick," Thomas Boston, Munro asserts that during this time "the Kirk was particularly powerful in the parish of Ettrick." She dramatizes him, writing of his awareness of his own sinfulness "and knows too how swiftly Grace may be withdrawn from him," describing him thus in a single summative paragraph: "He strives, he falls. Darkness again" (*Castle Rock* 14, 15). Munro describes Boston's beliefs and his bleak family situation in detail—and even with a bit of humor—dealing most, as well she might from historical distance, with its doctrine of predestination: "the most desperate life, from any outside point of view. Only from the inside of the faith is it possible to get any idea of the prize as well as the struggle, the additive pursuit of pure righteousness, the intoxication of a flash of God's favor" (*Castle Rock* 17).[13] It is here, in the next paragraph, that Munro writes the already noted passage, "The past is full of contradictions and complications ..., " and she sets that passage up by writing that "So it seems strange to me that Thomas Boston should have been the minister whom Will O'Phaup listened to every Sunday"; "My ancestor, a near pagan, a merry man, a brandy drinker, one upon whom wagers are set, a man who believes in fairies, is bound to have listened to, and believed in, the strictures and hard hopes of this punishing Calvinist faith" (*Castle Rock* 17).[14]

Concluding with Boston, Munro turns back to her relatives as two final "Men of Ettrick": her distant cousin James Hogg and her great-great-great-grandfather, James Laidlaw, who as a widower in his fifties led a portion of his family to "America"—Canada—in 1818. The two were first cousins, and Munro sees them together since their personalities were out of place in the Ettrick Valley, "a place which had not much for their sort—that is, for the sort of men who do not take easily to anonymity and quiet lives." She continues, "Hogg escaped, into the uneasy role of the naïve comedian, the bumpkin genius, in Edinburgh, and then he escaped, as the author of *Confessions of a Justified Sinner*, into lasting fame." Munro sees James Laidlaw much the same but without the larger literary stage that Hogg found—his audacity was in "hauling up the more docile members of his family and carrying them off to America ... when he was old enough, as Hogg points out, to have one foot in the grave." Within her family Munro is well aware here and throughout *Castle Rock* that she is akin to these two distant ancestors. She is too, and always been, at variance from most Laidlaws, whom she characterizes as having "a strenuous dignity and control, a sort of refusal. The refusal to feel any need to turn your life into a story, either for other people or for yourself." Along with Hogg and Laidlaw though, she has just that need, she knows: "some of us have that need in large and irresistible measure—enough so as to make the others cringe with embarrassment and apprehension" (*Castle Rock* 20). Thus here with her two distant Ettrick forebearers Munro asserts concerns which infuse *Castle Rock*—throughout, but most especially in those pieces that treat of her own immediate family: "Working for a Living," "Fathers," "Lying under the Apple Tree," "The Ticket," and "Home," most especially the first and last.

Munro in this concluding section of "Men of Ettrick" tells of Hogg's mother Margaret Laidlaw Hogg, who "was famous locally for the number of verses she carried in her head," just the sort of person Munro met and uses in "Hold Me Fast, Don't Let Me Pass" who knows and recites the old ballads. Sir Walter Scott was assembling "the old songs and ballads which had never been written down" into *The Minstrelsy of the Scottish Border*. "And Hogg—with his eye on posterity as well as present advantage—made sure he took Scott to see his mother." Before this, pausing with Hogg, Munro admits that it "is most his writings I have to thank for what I know of Will O'Phaup," and continues,

> Hogg was both insider and an outsider, industriously and—he hoped—profitably shaping and recording his people's stories. And he had a fine source in his mother—Will O'Phaup's oldest daughter, Margaret Laidlaw, who had grown up at Far-Hope. There would be some trimming and embroidering of material on Hogg's part. Some canny lying of the sort you can count on a writer to do.
>
> (*Castle Rock* 21)

Here Munro is thinking of Hogg but also thinking of herself; for writing "Men of Ettrick" sometime in 2005 to introduce her book—a book that she was one she did for herself—she well knows that she is like Hogg in being "both insider and an outsider" in Huron County, Ontario, just as he was in Ettrick.[15] And in that "canny lying" reference she is also looking both back and forward, back to what she had already written and published, and forward to James Laidlaw's letter to William Lyon Mackenzie in "The View from Castle Rock" with its reference to Hogg "conning lies." An introductory essay, "No Advantages" treats necessary contextual material through its separate parts: geology and landscape; her "people" amid their actual beliefs and circumstances and, having learned of all this, the presence of these legacies still in Munro's own life.

"Her Almost Anthropological Long View": Of Remnants, "The View from Castle Rock," "Illinois," and "The Wilds of Morris Township"

When Tessa Hadley was reviewing *Castle Rock* she noted the parallel careers of James Hogg and Alice Munro, also recognizing that Munro saw and used them too. Just as Hogg fashioned himself a rustic amid "Edinburgh's literary culture" so too has Munro "positioned herself, mediating the old-fashioned rural Canada she grew up in for a sophisticated cosmopolitan readership." Taking up this idea more broadly than in just the book at hand, Hadley writes that Munro's "almost anthropological long view is so penetrating because of her vantage point between systems" (17). This is certainly true of the whole of Munro's oeuvre, but it is especially so in the making of *Castle Rock* with its long provenance, its imaginative and practical challenges which, in fact, portend Munro's late style. Hadley sees and articulates what is happening within the book she has at hand. Writing of Munro's descriptions of "Margaret Hogg's reluctance to let go of her ballads," Hadley notes "the authorial hesitation of Munro's storytelling, always ready to disclaim its own authority, its version of things, reflecting continually on the mysteries and processes and treacheries of fiction. It might have been like that, she warns, but it might not. Be careful. Who is she to say?" Making this sharp, well taken, and precise critical discrimination, Hadley gets to the core of what Munro had long envisioned and had accomplished in *Castle Rock* when she points to the description of Andrew's first visit to Edinburgh at ten years old and asserts that "Munro's telling of the past changes mode from something like an essay to story." Hadley aptly calls this act "that last dream leap into the past." This leap involves "a sign in the text that she's guessing," that she is making up Andrew's impressions during his trip (17). And not incidentally, those made-up impressions are found in the first paragraph of "The View from Castle Rock," both in the paragraphs Munro wrote at the behest of the *New Yorker* for their first publication there and, revised and expanded for the book, in *Castle Rock*. Hadley's points about Munro's methods are just those that Duffy would later notice and isolate.

When Munro had finished work on *Runaway* and turned to assembling the manuscript of *The View from Castle Rock* (2004–6) its epilogue was entitled "Remnants." For much of that time she envisioned that "Wenlock Edge" would be one of the stories included in the book but, when she decided against it in late 2005 in favor of "What Do You Want to Know For?," the latter was initially included as part of the epilogue. It did not remain there, placed at Gibson's suggestion to end the "Home" section, and the epilogue's title was changed from "Remnants" to "Messenger."[16] Such editorial history is needed to reemphasize Munro's November 2005 comment in a letter to Gibson that "it is difficult to decide what works in a book of this sort," but it is especially important to *Castle Rock* in its highlighting the idea of remnants (M&S Z106.1). Munro comes from a place, Huron County, where it was long the practice in newspaper obituaries and on tombstones to describe long-widowed women as "relics" of their long-dead husbands. Thus an informed reading of *Castle Rock* needs to recognize that what Munro is offering in this book, one she described as "'really important to me,'" is a succession of narratives in which she places herself as author and narrator among remnants—historical remnants she has researched and read about, remnants of persons and places she has known and experienced herself and, ultimately and most importantly, the textual remnants of a person and an imaginative writer named Alice Munro (Stoffman H10). She is, herself, still in the midst of her career.

In most ways "The View from Castle Rock," that is, the account of the Laidlaws' 1818 voyage from Leith, Scotland to Quebec, Canada, which follows "No Advantages," best establishes what Munro is doing in her long-imagined family book. She offers a telling passage about her methods there in two short paragraphs following her extended quotations from two letters by James Laidlaw, the first one written to his eldest son Robert back in Scotland and the second to the editor of *The Colonial Advocate*, who published it. Picking up Laidlaw's reference to his cousin the Ettrick Shepherd, Munro shifts to herself: "And I am surely one of the liars the old man talks about, in what I have written about the voyage. Except for Walter's journal, and the letters, the story is full of my invention." Then, in another comment made in just the provisional fashion Hadley notes, "The sighting of Fife from Castle Rock is related by Hogg, so it must be true." Following a white-space break, Munro takes the reader to "the graveyard of Boston Church, in Esquesing, in Halton County," her second, examining the stones and accounting as far as she is able for the subsequent lives of her emigrant ancestors, saving the news of young James's precipitate death until the final paragraph (*Castle Rock* 84, 84–7).

As Munro admits, the remnant textual details she had at hand—the letters specified and Walter's journal—were basis for the narrative she fashions, for the story she tells. She uses them, especially eight imbedded quotations from Walter's journal which she metes out rather like a succession of beads along a line with which to organize her story and to move the voyage along. The version in *Castle Rock*, when compared to its *New Yorker* predecessor, shows several additions to the text, detailing more about her characters and the circumstances of the voyage itself.[17] Adding to the quotations from Walter's journal, Munro imagines and writes the family's settling aboard ship, various sights happening then, the death and burial of a child at sea (itself portending young James' unexplained death at the story's end), the circumstances surrounding Andrew's wife Agnes giving birth to their second child, Isabel, aboard ship, and Walter's shipboard friendship with Nettie, a well-to-do and tubercular teenager traveling with her businessman father. That man offers Walter a job in Montreal which he declines and, as well, Munro creates a mutual attraction between the doctor who delivers Isabel and Agnes, his patient. He is tubercular too. Throughout, Munro creates through imagination the sights and sounds of the emigrant voyage and also each of her ancestors' characters, most especially James Laidlaw, the garrulous widowed father and grandfather.[18]

Munro continues in this same vein throughout the first section of *Castle Rock*, inventing fictional circumstances to shape the historical remnants she has, but as she moves through that section the tilt is toward memoir. "Illinois," the third piece in the book, begins with Munro's paraphrased gloss of a letter Andrew Laidlaw sent to his brother William in the Highlands in May of 1831, a letter she quoted in its entirety in "Changing Places" (201–2). Here, she summarizes, the brothers in Canada "complained of not hearing from him for three years, and told him that his father was dead." She then shifts to a summary of William's activities upon learning this news, writing that "It did not take him very long, once he was sure of that, to start to make his plans to go to America." "He had discarded the Ettrick Valley for the Highlands without the least regret, and now he was ready to get out from under the British flag altogether—he was bound for Illinois." She continues,

> They settled in Joliet, near Chicago.
> There in Joliet, on the 5th of January, in either 1839 or 1840, William died of cholera, and Mary gave birth to a girl. All on the one day.
> She wrote to the brothers in Ontario—what else could she do?—and in the late spring when the roads were dry and the crops were planted Andrew arrived with a team of oxen and a cart, to carry her and her children and their goods back to Esquesing.
>
> (*Castle Rock* 88–9)[19]

Beyond these facts, "Illinois" is Munro's fictional invention of her great-great-grandmother's trek from Illinois to Ontario with her brother-in-law and her children, Munro's own great-grandfather among them the second-youngest child. They travel along the route that later became the Chicago Turnpike, Michigan Highway 12, across the bottom of the state, the route Munro took herself when she sought Will Laidlaw's grave in Joliet in 2004. Munro imagines and recreates their trip, the oldest son Jamie disconsolate at leaving, walking ahead and then behind out of sight of the cart, ultimately concocting a kidnapping of his newborn sister Jane so that they would have to turn about. Amid a bit of intrigue his plan fails and his uncle sees through it.

As this plot and "Illinois" wind down, Munro shifts to wondering over what led Will to decide on the States over Canada, and also to have Andrew share in that musing. In a Munrovian flourish here she has a "sharp-faced red fox" watching the family during a rest stop "from the edge of the woods" (*Castle Rock* 109). Foxes are central to Munro's own experience and in her work, and foxes are yet to come when the first section of *Castle Rock* reaches "Working for a Living." Just after this reference, Munro focalizes her ending through Andrew's thoughts, which she doubtless shares, writing to the story's end in intricate and well-considered prose:

> He had seen enough of the Yankee people by now to know what had tempted Will to live among them. The push and the noise and the rawness of them, the need to get on the bandwagon. Though some were decent enough and some, and maybe some of the worst, were Scots. Will had something in him drawing him to such a life.
> It had proved a mistake.
> Andrew knew, of course, that a man was as likely to die of cholera in Upper Canada as in the state of Illinois, and that it was foolish to blame Will's death on his choice of nationality. He did not do so. And yet. And yet—there was something about all this rushing away, loosing oneself entirely from family and past, there was something rash and self-trusting about it that might not help a man, that might put him more in the way of such an accident, such a fate. Poor Will.

After a white-space break, concluding "Illinois," Munro continues with "And that became the way the surviving brothers spoke of him until the day they died, and the way their children spoke of him. Poor Will." These people, his own children among them, "may have felt a pall, of sadness and fatedness, that hung around any mention of his name," but his wife "Mary almost never spoke of him, and how she felt about him became nobody's business but her own" (*Castle Rock* 110). So "Illinois" ends.

Such quotation is needed here because this ending is most emphatically a late-style recursion, and that several times over. Just as Munro remembers and signifies her childhood memories of growing up on a fox farm here with the watching fox (see "Boys and Girls" [1964], *Dance*) these wonderings which eventuate to Mary's memories of Will recall other such endings. There is her story of Irish emigration to Canada, "A Better Place than Home," featuring another widowed Mary. Or at the end of "Chaddeleys and Flemings: 2. The Stone in the Field" where Munro offers the newspaper obituary of a hermit. So too Mary in "Changing Places," who "like old James, was a person who had got her heart's desire" (206). The reference is to the letter Mary wrote to woo Will, for he was "her heart's desire." Here in "Illinois" Munro ends with Mary's mysteries, returning again to them in "Messenger" when she examines Mary's grave in the Blyth cemetery, "Mary who wrote the letter from Ettrick to lure the man she wanted to come and marry her. On the stone is the name of that man, *William Laidlaw. Died in Illinois*. And buried God knows where." Next to her is "the body and stone of her daughter Jane, the girl born on the day of her father's death, who was carried as a baby from Illinois." She died in childbirth at twenty-six. "Mary did not die until two years later. So she had that loss, as well, to absorb before she was finished" (*Castle Rock* 347, 348; original emphasis). Though Munro's remnants have told her a good deal about Mary Scott Laidlaw, as this book ends there is still a felt sense that she is "taking the mystery of her life with her."

A section toward the end of "Changing Places" accounting for the emigration to Will County Illinois of William and Mary Scott Laidlaw and their family in 1836 draws from a letter written by the second son, John (c. 1830–1907), to his younger brother Thomas (1836–1915), Munro's great-grandfather. Writing in 1907, "he was an old man" recording "everything he could recall about their time" in Illinois before they came to Ontario. Trying to remember the names of their neighbors there, he mentions "a Mr. Taylor lived about half a mile west 'in the direction of Father's Grave'" (203, 204). At this point in her essay Munro had not yet told of William Laidlaw's death from cholera so, heading in that direction, she continues in a new paragraph, "Father's grave. Yes. There was a canal being built at the time on the Des Plaines River—part of the system that would link Lake Michigan with the Illinois River … and William would get some work on it …." She wonders if he may have worked on the Caledonian Canal when it was built in the Highlands, but her salient wondering connects to the illness that killed him: "When he was at work he would have a source of drinking water other than the one he shared at home with his family, and that might explain why he got cholera and they didn't" (204). When she was introducing the elderly John Laidlaw's 1907 letter Munro also wrote that "The eldest son James had at that time been dead for fifty years so John was the only source" (203).

These two passages resonate in *Castle Rock*. By the time she wrote the second one in "Changing Places," Munro had already written and published "A Wilderness Station" in the *New Yorker* and in *Open Secrets*, the story she mentioned to Gittings in May 1992 as dealing with material from her projected family book. At its core is James Laidlaw's death from a falling tree while clearing land in Huron County in April 1853, the same story key to "The Wilds of Morris Township." The letter that John Laidlaw wrote to his brother Thomas in 1907, with its reference to "Father's grave," is what sent Munro to Illinois in 2004 to try to find that grave.

"The Wilds of Morris Township" begins with a brief account of William and Mary's children in Esquesing. Though they were "treated well" "there was no land coming to them. So as soon as they were old enough they set off for another wilderness." One of their cousins went with them, "Big Rob" Laidlaw, one of Andrew's sons, so called because "he had the same name as the third son of Will and Mary, who was now called Little Rob." Just as Munro had long done, "Big Rob took up the family custom or duty of writing his memories down when he was an old man, so that the people left would know what things had been like" (*Castle Rock* 111). She then offers six pages of quotation from the "Diary of Robert B. Laidlaw," a memoir he wrote in 1907 and one that was republished in *Blyth: A Village Portrait* (1977), a version she certainly saw when it appeared and one she likely owned. This was the second time Munro had used the text of this memoir; though names and details are changed, and she bends the material toward her own purposes, the February 1907 recollections at the outset of "A Wilderness Station" she attributes to George Herron and published in the Carstairs *Argus* are derived directly from Big Rob's memoir—specific echoes abound (*Open Secrets* 191-7). In "The Wilds of Morris Township" Munro quotes the entire memoir, doing some consistent but light editing throughout and deletes one sentence.[20] "And the place that now knows us, will soon know us no more," Robert B. Laidlaw (1828-1908) ends and Munro quotes, "for we are all old frail creatures" (Laidlaw 21, *Castle Rock* 117).

Though not as old as Big Rob was when he wrote his memoir about his pioneering Morris Township in the 1850s, Munro in her seventies, having had and survived heart surgery, doubtless empathized with his final sentence here as she quoted it. Ending her long quotation from it, Munro turns at once to "James, once Jamie, Laidlaw [who] died like his father in a place where no reliable burial records yet existed. It is believed that he was put into a corner of the land that he and brothers and cousin had cleared, then sometime around 1900 his body was moved to the Blyth Cemetery" (*Castle Rock* 117). In 1994 she told Turbide that she had not found his grave marked there, and makes no mention of one when she describes that cemetery in "Messenger," so a mystery remains (49).[21] Moving beyond James, Munro turns again to Big Rob, to his own life and family, noting that he

> was the father of many sons and daughters. Simon, John, Duncan, Forrest, Sandy, Susan, Maggie, Annie, Lizzie. Duncan left home early. (That name is correct, but I am not absolutely certain of all the others.) He went to Guelph, and they seldom saw him. The others stayed at home. The house was big enough for them. At first their mother and father were with them, then for several years just their

father, and finally they were on their own. People did not remember that they had ever been young.

(*Castle Rock* 117)

Munro is returning here to people and material she has explicitly used before in "Chaddeleys and Flemings: 2. The Stone in the Field" and will be seen in the balance of "The Wilds of Morris Township." Having catalogued Big Rob and his wife Christian McCollum Laidlaw's children and something of the family's history, Munro continues to describe and contemplate the lives they led:

> They turned their backs on the world. The women wore their hair parted in the middle and slicked tight to their heads, though the style of the day ran to bangs and rolls. They wore dark homemade dresses with skinny skirts. And their hands were red because they scrubbed the pine floor of their kitchen with lye every day. It shone like velvet.
>
> They were capable of going to church—which they did every Sunday—and returning home without having spoken to a soul.
>
> Their religious observances were dutiful but not in any way emotional.
>
> The men had to talk more than the women did, doing their business at the mill or the cheese factory. But they wasted no words or time. They were honest but firm in their dealings. If they made money it was never with the aim of buying new machinery, of lessening their labor or of adding comforts to their way of living. They were not cruel to their animals but they had no sentimental feelings for them.

These people, Munro's relatives, were ever in the thrall of their Presbyterian faith—which "was still contentious and cranky but did not lay siege to the soul as fiercely as it had done in Boston's day"—"they had constructed a life for themselves that was monastic without any visitations of grace or moments of transcendence" (*Castle Rock* 117–18).[22]

As seen here and as she had done previously in "Chaddeleys and Flemings: 2. The Stone in the Field," Munro is most focused on wondering over her relatives' lives as she describes them. Imagining those lives in the same way she imagined the trek from Illinois to Ontario, here Munro creates the family circumstances when one of them deviates from the siblings' "monastic" way of life. She details their reactions when Forrest sets to work building a house for himself on their land, digging a hole for the foundation, laying the stone, erecting the building. "He did not stop doing his share of the farm chores, but worked on this solitary project late into the night" (*Castle Rock* 119). Forrest deviated, and Munro traces the changes. He eventually got a job in town and their sister Lizzie, who had been assigned the job of looking after Forrest's clothing, came over to his house and joined him. As time passes and the siblings aged, Forrest and Lizzie came to be seen almost as a couple, though everyone knew they were brother and sister. Eventually "Forrest gave up walking to his job, and on Saturday nights he and Lizzie rode to town to shop" in the buggy they had purchased. "Lizzie reigned in her own house like any married woman" (*Castle Rock* 125).

Once this story ends she turns to "Working for a Living"—her 1981 memoir, a serene and understanding celebration of each of her parents—to conclude the "No Advantages" section of *Castle Rock*. But before she gets there, Munro shifts after a white-space break to each of her parents in their turn, ending "The Wilds of Morris Township" with each parent reacting to Forrest and Lizzie: "'They were devoted to each other,' said my mother, who had never actually met them, but was generally in favor of brotherly-sisterly relationships, unsullied by sex." "My father had seen them at church, when he was a child, and might have visited them a couple of times, with his mother." This contrast between her parents' separate attitudes is a difference crucial to the whole of Munro's oeuvre, the mother ever a looming difficult presence, the father a thoughtful one. But each person is present, necessary for myriad reasons to Munro's imaginary. Here she concludes with her father, who possesses a mystification equal to her own: "He did not admire them, or blame them. He wondered at them." Shifting to a new paragraph, the end to her story, Munro quotes him on these relations too: "'To think what their ancestors did,' he said. 'The nerve it took, to pick up and cross the ocean. What was it squashed their spirits? So soon'" (*Castle Rock* 125-6).

Just when Munro was still very much in the midst of rediscovering her family material, having returned to Ontario and to Huron County in the 1970s, she has the father in "Chaddeleys and Flemings: 2. The Stone in the Field," more of a fictional character than this one but still fundamentally her own father, say much the same thing as Robert Eric Laidlaw says here to end "The Wilds of Morris Township": "'But it's a wonder how those people had the courage once, to get them over here. They left everything.'" He then recounts the move to Morris and James Laidlaw's accidental death, then three deaths from cholera the next year, so the great-grandfather "'and his wife were left alone, and they went on clearing their farm and started up another family. I think the courage got burnt out of them. Their religion did them in, and their upbringing. How they had to toe the line. Also their pride. Pride was what they had when they had no more gumption'" (*Moons* 30-1). When Munro wrote this sometime in 1977, the idea of *The View from Castle Rock*, her family book, was nascent but real.[23] Her father had recently died in August 1976, she had been living in Huron County again for about two years, and the fiction she was writing then was a daily rediscovery of her home place. For the first time she had an agent; the *New Yorker* and other commercial magazines were interested in her stories; *Who Do You Think You Are? / The Beggar Maid* was coming together (see Thacker *Alice* 336-65). The historical passage that she wrote then in "Chaddeleys and Flemings: 2. The Stone in the Field," just quoted, amounts to a harbinger of Munro's direction toward *The View from Castle Rock*. That book, in turn, is beckoning entrance to Munro's still developing late style.

A Writer in the Midst of Her Own Material: Returning to "Working for a Living," Writing "The Ticket," Returning "Home"

The father's description of their ancestors to his narrator daughter in "Chaddeleys and Flemings: 2. The Stone in the Field" is a synecdoche for Munro's aesthetic direction as she returned to Huron County to live and as her career progressed. In one of the preliminary versions of "The Moons of Jupiter," when Munro intended to include it in the book which became *Who Do You Think You Are? / The Beggar Maid*, a version narrated in the first person by Janet (and so the same narrator as in both versions of "Chaddeleys and Flemings"), Munro has her narrate a scene in the legion hall in Dalgliesh during a visit to her widowed father. At one point, Janet writes, "My father introduced me to the wife of one of his friends—the men I knew, from long ago—and she said, 'Oh! You're the writer!' I was not very comfortable about being identified as a writer in the midst of what was, so to speak, my material" (Supplanted Bound Proof *Who* 29, Metcalf Collection; see Thacker *Alice* 341–52).[24]

As I wrote at the outset here, when I first met with Munro in August 2001 for purposes of *Alice Munro: Writing Her Lives* she told me that she had been revising what were then fugitive published pieces, among them "Home" (1974) and "Working for a Living" (1981).[25] Revised and inverted as to their published chronology, those two memoir stories came to be centrally placed in the structure of *Castle Rock*. In keeping with the genealogical chronology Munro was following, "Working for a Living" is aptly placed after "The Wilds of Morris Township" to end the "No Advantages" section while "Home," for its part, falls equally aptly between "The Ticket" and "What Do You Want to Know For?" as the penultimate story and titles the book's second section. Tracing Munro's writing trajectory, looking at where she was as a writer and in life during the early 2000s as she assembled her remnants into *Castle Rock*, she *was* in the midst of her material, her old life was still lying around her, as well as in the midst of her previous writing, and she certainly picked both up again.

The revisions Munro made to "Home" in August 2001 are readily evident; they are seen mostly in the deletion of the running author's commentary on what had been just written. The revised version, which first appeared in the *New Statesman* late in 2001 is, with minor further revisions, the version which appears in *Castle Rock*. Taking up "Working for a Living," the revisions are more integral and consistently define an authorial striving for greater perspective toward her parents, grandparents, and other relatives. More than that, the textual additions Munro makes to the memoir are telling, indications of both her greater perspective and need to better integrate the memoir into the book.

Without miring this in textual detail, a comparison of the two versions of "Working" shows Munro adding her own wonderings about facts. Talking about her father's schooling, she adds that "He was never very clear about how long he had stayed. Three years and part of the fourth? Two years and part of the third? And he didn't quit suddenly—it was not a matter of going to school one day and staying away the next and never showing up again" (*Castle Rock* 129). Turning from her father's history, Munro then takes up his parents, Sadie Code and William Cole Laidlaw, who were not compatible but did not argue. She was sociable; he was silent, a respected farmer but also a reader. In *Grand Street* she writes, "My grandfather diverged a little, learned to play the violin, married the tall, temperamental Irish girl with eyes of two colors. That done, he reverted; for the rest of his life was diligent, orderly, silent." With some differences in wording, this appears in *Castle Rock* too. But in the first version Munro tells of William's family's emigration "from the Vale of Ettrick, on a sailing ship, in 1818, to Quebec and then to the Scotch Block settlement in Halton County." Then the sons settle Morris in Huron County, "one was killed by a falling tree while they were clearing the bush," and more besides (*Grand Street* 15). In *Castle Rock* this history is replaced by almost a page on William Laidlaw's reading: "In the winter he managed to get all his work done—and well done—and then he would read. He never talked about what he read, but the whole community knew about it. And respected him for it. Munro then suggests some heavy titles and authors in the library then, wonders if he might have read Voltaire or Karl Marx, saying "It's possible." Her grandfather, by contrast, "got his work done first": "In no point of behavior did his reading affect his life" (*Castle Rock* 135).

Going back to the *Grand Street* text, still treating her father living with his parents in Blyth, in her 2001 and later revisions Munro shapes and adds, deepening the text. Some of her additions connect to other stories in *Castle Rock*—she writes of a "change in outlook from that of the man who went to Illinois"—and on that page too she admits that "When you write about real people you are always up against contradictions" (*Castle Rock* 136). And Munro adds material too that she had long since written but had not been included in the *Grand Street* version. Taking up her father's fox trapping, describing how the traps are handled, she then asks "How do you kill a trapped fox? You don't want to shoot him, because of the wound left in the pelt and the blood smell spoiling the trap. You stun him with the blow of a long, strong stick, and then put your foot on his heart" (*Castle Rock* 137; see Thacker *Alice* 38–9; 396/87.3: 5.11.8b).

While Munro has a good deal to say in "Working for a Living" about her grandmother Sadie, most especially her relations with her son and her husband, and the mutual antipathy she shared with her daughter-in-law, Munro's mother, the memoir in both of its versions focuses on two incidents. The summer Anne Chamney Laidlaw sold furs to American tourists at the Pine Tree Hotel in Muskoka, the summer of 1941, and a visit Munro made to her father's workplace on a family errand during the spring of 1949. Treating her parents' meeting and pairing, Munro remarks that when she thinks of them "before they became my parents … they seem not only touching and helpless, marvelously deceived, but more attractive than at any later time …" (*Grand Street* 17; *Castle Rock* 139).[26]

The episode focused on her mother begins in the same manner as "What Do You Want to Know For?," with Munro and Fremlin driving about their region and noticing something. Here it is "a store standing empty at a crossroads." "It seemed to me that I had been here once, and that the scene was connected with some disappointment or dismay" (*Castle Rock* 140). This recognition leads Munro to "remember everything" about that trip she had made with her father to Muskoka to gather Anne Chamney Laidlaw, hoping for the whole family's sake that she had sold the furs she had brought there. She had, and to get to that point Munro tells the whole story: why it was necessary, how her mother thrived doing it, how her grandmother, though she hated what her daughter-in-law was doing, came to Lower Town Wingham to look after the younger children. Describing things at home before she and her father drove to Muskoka, Munro adds this revision regard her father's relations with his mother, "My mother's absence brought a sort of peace—not only between them, but for all of us" (*Castle Rock* 148).

There is a critical moment in both versions of "Working for a Living"—critical for its initial memoir text, critical for Munro herself, and certainly critical for her late-style revision of the piece—when ten-year-old Alice and her father enter the dining room of the Pine Tree Hotel. Seeing them, a woman rose to meet them, and Munro continues, "The moment in which I did not realize this was my mother was not long, but there was a moment" (*Grand Street* 25; *Castle Rock* 150). The wording here is almost exactly the same in both versions, but in *Castle Rock* Munro's deeper renderings of the implications of the scene are palpable. To an original observation that her mother, who hoped to repeat these sales the next year, "couldn't have foreseen how soon the Americans were going to get into the war, and how that was going to keep them at home" (*Grand Street* 26–7) she adds, "how gas rationing was going to curtail the resort business. She couldn't foresee the attack on her own body, the destruction gathering within" (*Castle Rock* 152). Here again, reshaping "Working for a Living," the memoir which started as a fiction in the late 1970s, Munro finds herself once more confronting her mother, anticipating the Parkinson's Disease which in 1941 was about to besiege her. Munro had done so before; she would do so again until she reached "Dear Life," her final story about her mother.

The contradictory element in "Working for a Living" revolves around Anne Chamney Laidlaw then. Her character is presented there in ways her daughter denigrates—"She who had always had difficulty with her mother-in-law and her husband's family, who was thought stuck-up by our neighbors, and somewhat pushy by the town women at the church"—but also celebrates—"had found a world of strangers in which she was at once at home" (*Castle Rock* 153). Substantially, this passage is in the *Grand Street* version, and there too Munro makes her own rejection of her mother's sales success clear. Yet when revising in the early 2000s Munro emphasizes, elaborates, and makes her own understanding more subtle. After a white-space break, she continues:

> For all this, as I grew older, I came to feel something like revulsion. I despised the whole idea of putting yourself to use in that way, making yourself dependent on the response of others, employing flattery so adroitly and naturally that you did not even recognize it as flattery. And all for money. I thought such behavior shameful, as of course my grandmother did. I took it for granted that my father felt the same way though he did not show it. I believed—or thought I believed—in working hard and being proud, not caring about being poor and indeed having a subtle contempt for those who led easeful lives.
>
> (*Castle Rock* 153)

In both versions, Munro wonders if her father felt in any way the same, but in the revision she is more categorical. In 1941 the family needed Anne Chamney Laidlaw to succeed at that hotel, for they needed the money. "'But she had,' he said. 'She had it.' And the tone in which he said this convinced me that he never shared those reservations of my grandmother's and mine. Or that he'd resolutely put away such shame, if he'd ever had it." Then, just ahead of another white-space break, Munro offers a revision added in the early 2000s, a single-sentence paragraph, which gives us her own final truth about the matter: "A shame that has come full circle, finally being shameful in itself to me"

(*Castle Rock* 154). As this suggests, Munro turns her earlier feelings about her mother, and her father's view of his then wife's action, on their head. That she does, and does so just as she shifts to the 1949 visit to her father at work at the foundry suggests that her memory project in "Working for a Living" in its first published version continues into the revisions, but she does it best in its final form in *Castle Rock*.

The second part of the memoir focuses on Robert Eric Laidlaw's work life, and most especially on his dedication to the support of his family once the fox farm failed and his wife had gone inescapably into Parkinson's disease. At the same time, in the revisions to this section Munro may be seen bending the story in the direction of her own situation within the trajectory of *Castle Rock*. Needing to deliver a message that her father should stop by his mother's house on the way home after work, Munro rides her bicycle to the foundry. (The same mode of transport—likely the same bicycle—that Munro uses in "Lying under the Apple Tree.") Gone there for the first time, finding her father, seeing the particulars of his work there, Munro comes to and creates—in both versions—a deep appreciation for the life he had lived, the personal sacrifices he had made for all the family. She recounts, by way of the memoir's first ending, a night when her father had been forced to walk home through a massive snowstorm, when for a time he was trapped in its maw:

> He would die leaving a sick crippled wife who could not even take care of herself, an old mother full of disappointment, a younger daughter whose health had always been delicate, an older girl who was strong and bright enough but who often seemed to be self-centered and mysteriously incompetent, a son who promised to be clever and reliable but who was still only a little boy. He would die in debt, and before he had even finished pulling down the [fox] pens. They would stand there—drooping wire on the cedar poles that he had cut in the Austins' swamp in the summer of 1927—to show the ruin of his enterprise.
>
> 'Was that all you thought about?' I said when he told me this.
> 'Wasn't that enough?' he said ….

And continues to tell her how he managed to get home in that storm. While this exchange—it is in the first version too—has humor about it, Munro clarifies that she was thinking of his life apart from his family, about his life as a person: "I meant, was his life now something only other people had a use for?" (*Castle Rock* 166). This last question is the one that so struck Barber when she first read the memoir in 1980.

In the *Grand Street* version this question is followed by a space break and a single concluding paragraph comparing each parent's willingness to talk about these experiences in later years. They differed. With some small edits the same paragraph follows in *Castle Rock*, but after it and another space break, Munro takes up his work again, writing "And my father, as it turned out, had another occupation waiting for him." Not raising turkeys, which he did, but "It was after giving up such work that he took up writing. He began to write reminiscent pieces and to turn some of them into stories, which were published in an excellent though short-lived magazine. And not long before his death he completed a novel about pioneer life …." Beyond the description of this work Munro shifts to its effect on her father: "He told me that writing [*The McGregors*] had surprised him. He was surprised that he could do such a thing, and surprised that doing it could make him so happy. Just as if there was a future in it for him" (*Castle Rock* 167). She then quotes at some length from one of Laidlaw's published pieces, one she said is titled "Grandfathers." It was published in the *Village Squire* in November 1974 and it treats Robert Laidlaw's two grandfathers, Thomas Laidlaw—the baby carried from Scotland by William and Mary Laidlaw and the teenaged cook in the shanty pioneering Morris—and Thomas Code (1844–1927). Munro's quotation focuses on Thomas Laidlaw, and ends with a visit once paid to him by a rich and successful cousin from Toronto, another Robert Laidlaw. In the quotation Munro has edited the passage some from the source.[27] Once her father offers his memory of the two men visiting together, speaking to one another "in the broad Scots of the district from which they came," she interjects a paragraph to end "Working for a Living" and the "No Advantages" section of the book. Quietly, but with their ongoing presences and so the continuity of family history asserted, she writes:

> That is where I feel it best to leave them—my father a little boy, not venturing too close, and the old men sitting through a summer afternoon on wooden chairs placed under one of the great benevolent elm trees that used to shelter my grandparents' farmhouse. They spoke in the dialect of their childhood—discarded as they became men—which none of their descendants could understand.
> (*Castle Rock* 170)

This new ending to "Working for a Living" confirms Munro's purpose in her long-contemplated family book, for after detailing and precisely appreciating each of *her* parents as individuals, she isolates her father's happiness in discovering himself a writer in his last years. And she demonstrates his accomplishment. With this ending too, which largely ends her remembrances of her ancestors, she turns her attention to herself among Laidlaws. Opening the "Home" section—formerly called "Stories"—she turns to a succession of stories in which she herself is at the center. In each of them, she looks back and contemplates the discoveries she made then, the knowledge and perspectives she appreciates the better in the present as she assembled *The View from Castle Rock*.

Owing to chronology of composition and structure, only "The Ticket" has not yet received any sustained attention. This is apt, because "The Ticket" is the only story there that Munro appears to have written solely for *Castle Rock*.[28] More than that, its recursions are both central to Munro's late style and explicitly evident. Beginning as it does, "Sometimes I dream about my grandmother and her sister, my Aunt Charlie ..." (*Castle Rock* 255), it points back to these same women in "The Peace of Utrecht" and "Winter Wind" and, quite literally with its dreaming, the beginning of "Friend of My Youth." Munro's need for a new story here is evident, since the revised "Hired Girl" ends with the narrator—herself—still yet a teenager and "Home" beginning with Munro forty-one back in Ontario and separated from her husband. A bridge was needed. "The Ticket," treating as it does the time and circumstances of her wedding preparations—Alice Laidlaw married James Munro in late December 1951, when she was twenty—takes up a crucial time in her life. By that act, she clear-sightedly left her home place, its culture, and her family—most especially her ailing mother—behind to very consciously embrace her own life and career across the country in Vancouver (see Thacker *Alice* 104–9). This intention is evident in "The Ticket" since, along with her connections to her grandmother and her Aunt Charlie there, Munro recreates the person she was during the fall of 1951: her imaginings, expectations, and intentions. This was a time that led her to become Alice Munro, writer.

As she had done throughout, Munro focuses in "The Ticket" on familial and other pressures on her. After she recounts her dream of her grandmother (Sadie Code Laidlaw) and her aunt (Maud Code Porterfield)—"one younger, one older, than I am now," she explains that they "were packing the trunks I would take with me." She accounts for these trunks, mentioning that one was Aunt Charlie's gift. "'That's her wedding present?' my husband would say, later. 'A *trunk*?' Because in his family something like a trunk was what you went out and bought, when you needed it. No passing it off as a present" (*Castle Rock* 256; original emphasis). These two poles—the expectations of family and home, on the one hand, and those of her fiancé—drive the story Munro tells here, one quite literally based on her own circumstances then. "During the brief visit [Michael] had made to my home he had seen much that surprised him in an unpleasant way and that made him all the more resolute about rescuing me" (*Castle Rock* 260). This character is wholly based on James Munro who, for his part, came to be such husbands in Munro's fiction as Patrick in *Who Do You Think You Are? / The Beggar Maid* or Richard in "Chaddeleys and Flemings: 1. Connection."

Against such social expectations, Munro sets her "real work," her imaginings. Although most of her time at home was being spent on demanding housework—to Michael's dismay—and looking after her mother, she would "walk from our house on the far edge of town to the main street, where I did a bit of shopping and went to the library to return one book and take out another." She continues:

> I had not given up reading, though it seemed that the books I read now were not so harsh or demanding as the books I had been reading a year before. I read the short stories of A.E. Coppard—one of them had a title I found permanently seductive, though I can't remember anything else about it. 'Dusky Ruth.' And I read a short novel by John Galsworthy, which had a line on the title page that beguiled me.
>
> *The apple tree, the singing and the gold ...*
>
> My business on the main street finished, I went to visit my grandmother and Aunt Charlie. Sometimes—most times—I would rather have walked around alone, but I felt I could not neglect them, when they were doing so much to help me. I could not walk around here in a reverie, anyway, as I could have done in the city where I went to college.
>
> (*Castle Rock* 260–1; original emphasis)

After explaining why she could not do so in her hometown, Munro continues with yet another recursion: "And yet the town was enticing to me, it was dreamy in these autumn days" which, as I quoted the whole passage in the preface here, ends with "as I walked up the hill on Christena Street, toward my grandmother's house, I heard some lines in my head, the beginning of a story." A paragraph break, and then "*All over the town the leaves fell. Softly, silently the leaves fell—it was autumn.*" As I said above, substantially the beginning of Munro's "The Yellow Afternoon," written during the summer of 1951, never published but broadcast in 1955. Munro follows this with a bit of humor over her younger writing self, and recursively too, that there was no need to say that it was autumn: with leaves falling "it was foolish and self-consciously poetic to say so. Why else would the leaves be falling …"? (*Castle Rock* 261; original emphasis).

A. E. Coppard's "Dusky Ruth" is an inquisitive romantic story wholly in keeping with a young woman at twenty imagining her married future, a way for Munro to recapture just who she was and how she saw her life then as she anticipated as she dreamily walked about Wingham. So too Galsworthy's "The Apple Tree," which has as an epigraph a quotation from Gilbert Murray's 1911 translation of "Hippolytus of Euripides" as Munro remembers it.[29] Each textual reference, probably two things Munro actually read in 1951, then leads to her own most pressing concern: the fiction she was writing and would continue to write throughout her life. Images of narrators and other characters focused on writing are continual in her work, and this version of herself here in "The Ticket" following up on others, confirms yet again the recursive and autobiographical cast of her writing.

Within "The Ticket" Munro returns also to the characters of her grandmother and great aunt. In the case of her grandmother, the background and character of her marriage to William Cole Laidlaw are developed further than it had been in "Working for a Living" while here Munro goes into some detail about a relationship her grandmother had had with another man and broke off to marry her husband. Munro got much of this story from Aunt Charlie, whose own marriage she examines here too. As she writes,

> I had three marriages to study, fairly close-up, in this early part of my life. My parents' marriage—I suppose you might say that it was the most close-up, but in a way it was the most mysterious and remote, because of my childish difficulty in thinking of my parents as having any connection but the one they had through myself.

Once her mother "became sick—permanently sick, not just troubled with odd symptoms—the balance was altered." "From then on she was weighing the family down on one side and we—my father and brother and sister and I—were holding it up to a kind of normality on the other" (*Castle Rock* 273–4). After weighing all three of these marriages, Munro concludes with this passage, seeing the calm attraction everyone saw in Charlie and Cyril, her husband:

> I'm certain, though, that the other feelings I remember—the sense of obligation and demand that grew monstrously around my father and my mother, and the stale air of irritability, of settled unease, that surrounded my grandparents—were absent from that one marriage—and that this was seen as something to comment on, like a perfect day in an uncertain season.
>
> (*Castle Rock* 278)

All of this immediate family history is preliminary to Munro's own impending marriage to "Michael," James Munro. As well, too, she sees in her grandparents, especially, qualities that throughout *Castle Rock* she saw too in her ancestors from Scotland: a strict religiosity, reticence, hard work. Looking back to fall 1951 from the vantage point of 2005, Munro recalls herself then meaning "to hang on to [Michael] and to my family as well. I thought that I would be bound up with them always, as long as I lived, and that he could not shame or argue me away from them." She continues, writing of her thoughts of Michael / James then in a way that now might only an apology:

> And I thought I loved him. Love and marriage. That was a lighted and agreeable room you went into, where you were safe. The lovers I had imagined, the bold-plumed predators, had not appeared, perhaps did not exist, and I could hardly think myself a match for them anyway.
> He deserved better than me, Michael did. He deserved a whole heart.
> (*Castle Rock* 281)

With this retrospective admission, one she had already conceded in various ways, Munro recognizes just what she did when she married in 1951: she left her mother to her illness, her siblings and father to their responsibilities for her care in Munro's own stead and, equally, too, she admits to having married Michael / James without "a whole heart." In each case the problem is one of incomplete commitment. Munro had to become the writer she ultimately became. That goal was paramount.

After this passage Munro returns to her grandmother and aunt and then, detailing the scene in which her aunt surreptitiously slips her "Four fifty-dollar bills," she arrives at her title and the story's salient fact through Aunt Charlie's action: "'If you change your mind,' she said, still in a shaky urgent whisper. 'If you don't want to get married, you'll need some money to get away.'" Aunt Charlie's "eyes had gone pale with alarm at what she'd just said. And at what she still had to say, with more emphasis, though her lips were trembling. 'It might not be just the right ticket for you'" (*Castle Rock* 283).

While for some considerable time the Munros' marriage persisted, it ultimately was not "the ticket" for her as she well knew and had written about. So the reader of *Castle Rock* turns after "The Ticket" to "Home," where it is the early 1970s, Munro is back in Ontario, separated from James Munro, visiting her father and his second wife in Lower Town Wingham, being again within the culture of home after so long away. She also recognizes the advancing heart problems that would ultimately kill her father in 1976. There, myriad memories obtrude in Munro's imagination from first to last.

While she deletes the 1974 authorial commentaries in the 2001 revision of "Home" for its publication in the *New Stateman*, Munro retains a piece from the final commentary there. As "Home" has reached its final image, Munro writes in her own voice, "*There was something else I could have worked into an ending. I recognized, later, that the very corner of the stable where I was standing to spread the hay, and where the beginning of panic came on me, was the setting of the first scene I can establish as a true memory in my life*" ("Home" 74: *New* 152; original emphasis). Revising in 2001, awaiting surgery, Munro does just what she envisioned in 1974. She works on the scene of watching her father milk one of their two cows just as the especially brutal winter of 1934–5 approaches. In both the *New Statesman* and *Castle Rock* the remembered image of the scene is much the same as in the 1974 commentary—it is beautiful writing of a vivid scene in both versions—and yet there too Munro quite asserts her own presence, her own being, beyond the descriptive. To the existing 1974 sentence beginning "*Outside the small area of the stable ...*" (74: *New* 153), Munro made some small word changes and adds a reference to "the water tank where a kitten of mine will drown some years into the future" (*New Statesman* 93; *Castle Rock* 315). Perhaps a small addition, but indicative of her intentions in 2001, and then again as *Castle Rock* was being shaped. Munro puts herself amid her line of Laidlaws; she embraces her ancestral history.

That is just the point of "Home," and even more so the point of *The View from Castle Rock*. Written in 1973 and published the next year, "Home" is the anchor to Munro's family book. Its title encapsulates its central urge, one that, seen in relation to Munro's return to Ontario in 1972–3 and ultimately to Huron County in 1975, accounts for the fundamentally new way of writing she undertook when she returned there. The writing that she did after she returned to Huron—the descriptive photo text, "Places at Home," and then the fictions that produced *Who Do You Think You Are? / The Beggar Maid*—created a new depth in that work. Munro's decision in late 1978 to take *Who* off the press for restructuring and rewriting reveals a writer with an urgent imperative. That book—or those books—set Munro on a path to write her home place with precision, and with an emphatically singular depth of understanding, humane acceptance, and sharp complexity which far exceeded her early stories. Thus the stories found in volumes from *Who* to *Runaway*. But added to this authorial project, which Munro pursued from the writing of the original "Home" onward, there was the apparently ancillary but actively more central urge to write herself and her inheritance into her "kind of family book." In its complex and weighed provenance, the revisions that some of its fugitive pieces required as she awaited heart surgery in 2001, the circumstances she envisioned, all led Munro, contemplating her own end then, to a late style in that book that might well have proved to be her last. Seen contextually and biographically, *The View from Castle Rock* placed Alice Munro "in the midst of what was" her material, another imaginative Laidlaw writing her lives. It was not to be the end of her writing career as she envisioned it when she published *Castle Rock*. Rather, that book turned out to be the foundation for an emphatic late style that continued on for two more books based on her own "dear life," and those too of others. For Munro, ever and always, from first to last, "writing is the final thing."

Some last words about this most singular text, *Castle Rock*. "Home" does not end it, and even before the epilogue "What Do You Want to Know For?"—the memoir that Munro had so wondered over as to its inclusion—appears. It is there with its central mystery, a randomly found and difficult to re-find crypt that serves as synecdoche for its own immigrant history and, at some remove, as a synecdoche for Munro's own personal project in *Castle Rock*. It reveals Munro concluding her own story with Fremlin a new partner and she in her sixties, aware of final things through a cancer scare, itself a complement to the mysteries of the crypt. This leaves only "Messenger," formerly "Remnants," the epilogue to *Castle Rock*. There Munro does three things, each indicative of her personal project in *Castle Rock*. First she chronicles changes to the land in Huron, pointing to developments since her ancestors came to Morris in the early 1850s. Pausing to describe the shapings of the land her home place has seen, and the identifiable sites where homes once stood, she accounts for how it looks now through knowledge of what it had been. Then she tells us briefly of her trip to Illinois during the summer of 2004 in search of William Laidlaw's grave. She abandons that search but, tellingly, leaves readers with her mysterious sense that she had indeed found its location. Doubtless acknowledging her own activities throughout, Munro describes the genealogical urge.

Finally, Munro takes her readers to the Blyth Union Cemetery, her fourth in *Castle Rock*, where so many of her ancestors are buried, people who are characters in her book and, continuing on, tells of another: "Now all these names I have been recording are joined to the living people in my mind, and to the lost kitchens, the polished nickel trim on the commodious presiding black stoves, the sour wooden drainboards that never quite dried, the yellow light of the coal-oil lamps." Following these images, Munro takes her readers into "the stable warmed in winter by the bodies and breath of cows—those cows whom you still spoke to in words common in the days of Troy. *So—boss. So—boss*" (*Castle Rock* 348 original emphasis). These are the words a brother in "Fathers" uses to move cows (*Castle Rock* 180), but more emphatically this reminds us of three-year-old Alice Laidlaw watching her father milk their doomed cow in their barn in late 1934. After noting the "cold waxed parlor" in a remembered family home "where the coffin was put when someone died," Munro introduces "a magic doorstop, a big mother-of-pearl seashell that I recognized as a messenger from near and far, because I could hold it to my ear—when nobody was there to stop me—and discover the tremendous pounding of my own blood, and of the sea" (*Castle Rock* 348–9).[30] Her own blood. There she is, one of these people amid her own family: Alice Ann Laidlaw Munro.

4

"And Then Another Little Story Comes along and That Solves How Life Has Got to Be": The Recursions of *Too Much Happiness*

> *For instance, one day in winter, looking by chance out the back window of the library in the town hall, she saw a team of horses pulling a load of grain sacks on the municipal weigh scales. Snow was falling. The horses were heavy workhorses, which were rare now, except that some farmers used them in winter, on the roads that were not ploughed. The big grain sacks, the heavy obedient animals, the snow, made Rhea think suddenly that the town was muffled in great distances, in snow-choked air, and that the life in it was a timeless ritual. [….] A place of waiting, of loneliness, unfinished gestures. These feelings or visions didn't come so much from what she could see before her as they did from books that she had got to read from that same library—Russian stories and* Winesburg, Ohio.
>
> ("Spaceships Have Landed," Paris Review 276, 277)

This passage is a unique crux in Munro's serial publication. By late December 1992 Munro had completed six of the eight stories which were to be included in her next collection, *Open Secrets* (1994). She was then at work on "Spaceships," the next one, and could see her way toward the final story, "Vandals" (Munro to Barber December 11, 1992; 883/11.5.2).[1] Of the eight stories in the book, only "Spaceships" was not bought by the *New Yorker*; it first saw print in the *Paris Review*, which published it in 1994 accompanied by a Munro interview by Jeanne McCulloch and Mona Simpson as part of its "The Art of Fiction" series. The editor, George Plimpton, took the story on the condition that Munro cut its first six pages, which detail a scene in a speakeasy; she agreed, but then reinstated the passage in *Open Secrets*. To restructure the story for the serial after this opening cut, Munro wrote and inserted a long paragraph as a bridge there, one that was not included in the book (see Thacker *Alice* 449; Martin and Ober "Small-Town Historian").

My epigraph here is taken from that paragraph, and I begin this chapter with it as a way of suggesting where Munro was going in 1992–3 and where, recursively, she had already been. A few years later she would return to this scene in the introduction to her first *Selected Stories*, describing it at greater length and in her own voice, admitting that it was something she had seen when she "was around fifteen years old." There she wrote that she "saw it alive and potent, and it gave me something like a blow to the chest," asking also, "How can you get your finger on it, feel that life beating?" (xvi). When she describes Rhea's "feelings or visions" coming not from the life around her but rather "Russian stories and *Winesburg, Ohio*," Munro returns to the first fictional version of "Working for a Living"—circa 1979—when Janet travels home after withdrawing from the university, and sees her hometown in exactly the same way (for example 38.10.37.f5).[2]

In the *Paris Review* interview Munro remarks that "[r]eading was my life really until I was thirty. I was living in books." Thus Janet in the fictional "Working," Rhea here in her bridge meditation on her home place and, as just seen, a thinly veiled Alice Munro, recalling her own reading and writing in 1951 in "The Ticket." During this interview too Munro was still trying to envision a form for *Castle Rock* since she talks about that project, and she addresses the rest of her career, contemplating an eventual end to her writing. "The only thing I've ever had to fill my life has been writing," she said (McCulloch and Simpson 255, 263). Just now, leaving *Castle Rock* and turning to Munro's final two books, this interview—which happened about the same time Munro spoke to Gittings—is prescient in a way that takes Munro's late style into *Too Much Happiness* and finally into *Dear Life*. There Munro told McCulloch and Simpson of the challenges she was dealing with in shaping *Castle Rock*—"I've made a couple of attempts to plan a book, the sort that everybody's writing about their family. But I haven't got any framework for it, any center." The interviewers then prompt her, asking about "Working for a Living," and she responds, "Yes. I'd like to do a book of essays and include it." Still thinking of this project, Munro remarked to them, "It would take a while. I keep thinking I'm going to do something like this, and then I get the idea for one more story, and that one more story always seems so infinitely more important, even though it's only a story, than the other work." Citing a recent interview she had read with William Trevor—another influence—Munro says to end the interview, "and then another little story comes along and that solves how life has got to be" (263–4).

Making *Too Much Happiness*: "no story is never really over"

When "The Ticket" and "What Do You Want to Know For?" were submitted to the *New Yorker* on they arrived there along with another manuscript story titled "Dimension" (Shannon Firth to Deborah Treisman November 30, 2005; *New Yorker* files).[3] By then "Wenlock Edge" had been accepted by the magazine and was in proof and so moving toward its first publication in the December 5, 2005 issue (Edited Proof November 10, 2005; *New Yorker* files). "Dimension," after appearing in the *New Yorker* (June 5, 2006) with that title, would be renamed "Dimensions" and become the opening story in *Too Much Happiness* (2009).[4] Then there was "Wood," still being revised after the almost thirty years since it had first been in the magazine in 1980, destined finally to make the cut for the next book. *Castle Rock* finally finished and about to be published in 2006, Munro's stories did keep coming along.

The flap copy in the Canadian first edition of *Too Much Happiness* speaks of Munro "flirting with the idea of retirement" but then asserts that, even so, "Alice Munro's back" and continues to characterize the ten stories in the collection. Relations between and among stories after the experience of making *Castle Rock* and the two books after that flirtation show Munro's late style at its most recursive. Her hand is sure and precise, echoes and allusions to other stories and situations abound, and so Munro may be seen using these two books as summary to a writing career that kept on prolifically. And she would continue after *Castle Rock* with the new: each of her last two books offers a singular textual presence, a different Munro. In *Too Much Happiness* it is the long title story, one that tells of the last days of the renowned Russian mathematician, Sophia Kovalevsky, while in *Dear Life* it is that book's "Finale," Munro's quite conscious final word on her material, her writing, and her life. Four connected stories which take her back finally to her youth among her first family, living along the Maitland River in Lower Town Wingham. Marking my direction here, this chapter chronologically surveys the stories in *Too Much Happiness* but for the title story, which will be held back for the final chapter and treated along with the "Finale" to *Dear Life*.

As she turned to the two books she would produce after *Castle Rock*, all "last ones," Munro was thinking of final things, looking back as she looked forward (see Munro "Writing"; Thacker *Alice* 532–4). Beyond Gorra's review of *Too Much Happiness*— already quoted and about to be drawn from again—two others make points that, within the valedictory air surrounding its reviews, need to be noticed here as the stories in that book are taken up. Asserting that Munro is "a writer who isn't too modest—one possessed of a fearless, at times, fearsome ambition"—Leah Hager Cohen notes the "domesticity" of Munro's home place in her work. And she says further that Munro "has staked her claim on rocky, rough terrain" and that this writer "flays this material with the unflinching efficiency of a hunter skinning a rabbit" (9). Just so. And Michiko Kakutani isolates an element of Munro's late style—though she does not call it that— writing that "In recent stories, however, there has been a pronounced tendency on Ms. Munro's part deliberately to stage-manage her people's fates." This creates suspense, Kakutani concedes, but it also creates "tales that can feel implausible and contrived": "the willful melodramatics of these tales make them far cruder than Ms. Munro's best work" (C6). In *Too Much Happiness* this experienced reviewer excepts the title story and "Fiction" from this judgment, yet her criticism of the balance stands fair enough, and one continued into *Dear Life*. What Kakutani calls "willful dramatics" is to be found in Munro's late-style books, especially the last two, for within them she has moved beyond plot. Or, in Cohen's phrasing, Munro is too busy skinning rabbits. Given this author's own history, though, those rabbits might be better seen as muskrats, or mink or, especially, foxes.

Following Munro's progress chronologically, "Wood" demands especial prominence. This story is, oddly, an instance of both early and late styles. After its initial publication Munro revised it several times, it was often considered for inclusion in collections and, when it was finally included in *Too Much Happiness*, it might have been excluded again. Originally, "Wood" "came along" during what was arguably Munro's first truly fecund period, the late 1970s; an outpouring owing to her return to Huron County. In the midst of this "Wood," in the *New Yorker* and also quickly republished in two best-stories volumes, one in Canada, another in the United States, has been a unique presence.[5] As McGrath was preparing it for publication, he noted her activity by commenting, "You're working so fast these days that I can barely keep up" as he sends the latest "Wood" back to her (June 6, 1980; *New Yorker* records). The month before, at the end of a letter primarily concerned with "Dulse" (first published just prior to "Wood," July 21, 1980), McGrath tells her that "we're very taken with WOOD. It's an unusual story—surprising and oddly compelling—and needless to say, we're delighted to have it" (May 2, 1980; 38.2.4.5). Once he had started editing the story, McGrath wrote that "those two or three pages where you do nothing more than describe trees, are perhaps my favorite part of the whole story" (May 21, 1980; 38.2.4.6).[6]

"Wood" is the story of Roy Fowler, a sign painter in Logan, Ontario. Married and childless, he and wife live amid her large extended family and, while they accept Roy, he usually retreats to his workshop during family gatherings. He is good at his work, but Roy's real passion is for different types of hardwood, an enthusiasm known about but not spoken of by others, so he often goes off to the bush to cut and down trees, sawing them up and hauling the cordwood out. He loves trees, and often imagines the different types together in the forest: "Roy's thoughts about wood are covetous and nearly obsessive, though he has never been a greedy man in any other way" (*New Yorker* 48; see *Happiness* 232). He is happiest when he is off in the bush alone, although his wife worries about accidents. "Wood" treats an accident that befalls Roy—of a late autumn afternoon, a first snow falling, Roy slips and falls, breaking an ankle, and so is forced to crawl back to his truck, escaping the danger and getting out. In the 1980 version he does this alone, but in the 2009 version his worried wife, Lea, anticipates trouble and comes to his rescue. In that version Munro drops his last name and changes his occupation from sign painter to "upholsterer and refinisher of furniture" (*Happiness* 225).[7] She also develops Roy's wife's character. Commenting on the numerous iterations of the story within Munro's various collections, Ann Close has said "I can't tell you how many times we put "Wood" in a collection and then took it out." Munro rewrote it "every time and it finally got to be better; it was always kind of an interesting story, but it finally got to be, I think, a really wonderful story" (July 21, 2010).

The two versions of "Wood" have received important critical attention from Lisa Dickler Awano and from Héliane Ventura. Awano interviewed Munro about this story alone. There Munro explains that her father's woodcutting was a part of her childhood, certainly, but for the story she got her specific information from Fremlin, who himself went to the bush to cut and haul their firewood (61–2). This is borne out by archival drawings in a notebook—in another hand, probably Fremlin's—of a first cut, a felling cut, a partially down tree still on its stump with its top lodged in surrounding trees, an undercut, and sidesplitting. These drawings are followed by detailed notes, in Munro's hand, on cutting techniques, types of trees, the texture of the different barks, the machine requirements of cutting and getting out a cord a day, and the humped quality of the ground in the bush. Much of this material is in the story; it forms the basis of the descriptions of different trees that McGrath commented on (38.12.1; see also 38.10.32).

Munro also tells Awano that the first version "was something that I was taking from life. I knew the people in the story. And I didn't want to probe much deeper with them, because all I got from them, in fact, is what is in the story—which is more or less a trick story—you know, about how it's himself that Roy is chasing after." That is, Roy becomes concerned about a rumor that he has a competitor for a particular stand of trees; this rumor, he eventually realized, is based on his own plans, misunderstood. Continuing with Awano, Munro tells her that she passed "Wood" over so many times, despite attempts at a revision, because she "decided it had not enough weight as a story," that "it just didn't have enough layers to be interesting to *me*" (48; original emphasis).[8] At the same time too, Close mentioned that throughout the years since its *New Yorker* publication the prototypes for the characters in "Wood" were still living (Close to Thacker August 30, 2013) and Barber, for her part, once wrote, "It was Alice who wasn't ready to reprint 'Wood'" (email April 18, 2010). Close agreed too that Munro's assessment of the first version as slight was correct, but that when it was revised and placed in a key structural position in *Too Much Happiness*—where it precedes the title story—"Wood" became quite another thing, critical to that volume (Close interview July 21, 2010; see Thacker *Alice* 559–60).

In a note to her article Ventura comments that the "ending of the story is very much revised in the 2009 version," arguing that Roy, having been rescued by his heretofore depressed but now revitalized wife, is Munro's "profound equivocation" which ends that version. Safely in his truck, about to be driven to the hospital by Lea so that his injury could be addressed, "He lowers the window and cranes around, getting snow in his face. He looks at the wood from which he has just been rescued and exclaims 'The Deserted Forest.' The story finishes on this cryptic exclamation, the origin of which is neither explained nor elucidated, leaving the reader with a conundrum to grapple with" (437, n. 27, 431). This ending is abrupt, certainly, and it does leave a reader unaware of its intended meaning. Ventura then proposes a compelling and apt source for this phrase: Khalil Gibran's poem "The Beauty of Death," where a person about to die stipulates "the deserted forest" as his burial place.

Earlier in both versions of "Wood," after he has fallen and broken his ankle and is lying on the forest ground, Roy sees a large bird, perhaps a hawk, but actually a buzzard. When she attempted a revision to include the story in *Friend of My Youth*, using a photocopy of the text from *Best Canadian Stories, 81*, Munro deleted the single-word sentence that ends the first version—"Safe"—and writes "That wealth of trees behind him, in the mild snow. The windless day just before the winter. Himself, under the buzzard's eye" (M&S Z39.5). When *Too Much Happiness* was being produced, the final sentence of "Wood" was "'The Deserted Forest,' as if to put the cap on something, ~~like one of those sad old schoolroom quotations~~" (M&S Z119.21). The final phrase here is omitted from the 2009 version, but its existence as a possibility points back to the scene in "The Ottawa Valley" where the characters take turns reciting "sad old schoolroom quotations" and, as will yet be seen, it points forward to poetry read in "Wenlock Edge" and in "Face" in *Too Much Happiness*. Joined too with the buzzard in the story, with Ventura's effective elucidation of the Gibran poem as Munro's reference, and the many deaths in *Too Much Happiness*, whether possible, impending, or actual, Munro's revisions to "Wood" deepen the story, adding layers to the wife Lea's character especially, but those added layers are evident throughout and most particularly at its cryptic ending. That ending from Gibran leaves Roy wondering, Munro wondering, and readers wondering too. Finally well placed in *Too Much Happiness*, "a really wonderful story," the revised "Wood" stands beacon for that volume and for its author's continuing late style. Its unique provenance—with its beginnings in Munro's late 1970s period and, much revised, as a late-style story finally collected—confirms its singularity.

"Wenlock Edge" was held out of *Castle Rock* and included in *Too Much Happiness*. There, its ending was changed from that found in the *New Yorker* version (December 5, 2005), which reads "I kept on learning things. I learned that Uricon, the Roman camp, is now Wroxeter, a town on the Severn River" (91). The reference here is to A. E. Housman's poem XXXI in *A Shropshire Lad* (1896) beginning "On Wenlock Edge the wood's in trouble" (42), a poem which figures centrally in Munro's story. This crux is notable because it is indicative of Munro's later work: by telescoping here back to Roman times, by invoking poetry she knows well (Munro once told me that she could recite a considerable portion of *A Shropshire Lad* from memory), she lends her story an historic depth, a wisdom which resonates. Life is life, people are people, human issues are the same.

Examples of this are regular in late Munro: in "Hateship, Friendship, Courtship, Loveship, Marriage" (2001), Munro ends the story with a direct quotation from Horace's famed "seize the day" ode. In 2004 Munro published the Juliet Triptych, three connected stories sharing the same protagonist who, in the first story, "Chance," is reading *The Greeks and the Irrational* while on a transcontinental train to Vancouver. "Deep-Holes" (2008) and "Axis" display a deep geological awareness. And then there is the title story of *Too Much Happiness*: an extended historical fiction focused on the life and death of a nineteenth-century Russian mathematician, Sophia Kovalevsky; like nothing else Munro had ever done, certainly, but also a story which occasions long perspective. When Cohen reviewed *Too Much Happiness* she wrote of "the sensation, when reading, that your own mind is giving birth to the words as they appear on the page" (1); commenting on this in a letter to the editor, a Classics professor responded to connect this effect in Munro to Longinus' *On the Sublime*: "It is easy to imagine" Longinus "citing a passage in Munro" (Roberts).

Discussing "Wenlock Edge," Close said that she thought it better in the 2009 collection. "It was more like the other stories in *Too Much Happiness*" (July 26, 2010). That is fair enough, but the explicitly autobiographical cast of the story—apart from its central scene in which the unclothed narrator dines with a much older man, wholly clothed, and at his request reads aloud from Housman's *A Shropshire Lad*—suggests that "Wenlock Edge" might well have been placed appropriately in the "Home" section of *Castle Rock*. Its narrator clearly is Alice Laidlaw, a student at the University of Western Ontario with her living circumstances and serious mien. She works in the cafeteria, just as Munro did herself. And in the version first submitted to *New Yorker*, dated July 16 [2005], the narrator comments toward the story's end when she is talking to her cousin Ernie after Nina had left him:

> I was full of other news I wasn't ready to divulge. My life had turned around. A boy, a senior student, had asked me out. He saw in me simplicity and youth and purity— though of these three things only youth was really there. Handsome, determined, magically deluded, he claimed that he had fallen in love with me while watching me in the cafeteria. A girl like me doing work like that had touched his heart.
>
> (*New Yorker* files)

This is a reasonably accurate description of Munro's meeting and eventual relation with James Munro then, though she drops this paragraph—and so the suitor—from a submitted revision two weeks later (August 1, 2005; *New Yorker* files).

By placing "Wenlock Edge" during her undergraduate years Munro recreates herself doubly: recalling a time she loved, "being in that atmosphere, having all those books," "to have that concentration of your life, that something else was the thing you got up in the morning to do, and it was all reading and writing, studying" (Thacker interview April 2004). Throughout the story the narrator is at work on an essay on *Sir Gawain and the Green Knight*, one she is confident will receive an A, and when Mr. Purvis asked her after their dinner to read aloud from A. E. Housman's *A Shropshire Lad*, she readily acknowledges her familiarity with that famous collection. "I knew it. In fact I knew many of the poems by heart" (*Happiness* 82). But more than the circumstance of those years, Munro recreates herself—her values and mores—as the wondering young adult she was then. When she describes the boy's sense of her, the narrator asserts that then she was neither simple nor pure. The extended scene in "Wenlock Edge" when she agrees to take off all of her clothes during the dinner with Mr. Purvis complements this admission, as does her wicked action of informing Purvis of Nina's whereabouts in Ernie's home.

From January to April 1980 Munro was Distinguished Visiting Artist in the Department of Creative Writing at the University of British Columbia, a position she took mostly to be near her youngest daughter, then a teenager living in Victoria. This time in Vancouver led to a three-page autograph notebook fragment from the early 1980s of a story in which a narrator—probably Janet from the initial *Who/Beggar*—tells about a coincidence "twenty-seven years old." Continuing, she writes that "I was in Vancouver last winter to teach, or run, or be present at, a poetry workshop and one of the girls, or young women there, asked me to go and have supper with a group of her friends, all women, who met and talked about their writing in one another's houses." She goes along with this group to an apartment in Kitsilano and realizes first that they are near a place she once lived with her husband in the early fifties and then, once they arrive, she discovers that the apartment is in the same house where she lived. After they ate, the hostess, a "blonde young woman in jeans," "read some poems, then threw them down and talked about her life, how she had gone to live with a millionaire when she was seventeen and the millionaire had made her sit naked on the patio drinking cocktails, how she had gone to Japan for an abortion and fallen in love" (38.11.5.f3). These are Nina's circumstances in "Wenlock Edge," and Munro transformed them into her narrator's, imagining herself as an undergraduate doing such a thing at its dinner with Purvis, also a millionaire. In 2004 Munro told me that this episode of the writers' gathering happened to her, though not in the same house she had lived in but in the same neighborhood, when she was there in 1980. She also said she "had been trying to do something with the story [the woman told them at the gathering] for the last year. She always had to eat dinner naked" (Thacker interview April 2004). Thus "Wenlock Edge."

As she was working on it, Munro decided to change the ending once the first version had been submitted to the *New Yorker*. There the narrator prepares an envelope by placing Ernie's address in it, stamps it, and contemplates dropping it in the mail chute. But then she says, "I swear I didn't send it." "I was released from what I had wanted and meant to do and I tore the envelope in half and crumpled up the halves ....

I had crumpled and torn it in case I might want and mean to do such a thing again. I had wasted a stamp." That version then ends, after a white-space break, with these single-sentence paragraphs:

> And a few days after that Michael spoke to me in the cafeteria and I agreed to go out with him before I knew his name.
>   Mr. Purvis popped up in my mind every once in a while but I slapped him down.
>   I discovered that Unicon was Wroxeter, a Roman camp on the Severn river.
> (29, July 16 [2005]; New Yorker files)

By the August 1 revision—sent to the magazine on August 15—Munro had eliminated Michael and reversed the narrator's action; in it, and all subsequent endings, the letter is sent. After dropping it in the chute, the narrator looks about at the other students around her in the arts building, "Most of them on a course, as I was, of getting to know the ways of our own wickedness." This is followed by a single-sentence paragraph: "Unicon is Wroxeter, a Roman camp on the Severn river" (29, August 1, 2005; *New Yorker* files).

    Carefully following these changes reveals Munro repeatedly shaping her last word, the final sense she creates in "Wenlock Edge." Two days after she had read Housman to Purvis, after she went back their room that night and discovered Nina was gone, having gone off to Ernie's that night, and after she spent Sunday working on her paper amid the tumult caused by Purvis' assistant frantically searching for Nina, the narrator hears from Nina by phone and takes things to her at Ernie's. Then back at the university she goes to work in the cafeteria and, afterwards, she sees a notice for "a free recital of songs composed to fit the poems of the English Country Poets":

> I had seen this notice before, and did not have to look at it to be reminded of the names Herrick, Housman, Tennyson. And a few steps into the tunnel [that led to the arts building] the lines began to assault me.
>   *On Wenlock Edge the wood's in trouble*
>   I would never think of those lines again without feeling the prickles of the upholstery on my bare haunches. The sticky prickly shame. A far greater shame it seemed now, than at the time. He had done something to me, after all.
> (Happiness 90; original emphasis)

Then follow three more quotations from *A Shropshire Lad*, the first counterpointed with "No." The second with "No, never." And the third with "No. No. No." "I would always be reminded of what I had agreed to do. Not been forced, not ordered, not even persuaded. Agreed to do." "Nina would know." She would tease her about it. "Her teasing would have in it something like the tickling, something insistent, obscene. Nina and Ernie. In my life from now on" (*Happiness* 91).

    This is the fulcrum point to the story. Here Munro creates the circumstances which lead the narrator to mail her letter and so inform Purvis of Nina's whereabouts, effectively getting Nina out of her life, something she much prefers. And as the ending is adjusted through its various iterations, it is balanced between what is described as her "wickedness"—in all the extant versions of the story the first paragraph ends with her asserting "I had a mean tongue" (*Happiness* 64)—and her discovery of the meaning and location of Uricon in the primary Housman poem quoted (XXXI).

At the *New Yorker* Treisman gave the story its usual edit with many suggested changes—additions, re-phrasings, and deletions—and clearly she and Munro went over them on the telephone since many of them are x-ed out, indicating Munro's rejection of them.[9] The last two sentences, as set, are paragraphs that read "Most of them [other students] on a course, as I was, of getting to know the ways of their own wickedness." And "Uricon is Wroxeter, a Roman camp on the Severn River." Editing this last sentence, Treisman suggests adding this subordinate phrase after "Uricon": "I learned before the end of the semester," commenting "Or some such—it feels a little too unmoored as is." Whether originating with Munro or Treisman, the ending that ran in the *New Yorker* then follows in the latter's hand: "I kept on learning things. I learned that Uricon, the Roman camp, is now Wroxeter, a town on the Severn River" (*New Yorker* proof, November 10, 2005, 26–7; *New Yorker* files; *New Yorker* 91). A later proof, also edited by Treisman though less heavily and dated November 18, 2005, shows that Munro accepted most of these changes, including the new final sentence, for the serial version (*New Yorker* files).

Yet here too and in keeping with Munro's practice, it is possible to see a reversion to her originally submitted version of "Wenlock Edge" as it was shaped for *Too Much Happiness*. Most—though not all—of Treisman's edits drop away and the published text in the book is closer to submitted. And Munro returned to the ending again. In the setting copy of the manuscript, after "people passing me on the way to classes, on the way to have a smoke and maybe a game of bridge in the Common Room," Munro wrote "That was all." It was followed by a space break, and then:

> Uricon is now the village of Wroxeter, on the Severn River. Wroxter [sic] is also a village in Ontario, on another river.
> Names are sturdy and persistent. Like our wickedness.
> To learn the ways of our own wickedness.
>
> (127, Setting copy, Msc343.1.3-1.4)

All of this is crossed out in what looks Munro's hand. Emphasizing "wickedness" through its repetition and, as well, bringing it home by mentioning Ontario's Wroxeter, a town on the Maitland river just east of Wingham. The story was set for *Too Much Happiness* ending "on the way to have a smoke and maybe a game of bridge in the Common Room." Reading page proofs dated May 14, 2009, Munro added the sentence which now ends the story: "On their way to deeds they didn't know they had in them." She does so with a note about it to her editors, "ungrammatical never mind" (MsC 343.1.5).

As Munro moves toward this eventual ending, just before the narrator describes her actions surrounding the spiteful and revelatory letter she prepared and mailed, she has her narrator say "That day in the library I had been unable to go on with Sir Gawain. I had torn a page from my notebook and picked up my pen and walked out" (*Happiness* 93). That she could not go on with *Sir Gawain*, with poetry, connects directly to the narrator's transformed feelings toward *A Shropshire Lad* after reading from it to Purvis, and to the two published endings of "Wenlock Edge," the first citing wickedness and Housman, the second "deeds they didn't know they had in them." Wicked deeds like the narrator's here, probably, but revelatory and affecting in more than moral terms. What Munro is after here is the wellspring of poetry, the affects of being. The unchanging nature of humanity whatever the time, whatever the circumstances. That Munro began with an explicit invocation of Housman's poetic wisdom, but then backed away, and settled on to the effects on the narrator as she realized—over the retrospective recollection from three decades before—the ways her experience of reading Housman to Purvis changed her. Matured her. Hardened her. That the detailed provenance of surrounding the ending of "Wenlock Edge" shifted so, and it reveals a writer in the throes of her late style getting the exact effects she needs. And that *Sir Gawain and the Green Knight* and, especially, *A Shropshire Lad*—two famed texts in the tradition Munro has long worked—define the poetic wisdom and long view that she herself realizes through that late style is clear (see Luft).

Thus even before she had finished *Castle Rock*, and despite her flirtation with retirement after it was done, new stories kept pressing. After "Wenlock Edge" was in the *New Yorker* it was followed—again, also before *Castle Rock* was published—by "Dimension" there in June. As it happened, I saw Munro briefly just after it appeared in Bayfield, in Huron County, a place specifically mentioned in the story and, after I commented that I had just read it, she replied, "That must have been an upper." No. "Dimension," and then the retitled "Dimensions" that opens *Too Much Happiness*, is focused on a woman, Doree, dealing as best she is able with her new life after her abusive husband, now in a mental institution, murdered their three small children. After an argument and a night away she came home in the morning to find them dead, her husband sitting outside the house. (Munro had explored similar circumstances in "Runaway" [2003], though there the only death is—perhaps—a pet goat.) Her focus in "Dimensions" is on Doree's life afterwards, treating two journeys to see her husband Llyod in the institution. The story begins:

> Doree had to take three buses—one to Kincardine, where she waited for the one to London, where she waited again for the city bus out to the facility. She started the trip on a Sunday at nine in the morning. Because of the waiting times between buses, it took her till about two in the afternoon to travel the hundred-odd miles. All that sitting, either on the buses or in the depots, was not a thing she should have minded. Her daily work was not of the sitting-down kind.
>
> She was a chambermaid at the Blue Spruce Inn. She scrubbed bathrooms and stripped and made beds and vacuumed rugs and wiped mirrors. She liked the work—it occupied her thoughts to a certain extent and tired her out so that she could sleep at night.
>
> (*Happiness* 3)

When she and Ann Close were assembling *Too Much Happiness* Munro wanted "Dimensions" to be first. Close agreed (July 21, 2010). As this beginning shows, readers of "Dimensions" enter Munro's place and world—the three buses have been seen before, in "Home," though their direction is reversed. Doree and her work are matter of fact, as is her neutral destination, "the facility." She seems a Munrovian character. Another story placed in Alice Munro Country since Kincardine and London are named here yet traveling with Doree the reader does not know until pages in just where she is heading. The facts emerge, both regarding what has happened and Doree's present situation. Then Lloyd in the facility himself, the disturbing writing he sends her. Then another bus heading toward another visit, this one interrupted near Bayfield, where Doree aids another person, a young man in an accident. Munro describes Doree's ministering to him and writes "that everything in the world outside the boy's body had to concentrate, help it not lose track of its duty to breathe" (*Happiness* 33). Doing so, she affirms life and through that decides as "Dimensions" ends not to go on with the bus to London to visit Lloyd. In that moment another life changed.

Michael Gorra wrote in his review that "[m]ost readers will find themselves absorbed—indeed ravaged—by this book's first story, 'Dimensions,'" and he asserts too that the "collection does show the blend of continuity and change that one wants and hopes to find in a late book by a master" ("Mortal" 4, 3). Age "has given her a new subject," and unlike others "she does not seem to rage at the indignity of years": "if I had to reduce the concerns of *Too Much Happiness* to a single word, it would be 'mortality'" ("Mortal" 4). This he asserts by pointing to "Free Radicals" (2008) and emphasizes its ending. That story ends with "a two-word paragraph which feels like no ending at all: 'Never know.'" Then in a line I have come to love in its aptness, Gorra maintains that "Munro has always had an ability to take a narrative corner at speed" ("Mortal" 4). Of the book at hand, he continues, writing "But the corners are now tighter than ever, single words or sentences that seem marked by an epigrammatic impatience with the whole business of endings; as though every tale might allow for an alternative version and no story is never really over." This is just what is found in the text of "Wenlock Edge," and he goes on to note that "Fully half the pieces in *Too Much Happiness* finish with such one-sentence paragraphs, endings that don't feel open so much as jagged or bitten-off." Finally, another aptness: "I wonder if this abruptness might be something like the formal expression of Munro's own age; and a sense of no time to waste, a sense too that all conclusions are arbitrary. Any given moment might serve to close things down. Not all of them work" ("Mortal" 4).

Other observations might be cited, but these quotations define the effects Munro creates through her late style and most especially in *Too Much Happiness*. They offer a fabric of allusive textures which remind readers of previous Munrovian situations while exploring other circumstances anew. "Free Radicals" also offers three violent deaths but they, as in "Dimensions," are not the point of the story. Rather, Munro focuses on her protagonist, Nita, a widow alone fighting cancer, who offers an intruder a version of her own story—its veracity is unclear, so that offering may well be borne of Nita's own wickedness—as a way of avoiding being murdered herself. She avoids violent death, and her life continues, whatever the cancer may do. "Child's Play" (2007) recalls the cruelty of two young girls at camp toward another girl, whom they drown and, though sharing that connection throughout life, suffer no consequences for their action. It is reminiscent of "Open Secrets" (1993) where a young girl mysteriously disappears forever amid a morning girls' hike, but "Child's Play" focuses deeply and enigmatically on the murderers' subsequent lives.

"Child's Play" was followed in *Harper's* by "Fiction" (2007). There the protagonist, Joyce, rediscovers a former student, the daughter of a woman who years before had supplanted her with a longtime lover; Joyce sees her at a party and is told she writes and has just published a book. Discovering it in a store, she buys a copy and, looking at it, thinks, "*How Are We to Live* is a collection of short stories, not a novel. This in itself is a disappointment. It seems to diminish the book's authority, making the author seem like somebody who is just hanging on to the gates of Literature, rather than safely settled inside" (*Happiness* 52). Here Munro is harkening back to herself in the late 1950s, when she struggled to write a novel, but managed only stories. By the time she wrote "Fiction" in the 2000s, such a comment is both self-revelatory and a wry joke.

In bed that night with her husband, Joyce begins to read the book, not yet having discovered that she herself appears as a central figure in one of its stories. She looks at and evaluates the author photo and, while her husband talks of something else,

> Joyce shifts her knees so that she can position the book against them and read the few sentences of the cover biography.
> *Christie O'Dell grew up in Rough River, a small town on the coast of British Columbia. She is a graduate of the UBC Creative Writing Program. She lives in Vancouver, British Columbia, with her husband, Justin, and her cat, Tiberius.*
> (*Happiness* 50; original emphasis)

As with the joke about the expectation of a novel, Munro is looking back here to another story about writers and their ways: "Material." Narrated by a writer's former wife who discovers and reads a story by her former husband, Hugo, Munro has that narrator contemplate the author biography she finds in the book. There, however, and with considerable venom, the narrator dissects the biography, sneering at its pretensions: "But listen to the lies, the half-lies, the absurdities" (*Something* 29). After over a page of such dissection, the narrator concludes: "Look at you, Hugo, your image is not only fake but out-of-date. You should have said you'd meditated for a year in the mountains of Uttar Pradesh; you should have said you'd taught Creative Drama to autistic children; you should have shaved your head, shaved your beard, put on a monk's cowl; you should have shut up, Hugo" (*Something* 31). This narrator goes on to read the story she found in this short-story anthology, one based on a woman they both knew early in their marriage, when Hugo was a graduate student and the narrator was pregnant. She finds it to be quite good. But though she tries, she cannot bring herself to write and tell him so, for like her husband and so like men generally, Hugo is "not *at the mercy*." "I do blame them. I envy and despise" such men, she says (*Something* 44; original emphasis).[10]

Revisiting "Material" over thirty years later in "Fiction," Munro offers quite a different perspective. The narrator at the end of "Material" is roiled, but not so Joyce. She has taken her copy of *How Are We to Live* to a book signing at the store where she purchased it and, commenting to O'Dell on the story drawn from their shared experience and offering the author a present, she realizes, "There is not a scrap of recognition in the girl's face. She doesn't know Joyce from years ago in Rough River or two weeks ago at the party. You couldn't even be sure that she had recognized the title of her own story. You would think she had nothing to do with it. As if it was just something she wriggled out of and left on the grass" (*Happiness* 62–3). As in "Material," Munro undercuts the writer here—in both stories she acknowledges her own implications in these equations—yet Joyce is not upset, only affected by the sharp realization she has had; after a break in the text, though, this is how "Fiction" ends: "Walking up Lonsdale Avenue, walking uphill, she feels flattened, but gradually regains her composure. This might even turn into a funny story that she would tell someday. She wouldn't be surprised" (*Happiness* 63).[11] The matter-of-fact tone, the ending without emphatic insight, typifies late Munro: this incident has happened; it holds Joyce's attention briefly. Life goes on.

The next story, "Deep-Holes" also takes up distant lives through the lifelong estrangement of a son within a family—something that Munro had done before in "Silence" (2004), the third story in her Juliet Triptych. It is a story informed by her interest in geology since it begins with Alex and Sally heading off with their two young sons and infant daughter for a family picnic to Osler Bluff—a noteworthy place along the Niagara Escarpment near Georgian Bay off Lake Huron. Alex is a geologist and the picnic is in honor of his first solo article—they have chosen Osler Bluff because it "figured largely in the article, and because Sally and the children had never been there" (*Happiness* 96). Munro is not drawn to overt symbolism, but she chooses her materials with discernment, so the family's first arrival at Osler Bluff is inescapably laden with the implications of the title, "Deep-Holes."

Nine-year-old Kent eventually falls in one of the holes and must be rescued by his parents—he is seriously injured and undergoes a protracted recovery. Through that recovery "Deep-Holes" then shifts to Kent's subsequent history and to his eventual disappearance. Alex's actions that day at Osler Bluff saving Kent recall Munro's earlier story, "Miles City, Montana," a story based on an actual Munro family incident, a near drowning, in 1963 (see Thacker *Alice* 126–7, 171–2).

After years with no word and after his father is dead, Kent is discovered by his sister living in Toronto as a monk. When the family finally makes contact, Kent tells his sister that "He had often passed the building Savanna worked in and had spotted her a couple of times on the street. Once they were nearly face to face at an intersection. Of course she wouldn't have recognized him because he was wearing a kind of robe," Savanna reports to Sally. Telling her mother of her first conversation with her brother, Savanna says too that Kent told her "all he meant to tell her." Kent told her that their mother could come see him, and Sally does. It does not go especially well, and she settles, on parting, for "'Maybe we'll be in touch'" (*Happiness* 107–8, 116).[12]

"Something happened here": "Face" and "Some Women"

When she sent the edited proof of "Deep-Holes" to Munro, Treisman explained that she had "found a spot in the magazine before 'Face,' simply because it's a little shorter." This suggests that they had seen and bought "Face" first. She also explains her thoughts on the editing of "Deep-Holes," including the ending and, referring to "Silence" which she had edited in 2004, also wrote, "I really love how this story echoes Juliet and her daughter—and balances it with a much more male version of the abandonment" (June 10, 2008;

New Yorker files). And the image of Kent and Savanna meeting by chance after long separation in Toronto is one that Munro had long imagined and uses also in "Face." It is one that she would use yet again in "Amundsen" (2012) in *Dear Life*. In "Face" there is an unnamed male first-person narrator who begins with his own birth and tells his life story casually, asserting that "I am convinced that my father looked at me, stared at me, saw me, only once. After that, he could take for granted what was there." "I know what he said. Or what [my mother] told me he said. 'What a chunk of chopped liver.' Then, 'You don't need to think that you're going to bring that into the house.'" The problem here was—and is still—a birthmark on the narrator's face: "not red, but purple. Dark in my infancy and early childhood, fading somewhat as I got older, but never fading to a state of inconsequence, never ceasing to be the first thing you notice about me, head-on, or are shocked to see if you have come at me from the left, or clean, side" (*Happiness* 140–1). By this Munro takes up the tradition of such stories as Hawthorne's "The Birthmark" from *Mosses from an Old Manse* (1846) or Cather's "The Profile" (1907).[13] Thus marked and described, her narrator then accounts for his subsequent distant relation with his father, his parents' strained marriage, and his mother's attempts to shield him from the scorn of other children. Growing up "on cliffs above Lake Huron, in the Victorian house my grandfather had built facing the sunset," the family's "Prosperity was ebbing as the twentieth century progressed, but the big house was still there, the cook and the gardener," and the narrator notes that "my father's most vivid quality was a capacity for hating and despising" (*Happiness* 141–2). The man did this in the midst of an indolent life of minimal work and much sport—golfing and sailing.

This is context. "Face" focuses on the narrator's childhood relations during the early 1940s with Nancy, who is about the same age. She is his primary playmate and the daughter of Sharon Suttles, a widow who lived on the property, who worked in his father's insurance office and, the narrator still recalls, had an ill-defined relationship with his father. After the narrator provides an extended account of their games together, still wondering, "I cannot bring Nancy's face to mind so clearly as I can her mother's. I think her coloring was, or would in time be, much the same. Fair hair naturally going brown, but now bleached by so much time in the sun" (*Happiness* 153). Two things are happening here: Munro is setting the stage for the crucial occurrence in the narrator's life and, because he is still striving to recall Nancy's appearance, confirming an ongoing connection with her.

The crucial occurrence was when, playing together in the cellar, the two get into stored paint. The young narrator uses some to write graffiti while Nancy paints her own face red so, she thinks, she can have a birthmark like his too: "'Now I look like you,' she said, drawing the brush down on her neck. 'Now I look like you.' She sounded very excited and I thought she was taunting me, but in fact her voice was bursting with satisfaction, as if this was what she had been aiming for her whole life" (*Happiness* 154–5). The young narrator "did not believe that any of [his] face was red." "I believed my birthmark to be a soft brown color, like the fur of a mouse." Outraged at Nancy's action, he fled and found his mother:

'Not red,' I shouted with gulps of angry tears. 'I'm not red.' She came down the steps with a shocked face but so far no understanding. Then Nancy ran out of the cottage behind me all amazed, with her garish face. My mother understood. 'You nasty little beast,' she cried at Nancy, in a voice that I had never heard. A loud, wild, shaking voice.

(*Happiness* 155–6)

Things get worse, as the narrator recalls, and Nancy and her mother are immediately banished from the cottage on the property. Never to be seen again, though he did not realize that then.

Telescoping time, Munro shifts to the day after the narrator's father's funeral when he is in university—he goes out to dinner with his mother who, once they are settled into the restaurant, says, "'There is something I think you ought to know.'" Continuing this scene, the narrator comments, "These may be among the most unpleasant words that a person has to hear." Munro, an author who wrote and published a story (and a book) entitled "Something I've Been Meaning to Tell You" then has the mother tell him of another action Nancy took:

Nancy and her mother had gone to live in an apartment that belonged to my father, on the Square. There in the bright early fall morning Nancy's mother had come upon her daughter, in the bathroom, using a razor blade to slice into her cheek. There was blood on the floor and in the sink and here and there on Nancy. But she had not given up on her purpose or made a sound of pain.[14]

"'It was the same cheek,' she said. 'Like yours' (*Happiness* 158, 159, 160).

Throughout "Face" the narrator makes it clear that, having returned to his boyhood home in what appears to be Goderich for a purpose, to clean the house out so as to prepare for its sale, memories have filled his mind, coming unbidden. Thus after the scene at the restaurant, he steps ahead in time and remarks of his mother, "I don't know what bearing it has on anything, but I have to say that my mother changed completely in extreme old age, becoming ribald and fanciful" (*Happiness* 160). This accentuates a sense that grows on the reader as the story progresses: that this narrator is attempting to figure the meanings of these memories for himself. Thus his wonderings about what motivated his father, his mother, Nancy, and others.

Standing apart, this single paragraph about his mother in old age points directly to the core of "Face," which is still yet to come. During the late 1960s, after she had borne her third daughter, Munro began writing poetry herself; she even published a poem under her mother's maiden name as pseudonym (see Thacker *Alice* 125–6). Poetry figures in "The Ottawa Valley," "Lying under the Apple Tree," and "Wenlock Edge," but in the balance of "Face" poetry is critical to its meaning, its essential mass. As Tracy Ware has remarked, comparing "Face" to a similar story which followed it, "Pride,"

"Face" is a full narration with rich details and many allusions (the poetry reciting at the end enables Munro to bring in a small library of references). "Pride" is a minimal narration that must suit Munro's purpose for this narrator, but I am tempted to take the two stories as typical of their volumes: the stories in *Too Much*

Happiness are consistent with the work of Munro's great phase; the stories in *Dear Life* are much pared down.

(email June 4, 2020)

Ware's assertion is absolutely right. After the narrator gives the paragraph on his mother "in extreme old age" there is a design break and he continues "A few days ago I was stung by a wasp while clearing out some rotten apples under one of the old trees. The sting was on my eyelid, which rapidly closed." He gets himself to the hospital, where he is treated, both eyes bandaged, and kept overnight. After "what they call a restless night" a woman walks into his room and he says, "and I had the feeling that she was not a nurse." Thinking that she had come to check on his vital signs, he offers his arm and the woman responds, "'No, no,' she said, in her small persistent voice. 'I've come to read to you, if that's what you would like. Sometimes people like it; they get bored lying there with their eyes closed.'" "'I like poetry'" he says, and the woman responds, "'You don't sound very enthusiastic.'" He then thinks, "I realized that this was true, and I knew why. I have some experience reading poetry aloud, over the radio, and listening to other trained voices read, and there are some styles of reading I find comfortable, and some I abhor" (*Happiness* 161). He is referring to his long career as a radio dramatist and announcer, literally, but more than that Munro is here creating a scene which is untethered: he cannot see this person, he has gone in and out of consciousness, and the woman infers his real enthusiasm. She may be imagined or, more precisely, this may be a dream. In January 2008, when the *New Yorker* was probably considering a revised second version of "Face," Munro sent Treisman a new ending as "a possible clearing-up," she wrote in a cover letter, and then commented "In a way, it doesn't matter if it was a dream. She is in his life (again?)" [.] (January 14, 2008; *New Yorker* files).[15]

Thus this unseen reader is either Nancy returned literally or Nancy imagined by the narrator. Regarding the reading of poetry, the woman suggests, "'I could read you a line or two, then I stop and see if you can do the next line. Okay?'" He agrees. Her initial offering is the first line of the Scots "Ballad of Sir Patrick Spens"—he immediately replies with the second. With this, Munro is once again back to her own "old schoolroom quotations" seen in the "The Ottawa Valley" and referred to again in "Wood." This ballad is the first poem in W. J. Alexander's *Shorter Poems* (1924, 1932), probably the book young Alice Laidlaw read herself. This recollection then is the narrator's and Munro's own. The two continue in the same vein, with the narrator reciting a succession of poems from memory, which he names. Having gone from one poem to the next, the woman—the real Nancy or her imagined apparition—comments:

"You're getting short of breath," she said. Her little quick hand was laid on my mouth. And then her face or the side of her face, laid on mine. "I have to go. Here's another just before I go. I'll make it harder because I won't start at the beginning.

'None will long mourn for you,/Pray for you, miss you/Your place left vacant—'"

"I've never heard that," I said.

"Sure?"

"Sure. You win."

(*Happiness* 162)

Following this, Munro shifts from this unidentified poem to metaphor embodying the narrator's wonderings, his state of mind as he lay in that hospital bed, his imaginings:

> By now I suspected something. She seemed distracted. Slightly cross. I heard the geese calling as they flew over the hospital. They take practice runs at this time of year, and then the runs get longer and one day they're gone. I was waking up, in that state of surprise, indignation, that follows a convincing dream. I wanted to go back and have her lay her face on mine. Her cheek, on mine. But dreams are not so obliging.
>
> <div align="right">(<i>Happiness</i> 162–3)</div>

There is a white-space break here, and the narrator, still wondering, looks once he is home to find "those lines she had left me with in my dream" and, not finding them, he "began to suspect that the lines did not belong to a real poem at all, but had just been devised in the dream, to confound me." A single-sentence paragraph follows here, asking "Devised by whom?" (*Happiness* 163).

There are no answers to this poem's identity nor to this question so the reader wonders with the narrator. He eventually discovers the poet's identity when, while "getting some old books ready to donate to a charity bazaar, a piece of brownish paper fell out, with lines written in pencil." Not his mother's hand, nor his father's. "Whose, then? Whoever it was had written the author's name at the end. Walter de la Mare. No title. Not a writer whose works I have any particular knowledge of." Still not knowing, still wondering. But then the narrator realizes that he had written this himself: "But I must have seen the poem at some time, maybe not in this copy, maybe in a textbook. I must have buried the words in a deep cubbyhole of my mind. And why? Just so that I could be teased by them, or teased by a determined girl-child phantom, in a dream?" (*Happiness* 163). The phrase here, "maybe not in this copy," should have been deleted, for when Munro submitted "Face" to the *New Yorker* this paragraph included this sentence: "But it seems I must have found this page before, in this book called The Happy Warrior, that I was sure I had never read, written by someone I had never heard of, named A. S. M. Hutchinson" (23, revised submitted manuscript, January 14, 2008; *New Yorker* files). The "But it seems …" became the passage beginning "But I must have …" just quoted. Without identifying de la Mare's poem by its title, "Away" (1938), Munro then quotes the whole of the poem. (Her preference, in keeping with her narrator's character, was to offer it largely without its punctuation.)[16]

While "Away" does not appear in Alexander's *Shorter Poems* Walter de la Mare does. Deluged by memories of his childhood and, particularly, of Nancy and her desire to "look like" him, the narrator wonders over the whole of his life, its meanings and now, his eventual death. Thus the autumnal disappearance of those geese over the hospital, the disappearance of his parents, the uncertain though pressing imagined presence of Nancy, her face upon his. All of these emotions are encapsulated, made vivid, by de la Mare's "Away," its point best found in its opening and ending lines: "'*There is no sorrow/Time heals never/No loss, betrayal/Beyond repair*'" as it begins and, as it ends, "*None will long mourn for you/Pray for you, miss you/Your place forgotten/You not there*" (Canadian M&S *Too Much Happiness* 162; original emphasis).[17] As the poem describes, the narrator of "Face" is heading, as everyone is, toward the final oblivion of death: "You not there."

Again, the story's ending: when Munro submitted "Face" to the *New Yorker* the de la Mare poem was followed by a three-sentence paragraph: "By this time I had decided not to sell the property. Something happened here. So I will stay" (24, *New Yorker* files). Just after, when Munro sent Treisman her "possible clearing up" on January 14, 2008, she had revised that ending: "I had decided to stay" and then a new paragraph, "Something happened here. There are places, or maybe a place, where something has happened in your life, and then there are all the other places. I quite agree with the last lines of the poem but the fact is. I am still here. And I don't much care what definition is put on things. Dreams happen too" (24, January 14, 2008; *New Yorker* files). Still thinking about "Face," Munro sent Treisman a revised ending—five manuscript pages—in August and there added the three paragraphs after "all the other places," which end the published story. The first treats the possibility of running into "Nancy—on the subway, for instance, in Toronto" where he had long lived, "both of us bearing our recognizable marks" on their faces, "we would in all probability have managed only one of those embarrassed and meaningless conversations, hurriedly listing useless autobiographical facts." "We would have been shocked, hearty, dying to get away." In the following revision the next paragraph, the narrator's question—"You think that would have changed things?"—is answered with "No. Or only for a little. No" (24, August 3, 2008; *New Yorker* files). That was revised when Munro and Treisman worked on the ending in proof, becoming the printed ending ("The answer is of course, and for a while, and never" [*New Yorker* 67, *Happiness* 163]).[18] So writing, Munro and her narrator get to just where he is in "Face": Nancy, long gone, may have been in the hospital, but more likely as the narrator says was probably a dream, a person who brought the whole of de la Mare's "Away" up from the his memory and so brought it back to him. Her marked face, her cheek, on his marked face. Always there, a vivid memory, and long gone away. "Something happened here" and because it has, he needs to stay (*Happiness* 164).[19]

But for "Too Much Happiness," held for the final chapter here, the next and last story in the collection is "Some Women" (2008). It begins with this sentence: "I am amazed sometimes to think how old I am"; it ends with another, a single-sentence paragraph: "I grew up, and old" (*Happiness* 165, 188). But for the remembered actions of a single long-ago summer which make up the story, this narrator tells the reader nothing else of her life story, though there are many indications of retrospection and implied subsequent experience throughout the tale she tells—she comments from mature years later on the memory of what happened during that long-ago summer. When he reviewed the book Gorra singled this story out, noting each of these sentences, calling the last one a "trap door," and asking "What did the narrator learn that summer that has to do with the fact of her own old age? What prompts her memory?" Acknowledging that some might say that these questions "must remain unanswered," he asserts nevertheless that the "fact that we ask them is, however, one mark of Munro's power. We ask, and trust the narrator precisely because she gives no answers; trust that she herself knows, even if she can't or won't tell us" (3). In his next paragraph, Gorra makes the assertion, already noted, that if he "had to reduce the concerns of *Too Much Happiness* to a single word, it would be 'mortality'" ("Mortal" 4).

Here again in "Some Women" there is a death, this one from leukemia and one impending throughout the story but ultimately eventuated as it ends. The patient's circumstances are announced in the last sentence of the first paragraph in which the unnamed narrator remembers how things were when she was young: while sometimes those with polio recovered, "people with leukemia went to bed, and after some weeks' or months' decline in a tragic atmosphere, they died." The patient here is Bruce Crozier who had been a fighter pilot in the Second World War, came home, graduated from college, married, and was stricken—because of his illness, the narrator says, "I got my first job, in the summer holidays when I was thirteen" (*Happiness* 165). The circumstances of the job, the people she meets and wonders over, the dénouement of the conflict during that summer years ago: these together are the crux of "Some Women." Not the balance of her own life. And as the title asserts, what Munro is narrating altogether is the behavior of women around a man, his illness notwithstanding and to one side; primarily the three the narrator observes around Crozier, but the narrator and her mother too.

The absence Gorra points to in "Some Women" needs to be emphasized. In many ways it is an especial embodiment of Munro's artistry and of her late style. Or, in keeping with Ware on the ending of "Face," another key example of Munro in her major late phase: recursion is evident in this story, most especially in its "distinctive retrospective narrative approach," as I called it in 1983 in my first critical article on Munro (Thacker *Reading* 23; see 23–44, 271–2). In fact, had "Some Women" been available to Munro in 2006, it would have fit comfortably into the "Home" section of stories in *Castle Rock*. The unnamed narrator in "Some Woman" appears to be Munro herself, retrospectively remembering or imagining these experiences from over sixty years before, when she was thirteen.

Unlike such autobiographical stories as "Hired Girl" and others, I write here with no idea whether the first job Munro describes in "Some Woman" had any basis in fact, though I am inclined to think not. Munro turned thirteen on July 10, 1944, so the timing of Crozier's war experience, and then his subsequent education and marriage once returned, does not seem quite right. The narrator first describes the circumstances of her employment—that is, the house, the invalid's stepmother, old Mrs. Crozier, "stumping" about the house with her cane; young Mrs. Sylvia Crozier, Bruce's wife, there too.

Early on she also tells of her mother's interest in the patient's sleeping arrangements and of an uninvited visit she made on the first day the narrator she was working at the Croziers'. She explains:

> My mother had an idea of going into the antique business, so she was very interested in getting inside of that house. She did get in, once, during my very first afternoon. I was in the kitchen, and I stood petrified, hearing her "yoo-hoo" and my own merrily called name. Then her perfunctory knock, her steps on the kitchen stairs. And Old Mrs. Crozier stumping out from the sunroom.
>
> My mother said that she had just dropped in to see how her daughter was getting along.
>
> "She's all right," said Old Mrs. Crozier, who stood in the hallway blocking the view of antiques.
>
> (*Happiness* 166)

In "Chaddeleys and Flemings: 2. The Stone in the Field," the story begins with the narrator saying of her mother that she "was a businesswoman really, a trader and dealer. Our house was full of things that had not been paid for with money, but taken in some complicated trade, and that might not be ours to keep." She details various things that came and went, concluding the opening paragraph, "We were living in a warehouse" (*Moons* 19). Asked about this, Munro commented that her mother did trade some in antiques, that "she didn't view it as a business, but she was very interested," and that "if she hadn't been coming on with Parkinson's as she was, she could have easily done that and done well. That was the kind of person she was" (Thacker interview September 2013).

Thus the autobiographical basis of the narrator's mother in "Some Women." The narrator continues:

> My mother made a few more mortifying remarks and took herself off. That night she said that Old Mrs. Crozier had no manners because she was only a second wife picked up on a business trip to Detroit, which was why she smoked and dyed her hair black as tar and put on lipstick like a smear of jam. She was not even the mother of the invalid upstairs. She did not have the brains to be.
>
> (We were having one of our fights then, this one relating to her visit, but that is neither here nor there.)
>
> (*Happiness* 167)

This version of Anne Chamney Laidlaw, who appears in such stories as "Walker Brothers Cowboy" and, as will be seen in my final chapter, in "Voices" in the "Finale" of *Dear Life*, is yet without Parkinson's disease. That came soon enough; it is described in one of the ending codas to "Some Women." Munro's retrospection—she was indeed old as she wrote this, probably about seventy-five, her mother gone since 1959—is not caustic but it is matter of fact. Equally too, remembering her mother's behavior then, Munro asserts common cause with her as she has her narrator begin the next paragraph: "The way Old Mrs. Crozier saw it, I must have seemed just as intrusive as my mother, just as cheerily self-regarding" (*Happiness* 167).

Discussing "Fiction," I noted the joke Munro offers there, deprecating short-story writers. Here in "Some Women" there is another wryness, since the plot hinges on a key; thus though not a novel, the story is nevertheless something of a *roman à clef*. As she concludes the paragraph in which she retrospectively admits her own intrusiveness, the narrator illustrates it by commenting that on her

> very first afternoon I had gone into the back parlor and opened the bookcase and stood there taking stock of the Harvard Classics set out in their perfect row. Most of them discouraged me, but I took one out that might be fiction, in spite of title in a foreign language, *I Promessi Sposi*. It appeared to fiction all right, and it appeared to be in English.
>
> (*Happiness* 167)

Here Munro asserts a succession of contextual points which define the narrator and those she is working among. Alessandro Manzoni's *I Promessi Sposi* (1827)—translated as *The Betrothed*—is often cited as the most famous Italian novel, one treating love and political power; it is indeed a volume in the *Harvard Classics* (1909) series. That the Croziers have a set is more an indication of wealth than intellectual interest; this is in contrast to Bruce Crozier's sickroom reading which is 1940s topical and contemporary. Finding the narrator reading *I Promessi Sposi*, Mrs. Crozier inquires where she got it, for she seemed to think reading itself "an activity too foreign for contemplation," and "said that if I wanted a book I should bring one from home" (*Happiness* 167).

The job the narrator does is occasioned by Mrs. Sylvia Crozier's teaching two days a week at the university she and her husband attended—thus making her unavailable to look after him—and that is a matter for judgment: those around her thought she was not doing her wifely duty. "People were just down on her because she had got an education." "One day," the narrator says, "I tried a conversation with Young Mrs. Crozier, or Sylvia. She was the only university graduate I knew, let alone being a teacher. Except for her husband, of course, and he had stopped counting." The narrator asks her a question about Toynbee, gets a perfunctory reply, and thinks "None of us mattered to her, not me, or her critics or defenders. No more than bugs on a lampshade" (*Happiness* 168-9).

"What Old Mrs. Crozier cared about really was her flower garden." She has a man—a neighbor of the narrator's—who comes and helps with it. The narrator asks "if I could pick a bouquet to brighten the sickroom. 'They'd only die,'" Mrs. Crozier replied, "not seeming to realize that this remark had a double edge to it, in the circumstances." Bruce "had stopped counting," Sylvia thought all of them insignificant, and Old Mrs. Crozier is impervious to context. Remembering her young self watching and interacting with these people, gauging their motivations, Munro or the narrator still wonders.

Into this circumstance, into Bruce Crozier's "decline in a tragic atmosphere," a new person arrives, the narrator reports, calling "'Dorothy,' which I had not known was Old Mrs. Crozier's name." Describing the voice she heard and the sounds of arrival, the narrator says it "was a woman's or a girl's, and it was bold and teasing all at once, so that you could almost feel this person tickling you." This woman is Roxanne, Old Mrs. Crozier's masseuse, and her arrival both changes the story's direction and deepens it. The narrator has never seen anyone like her, and realizes quickly that Roxanne also "had sized me up, apparently, as somebody who was willing to take orders—especially, perhaps, orders in such a coaxing voice. And she was right, though maybe she didn't guess my willingness had more to do with my own curiosity than her charm." Munro offers Roxanne as a paragon of youthful sexuality, recalled quite specifically:

> She was tanned this early in the summer, and her pageboy hair had a copper sheen—something you could get easily nowadays from a bottle, but that was unusual and enviable then. Brown eyes, a dimple in one cheek, such smiling and teasing that you never got a good-enough look at her to say whether she was really pretty, or how old she was.
>
> Her rump curved out handsomely to the back instead of spreading to the sides.
>
> (*Happiness* 170)

There ensues the plot that is the balance of the story, a plot which has the narrator retrospectively recall what happened then. Roxanne sets about giving Mrs. Crozier her massage, and the narrator recalls when she saw them for the first time, "I saw Old Mrs. Crozier stretched out on a daybed on her stomach, head turned away from me, absolutely naked. A skinny streak of pale flesh." This scene itself is a shock to her: "I sat on the top step and listened to the sounds of massage. Thumps and grunts. Roxanne's voice bossy now, cheerful but full of exhortation." "Old Mrs. Crozier was making little yelps. Sounds of complaint and gratitude" (*Happiness* 171, 172).

Just after, while reading magazines, the narrator hears Roxanne and Mrs. Crozier coming upstairs, so she "slid the magazines back into their place in the cupboard that would have been coveted by my mother, and went into Mr. Crozier's room. He was asleep, or at least he had his eyes closed." Mrs. Crozier came up the back steps, "with her slow and threatening cane steps. Roxanne running ahead, and calling, 'Look out, look out, wherever you are. We're coming to get you wherever you are.'" Bruce Crozier's eyes open, and the narrator notes "Beyond his usual weariness was a faint expression of alarm." Roxanne "burst into the room." She and Bruce are introduced, she comments on his poor shave, seeing that he did it himself. She then asks the narrator, "'When you're getting her water, how'd you like to heat some up for me and I'll undertake to give him a decent shave?'" (*Happiness*, 172–3).

Munro's use of "undertake" here, like her reference to "bugs on a lampshade" regarding Sylvia's disdain, as well as the reference to the narrator's mother and antiques keeps the characters' situations and attitudes alive. Bruce is dying of leukemia, people think Sylvia is neglecting her duties, the mother has her own agenda, Old Mrs. Crozier is abrupt and assertive—and the narrator endeavors to understand it all. When Roxanne comes Mrs. Crozier thinks it a good idea to have her entertain Bruce, to play Chinese checkers—surprisingly, Mrs. Crozier makes a joke, saying that "she never understood the game or been able to keep her marbles straight" (*Happiness* 174–5). The narrator takes exception to this activity, saying "If ever there was a time for him to become irritable, it is now. Being forced to play a silly game on his deathbed, when you could feel his fever in the sheets." Yet she sees too that Bruce is attracted to Roxanne, that when she gets the name of Alexander the Great wrong, "I realized something when I looked at Mr. Crozier at that moment. Something shocking, saddening." Here is a revisiting of the narrator's knowledge in "Hired Girl." Continuing in a new paragraph, she explains, "He liked her not knowing. I could tell. He liked her not knowing. Her ignorance woke a pleasure that melted on his tongue, like a lick of toffee" (*Happiness* 175). Roxanne—whose name is that of the wife of Alexander the Great, as the narrator knows, a figure whom Roxanne called "Great Alexander"—is evidently attracted to him too.

So much so that over time a scene ensues. "I had a feeling there was mischief stirring, but I could not pin it down" (*Happiness* 179). They settle into a regular routine that summer, one in which Roxanne's visits are central.

> I began to understand that there were certain talkers—certain girls—whom people liked to listen to, not because of what they, the girls, had to say, but because of the delight they took in saying it. A delight in themselves, a shine on their faces, a conviction that whatever they were telling about was remarkable and that they themselves could not help but give pleasure.

Mr. Crozier for his part listened, he

> sat propped up on his pillows and looked for all the world as if he was happy. Happy just to close his eyes and let her talk, then open his eyes and find her there, like a chocolate bunny on Easter morning. And then with his eyes open follow every twitch of her candy lips and sway of her sumptuous bottom.[20]

And "Old Mrs. Crozier would rock slightly back and in her curious state of satisfaction" The narrator wonders if Rozanne is being paid for all this time and, "if she wasn't, how could she afford to take the time." "Why?", she wonders (*Happiness* 177–8).

"Summer school at the college would end after the second week of August and Sylvia Crozier would be home every day" and the narrator's job would end. That Munro describes Sylvia by her full name here suggests the transitional point achieved. Roxanne keeps up her entertainments of Bruce, even though "Anybody could see how he was failing. There were hollows in his cheeks like an old man's and the light shone through the tops of his ears as if they were not flesh but plastic. (Though we didn't say 'plastic' then, we said 'celluloid.')." The last day of this arrangement sees Old Mrs. Crozier sending her man to the bakery for macaroons, telling Roxanne "'I thought we'd have a treat, like something special,'" and the two agree that it is the "'Last day before [Sylvia] parks her butt here permanently,'" as Roxanne says (*Happiness* 179, 180).

On this day the dénouement of "Some Woman" occurs. Bruce calls the narrator to his room and "told me to go to the bureau across from his bed and open the left-hand little drawer, and see if I could find a key there." She does this, and then "he wanted me to go out of this room and shut the door and lock it. Then hide the key in a safe place perhaps in the pocket of my shorts." "I was not to let anybody know I had the key until his wife came home, and then I was to give it to her." "Okay. All the time he was talking to me there was a film of sweat on his face and his eyes were bright as if he had a fever. 'Nobody is to get in'" (*Happiness* 181–2). She agrees, locks the door, and hides the key.

When Roxanne comes upstairs after the massage, she finds the door locked, cannot get Bruce to open it, and then puts her mouth to the keyhole and pleads, and "she sounded as if she was saying her prayers." Consternation ensues. Roxanne questions the narrator about the locked door and, having heard a "commotion," Old Mrs. Crozier comes up. Roxanne kicks the door, wanting to break in, wanting to call the police to come through the window, apparently concerned that Bruce might harm himself. Old Mrs. Crozier wants none of this, telling her that the locked door was his decision, and that Roxanne had "'better just take yourself away before you forget whose house this is.'" She does. Old Mrs. Crozier "stood at the locked door and said one thing. 'Stronger than you'd think,' she muttered." Then she goes downstairs and outside to her garden. The narrator, finding the macaroons on the kitchen table, ate two. "I ate them hoping that pleasure would bring back normalcy, but I barely tasted them. Then I shoved the box into the refrigerator so I would not hope to turn the trick by eating more" (*Happiness* 183–5). Sylvia arrives home, gets the key and an explanation of what happened from the narrator, talks first to Bruce (afterwards "she looked shocked but unable to resist her happiness"), then with Old Mrs. Crozier, upset by what happened, and she then takes the narrator home for the final time. Sylvia tells her that she did the right and loyal thing, saying that "Mrs. Crozier and Mrs. Hoy were certainly trying their best, but Mr. Crozier just didn't feel that he wanted them around anymore. He just had enough of them. You understand?" Then in a passage which captures Munro's essential retrospective meanings, the narrator is still wondering:

> She did not seem to know she was smiling when she said this.
> Mrs. Hoy.
> Had I ever heard that name before?
> And spoken so gently and respectfully, yet with light-years' condescension.
> Did I believe what Sylvia had said?
> I believed it was what he had told her.
>
> (*Happiness* 186–7)

Roxanne, still upset amid her consternation, is seen by the narrator driving around as Sylvia drives her home making small talk about possible rain amid the summer's drought. There is a design break, followed by the narrator's remembered recreation of her realization of what had just happened as the apex of her discoveries about human beings that summer, a single, pointed, late-style paragraph:

> I understood pretty well the winning and losing that had taken place, between Sylvia and Roxanne, but it was strange to think of the almost obliterated prize, Mr. Crozier—and to think that he could have the will to make a decision, even to deprive himself, so late in his life. The carnality at death's door—or the true love, for that matter—were things I had to shake off with shivers down my spine.
>
> (*Happiness* 188)[21]

I have consciously paraphrased and quoted fully from "Some Woman" because, more than any other story from *Too Much Happiness*, it reveals the deep recursions of Munro's late style. This narrator sharply recalls the insight she got into human nature that summer when she was thirteen—the "winning and the losing" between the two women, Bruce's self-denial in the face of death—demands the pointed use of the retrospective technique Munro had refined throughout her career. More than that, it demands the absence of any other indication of the rest of the narrator's life: what she learned that summer was crucial, deeply held within a long-lived life. More than that again, "Some Woman" sees Munro returned to many other stories she had written and published: "The Peace of Utrecht," "Postcard" (1968), "Material," and "Chaddeleys and Flemings" primarily, but there are other echoes too. As the action in "Some Women" reaches its climax, the narrator disagrees with Roxanne's fears: "I believed it would quite absurd for a person with only a short time to live to commit suicide. It could not happen" (*Happiness* 185). Thus Munro consciously inverts what she had just offered in "Face": "Something happened here." But something *really* happened in "Some Women" too.

Stepping back from the core realization the old remembering narrator offers from all those years ago—the evidences of sexual attraction between Bruce and Roxanne which the narrator apprehends—Munro accounts for the subsequent lives of all these people, her deftly drawn characters, as she finishes:

> Sylvia took Mr. Crozier away to a rented cottage on the lake, where he died sometime before the leaves were off.
> The Hoy family moved on, as mechanics' families often did.
> My mother struggled with a crippling disease, which put an end to all her moneymaking dreams.
> Dorothy Crozier had a stroke, but recovered, and famously bought Halloween candy for the children whose older brothers and sisters she had ordered from her door.
> I grew up, and old.
>
> (*Happiness* 188)

Returning to the notion with which this discussion began, in "Some Women" Munro has again gone back to her young adolescent years of the mid-1940s. Whether its circumstances owe to any autobiographical experience or not, its severe focus on the narrator's retrospection, on her still ongoing wonderings about these people, both individually and together, is what drives the story. Throughout, she is its subject. Her growing understandings of human interaction, her better wisdom, are Munro's focus: that is what is created. Detailing her growing thirteen-year-old understandings then—what she saw in each person's character and in the lure of sexual attraction, the whole framed by her mother's strong presence and even more so here, Old Mrs. Crozier's—the narrator defines the entire episode as a major lode in her own development. Her own presence as an old person, framing the action, wondering over and still shaping its significances, animating the whole of "Some Woman." No more about her subsequent life is needed. Like the end of "The Ottawa Valley," Munro ends by writing again about her mother, for she is a presence who plays a part here too, but here the "whole journey has been undertaken" to capture herself, the narrator (*Something* 246).

Taken together, the stories collected in *Too Much Happiness*—save the title story—reveal Munro's art at its most consciously recursive. Ever, she revisits materials she has used before, taking a different angle toward them, discovering yet again "the rest of the story," as she said of that seen image of the work horses pulling grain sacks at the town scales in winter, used first in the *Paris Review* version of "Spaceships Have Landed," returned to again in 1997 in her introduction to the first volume of her *Selected Stories* (xvi). "Wood," repeatedly revised and considered but finally collected, takes Munro back to her fecund late 1970s when one story followed another, and appears again in a different, deepened form. With its connections to *Castle Rock* and the time Munro was publishing "Wood," "Wenlock Edge" is a story which revisits Munro's university years, a time she was not yet done with, and like "Some Women," tracks the narrator's self-discoveries retrospectively, gauging what she learned and knows now against what occurred then. As Gorra said in his review, "no story is ever really over": mortality looms.

5

"It Seemed as If We Had Gotten Time Back, as If There Was All the Time in the World": The Gathering of Stories before the "Finale" in *Dear Life*

> *When I went home to Dalgleish on the bus I thought I was making a momentous journey. Picture it: the darkening fields, the northward road, the shabbier and more hopeless villages. The bus only ran once a day, in the late afternoon. I ran down the drive from the university to catch it. This was a small unimportant university at that time; its standards were middling at best, and it was known mostly for its football team, some new, and, as it was said, solidly career-oriented courses—Business Administration, Secretarial Science—and the fact that you could usually get into it if you failed to get into the University of Toronto. But the Arts Building had a Gothic tower, the great hall where we wrote our examinations let in stained light through high mullioned and crested windows, making me think of St. Agnes' Eve (and the windows in the library stacks, looking out on ploughed Ontario fields) were designed for firing arrows through. All this had its effect on me, I was more susceptible than most. I read poetry a lot of the time. Yeats. I read Yeats going home to Dalgleish on the bus while the light lasted.*
>
> *… … …..*
>
> *When it was too dark to read Yeats I was just as happy looking out the bus window, seeing my own face on the snow or the brown bog that could not have been unlike Yeat[s]'s west of Ireland.*
>
> (37.19.57)

This epigraph is most of a fragment beginning that Munro wrote sometime before 1978. It breaks off just after this, but not before the narrator mentions that it is 1950—one of the two years that Alice Laidlaw attended university. The Munro Fonds includes scores of such abandoned beginnings, many not more than a sentence or two, few longer than a typed double-spaced page. This one is here because it has Munro back on a bus to Wingham in 1950—Dalgleish its frequent 1970s and later renaming—just as she was in 1972 in "Home" and, later, as she was in the beginning fictional manuscript versions of "Working for a Living."[1] And this same 1950 bus ride, modified a bit, begins "Axis," a story she published in 2011 in the *New Yorker* but kept out of *Dear Life*; that story also includes another bus ride and a train journey too, each of them key to its plot and revelations. That in this fragment the narrator is reading Yeats is apt: Wendell Berry once wrote that "We think of a poem and in the same thought think of what it is about, if it is about anything. Literature involves more than literature, or we would not be grateful for it" (87). This is a comment that seems especially particularly true for Munro, whose work has evoked gratitude along with deep admiration.

Take Yeats here: Michael Gorra comments that as a reader of each of Munro's late stories he "will remember its emotional terrain, as [he remembers] lines and fragments from this Yeats poem or that; a twist of the voice, an intonation separate, perhaps, from any actual words." "Each of these stories," he continues, "is like a chip off some massy substance, a piece that implies the whole. Every one of them seems reinforced by the echoes of another, and to read Munro now, to visit and revisit this house or that marriage, seems like immersing oneself in a great poet's collected works, a chance to inhabit a mind, a sensibility, that is larger than any of its individual iterations" ("Mortal" 4). Exactly so. Here Gorra describes the experience of all who have immersed themselves in Munro's writings. When, in 2010, I told Munro about Gorra's comparison of her stories to Yeats' collected works, her pleasure was evident, for she said she had not seen the review (Thacker interview). Well she might have been, with her 1950 readings of Yeats in the midst.[2]

Thus before turning at last to Munro's "Finale" in *Dear Life* as her own finale, and just before that to her titular "Too Much Happiness" which ends her penultimate late-style collection, it seems fair first to ask following Berry just what the balance of *Dear Life* involves and just how, once that question has been asked and answered, it sets up the "Finale." Given Munro's lengthy histories with the endings of her stories, the construction of an avowed and self-conscious finale to end what she saw as her final collection was one gone about methodically. She moved through *Dear Life* toward the "Finale" and toward that finale's finale: "Dear Life," the story, with a sharp precision.

The volume is the apogee of Munro's writing career, a deeply recursive one that has involved continued looking back—remembering, revisiting, reshaping: her late style. While not avowedly autobiographical in any clear way, the ten stories that precede the "Finale" in *Dear Life* are reminiscent of the whole of Munro's oeuvre (see Thacker "This" 30–5, 37n11). Echoes of previous stories and other connections abound. "Pride," as has been noted, seems to bear some direct connection to "Face"; in a *New Yorker* interview published online just as *Dear Life* appeared, Munro commented that her "favorite scene" is that story's ending "where the little baby skunks walk across the grass" (Treisman interview).[3] As the narrator and a friend watch this, he ends the story by saying, evenly but not emphatically or with any particular insight, "We were as glad as we could be" (*Dear Life* 153). Their lives continue. So these stories bear the weight of those that have preceded them and readers feel that weight. In that same interview, Munro also comments that of the stories in the collection she is "partial to 'Amundsen'—it gave me so much trouble" in its revision. "The girl has her first experience with a helplessly selfish man—that's the type that interests her" (Treisman interview). That story ends with the briefest of reunions as, years later, the two principals spot each other crossing a crowded Toronto street. They speak without stopping and move on. Seeing him again, the man who sent her away years before, the narrator reacts again to the way "one of his eyes opened wider": "And it always looked so strange, alert and wondering, as if some whole impossibility had occurred to him, one that almost made him laugh" (*Dear Life* 66). Throughout Munro's wonderings have been evident in late-style stories: she uses the word here in a crucial passage. There are other instances in *Dear Life*.

"Axis" and "Corrie"

Understanding the recursive weight of the stories preceding those forming the "Finale" to *Dear Life* is best done by looking at them largely chronologically and, ironically, looking first at "Axis," an anomalous story in the late Munro oeuvre. It was published in the *New Yorker* but, though originally slated for inclusion in *Dear Life* and considerably revised toward that end after its appearance in the magazine, it was ultimately left out in deference to Fremlin.[4] As such, "Axis" is both a singular fugitive late-style story and a synecdoche of that style. It is also a synecdoche of the geological knowledge Munro acquired from Fremlin after she moved back to Huron County in 1975, knowledge that is readily evident in another fugitive story, the early "Characters" (1978), as well as in "White Dump" (1986) and, as has already been shown, in "What Do You Want to Know For?" "Axis" typifies Munro's stories in its combination of autobiography, of biography, and of imagination—each one a narrative rendering of imagined possibility (Thacker "Introduction" 18, 12–17).[5]

Returning to the fragment used here as an epigraph and to the time of "Wenlock Edge," "Axis" takes place mostly during Munro's time at Western Ontario, 1949–51. It returns to a bus ride then, beginning "[f]ifty years ago, Grace and Avie were waiting at the university gates, in the freezing cold." They were waiting for a bus, "[f]orty miles to go for Avie, maybe twice that for Grace." "Serious students," they "were carrying large books with serious titles." But more than this, each of these characters echoes Munro herself: "They were both farm girls, who knew how to scrub floors and milk cows. Their labor as soon as they entered the house—or the barn—belonged to their families. They weren't the sort of girls you usually ran into at this university." Not sorority girls, bent on finding a husband in the business school (63).

The plot of "Axis" focuses mostly on a visit Royce—Grace's boyfriend, a Second World War veteran, and near philosophy graduate—makes to her on the farm during the summer. Still a virgin, Grace has a plan to capitulate to his advances during his visit. In a wonderfully comedic scene, the couple is caught in bed by Grace's mother who is outraged at the discovery. Royce dresses and leaves, scorning both mother and daughter, angry and now forced to hitchhike back to the university town where he lives.[6] Munro describes the moments as he takes his leave: "When Grace heard him zip up his bag she turned over and put her feet on the floor. She was perfectly naked. She said, 'Take me. Take me with you.' But he had gone out of the room, out of the house, as if he hadn't even heard her" (67). At one point Munro thought of "Take Me with You" as a possible title for the story and queried Close about it. That title would have emphasized the elements of romance in the story, and there is also a subplot involving Avie and her boyfriend Hugo, by whom she gets pregnant and marries.

But the story is called "Axis." The reference is to one of two major geological facts of southern Ontario: the Frontenac Axis; the other one, the Niagara Escarpment, figures in the story too. Late in life, toward the end of "Axis," Royce and the by then widowed Avie inadvertently meet on a train heading east from Toronto toward Gananoque, his destination, and Montreal, hers. He tells her about his life, she hers. He taught geology, never married; she had six children, was a housewife and mother. Recalling their time together in college, Royce also tells her that, traveling on a bus on his way to visit Grace years ago, he looked out the window and saw Avie on the street in her hometown; after acknowledging and dismissing his connection with Grace then, he continues: "'Anyway, I saw you there on the sidewalk talking to somebody and I thought you looked just irresistible. You were laughing away. I wanted to get right off the bus and speak to you. Make a date with you, actually.'" Looking back now, Avie is torn; Royce wants to know if she thinks it a good thing that "'we didn't make contact?'" and Munro writes "She does not even try for an answer" (68). Royce leaves this question alone and closes his eyes, telling Avie to be sure to wake him "before we're into Kingston if I've gone to sleep,' he says. 'There's something I want to be sure to show you'" (69).

What Royce the geologist wants to show Avie is evidence of the Frontenac Axis. The train stops in Kingston and

> [w]hen the train starts up again, he explains that all around them are great slabs of limestone packed in order, one on top of the other, like a grand construction. But in one spot this gives way, he says, and you can see something else. It's what's known as the Frontenac Axis. It is nothing less than an eruption of the vast and crazy old Canadian Shield, all the ancient combustion cutting through the limestone, pouring over, messing up those giant steps.
>
> 'See! See!' he says, and she does see. Remarkable.
>
> (69)

From this scene Munro cuts back to a letter Avie received from Grace after she had married and moved to Northern Ontario where Hugo was teaching. Grace congratulates her and then tells Avie that she has dropped out of school "'due to some troubles I have had with my health and my nerves'" (69). Back on the train, thinking about this time, Avie "asks Royce if he heard anything from Grace, ever." He replies no and asks why she thinks he would have. "Axis" ends:

> "I thought you might have looked her up later on."
> "Not a good idea."
> She has disappointed him. Prying. Trying to get at some spot of live regret right under the ribs. A woman.
>
> (69)

Analyzing "To Reach Japan," J. R. (Tim) Struthers argues that in Munro's late work metaphor transmutes into allegory, and her use of the Frontenac Axis here is a vivid illustration of what he means ("Traveling"). Royce's enthusiastic exclamations as he points out evidence of "the vast and crazy old Canadian Shield" point to another experience he had during that visit to Grace, whom now he little remembers. Getting out of one of the cars he had hitched a ride in, Royce experienced his first geological epiphany:

> Then he got out, and he saw across the road in the cut of the highway a tower of ancient-looking rock that looked quite out of place there, even though it was capped with grass and a small tree growing out of a crack.
>
> He was on the edge of the Niagara Escarpment, though he did not know that name or anything about it. But he was captivated. Why had he never been told anything about this? This surprise, this careless challenge in the ordinary landscape. He felt a comic sort of outrage that something made for him to explore had been there for him all along and nobody had told him.
>
> Nevertheless, he knew. Before he got into the next car, he knew he was going to find out; he was not going to let this go. Geology was what it was called. And all this time he had been fooling around with arguments, with philosophy and political science.
>
> It wouldn't be easy. It would mean saving money, starting again with pimpled brats just out of high school. But that is what he would do.
>
> Later, he often told people about the trip, about the sight of the escarpment that turned his life around. If asked what he'd been doing there, he'd wonder and then remember that he'd gone up there to see a girl.
>
> (67)

Because Munro decided to withhold "Axis" from *Dear Life*, its final published form is in the *New Yorker*, yet there is manuscript evidence that she did considerable work revising it toward book publication. On a revision dated November 1, 2011—about ten months after its appearance in the magazine—Close suggested that Munro needed something more in the ending, by then slightly different from the one published in the *New Yorker*. Munro did this, adding a discussion about Grace between Avie and Royce on the train in which Royce explains, filled with his revelation and new resolve, that he imagined himself going back to rescuing Grace from her family in gratitude—this is the version entitled "Take Me with You." "'She was the one got me here, I thought'" (19). He credited her as the agent of his geological realization.[7]

In that revised manuscript too there is a rewritten version of Royce's realization, one Munro followed up with new material connected to his imagined romantic "rescue" of Grace. Here Munro is more geographically specific: a driver dropped Royce in Wiarton, Ontario at the foot of the Bruce Peninsula, near Owen Sound, where he noticed the cliff running along the south side of Colpoy's Bay—evidence of the Niagara Escarpment.[8] Seeing it, he wonders over the processes which produced it, thinking about the very existence of such a thing. His sense of geography was vague but for Toronto and London and points between. He asks the next driver who picks him up, one who knows the area, and who details and names the landforms Royce noticed. As the man does this, his descriptions create in Royce "some kind of sheer pleasure up his spine" ("Take Me with You" 12). This feeling, this moment, is the same one Munro describes in the published version of "Axis" as "surprise" at "this careless challenge in the ordinary landscape": "he was not going to let this go." His life is transformed with new purpose; this transformation is rather like the "eruption of the vast and crazy old Canadian Shield," the making of the Frontenac Axis, he shows and describes to Avie those years later on the train (*New Yorker* 67, 69).

When "Axis" was first submitted to the *New Yorker*, the story largely ended with the sighting and recognition of the Frontenac Axis from the train. Avie thanks Royce for showing it to her and, for his part, he acknowledges her thanks and does not seem to wish to talk further. Then there is a white-space break followed by this four-line, four-paragraph exchange: "'Do you know where Grace is?' Startled, she shakes her head. 'I thought you might.' No" (*New Yorker* files). Thus this first version ends with an indication that Royce may wish to reconnect as the story's final statement. While Munro and Treisman were working on it for the magazine, that ending was reversed—in its publication Royce dismisses the idea. Then in post-publication revision for its inclusion in *Dear Life* Munro returns and reverses herself again, with Royce thinking he would rescue Grace out of gratitude (Third November 1, 2011 version, "Take Me with You").

Such reversal is also to be seen at the ending of "Corrie," the earliest story collected in *Dear Life*, one first published in October 2010 in the *New Yorker*. After that appearance it was selected as a PEN / O. Henry prize story for 2012 and was republished in that collection with a different ending from the *New Yorker* version, and then again in *Dear Life* with yet a third ending. "Corrie" retrospectively tells the story of a protracted illicit relationship during the mid-1950s between an architect, Howard, married with children, and a lame (from polio) wealthy woman, Corrie, whom he first meets when they were young through a job renovating a small-town church. The affair continues for years, and the plot hinges on a putative blackmail scheme by a former servant, named Sadie in the first two versions and Lillian in the third, who threatens to expose them to Howard's wife. When Sadie / Lillian dies, Corrie apparently realizes that the blackmail was a sham, that Howard actually pocketed the cash she had supplied to him to pass on to the woman for her silence. The story ends before Howard confirms Corrie's realization one way or the other, but it is that recognition—and Corrie's understanding of it—which is the nub of the ending and so the story. Weighted with this new knowledge, Corrie wonders over just what to do: confront him, flee, or just continue on as they always have. Detailing the different effects created in each different ending, Lee Clark Mitchell argues that readers "waver among three different versions," calling them "productive contradictions" (70).

When Munro was getting to the point of drafting the ending that is, in fact, final to "Corrie"—the one in *Dear Life*—when the text of the book was being assembled, she sent an autograph version of the passage following the white-space break beginning "The briefest note, the letter tossed" (*Dear Life* 173–4). It is identical to what is published but for a deleted phrase at the ending of the last sentence in *Dear Life*: "When there could have been worse, much worse, ~~and her hands are like bouquets of surviving eggshells, that light~~" (2017.103.1.8).⁹ The ethereal reference here is to the morning light surrounding Corrie as she digests Howard's response to what she has written. The simile, itself jarring though suggestive of things broken (and perhaps *Humpty Dumpty*), is utterly equivocal as to what Corrie might do next, but the implication is that lives and a relationship continue together.

Other details, somewhat wayward, in "Corrie" seem to clinch this point. Owing to her ample personal means, Corrie has taken over the running of the town's library as a benefaction. It was "a Carnegie library, not easy to get rid of, even though few people used it anymore—not nearly enough to justify a librarian's wages" (*Dear Life* 165). When she learns that Lillian Wolfe—the putative blackmailer—has died and will be brought back to the town for burial, Corrie is minding the library. The fellow who cuts her grass stops by to tell her he would not be able to do so as planned that day because "He had to go to the cemetery and dig a grave. It was for someone who used to live around here, he said. Corrie, with her finger in *The Great Gatsby*, asked for the person's name." Munro focalizes Corrie's thoughts about returned corpses, thinking that such people "might have lived their entire lives in cities nearby or distant, and seemed quite satisfied in those places, but had no wish to stay there when they were dead. Old people got such ideas" (*Dear Life* 167). Confirming that the deceased was in fact Lillian Wolfe and that the funeral was that afternoon, Corrie thinks about how to tell Howard the news. She decides to write. So she "went back to *Gatsby*, but she was just reading words, she was too restless. She locked the library and walked around town" (*Dear Life* 168). Eventually Corrie finds her way to the post-funeral reception and learns more about Lillian's subsequent life, including details from the woman who employed her in Kitchener, that plant doubt in her mind; this person was no blackmailer.

In talking about her own town library, Munro has consistently noted that Wingham did not accept a Carnegie library when they were being established throughout North America—the town was not willing to take the responsibility for the building's upkeep, a requirement. As a lifelong avid reader, she resented her town's attitude and thought its niggling refusal indicated long-held hometown attitudes she despised. And by having Corrie take over the library too, Munro is reminding readers of an earlier story of hers, one her editor Close sees as beginning Munro's late style, "Carried Away," in *Open Secrets*. There the trajectory of Louisa's life is redirected when she quits her job and becomes a town's librarian; she finds a new life. Munro herself worked in libraries at university and in Vancouver (see Thacker *Alice* 91, 116). But of these details, the one that strikes most clearly is the mention of *The Great Gatsby* in connection with the beginnings of Corrie's epiphany. Here in a story of romance, though not in a romantic story, Munro points Corrie at a key moment to a novel that is seen as the quintessential meditation on romance, sexual attraction, and the aesthetics of that pull among people of means. Nick Carraway takes it all in as it ends tragically, he is left empty of emotion. So Fitzgerald's story ends ruefully, as does Munro's, each with obtained wisdom through what has happened. After she meditates on her discoveries, Corrie begins a letter to Howard; after two pages of Corrie's evening meditations over what she has inferred through the events of the day of the funeral, there is a white-space break and this follows:

> She goes to bed with the letter to him still unfinished.
> And wakes up early, when the sky is brightening, though the sun is not yet up.
> There's always one morning when you realize that the birds have all gone.
> She knows something. She has found it in her sleep.
> There is no news to give him. No news, because there never was any.

No news about Lillian, because Lillian doesn't matter and she never did. No post office box, because the money goes straight into an account or maybe just a wallet.

… … ….

She gets up and quickly dresses and walks through every room in the house, introducing the walls and the furniture to this new idea. A cavity everywhere, most notably in her chest. She makes coffee and doesn't drink it. She ends up in her bedroom once more, and finds that the introduction to the current reality has to be done all over again.

Another white-space break and then "[t]he briefest note, the letter tossed. 'Lillian is dead, buried yesterday'" (*Dear Life* 173). Corrie sends this.

"What are these moments that stand out, clear patches in your life—what do they have to do with it? They aren't exactly promises. Breathing spaces. Is that all?" So Munro wrote in "Circle of Prayer" in *The Progress of Love*. In that collection too she wrote in "White Dump" that a character "wouldn't be so astonished at the way the skin of the moment can break open" (*Progress* 273, 308; see Thacker *Reading* 73–7, 231–42). And here in her last book Corrie is at such a moment after she sends "the briefest note" with its potentially cataclysmic news to Howard. The house, its walls and rooms, knows the news, so Howard needs that news too. She "turns off the phone, so as to not suffer waiting. The silence. She may simply never hear again." But he does reply: "'All well now, be glad. Soon.'" Echoes of earlier stories are here: "Silence" and "Soon," both stories in the Juliet Triptych in *Runaway*; Munro tries to invoke "bouquets of eggshells" here before she deleted the metaphor, but the morning light in which Corrie experiences her breathing space remains to illuminate this scene as the story ends (*Dear Life* 174).

That reaction is envisioned and stated in the first *New Yorker* ending, where Corrie thinks, "If he doesn't know that Sadie is dead he will just expect things to go on as usual. And how would he know, unless he is told? And who would he be told by, unless by Corrie herself? She could say something that would destroy them, but she does not have to" (*New Yorker* 101). This equilibrium, which also ends the final version, is reversed in the intermediate *Pen / O. Henry* ending where Corrie envisions fleeing from the relation, so the story's last words are "Do it" (409).

"Having Gotten along as Best They Could": "Gravel," "Pride," and "Leaving Maverley"

The long perspective which characterizes the *Dear Life* stories preceding the "Finale" texture them in time, complexity, and recursion. When Munro was asked to comment on the provenance of "Corrie" for the *Pen / O. Henry* collection she responded with details pertinent both to her own perspective in 2009–10 and to late style:

> I don't remember whether I knew a Corrie, but I did know lonely, idle, small-town rich girls—just outside of their lives. I was not at all interested in them, being of Sadie's class myself. Then a cousin told me how she, working as a maid, saw a guest,

plus his wife, dining in her employer's house, and what a shock it was, because she had known him as the long-time gentleman caller of an unmarried, well-to-do woman in our town. The story came to me years after it happened, but it stuck. I put the foot on her [lameness from polio] quite naturally, no symbolic crap, then was embarrassed a bit but left it. Same way with Gatsby. Will anyone get that now?

I must say I like these characters. Him, too. Would be too boring to make him an utter stinker.

(author comment 427)

"Corrie" was followed in 2011 by five serial stories—four fictional and "Dear Life," personal history—mostly in the *New Yorker*, but "Pride" went to *Harper's*. The account Munro offered regarding the provenance of "Corrie" typifies her practice of recalling an incident (whether hearsay or autobiographical), centering on it at the core of story, and shaping it to her vision of it—or as close to that vision as she could get. Yet as a writer turning eighty after over sixty years of publication, the prolific production levels of 2011 and 2012 (which saw seven stories published as well as *Dear Life* itself) are remarkable, the effect too of all those years of writing on. Munro may be seen there quite clearly echoing herself, going back again, and in numerous ways, to ideas and situations she had worked on before and, also, published on before. Here too it is apt to note again a line which appears in passing in "Corrie," quoted above, "Old people get such ideas." Then there is that vexing opening sentence to "Some Women": "I am amazed sometimes to think how old I am." Munro agreed about the truth of that comment when I asked her about in 2010, and her repeated assertions of wanting to end writing after each of her last three books suggests, too, that she thought she had been writing long enough. Powerfully, *Dear Life* as a last collection finally managed the ending, the "Finale," she wanted.

Just after "Gravel" appeared in the *New Yorker* (June 27, 2011), I replied to questions from Charles May, a Munro critic and short-story expert, about it. He had written asking about the provenance of the story—he wrote that it seemed "more like early Munro than late Munro—short, focused, single event." My response to May then gets at just where I was, and we Munro critics were, as she showed her directions as she moved toward that final collection. I wrote:

The story itself—which I also like very much: the last paragraph / section is eerily haunting—does take up characters and incidents reminiscent of early Munro, but I was most struck by the many ways Munro is echoing herself: "The Time of Death" (1956), "Miles City, Montana" (1985), "The Children Stay" (1997). The Mother's transformation—dressing younger, keeping up with trends—while married to a stodgy husband is, again, Alice and Jim Munro in Victoria in the 1960s. Two other things really seem pressing: the way she creates the narrator's long perspective, for she is convincing as an older narrator remembering experiences which occurred to her when she could scarcely understand them—Munro creates the inchoate presence of the child as narrator. Better, I think, than in "My Mother's Dream" (1998). Second: the dog. It may be that I've been reading Maxwell overmuch, but at the moment when Caro gets to the gravel pit, however that occurred, I was more worried about Blitzee, a presence Munro tells us no more about. What happened to the dog?

(Thacker to May, June 27, 2011)[10]

My final question then was not rhetorical, for the dog, Blitzee, appears briefly after the narrator's sister Caro throws herself into the gravel pit, ostensibly to save the dog, only to drown herself. There is no further mention of Blitzee.

"Gravel" begins matter-of-factly, "At that time we were living beside a gravel pit. Not a large one, hollowed out by monster machinery, just a minor pit that a farmer must have made some money from years before" (*Dear Life* 91). This is an immediate reminder of the circumstances of "Nettles" (2000, *Hateship*); later, there is another echo of that story when Neal—the lover of the narrator's mother—protests that he might have run over the girls playing in the lane; such a thing happens in "Nettles." "Gravel" is the story of two sisters whose mother works in theatre and meets an actor—the adults take up with one another, the mother gets pregnant, leaves her dour husband and their upper-middle-class home and life and moves into a trailer beside a gravel pit. Unable to clearly remember exact circumstances, the remembering unnamed adult narrator is haunted by her sister's seemingly intentional drowning in the gravel pit while the adults were stoned and having sex. Munro puts her reader mostly in the remembering narrator's mind, so that "Gravel" offers both distance from the described events and uncertainty about them. The story ends years later with a last meeting between the narrator and Neal, an old hippie, a type, who spouts a vague 1960s and '70s counterculture philosophy. Along with the absent mention of the dog, the mother's subsequent circumstances are not addressed either.

The dog's absence is worth noting because of what was happening with the *Dear Life* stories as they moved toward that collection. After "Gravel" appeared in the *New Yorker* in late June, when I was asking about stories for the forthcoming book, Close wrote that "Alice told me she'd done a lot of work under Deborah's prodding on one of the New Yorker stories. I think it was 'Gravel'" (August 3, 2011). The edited proof copies of the story bear this out: Treisman's edits are characteristically thorough, with many substitutions, re-phrasings, and deletions; the net effect is one of both tightening and distancing the narrator's rendering of her memories of this time. She was then pre-kindergarten and claims, throughout "Gravel," to not remember many things. Munro accepted most of these edits. The initial ending, the final paragraph / section set off by a white-space break, reads: "I see what he means, though. It really is the right thing to do. It just doesn't seem to apply to Caro and me." After two suggested deletions and one substitution here, Treisman wrote: "Alice: I feel it needs another beat or two here. Obviously Neal's philosophy can't work for Caro, who's dead. But where does this leave the narrator? It feels a little vague—in need of something a little more concrete." Munro responded to this request with a sentence which completed the edited paragraph as it was then, and which was carried into the magazine version and then, with only the addition of a single word, into *Dear Life*: "But, in my mind, Caro keeps running at the water and throwing herself in as if in triumph, and I'm still caught, waiting for her to explain to me, waiting for the splash" (15, 14 edited proof, June 1, 2011; *New Yorker* files; *New Yorker* 70; *Dear Life* 109).

Comparing these versions of the ending to the story is germane to Munro's late style and to "Gravel." Because of her numerous recursions in it, the need for much plot is deeply diminished. In fact, because Munro controls the narrator's perspective so absolutely—as I told May upon my first readings, she "creates the inchoate presence of the child as narrator" when it is quite clear that she is an adult striving to remember the events surrounding her sister's drowning. The effect of Treisman's edits and her prodding toward a more concrete ending—which Munro delivered with the envisioned splash (*Dear Life* 102)—again both demonstrate another instance of the very real effect serial editing had on Munro's late style and create a dreamlike, almost ethereal, atmosphere.

At the critical moment in the narrator's memory, the crux, when Caro enters the water of the gravel pit, she describes the circumstances, recalling that Caro had told her to "tell Neal and our mother something. That the dog had fallen into the water." She continues, in an extended back-and-forth way, ending:

> In my mind I can see her picking up Blitzee and tossing her, though Blitzee was trying to hang onto her coat. Then backing up, Caro backing up to take a run at the water. Running, jumping, all of sudden hurling herself at the water. But I can't recall the sound of the splashes as they, one after the other, hit the water. Not a little splash or a big one. Perhaps I had turned toward the trailer by then—I must have done so.
>
> When I dream of this, I am always running.
>
> (*Dear Life* 102)

The back and forth here creates uncertainty and contradiction—these all contextualize the workings of memory: the reader cannot judge what happened, neither to Caro nor to Blitzee. This crux embodies the narrator's imagination, for just after this she writes that "What I really did was make my way up the little incline towards the trailer": "I sat down and waited for the next thing to happen" (*Dear Life* 103). "What I really did" is the same as when Munro, as Duffy points out, breaks her narrative in "The View from Castle Rock" and writes of James Laidlaw's letter being in *Blackwood's Magazine* "where I can look it up today" (*Castle Rock* 83; Duffy 376). And then Munro follows that statement with a variation of a line more recently used in "Face": "Something happened here" (*Happiness* 164). She sat waiting "for the next act in Caro's drama. Or the dog's." Shifting from this crucial moment in her past to a more recent one, the narrator writes that she "went to a professional person about this once and she convinced me—for a time, she convinced me—that I must have tried the door of the trailer and found it locked." With more information dimly remembered, and commenting too of "So many games, with Caro," a reader recalls that the mother and Neal were stoned and so slow to act, to go find Caro's lifeless body (*Dear Life* 103).

In between "Gravel" and its predecessor, "Axis," Munro published "Pride" in the April 2011 issue of *Harper's*. Having published "Face" in 2008, the editors at the *New Yorker* passed on it, for it is a story reminiscent of that one. Munro again offers a first-person adult male narrator who has a physical facial flaw—a harelip—who tells of his friendship with a woman, Oneida. Like Corrie, she was of the town's prominent family. Her father "ran the bank," "a man born to be in power" (*Dear Life* 134, 135). And as in "Face" too, the narrator tells the story of his life, and of a good deal of the changes seen in his town over his lifetime. A bachelor who lived with his mother until her death, he tells of the thirties and the war years, bringing the story into the postwar years. Beyond "Face" and "Corrie," there are echoes of numerous previous works.

Readers are told how Oneida's father during the thirties got involved in a scheme, "the resurrection of the steam-driven car, such as had been around at the turn of the century." This type of car figures in Munro's "A Wilderness Station," and here in "Pride" it accounts for the disgrace of Oneida's father, who made the positive decision on the bank's loan to support the car's manufacture but "he had also dipped improperly into bank funds" as his own contribution—thinking it could be paid back. Exposed after the scheme had collapsed, he is held responsible: "The bank had lost a lot of money. There was talk not of cheating but of mismanagement. Somebody had to be punished. Any other manager would have been out on his ear, but given it was Horace Jantzen, this was avoided." He was assigned as manager in a small branch in a nearby town that did not need one; he sat all day, looked good, and did nothing, chauffeured back and forth by his daughter Oneida. "Surely he could have refused, but pride, it was thought, chose otherwise. Pride chose that he be driven every morning those six miles to sit behind a partial wall of cheap varnished boards, no proper office at all" (*Dear Life* 136).

One of Munro's interests in her later work was to tell something of the history of manufacturing in small-town Ontario—in *Open Secrets* there are characters named Doud whose family had and then lost a piano and organ factory—and of the history of those towns generally. In "Pride," the unnamed narrator tells that he has set himself to the task of town historian—like Del Jordan's Uncle Craig in *Lives*—although how much progress he has made is not clear. As in "Gravel," in "Pride" the narrator is unsure of his story. Describing how his harelip might have affected his draft status during the war, he holds that "I must have got my notice. I must have gone to the doctor to get an exemption. I simply don't remember" (*Dear Life* 138). He is vague too over his relations with Oneida during the years of the war and when his mother died, saying that "I must have run into Oneida during those years, and kept track of her life. I would have had to. Her father died right before VE day, mixing up the funeral with the celebrations in an awkward way" (*Dear Life* 140).

This is all background to the story proper, which is focused on the growing friendship between the narrator and Oneida in later years, after each of their remaining parents has died. It really begins when Oneida stopped the narrator—a bookkeeper—on the street to ask his advice about selling her house. He does give advice; she ignores it and takes a low price from a questionable person, who immediately pulled it down to replace it with an apartment house. Separately and for their own reasons, each character eventually moves in there.

As the two are drawn together, Munro focuses on their different characters, and the narrator's own pride figures in when he takes exception to something Oneida says about his habit of using old nicknames. "All my school years had been spent, as I saw it, in getting used to what I was like—what my face was like—and what other people were like in regard to it. I suppose it was a triumph of a minor sort to have managed that, to know I could survive here and make my living and not continually be having to break new people in." He wonders further about Oneida's opinions, since "[i]t didn't seem to me that she was settled yet. Actually now that the big house was gone, a good deal of her was gone with it. The town was changing, and her place in it was changing, and she hardly knew it." Following this comment the narrator telescopes the changes in the town over three decades—the fifties through the seventies—changes he holds Oneida has missed: "But she hadn't altogether caught on. There was still that strange hesitation and lightness about her, as if she were waiting for life to begin" (*Dear Life* 144).

It does. Despite the narrator's pride, the two are drawn together inexorably. They adopt a regular evening routine of eating and watching television and, when he has some sort of attack, she stays on at his house and nurses him. After this, Oneida makes a proposal: "the gist of it was that she was prepared to move in." After explaining her thinking, the narrator continues:

> Another thing she said was that we were not entirely capable of looking after ourselves. What if I had got sick and been all alone? What if such a thing should happen again? Or should happen to her?
>
> We had a certain feeling for each other, she said. We had a feeling which was not the usual thing. We could live together like brother and sister and look after each other like brother and sister and it would be the most natural thing in the world. Everybody would accept it as so. How could they not?

"At this," the narrator recoils: "I felt as if I had been thrown down into a cellar and a flat door slammed on my head." But the narrator does not say this. Pronouncing Oneida's proposal impossible, he lies to her, telling her that he had sold his house. Trapped in that lie, he then actually does so. "And then I had to face the job of dealing with all that had been accumulating since my parents moved in on their honeymoon" (*Dear Life* 148, 149). That is, this narrator is faced here with the same situation as the narrator in "Face." Needing a place to live, he arranges to move into Oneida's apartment building.

At end of "Pride" the narrator and Oneida are together in his house while he is working at clearing it out. "Oneida was looking better than formerly when she showed up in the midst of my packing and discarding. She'd had her hair done, and the color changed somewhat, maybe browner. 'You mustn't throw everything out in one fell swoop,' she said. 'All you'd collected for that town history.'" In reply, he says he "was being selective, though that was not entirely true. It seemed to me that both of us were pretending to care what happened, more than we really did." He had lost interest in his history since "it seemed as if one town must after all be much like another." She was about to go off on one of her trips. There together, Oneida "gave a most unusual little shriek or cry and then put her hand to her mouth and moved with large cautious steps to my window. 'Careful, careful,' she said. 'Look, look.'" So orchestrated, this scene arouses curiosity, perhaps concern. But Oneida is "laughing almost soundlessly" and she reveals, in the birdbath he had just filled that morning, five little skunks, "Flashing and dancing and never getting in each other's way ...." "While we watched, they lifted themselves up one by one and left the water and proceeded to walk across the yard, swiftly but in a straight diagonal line. As if they were proud of themselves but discreet. Five of them." Looking at Oneida, the narrator says that "Her face looked dazzled" (*Dear Life* 152–3). In 2012 Munro told Treisman that this was her favorite scene in *Dear Life*.

"Pride" ends, in both its published forms, with a single-sentence paragraph: "We were as glad as we could be." That ending came after Munro finished the story, since an earlier draft—probably the one submitted to the *New Yorker* and eventually to *Harper's*, ended with the published penultimate paragraph: "I thought she might say another thing, and spoil it, but no, neither of us did" (2017.103.1.8). Early in "Images," one of the three stories that Munro wrote in 1967 to complete her first book, *Dance of the Happy Shades*, the narrator, recalls a detailed family scene and writes of "all this life going on" (*Dance* 31). So it is too, still, in "Pride" with "We were as glad as we could be": the narrator and Oneida, together, sharing a communion moment, seeing those skunks. Their lives going on yet circumscribed by age, as glad as they could be. So "Pride" ends, a story without a great deal of plot but with much description and perception, with aged and still aging characters, together, their lives still "going on": it is a late-style story that not so much concludes as it stops. Like dear life itself.

The publication of "Pride" in the April 2011 *Harper's* was followed in the *New Yorker* by "Gravel" in late June, the personal history "Dear Life" (September 17, 2011), and another fictional story that year, "Leaving Maverley" (November 28, 2011).[11] It is set just after the Second World War in a Wingham-like town in Ontario. It begins seeming to focus on a man who runs the Capital theatre in Maverley; it shifts and then seems to be focusing on a teenaged girl hired as a ticket-taker, but ultimately it alights on Ray Elliot, the town's "night policeman." He "had taken the job so that he would be able to help his sick wife manage for at least some part of the daytime." Her name is Isabel—a reference to Munro's relative born at sea in 1818. The two met after the Second World War when, delayed by his service, Ray was finishing high school and Isabel was his married teacher; as it happened, she then left her husband, also a veteran, for Ray. She becomes chronically ill with "something called pericarditis. It was serious and she had ignored it to her peril. It was something she would not be cured of but could manage, with difficulty." Isabel and Ray "had no children and could get talking anytime about anything. He brought her the news of the town, which often made her laugh, and she told him about the books she was reading" (*Dear Life* 69, 70–1). These two follow the doings of the girl hired to take tickets, Leah, who at first seems to be just the eldest child of a religious family dominated by the father. Ray and Isabel wonder over her personality and characteristics. But then she elopes with the visiting son of the United Church minister, has two children with him elsewhere, and sometime later returns to Maverley with her children, by then estranged from her husband. She then has another affair with the new United Church minister—and a scandal too since the minister announces their liaison from the pulpit. Once again, "all this life going on."

This complicated plot and this summary reflects Munro's late-style recursive purposes. Reading the stories in *Dear Life*, especially the ten which precede the "Finale," it is clear that for Munro plot is less imperative than are the contextualizations of moments, or of images as in "Gravel" and "Pride," which embody characters' beings. Their understandings. In five of these stories funerals are either anticipated, invoked, or depicted and in "Leaving Maverley" Isabel's long-expected death finally occurs, leaving Ray bereft, stunned, yet wondering. And as seen throughout Munro's career, several train trips (and another transcontinental one in "To Read Japan") lead to new beginnings, to adventures, to life going on yet. Seen biographically, echoes of other stories—in manuscript and published—are continual and never far distant, and Munro's Huron County home place provides setting and the remembered years of her life there through time. This is true not only in the ten recursive stories but also, and most essentially, in the four *"not quite stories"* in the "Finale" (*Dear Life* 255; original emphasis). All this is seen in a published comment Munro made when "Leaving Maverley" was republished in the 2013 *O. Henry Prize Stories* volume. Beginning "My husband's father was a night cop," who "used to get some warm moments from cold nights walking the streets by ducking into the Lyceum Theatre," Munro comments too that he "was a well-read school dropout (a common thing in those days—lack of funds) and took a dim view of the plots, but had fun." Having asserted this central fact, she expands by developing it and placing it amid Huron County cultural knowledge:

> Also a World War II scandal, a married teacher leaving respectable husband for penniless young vet—somehow I just wound these up and the girl appeared—plenty of dour Christians in that (my) home town, and I went along to see what would happen to them—the preacher getting in, then out—and the two shorn creatures left at the end. Not completely shorn, though, having got along the best they could.
>
> (author comment 437)

In the story Leah's disappearance is detailed—the first shut-down lake-effect snowstorm of the year provides drama, since she may have been enveloped and frozen—and then discovery of her elopement with the minister's son. Ray and Isabel talk about what happened, and they wonder what will happen next. Munro keeps the focus on Ray and his sick wife: Isabel takes a turn for the worse, is moved to a hospital in the city, and eventually goes into a coma. Ray stays with her, taking a job in the hospital. Working there after Isabel's situation has been long unchanged, Ray meets Leah again. She happens now to work in the same hospital. Leah tells him the rest of her story in a happenstance meeting just before Ray discovers that "Isabel was finally gone. They said 'gone,' as if she had got up and left. When someone had checked on her about an hour ago, she had been the same as ever, and now she was gone" (*Dear Life* 89).

Once when Munro was being interviewed for a 1973 M. A. thesis, she noted that as we age "'life becomes *more* mysterious and difficult,'" and that "'writing is the art of approach and recognition. I believe that we don't solve these things—in fact our explanations take us further away'" (see Thacker *Reading* 73 and *passim*). Here is Munro's "approach and recognition" to life itself in "Leaving Maverley." Just after the passage in which Ray learns of Isabel's death she offers three critical brief paragraphs, the first two each a single sentence: "He had often wondered what difference it would make." And "But the emptiness in place of her was astounding." And, after a paragraph of detail describing Ray's adjustment to this new fact while a nurse spoke to him, this: "He'd thought that it had happened long before with Isabel, but it hadn't. Not until now." Concluding "Leaving Maverley"—its title continuing to accrete resonance as it continues to be read—Munro tells us that Ray made arrangements "for the remains" and offers this extended ending:

> And before long he found himself outside, pretending that he had as ordinary and good a reason as anybody else to put one foot ahead of the other.
>
> What he carried with him, all he carried with him, was a lack, something like a lack of air, of proper behavior in his lungs, a difficulty that he supposed would go on forever.
>
> The girl he'd been talking to, whom he'd once known—she had spoken of her children. The loss of her children. Getting used to that. A problem at suppertime.
>
> An expert at losing, she might be called—himself a novice by comparison. And now he could not remember her name. Had lost her name, though he'd known it well. Losing, lost. A joke on him, if you wanted one.
>
> He was going up his own steps when it came to him.
>
> Leah.
>
> A relief out of all proportion, to remember her.
>
> (*Dear Life* 89–90)

Leah, who knew about Isabel's protracted illness and of Ray's presence as a co-worker in the hospital, had suggested their getting together occasionally for a meal; he is not interested, preferring to stay alone. These two are "the shorn creatures at the end," as Munro wrote.

This ending is unusual in Munro's stories because it is exactly the same as that found in the *New Yorker* (71). When Munro submitted story this was its ending after a white-space break:

> The girl. He could not at the moment recall her name. An expert at losing, she was. Himself a novice by comparison.
>
> Name lost. It would come to him.
>
> He and Isabel would laugh and stamp the floor and go into a pantomime of despair and sometimes remember at exactly the same moment, together.
>
> Leah.
>
> (n.d.; *New Yorker* files)

On September 7, 2011, Munro faxed a two-page revised ending to the *New Yorker* which is close to the published ending, Ray thinking only of the girl's lost name and making no mention of Isabel. Then on the 12th she faxed a full revised draft with yet a new ending, Isabel back:

> He was going up his own steps, taking out his key.
>
> "Leah," said Isabel.
>
> Yes.

The 13th brought another twenty-page faxed revision and here Isabel's presence in the remembering of Leah's name is gone again. But for small wording and punctuation, this is the published ending (*New Yorker* files).

Beyond endings, what Isabel's final back-and-forth presence demonstrates is that Munro wavered between Ray as a person still infused with his dead wife's being— aptly so since she had been long gone during her four years in a coma yet he did not leave her—and with Ray alone, left only with himself, with his own mystery. That she decided finally on the latter to end "Leaving Maverley" is indicative of where Munro was heading through all the recursive late-style stories in *Dear Life* as 2011 closed. When she saw Treisman's edits Munro accepted almost all of them for the serial and carried them forward into *Dear Life* (November 3, 2011 proofs; *New Yorker* files).

The Seven Recursive Returns of 2012

During 2012 Munro published seven stories in serials, with two—"Haven" and "Amundsen"—in the *New Yorker*, while another, "Train," went to *Harper's*, two more went to *Granta*—"In Sight of the Lake" and "Night"—and two others were in serials new to her: *Narrative*—"To Reach Japan"—and *Tin House*—"Dolly." This flurry of productivity anticipated that fall's publication of *Dear Life*—the need to have the serials in print before the book came out. Seen and understood together these 2012 stories show Munro working recursively and usually at the separate phases of her life and career, covering the full range, with the two *New Yorker* stories and "Night" told from a remembering young girl's point of view; "To Reach Japan" and "Train" focused on adults' whole lives; and "Dolly" and "In Sight of the Lake" taking up old age and characters continuing on, with the latter concerned with the debilitations of memory loss, a conscious anticipation by Munro of her own circumstances. At the same time "Dolly" was placed in *Dear Life* just before—and so introduces—the book's "Finale." It, like "Axis," uses Fremlin's history and there are also echoes of previous situations included and, in one instance, "Train," where Munro explicitly returns to and finally used material she had drafted and re-drafted in the later 1950s into the '60s. Altogether, these final stories reveal Munro writing on still as she had always done: in their variety and in their similarities to stories that preceded them they both encapsulate her late-style writing and, with that "Finale," are a conscious final statement.

"Haven" begins, like "Some Women," with a direct matter-of-factness:

> All this happened in the seventies, though in that town and other small towns like it, the seventies were not as we picture them now, or as I had known them even in Vancouver. The boys' hair was longer than it had been, but not straggling down their backs, and there didn't seem to be an unusual amount of liberation or defiance in the air.
>
> My uncle started off by teasing me about grace. About not saying grace. I was thirteen years old, living with him and my aunt for the year that my parents were in Africa. I had never bowed my head over a plate of food in my life.
>
> (*Dear Life* 110)

Another strategically decided thirteen-year-old in a new situation—like "Some Women"—discovering a new place. Here the subject of discovery is the marriage of the narrator's Aunt Dawn and Uncle Jasper and, as Munro demonstrates in the scene which follows the passage that opens the story, her childless uncle's dominance of his home. The "Haven" of the title is the haven that a woman was traditionally expected to provide for a man—and the couple's last name, Cassel, becomes an explicit pun mentioned in "A man's home is his castle" (*Dear Life* 125). The narrator discovers that providing that haven was a challenge for her Aunt Dawn, given Uncle Jasper's behavior. "'Dawn's life is devoted to her husband,' my mother had said, with an attempt at neutrality. Or more dryly, 'Her life revolves around that man.' This was something that was said at the time, and it was not always meant as disparagement. But I had not seen before a woman of whom it seemed so true as Aunt Dawn" (*Dear Life* 112–13).

The narrator's mother went on to say that things "would have been quite different ... if they'd had children." To this, the retrospective narrator recalls and asserts, "Imagine that. Children. Getting in Uncle Jasper's way, whining for a corner of their mother's attention. Being sick, sulking, messing up the house, wanting food he didn't like. Impossible. The house was his, the choice of menus his, the radio and television programs his. Even if he was at his practice next door, or out on a call, things had to be ready for his approval at any moment" (*Dear Life* 113). Jasper is the town doctor, and so prominent, and the narrator notices that his demeanor in the office—where she has to go early in her stay because of injuries from a bicycle accident, another girl on a bike—is not so dominant there.

Most of "Haven" has to do with two incidents involving Jasper's older sister Mona, a professional violinist estranged from her brother (this circumstance owes to Fremlin's history too [Thacker interview June 2003]). When she comes to the town for a performance, Dawn arranges a reception for her and for the other players without her husband's knowledge. Arriving home from a meeting, he finds his sister and the others still playing. He behaves boorishly, mocking classical music to the narrator. An unpleasant scene. Not too long after this Mona dies and, like the woman in "Corrie," is brought back to be buried at the family's former Anglican church—now the "Church of the Hosannas." Jasper orchestrates another scene, this time at the funeral, again to mock his sister's pretensions in music. He has his office assistant, who plays organ at a fundamentalist church, play "The Old Rugged Cross" instead of the intended program. When, amid his own boisterous singing, Jasper discovers that Dawn has not joined in, he is probably disappointed at that fact, the narrator infers. But another possibility is offered in the penultimate paragraph of the story: "Or perhaps [Dawn] realized that, for the first time, she didn't care. For the life of her, couldn't care" (*Dear Life* 132).

Writing earlier in the story, meditating on the disrupted performance she witnessed, and Mona, about whose death they have just learned, the narrator notes her own transformations while living apart from her own family that year:

> Some of my ideas had changed during the time I had been living with my aunt and uncle. For instance, I was no longer so uncritical about people like Mona. Or about Mona herself, her music and her career. But I did not believe that she was—or had been—a freak, but I could understand how some people might think so. It wasn't

just her big bones and big white nose, and the violin and the somewhat silly way you had to hold it—it was the music itself and her devotion to it. Devotion to anything, if you were female, could make you ridiculous.

Just after this paragraph the narrator offers a disturbing—to her—account of overheard Sunday morning sex coming from her aunt and uncle's bedroom. She describes her own reaction, "I had heard sounds such as I had never heard from my parents or from anyone else—a sort of pleasurable growling and squealing in which there was a complicity and abandonment that disturbed and deeply undermined me" (*Dear Life* 128).

Both of these passages end in ways wholly Munrovian. Mona's devotion to music is paralleled—Munro well knew when she wrote this in 2011 or early 2012 sometime—by her own devotion to reading and writing. Admitting that devotion often, and well aware of how such intellectual pursuits were seen in the culture she was born to, she knows she is implicated fundamentally. The second passage—a thirteen-year-old's disturbance over sexual attraction and passion, is yet another of her great concerns as a writer and as a woman. Munro has long been seen as pioneer writer on the subject of female sexuality and infidelity.

When Munro wrote of "Amundsen" to Treisman, she said that there "the girl has her first experience with a helplessly selfish man." There too Munro remarked that she is "partial to 'Amundsen'—it gave me such trouble" (Treisman interview). Beginning as a story called "Like a Russian Novel," "Amundsen" is set during the Second World War at a tuberculosis sanatorium within driving distance of Huntsville; Ontario's rural sanatoria were in that area, and in the story Munro uses the Ontario Northland railway connecting these places to good effect. A young woman, the narrator, Vivien (or Vivi), interrupts her studies in Toronto and takes a job teaching the patients there; arriving by train during winter, she meets a raucous high-school girl, Mary, and the head physician, Dr. Alister Fox, a well-read discomforting person who is wry, demanding, and eventually interested in marrying her.

Munro concerns herself with Vivien's discoveries of the place, methods for teaching the students within the circumstances of their disease and with the doctor's advice, and connecting some to Mary. The doctor invites Vivien to dinner and ultimately takes her to bed with a promise of marriage. Not too long later, the couple head to Huntsville planning to marry; they prepare to do so, obtaining a license and intending to visit a justice of the peace. But, when they are parked in the car, Munro moves ahead to an interaction between Alister and another man, who interrupts them when they are talking—rather, when he is telling her something. "What he was saying then had been terrible but his tight grip on the wheel, his grip and his abstraction and his voice had pain in them. No matter what he said and meant, he spoke out of the same deep place then, that he spoke from when he was in bed with me" (*Dear Life* 61). Only then does Munro go back to what Alister actually said previously: "I can't do it, he has said. He has said that he can't go through with this. He can't explain it." Then, after telling her that he is going to take her to the station and put her on a train to Toronto, there is a "new tone in his voice, almost jaunty. A knockabout tone of relief. He is trying to hold that in, not let relief out till I am gone" (*Dear Life* 62).

Vivien watches from the station while waiting for the train, thinking that he might change his mind and return. He does not. While he has explained, she still wants to know why. She boards the train and happens to run into Mary, again raucous, this time with a group of teammates after a high school game riding back to Amundsen. She notices that Vivien is dressed up but does not especially care. A white-space break—both in the *New Yorker* and in *Dear Life*—and then, "For years I thought I might run into him. I lived, and still live, in Toronto. It seemed to me that everybody ended up in Toronto at least for a little while." "It finally happened. Crossing a crowded street where you could not even slow down. Going in opposite directions. Staring, at the same time, a bare shock on our time-damaged faces. He called out, 'How are you?' and I answered, 'Fine.' Then added for good measure, 'Happy.'" The narrator then writes that this was not, strictly speaking, true (*Dear Life* 65). Munro then focuses on that moment:

> It still seemed as if we could make our way out of that crowd, that in a moment we would be together. But just as certain that we would carry on the way we were going. And so we did. No breathless cry, no hand on my shoulder when I reached the sidewalk. Just that flash, that I had seen in an instant, when one of his eyes opened wider. It was the left eye, always the left, as I remembered. And it always looked so strange, alert and wondering, as if some whole impossibility had occurred to him, one that almost made him laugh.
>
> (*Dear Life* 66)

When the *New Yorker* version of this story ends, it is followed by "That was all. I went on home." A paragraph break, and then "Feeling the same as when I'd left Amundsen. The train dragging me, disbelieving. Nothing changes, apparently, about love" (69). Preparing the story for *Dear Life*, Munro made yet one more change in proofs; there is no "That was all," no mention of going home, but "[f]or me, it was the same as when I left Amundsen, the train dragging me still dazed and full of disbelief." Another paragraph break and then, in what appears to be consciously awkward phrasing, "Nothing changes really about love" (*Dear Life* 66).

Munro made reference to such chance meetings in two stories in *Too Much Happiness*, but such occasions are found also throughout her archival manuscripts. In the 1970s when she was writing the stories intended first for *Who Do You Think You Are?* but which ultimately found their way into *The Moons of Jupiter*, Munro had a notebook draft beginning "Crossing a street in Edmonton I met a man I hadn't seen for fifteen years. We didn't recognize each other immediately. We slowed, looked back, uttered names, then ran to one curb where we embraced" (38.12.1). They go inside for coffee and catch up; each is divorced and has done other things since years ago.[12] None of this in late-style "Amundsen." There it is a crucial moment recalled, balanced by the same sort of illuminated moment of seeing each other crossing the street, Vivien's realization that she has never lost her attraction to Alister.

When Ann Close sent Munro the copy-edited manuscript of *Dear Life*—her cover letter is undated but this would have been in spring 2012—she commented in passing that "Doug is worried about the reception of In Sight of the Lake, but as usual with one we worry about I think there will be a batch of people find it their favorite story." There too Close calls "In Sight of the Lake" a "heavily revised" story—she later told me that Munro had revised it eight times (November 10, 2021). First published in *Granta* early in 2012, it is an unusual story in *Dear Life* and in Munro's oeuvre generally. It begins, "A woman goes to her doctor to have a prescription renewed. But the doctor is not there. It's her day off" (*Dear Life* 217). But the story ultimately does an about face at its conclusion. The reader spends most of the story following this person's search for the office of the doctor she is seeking, even asking advice from a man she meets on the street in the strange town where she goes to find the doctor's office; he suggests that she try the nursing home out on the highway. This man, who "has come along one of the paths, carrying a pair of shears"—an echo from one of Munro's very early stories, "The Time of Death"—makes this suggestion and she follows it (*Dear Life* 224; *Dance* 98–9). When she finds the home and enters it, the whole narrative is undercut: this narrator is in fact a memory-afflicted patient in the home itself.

She gets into the building, finds no one, and when she tries to get out she cannot: "She opens her mouth to yell but it seems that no yell is forthcoming. She is shaking all over and no matter how she tries she cannot get her breath down into her lungs. It is as if she has a blotter in her throat. Suffocation." "Her heart is pounding but she is nearly safe." But after a white-space shift, a woman asks her, "'What are we going to do with you?' says Sandy. 'All we want is to get you into your nightie. And you go and carry on like a chicken that's scared of being et for dinner.' 'You must have had a dream,' she says. 'What did you dream about now?'" Nancy replies, "'It was back when my husband was alive and when I was still driving my car'" (*Dear Life* 232). So readers found her doing early in the story but now, as Munro makes clear, Nancy's life was indeed "*but a dream*," as Munro wrote to end "Chaddeleys and Flemings: 1. Connection" (*Moons* 18; original emphasis).

Of the three remaining 2012 stories in *Dear Life* yet to be considered here, two demonstrate Munro's recursive methods emphatically while also showing remembrance and history: "To Reach Japan" and "Train." The third, "Dolly," is important for its contextual effects in the structure of *Dear Life* while showing recursive elements too. "To Reach Japan" was first published in *Narrative* in January 2012. Just after it appeared I wrote to Ann Close about it—she was then in the early stages of assembling *Dear Life*—because I knew of and was watching for "Train" at *Harper's*. Since both stories feature train travel, I thought there may have been a change in title or perhaps a shift of serial publisher. Close replied that none of that was so. Confirming that there were two different stories, Close commented that she thought "To Reach Japan" to be "vintage Alice" and also wrote that "if we weren't calling the collection 'Dear Life,' we were going to call it 'To Reach Japan'" (January 30, 2012). It was selected to open *Dear Life*.

The story begins with a departure from Vancouver on a transcontinental train to Toronto. Greta and her young daughter Katy are seen off by Peter, Katy's father and Greta's husband, an engineer. She is a poet and so echoes Lydia, the focalized character in "Dulse" (*Moons*). Peter is traveling far up north on a summer job and Greta and Katy, for their part, are heading to Toronto for the summer to house sit (something Munro did herself in 1972). After setting this departure scene Munro leaves it, writing, "When Peter was a baby, his mother had carried him across some mountains whose name Greta kept forgetting, in order to get out of Soviet Czechoslovakia into Western

Europe." Peter's father "had been sent to a sanatorium" and "was to follow them when he could, but he died instead" (*Dear Life* 4). This background is as much about Peter's mother as it is about him, and then Munro shifts to a literary party Greta attended near the university—she had been invited because she had published in a Toronto magazine called *The Echo Answers*. There she drinks too much punch and meets a man, Harris Bennett, a journalist from Toronto. She is attracted to him (and he she) and accepts the ride home to North Vancouver he offers. They drive through the city and across the Lion's Gate Bridge. That is that.

Yet it is not. Greta subsequently longs for him: "During the coming fall and winter and spring there was hardly a day when she didn't think of him. It was like having the very same dream the minute you fell asleep." And "[s]he nearly wept with longing. Yet all this fantasy disappeared, went into hibernation when Peter came home. Daily affections sprang to the fore then, reliable as ever" (*Dear Life* 13). Once the summer's arrangements in Toronto are confirmed, Greta "found herself writing a letter. It didn't begin in any conventional way. No Dear Harris. No Remember Me." Instead:

> *Writing this letter is like putting a note in a bottle—*
> *And hoping*
> *It will reach Japan.*
> Nearest thing to a poem in some time.
>
> (*Dear Life* 14; original emphasis)

Munro returns to the train heading east with Greta and Katy aboard. Details of that mode of travel ensue; Greta and Katy meet a young couple, Greg and Laurie, whose work is entertaining preschool children—and they set about doing that for Katy. They have recently broken up a relationship; Laurie leaves the train in Jasper and Greg continues on to Saskatoon. After Laurie leaves, Greta and Greg drink together. With Katy sleeping in the berth beside them they begin intimacies and, pressing forward, they move to Greg's berth, leaving Katy sleeping in Greta's. She returns to find Katy gone and engages in a frantic search until she finds her sitting in the space between two rail cars.

Greta upbraids herself as a mother for this episode, but then Munro carries such self censure deeper, articulating Greta's immediate direction in life:

> Other thoughts had crowded the child out. Even before the useless, exhausting, idiotic preoccupation with the man in Toronto, there was the other work, the work of poetry that seemed that she had been doing in her head for most of her life. That struck her as a new traitorous business—to Katy, to Peter, to life. And now, because of the picture in her head of Katy alone, Katy sitting there amid the metal clatter between the cars—that was something else that she, Katy's mother, was going to have to give up.
>
> A sin. She had given her attention elsewhere. Determined, foraging attention to something other than the child. A sin.
>
> (*Dear Life* 28)

This is a passage of autobiographical recursion. Munro is remembering detail from her own transcontinental train trips east with her daughters (in 1956—the last time she saw her mother alive—with Sheila, in 1959 with Jenny too, and in 1971 she took them by train, sharing a room with her youngest daughter, then about five) (Thacker *Alice* 126-7, 235). She is doubtless embellishing in "To Reach Japan," yet at the center of this passage is Alice Munro, young mother, woman, and writer. The comment on poetry echoes this passage, quoted above, from "Miles City, Montana" where the narrator speaks of her "real work" as a process of "sort of wooing distant parts of myself" (*Progress* 88). So Munro still was doing in 2011 as she remembered and wrote "To Reach Japan," a story which is recursive and autobiographical. The story is set about 1960: "In the decade that they had already entered but that she at least had not taken much notice of, there was going to be a lot of attention paid to this sort of thing. Being there was to mean something that it didn't used to mean. Going with the flow" (*Dear Life* 20).

Anticipating the 1960s, a crucial time for Munro personally, "To Reach Japan" makes repeated returns to past autobiographical facts and texts. The party where Greta meets Harris Bennett is based on parties held then and there by Robert Weaver, literary producer for the CBC and editor of the *Tamarack Review*, which Munro attended. At that party Greta drinks "Pimm's No. 1 and grapefruit juice, downed in a hurry," for it was a hot day and she had just walked a distance (*Dear Life* 9). Munro drank the same thing with Ginger Barber at a party where the two met (Thacker *Alice* 310-11). Harris Bennett is based on a neighbor of the Munros' in West Vancouver, a journalist and the first professional writer she knew; she was attracted to him but said it did not go beyond flirting (Thacker interview June 2003). Peter's history is a more detailed version of Gabriel's in "Material." And, as already indicated, train travel east figured in the British Columbia years.

These echoes notwithstanding, when Munro came to write "To Reach Japan" what she was doing was less a reworking of old material than it was a fresh story which adds identifiable autobiographical details. Its ending, likely what Close was thinking of when she called it "vintage Alice," captures this late recursive technique. There is a design break just after Munro wrote, for the second time, "A sin" (*Dear Life* 28), and Munro shifts to describe Greta and Katy's arrival in Toronto's Union Station precisely; there "was summer thunder and lightning. Katy had never seen such commotion on the West Coast ...." Katy was concerned too, for Munro noted "the still greater, electrically lit darkness they encountered in the tunnel where the train stopped." Once they got into the terminal,

> There the people who had been walking in front of them began to peel off, to be claimed by those who were waiting, and who called out names, or who simply walked up and took hold of their suitcases.
>
> As someone now took hold of theirs. Took hold of it, took hold of Greta, and kissed her for the first time, in a determined and celebratory way.
> Harris.
> First a shock, then a tumbling in Greta's insides, an immense settling.

Katy pulls away from her mother's hand but "didn't try to escape. She just stood there waiting for whatever had to come next" (*Dear Life* 29–30).

However much this recursive late-style story reminds of other Munro stories and autobiographical details, this moment with Katy "waiting for whatever had to come next," is what "To Reach Japan" accomplishes: a breathing-space moment, perhaps an epiphany but certainly a moment of insight, in which all of these characters' lives are laid bare as they move into the future.

Among the novels Munro worked on from the later 1950s into the '60s was one called "The Boy Murderer." It features a character named Franklin coming home from the Second World War who jumps off the train before it gets to his hometown, Goldenrod. The archives reveal that Franklin and his circumstances became something of a continuing presence in Munro's writing then. No such novel ever emerged, but there is evidence that Franklin was present in some of the stories which appeared in *Dance,* in *Lives of Girls and Women*, and in *Who Do You Think You Are?* / *The Beggar Maid* (see, for examples, 37.10.42, 37.14.23.5, 37.14.24.1, 37.16.28, 37.13.28). There is also a scene involving this Franklin which anticipates the opening of "Miles City, Montana," and he figures as well in draft versions of "The Progress of Love" (see Thacker *Reading* 154–9).

Suffice to say, when Munro came to write "Train," she had been thinking about Franklin jumping off that train for some considerable time. When that story was included in *The Best American Short Stories 2013* Munro commented that it "examines a man's desire to avoid his past mistakes by essentially becoming someone new, someone in whom others can place trust and belief and even memories of loved ones now gone. To atone is so often to assume a new, cleaner identity. To attempt, of course, to begin again" (author comment 333). In it Jackson—not Franklin—jumps off the train coming home before he gets to his town and, immediately ascertaining his new surroundings after landing, wonders "What are you doing here? Where are you going? A sense of being watched by things you didn't know about. Of being a disturbance. Life around coming to some conclusions about you from vantage points you couldn't see" (*Dear Life* 177). Munro concentrates on action, sidestepping Jackson's motives for his leap, leaving those aside until later in the story. He wants to avoid Ileane, a special friend at home he has been corresponding with during the war, one who is awaiting his return at the station there. While they attempted sex just before he left, "It was a disaster" (*Dear Life* 213)—either because of Jackson's homosexuality or, equally possible, the sexual abuse he had suffered as a child from his stepmother. Ileane is avoided by Jackson's leap and, because of it, a new life ensues. He never does return to his hometown.

Just after, as Jackson starts to comprehend his new circumstances and his new life, he hears an unidentifiable sound along a nearby road:

> The road rose up a hill, and from over that hill came a clip-clop, clip-clop. Along with the clip-clop some little tinkle or whistling.
>
> Now then. Over the hill came a box on wheels, being pulled by two quite small horses. Smaller than the one in the field but no end livelier. And in the box sat a half dozen or so little men. All dressed in black, with proper black hats on their heads.

> The sound was coming from them. It was singing. Discreet high-pitched little voices, as sweet as could be. They never looked at him as they went by. That chilled him.
>
> (*Dear Life* 180)

Munro offers this image within Jackson's life as another talismanic moment, an image akin to the baby skunks at the end of "Pride." Here Jackson begins the new life Munro describes—living platonically there for seventeen years with a woman, Belle, whom he happens upon, making himself useful about the place, so that the pair are thought of locally as adult siblings. She is a character seen long before as Aunt Dodie in "The Ottawa Valley" and, Munro later reveals, is herself haunted by sex. In her case it was an incestuous attraction felt by her father, who then because of shame commits suicide by throwing himself before a train. Jackson ultimately abandons Belle to her fate when she is being treated in a Toronto hospital and begins another life there. He becomes the manager of an apartment house Munro calls the Bonnie Dundee—a poem by Sir Walter Scott and often a song. When Ileane very coincidentally emerges there from his past, he flees again, taking yet a different train north. On it, "He slept off and on during the night and in one of those snatches he saw the little Mennonite boys go by in their cart. He heard their small voices singing"; "In the morning he got off in Kapuskasing. He could smell the mills, and was encouraged by the cooler air. Work there, sure to be work in a lumbering town" (*Dear Life* 216). This story, replete again with the beginnings of a new life in a new place, is certainly based on the sort of coincidence Michiko Kakutani criticized when she reviewed *Too Much Happiness*. With her next story, "Dolly," Munro is again about to hang another story on a central coincidence. But plot coincidences are not the point within Munro's late style, as she said when she commented on "Train." Fleeing Toronto and his past for Kapuskasing still recalling in his dreams the attracting image of the Mennonite boys going by on their wagon, Jackson again leaves past mistakes behind. As Munro said, "To atone is so often to assume a new, cleaner identity." So she created Jackson first leaping from one train to avoid Ileane and, years later, arriving that morning in Kapuskasing on another train, having again avoided Ileane in Toronto. Munro also held that 'the desire to escape and rebuild is something I find interesting' (author comment 333).

When "Dolly" first appeared in *Tin House* in 2012 it had a very different ending than it has in the book version—the narrator describes herself as "a perfectly ordinary and savage woman," and the final paragraph reads "That made me think about the conversation we'd had earlier in the fall and our notion of being beyond all savagery and elation" (80). That ending is more abrupt than that found in *Dear Life*, itself more equivocal and in keeping with other and more balanced endings in late Munro. In the *Tin House* version too, the protagonist's name is Jackson, though the two Jacksons do not seem to be the same man. This duplication pointed out, Munro aptly enough changed the name of the man in "Dolly" to Franklin.

"Dolly" owes to Munro's life with Gerald Fremlin in Clinton between 1975 and 2013, when he died. "That fall there had been some discussion of death," the book version begins. "Our deaths. Franklin being eighty-three years old and myself seventy-one at the time, we had naturally made plans for our funerals (none) and for the burials (immediate) in a plot already purchased. We had decided against cremation, which was popular with our friends. It was just the actual dying that had been left out or up to chance" (*Dear Life* 233). While biographical specifics are a bit off here, the general outline is one consistent with Fremlin and Munro's circumstances as the 2010s began; Fremlin was older, had served overseas during the war, and returned and went to university where he published some poetry—all details consistent with Franklin. Also, they had been living together for some time and, given age and infirmity, were certainly aware of mortality. They had also purchased a cemetery plot.

Beyond anticipation of death, the story begins also with the two thinking about a suicide pact—they find a suitable out-of-the-way road where they might park, commit suicide, and expect their bodies to be discovered in good time. In early drafts this pact is a framing device, but in the published versions the frame is not closed. The narrator realizes that her life with Franklin is still being lived. The "discussion of death," Munro makes clear, seems to foreshorten the realities of ongoing life—what in the *Tin House* version she calls "our notion of being beyond all savagery and elation." Before this the narrator comments that "it had seemed as if we had gotten time back, as if there was all the time in the world to suffer and complain" (80).

The plot—with the narrator and Franklin coincidentally running across a former girlfriend of his from the war years, Dolly, and, as it moves forward, the narrator misapprehending his feelings and actions toward her and about her, so much so that the narrator flees their home for a bit out of jealousy—is less of the moment in "Dolly" than their reaction to that plot. It is when the narrator returns home to find Dolly gone to North Bay to live with a daughter she comments in the *Tin House* version that she "was a perfecting ordinary and savage woman" (80). This phrasing was dropped for *Dear Life* but the scene toward the end in which Franklin "put his arms around me, lifted me down from the chair" from which she was replacing just-washed jars is critical. "'We can't afford rows,' he said. No indeed. I had forgotten how old we were, forgotten everything. Thinking that there was all the time in world to suffer and complain" (*Dear Life* 253). Both versions of this scene end with the narrator's attention shifting to the key she had shoved through the mail slot when she left, and that leads to her thinking about the denouncing letter that she had mailed—another letter, as in "Wenlock Edge." She acknowledges that she needs to intercept it:

> Supposing I should die before it came? You can think yourself in reasonable shape and then die, just like that. Ought I to leave a note for Franklin to find, just in case?
>
> If a letter comes addressed to you from me, tear it up.
>
> The thing was, he would do what I asked. I wouldn't, in his place. I would rip it open, no matter what promises had been made.
>
> He'd obey.
>
> What a mix of rage and admiration I could feel, at his being willing to do that. It went back though our whole life together.
>
> (*Dear Life* 253–4)

So "Dolly" ends in *Dear Life*.[13] About a year after the book's publication, Close commented on the story in a way that exactly captures its intentions and meanings: "'Dolly, as I read it now, is a story about the persistence of love in all its "savagery and elation," as she said in one version. Even as they grew older that passion remained (September 4, 2013).[14] That is just what Munro constructs here; that is what she presumably felt for Fremlin throughout their years together; that is what growing old together in such a relationship means.

Whatever the personal experiences which led to the story's imagined situations, Munro in publishing "Dolly" at age eighty-one offers an assertion that life, with its vicissitudes, is the same, it continues on, until it does not. Munro thus ends the story placed just before the "Finale" of *Dear Life* with a sharp, even caustic, image of herself as she was entering her ninth decade. That one is followed, as the reader moves to the "Finale" after reading Munro's author's note presenting those "*not quite stories*," to what is her ultimate recursion: four pieces linked by her return to herself as she was as a child and as a young girl (*Dear Life* 255; original emphasis). Set when she was living at the family fur farm along the Maitland River—her essential recursive ruminative place where, as she wrote in 1974 just after she had returned to Ontario, "everything here is touchable and mysterious." Those four stories, however "*not quite*," end *Dear Life* and so end Munro's career as a writer. As she wrote for the online interview about *Dear Life* just as it was being published, "the last things in the new book were all simple truth" (Treisman interview).

6

"Simple Truth": "Too Much Happiness" and the "Finale" to *Dear Life*

> *When my mother was dying, she got out of the hospital somehow, at night, and wandered around town until someone who didn't know her at all spotted her and took her in. If this were fiction, as I said, it would have been too much, but it is true.*
>
> *("Dear Life," New Yorker 47)*
>
> *... ... .*
> *I have never kept diaries. I just remember a lot and am more self-centered than most people.*
> *My mother, I suppose, is still a main figure in my life because her life was so sad and unfair and she was so brave, but also because she was determined to make me into the Sunday-school-recitation little girl I was, from the age of seven or so fighting not to be.*
> *I have used bits and pieces of my own life always but the last things in the new book were all simple truth.*
> *As was—I should have said this—The View from Castle Rock, the story of my family as much as I could tell.*
>
> *(Treisman interview)*

This initial epigraph ended "Dear Life" when it was first published in September 2011 but, as that piece was revised to become the last of the four stories in the "Finale" to Munro's final collection, *Dear Life*, it was deleted. The penultimate paragraph in the *New Yorker* now ends the book with these two sentences: "We say of some things that they can't be forgiven, or that we will never forgive ourselves. But we do—we do it all the time" (*Dear Life* 319). Asked about this omission after the book appeared in 2012 Munro commented that she decided it better not to introduce anything so harrowing just as she and her readers reached the end. Ann Close agreed (Thacker interview September 2013; Close email September 17, 2013). Yet Anne Chamney Laidlaw's winter escape from the hospital in very early 1959 first appeared in "The Peace of Utrecht" in 1960 and, in 2002, during celebrations for the dedication of the Alice Munro Garden in Wingham on Munro's seventy-first birthday, the woman who took her mother in that night approached Munro directly to ensure that she knew just what had happened (see Thacker *Alice* 149). As ever, Munro's mother "looms too close, just as she always did" (*Something* 246). Throughout Munro's work, versions of her mother, healthy or infirm, are readily present. When I first read a *New Yorker* proof of "Dear Life" in August 2011 prior to its publication—as "personal history"—I recognized what was there but, like everyone, I did not yet know that "Dear Life" would prove to be Munro's final published version of her mother and, as well and more pointedly, of herself.[1]

Heading the "Finale" to *Dear Life*, Munro wrote that "*The final four works in this book are not quite stories. They form a separate unit, one that is autobiographical in feeling, though not, sometimes, entirely so in fact*" (*Dear Life* 255; original emphasis). Two essential points from what Munro wrote here: together, they are a unit and the material is autobiographical—at least in feeling if not in fact. Presenting the stories in the "Finale" as such, Munro continues a practice which began with *The Love of a Good Woman*—from that collection on she included a long piece in each book. This practice is a feature of Munro's late style. These longer pieces, replete with breadth of treatment and singular imaginative range, encapsulate that late style. No more so than in the last two books, "Too Much Happiness" a major story, the "Finale" a gathering of four stories, each placed to anchor its volume.

"Too Much Happiness": "Sheets of Clear Intelligence, a Transforming Glass"

"Too Much Happiness" demands separate examination because of its length and unusual subject matter. The story—or novella, as it was presented by *Harper's* when first published in August 2009—was composed just after *The View from Castle Rock* amid the mix of the other stories in *Too Much Happiness*, likely in the autumn of 2006 or during early 2007. On July 30, 2007, Munro sent a largely complete manuscript copy of it to Barber, writing "So—I thought I'd send you this totally unplaceable piece—also went to Doug & Ann & I will send it to Jennifer even though its quite unsaleable due to the fact it is a) not fiction, b) not verifiable biography but c) a mixture of both & I don't even know if this is *legal*" (2015.062.1.4; original emphasis). It was then titled "By the Danish Islands," but by November 2007 Walsh submitted it to the *New Yorker*, along with "Free Radicals," as "Too Much Happiness" (*New Yorker* files). They took "Free Radicals" though not "Too Much Happiness."[2] Munro's uncertainties about the story are genuine, and they define the audacity of her project. She had done similar things before with distant historical materials, but in "Too Much Happiness," by taking up the life of the well-known mathematician and writer Sophia Kovalevsky, Munro steps into another sphere altogether.

Monika Lee has called the story a "precise but non-linear novella," noting that Munro said *Too Much Happiness* "would be her last book" and that "one way of reading the concluding novella would be to see it as a possible coda or literary epitaph to her writing career, with the prodigiously talented and heartbroken Sophia Kovalevsky as a stand-in of sorts for the talented but misunderstood Munro" (389, 391). While I very much doubt this reading's conclusion—that Munro was drawn to Kovalevsky because she felt "misunderstood" herself—Lee finds parallels between the two which Munro doubtless recognized as she was drawn into Kovalevsky's world and biography. Stating that Munro was attracted to that world because the story "explores mathematics as metaphor," Lee treats Kovalevsky's biography, and her mathematical and literary work too, arguing for what she calls "Munro's partial differential narrative technique" (394). Or, as Duffy writes, here Munro "emerges as a producer of multivalent narrative, in which the factual and the imaginative exist within an equivalency" (377).

When "Too Much Happiness" was first published, and then again in the book version, Munro included an acknowledgment outlining how she came upon Kovalevsky by chance and explaining that the "combination of novelist and mathematician immediately caught my interest, and I began to read everything about her I could find. One book enthralled me beyond all others, and so I must record my indebtedness, my immense gratitude, to the author of *Little Sparrow: A Portrait of Sophia Kovalevsky* (Ohio University Press, 1983), Don H. Kennedy, and his wife, Nina, a collateral descendent of Sophia's, who provided quantities of texts translated from the Russian, including portions of Sophia's diaries, letters, and numerous other writings" (*Harper's* 72, *Happiness* 307). Beyond its evident sincerity, this explicit acknowledgment of the Kennedys' book both points readers to it and encourages comparison of the two texts—in fact, the price of used copies bumped up after Munro's story appeared.[3] Thus various passages in Munro's story—and numerous factual details—may also be found in the Kennedys' biography. While I have argued that Munro's decision to write a story set in late-nineteenth-century Europe may have been in some sense an assertive response to the tepid critical reception *Castle Rock* got, with some critics complaining of the narrowness of Munro's Huron County world, the place of "Too Much Happiness" in her oeuvre is more complicated (see Thacker *Alice* 544–7, *Reading* 227–30). That Munro, whose reading and interest in Russian literature go back to her high-school and university days, who has referred to it in her own writing, and who was famously dubbed by Cynthia Ozick during the late 1980s as "our Chekhov," would be drawn to Sophia Kolvalevsky is not surprising. And Kovalevsky, a woman who knew such people as Dostoevsky (who once proposed to her sister), Turgenev, and Ibsen, was doubtless of interest. "Sophia did not become a close friend" of Ibsen's, the Kennedys write, "but did penetrate his austere exterior to the warm and gentle man within. She of course agreed with the themes of his famous plays. It was Ibsen who advised [Kovalevsky's friend and coauthor] Anna Charlotte [Leffler], when in later years he learned she was writing her recollections of Sophia that the latter could only be depicted in a highly poetic manner" (Kennedy 273). So for "Too Much Happiness," Munro reshapes and retells this story by way of her own researches and understandings. Coupled with Kovalevsky's biography and literary aspirations, there were her accomplishments as a significant mathematician: describing her reception in Paris in December 1888 when she accepted the Bordin prize from the French Academy of Science, the Kennedys write that by it "she received the highest scientific recognition ever accorded a woman to that day, and for long after" (Kennedy 288).

These and other borrowings can be seen throughout "Too Much Happiness." The epigraph quotation from Kovalevsky with which Munro opens, which asserts that mathematics is a science which "*requires great fantasy*," is taken from an 1890 letter quoted in *Little Sparrow* (*Happiness* 247; original emphasis; Kennedy 264). Beginning the text of the story proper and the first of its five sections, Munro writes:

> On the first day of January, in the year 1891, a small woman and a large man are walking in the Old Cemetery, in Genoa. Both of them are around forty years old. The woman has a childishly large head, with a thicket of dark curls, and her expression is eager, faintly pleading. Her face has begun to look worn. The man is immense. He weighs 285 pounds, distributed over a large frame, and being Russian, he is often referred to as a bear, also as a Cossack. At present he is crouching over tombstones and writing in his notebook, collecting inscriptions and puzzling over abbreviations not immediately clear to him, though he speaks Russian, French, English, Italian, and has an understanding of classical and medieval Latin.
>
> (*Happiness* 247; see Stillman 35, Kennedy 310)[4]

She continues with this overview description of Maxsim Maxsimovich Kovalevsky for several lines and, at its conclusion, tells the reader that "The woman with him is also a Kovalevsky. She was married to a distant cousin of his, but is now a widow" (*Happiness* 248).

With this, Munro shifts to an interchange between the two, with the woman speaking to the man "teasingly," saying, "You know that one of us will die," she says. 'One of us will die this year.' Only half listening, he asks her, Why is that?': "'Because we have gone walking in a graveyard on the first day of the New Year.'" This folk belief seems news to him, but she asserts that she had known about it since "'before I was eight years old.'" He says that girls get such notions from "kitchen maids" but "boys in the stables" do not hear such things and she asks, "'Boys in the stables do not hear about death?'" He thinks not. Then to close the opening text of this scene—a white-space break follows—Munro writes, "There is snow that day but it is soft. They leave melted, black footprints where they've walked" (*Happiness* 248). Thus readers begin in a cemetery, immersed in an imagined and developed recreation of a scene she found described in *Little Sparrow*, at least, and perhaps elsewhere.

In a cemetery reading tombstones, death, black footprints in the snow. The narrative of "Too Much Happiness" begins in a manner consistent with Munro's late style. Through its story and affect as well as her acknowledged use of mortality, such concerns seem to be accelerating. "People are curious," Munro has her narrator in "Meneseteung" write in the penultimate paragraph there, herself a curious person putting together the imagined story of the poet Almeda Joynt Roth in many of the same ways as this more extended treatment of Kovalevsky. "A few people are," she continues: "They will be driven to find things out, even trivial things. They will put things together. You see them going around with notebooks, scraping the dirt off gravestones, reading microfilm, just of the hope of seeing this trickle in time, making a connection, rescuing one thing from the rubbish" (*Friend* 73). Duffy's excellent analysis of "Too Much Happiness" as narrative historicism details its precise links to "Meneseteung," a story Munro wrote as she was concurrently embarking on the research trajectories which led to *The View from Castle Rock*.

In that book readers see Munro, like her characters here, in a succession of cemeteries in Scotland and Ontario seeking the remains of her people. Besides her family researches there, Munro may also be seen then embarked on other investigations of her own choosing, her own interest, as she discovers the history of the crypt in Sullivan Township in Grey County, Ontario in "What Do You Want to Know For?". She links these researches to her own life there—driving and looking about with Fremlin amid a very real health scare which portends her own end—as she discovered that history. And after all the reconstructive work required for *Castle Rock*, here at the beginning of "Too Much Happiness" Munro returns to a cemetery, far away in space and time, as she begins another excavation: that of the end of Sophia Kovalevsky's life in Stockholm in February 1891. The Kennedys, she acknowledges, tell a far broader version of this story in *Little Sparrow*. Taking often from their story, Munro creates her own late version, an amalgam, as she told Barber in 2007, "a mixture of both" fact and fiction. For Munro in "Too Much Happiness," the Kennedys provide the skeleton story she shapes and tells.

In their epilogue, the Kennedys pose three central questions about Kovalevsky that they had endeavored to answer: "Was she happy? Did she contribute to knowledge? Did her life benefit others?" They proceed to answer these questions, writing that "Sophia experienced less than a reasonably happy life. When at the end she exclaimed, 'Too much happiness,' seemingly she meant that the happiness she believed she had found at last was being snatched away, as though she did not really deserve it" (Kennedy 318).

Beginning with the fantasy Kovalevsky saw in mathematics in her epigraph, rooting it in the cemetery scene featuring Maxsim's concentration on its gravestones, Munro offers a succession of images to wonder over at the beginning of "Too Much Happiness." The folk belief Sophia teases Maxsim about, that one of them will die that year, coupled with the black footprints they leave in the snow, opens the way into Munro's multivariant narrative in which mathematics is a metaphor, a fantastic metaphor for being itself. Shaping the historical information she found, imaginatively filling in gaps and creating scenes like this, Munro may be seen quite within the throes of her late style. Death and mortality are at its very core.

So too the placement of the story or novella, "Too Much Happiness," within the book itself. When she described pulling the collection together—specifically, arranging its stories—Close commented that Munro wanted to open it with "Dimensions" and, when then she first read "Too Much Happiness," she said, "[I]t had to be at the end; it was too long a story and too important." Then there was "Wood." Munro and her editors decided, once they had agreed to include the oft-revised story, that "Wood" was best placed just before "Too Much Happiness." This left it—a normative Huron County Munro story, certainly—introducing a long story, a novella, as far distant from Huron and Ontario as Munro had ever been, really. And as has been noted and will be detailed below, this relation presaged the comparable effects created too in *Dear Life* by the placement of "Dolly."

Following the imagined though historically grounded scene in the cemetery on New Year's Day, after a white-space break, Munro turns to the couple's meeting and to the blossoming relationship they began in Stockholm, where Sophia Kovalevsky was the first woman to hold a chair in mathematics at a European university. Detailing this time, when she "was so sure of herself then, and especially sure of him," Munro turns again to poetry:

She wrote a description of him to a friend, borrowing from De Musset.

> *He is very joyful, and at the same time very gloomy—*
> *Disagreeable neighbor, excellent comrade—*
> *Extremely light-minded, and yet very affected—*
> *Indignantly naïve, nevertheless very blasé—*
> *Terribly sincere, and at the same time very sly.*

The recipient of these lines was Anna-Charlotte Leffler, and they are quoted as here in Kovalevsky's letter. She was describing Maxsim and, after quoting De Musset, she wrote, "And a real Russian, he is, into the bargain" (*Happiness* 249; original emphasis; Kennedy 282). Writing still to this friend Kovalevsky confesses further in Munro's story that she has "'never been so tempted to write romances, as with Fat Maxsim.' And, 'He takes up too much room, on the divan and in one's mind. It is simply impossible for me, in his presence, to think of anything but him'" (*Happiness* 249; Kennedy 281). The Kennedys make it clear that Kovalevsky was "madly in love with an elusive Russian," that she was seeking during this time "love again and glory, too," that she was "distracted by her thoughts of Maxsim," and "she could neither live with Maxsim nor without him" (Kennedy 274, 279, 301). While Munro makes it clear that the relationship was not altogether serene, the Kennedys describe and point up disagreements between the two. Once when they were together and Maxsim "was 'nervous and quite unbearable,'" so Kovalevsky wrote to a Mr. H. in Berlin—only his initial is known—that even so "'Here everything is so astonishingly beautiful that, contrary to the poet, one always thinks—happiness is where we are'" (Kennedy 306).

These remembrances of complete infatuation are overshadowed by Kovalevsky's awareness that "[t]his was at the very time when she should have been working day and night, preparing her submission for the Bordin Prize" in mathematics which, even so, she would ultimately win. "Two triumphs—her paper ready for its last polishing and anonymous submission, her lover growling but cheerful, eagerly returned from his banishment and giving every indication, as she thought, that he intended to make her the woman of his life." But this was not to be: "The Bordin Prize was what spoiled them." Having won it, Kovalevsky accepted its accolades and while "she was basking Maxsim decamped" (*Happiness* 249, 250). "He had felt himself ignored," Munro writes (*Happiness* 250).

She is taking directly from *Little Sparrow* to shape materials there into the version of Kovalevsky's last days, infused with deep retrospection about the latter's own past life and circumstances. Describing her relations with Maxsim then, the Kennedys write that he was "a wary bachelor," that "he expected an affair, whereas she aimed at marriage" (Kennedy 283). So Munro's subject here is also the relations between men and women then; because of Kovalevsky's abilities in mathematics, she is seen as "an utter novelty, a delightful freak, the woman of mathematical gifts and female timidity, quite charming, yet with a mind most unconventionally furnished, under her curls." Having left for his own estate, Maxsim wrote "cold and sulky apologies" and "at the end of his letter one terrible sentence"—a paragraph break, then: "'If I loved you I would have written differently'" (*Happiness* 250–1). Maxsim wrote the very sentence Munro highlights here when, after she learned of the Bordin prize, she took a leave from Stockholm in hope of a chair in France. Criticizing her at this news and self-justifying, he also wrote, "'You have written me many stupid things, unjust and undeserved reproaches, and generally have disclosed yourself to be, in the fullest sense of the word, a woman.'" French promises are not to be believed, he maintains, and "'In view of this, thinking that the expectation of a mutual life was a deciding factor for you, I preferred to disappear temporarily. My advice to you now—return to Stockholm where your little daughter lives and where your friends are waiting.'" Maxsim follows this with the "one terrible sentence" Munro notes. The Kennedys then assess his attitude: "Her mathematical glory meant little. She had been rejected as a person. She who had expected devotion, while holding much of herself in her own keeping, had been abandoned" (Kennedy 289–90).

Thus drawing on *Little Sparrow* and other sources to create a narrative in which Kovalevsky's life from her girlhood to its end is recalled while, concurrently, Kovalevsky returns to Stockholm in the present, Munro examines that life through focalized retrospection and through her character's movements. Memories of her significant relations are told: with her sister and her parents, the circumstances of her "white marriage" to Vladimir Kovalevsky so as to be allowed as a woman to leave Russia and study abroad, that study and her growing reputation as a mathematician, her return to Russia and the birth of her daughter, her sister and brother-in-law's deep involvement in the revolutionary work of the French Commune, her husband's difficulties and eventual suicide. And while Munro does not dwell on them, there are references to Kovalevsky's published writings, her fiction, memoir, and reviews too.[5] All these recollections are interleaved smoothly, almost serenely, as the narrative of "Too Much Happiness" proceeds, deepening the sense of Sophia Kovalevsky's biography and being.

The opening scene in the Genoa cemetery is followed by another visit with Maxsim at his estate in France, during which the lovers get back to harmony and decide to marry in the spring. That determined, it is followed by an account of Kovalevsky's return journey by train and ferry to Stockholm, with stops in Paris and Berlin but, owing to a perceived threat of a smallpox epidemic there, she is warned off her original itinerary by a doctor she meets on the train, so she does not go through Copenhagen. That journey creates the arc of "Too Much Happiness." The first visit in Paris is primarily to her dead sister Aniuta's husband and their son while the second, in Berlin, is with her mentor, Karl Theodore William Weierstrass, and with his two sisters, Clara and Elisa. As she embarks on this trip, accompanied by Maxsim from Nice to Cannes, Sophia still wonders about his commitment to marry. This is so, even though "[s]he has already written to Julia," a friend she lived with in Berlin when they were students, "saying that it is to be happiness after all. Happiness after all. Happiness." This passage is followed by a white-space break and, tellingly, the next text begins "On the station platform a black cat obliquely crosses their path. She detests cats, particularly black ones. But she says nothing and contains her shudder." Parting in Cannes, he "kisses her with decorum but with a small flick of his tongue along her lips, a reminder of private appetites." This scene is entirely imagined by Munro. Just after it she finishes the first section of the story—which concerns itself most with the relationship with Maxsim as an instance of the relations between men and women then—with this detail once the two have parted: "At least she has time now to discover that she has a sore throat. If he has caught it she hopes he will not suspect her" (*Happiness* 254, 255).

This sore throat, which is referred to during the balance of Kovalevsky's journey back to Stockholm, bodes personal threat. First mentioned amid references to the black cat and her contained shudder, "Happiness after all," and the uncertain status of her relations with Maxsim, whom she thinks is "Spoiled and envious, actually" (*Happiness* 255), this scene ends the first of the story's five sections with a direction confirmed but also with much uncertainty. The second section takes up the stop in Paris to visit her sister's husband and son, neither of whom receives her warmly. Rudely criticizing her in various ways and telling her that "being a mathematician isn't necessary" when he accompanies her to the train, the nephew Uray takes the money she gives him nonetheless:

> Then he thanked her, hurriedly, as if this was against his will.
>
> She watched him go and thought it was quite likely she would never see him again. Aniuta's child. And how like Aniuta he was, after all. Aniuta disrupting almost every family meal in Palibino [her parents' family estate] with her lofty tirades. Aniuta pacing the garden paths, full of scorn for her present life and faith in her destiny which would take her into some entirely new and just and ruthless world.
>
> Urey might change his course; there was no telling. He might even come to have some fondness for his aunt Sophia, though probably not till he was as old as she was now, and she long dead.
>
> (*Happiness* 265–6; see Kennedy 296)

Mortality once more.

While in Paris too Kovalevsky sees another mathematician, Jules Poincaré, who complained "about the behavior of the mathematician Weierstrass, Sophia's old mentor, who had been one of the judges for the king of Sweden's recent mathematical prize. Poincaré had indeed been awarded the prize, but Weierstrass had seen fit to announce that there were possible errors in his—Poincaré's—work that he, Weierstrass, had not been given time to investigate" (*Happiness* 259). Although Sophia feigns ignorance about this academic dispute to Poincaré, she had actually sent a letter to Weierstrass teasing him about it and it illustrates a comment Urey makes. Probing her nephew's aspirations—he wants only to call out the stations on a bus, she is disappointed to discover—he remarks too that professors of mathematics concern themselves only with "getting prizes and a lot of money for things nobody understands or cares about and that are no use to anybody" (*Happiness* 265). Placating Poincaré, promising to discuss the matter with Weierstrass when she sees him in Berlin, Sophia continues:

> "And after all," she said to Jules, "after all you do have the prize and will have it forever."

> Jules agreed, adding that his own name would shine when Weierstrass would be forgotten.
> Every one of us will be forgotten, Sophia thought but did not say, because of the particular sensibilities of men—particularly of a young man—on this point.
>
> (*Happiness* 260)

Mortality once more, indeed more than that, oblivion, this time enmeshed in the petty concerns of academic judgments. But what really resonates in this passage is the word "forgotten" in the last sentence: that is the word Munro substitutes in her rendering of de la Mare's "Away" in "Face," making "Your place left vacant"—as it appears in the *Collected Poems*—into "Your place forgotten" in submitted manuscripts and in the Canadian edition of *Too Much Happiness*.

This substitution and repetition is not accidental. Here I have noted textual breaks within *Too Much Happiness*. Ailsa Cox, in an excellent discussion of Munro's late style in that book, writes of her "fragmentary paragraphs" and connects the "use of dreams, hallucinations, and other altered states" in the title story to other historical fictions Munro has done; "Too Much Happiness," though, is "less speculative than ["Meneseteung" or "Carried Away"], a fictional reconstruction that seems to follow the documentary evidence." They key to this style, this story, and indeed to this book, Cox argues effectively, is that Munro "presents time as a continuum, a seamless flow of experience" (278, 279).⁶ As Duffy maintains, Munro "produces narrative, period" (377). This is, quite in fact, just how Munro creates and maintains Kovalevsky's character and story in "Too Much Happiness." Speaking to Poincaré in Paris over his venal reaction to Weierstrass' comment surrounding the Swedish prize, thinking quite truthfully that "every one of us will be forgotten," Kovalevsky echoes de la Mare's poem within the reading field which is *Too Much Happiness* as narratives follow one another. Munro creates this sense just as her reader's apprehension of the doom towards which Kovalevsky was then traveling was becoming more acute within this narrative.

Leaving Paris for Berlin and her final visit to Weierstrass, Kovalevsky ruminates over past times there as the train leaves the station "with the usual groans and clatter," recalling

> How she used to love Paris. Not the Paris of the Commune where she had been under Aniuta's excited and sometime incomprehensible orders, but the Paris she had visited later, in the fullness of her adult life, with introductions to mathematicians and political thinkers. In Paris, she proclaimed, there is no such thing as boredom or snobbishness or deception.
>
> (*Dear Life* 267)

Here two moments are juxtaposed, her intellectual growth and potential achieved. Yet, Kovalevsky continues to think of her experience caustically; after a white-space break, Munro writes "Then they had given her the Bordin Prize, they had kissed her hand and presented her with speeches and flowers in the most elegant lavishly lit rooms. But they had closed their doors when it came to giving her a job. They would no more think of that than of employing a learned chimpanzee" (*Happiness* 267). With an echo of the first paragraph of her story "Material," Munro then details the assessments made by the wives of the male academics to differentiate between Kovalevsky's actual accomplishment and how she was assessed by others then. She thinks that her social standing among such women will be increased once she becomes "wife of a rich and clever and an accomplished man into the bargain" (*Happiness* 267, 268).

Before she reaches Berlin, her train's progress slowed by snow, Kovalevsky "thinks of the Weierstrass house, where she will sleep tonight" and recalls her first arrivals there, meeting Weierstrass' sisters and being appraised as a possible student.[7] Doubtful of her abilities, he sets a series of problems which, to his surprise, she brings back a week later with the correct answers. Still doubtful, thinking this may be someone else's work, Weierstrass demands step-by-step explanations from this girl in a bonnet, which in her enthusiasm she takes off and puts on the floor, displaying a head of curls. As she does, he hid "as well as he could his astonishment, especially at solutions whose methods diverged most brilliantly from his own" (*Dear Life* 271).

What Munro is doing here is precisely detailing the qualities which Weierstrass then discovered in Kovalevsky, those personal and intellectual attributes which both defined her as a potential brilliant mathematician and, given the mores of the Europe in the 1870s, uniquely set her apart from the woman of her time. In an extended passage, she gets right at Kovalevsky's being, intellectual abilities, and Weierstrass' comprehension of them. When he realizes the potential of the mind he has before him,

> He felt that he must soothe her, hold her carefully, letting her learn how to manage the fireworks in her own brain.
>
> All his life—he had difficulty saying this, as he admitted, being always wary of too much enthusiasm—all his life he had been waiting for such a student to come into this room. A student who would challenge him completely, who was not only capable of following the strivings of his own mind but perhaps of flying beyond them. He had to be careful about saying what he really believed—that there must be something like intuition in a first-rate mathematician's mind, some lightning flare to uncover what has been there all along. Rigorous, meticulous, one must be, but so must the great poet.
>
> When he finally brought himself to say all this to Sophia, he also said that there were those who would bridle at the very word, "poet," in connection with mathematical science. And others, he said, who would leap at the notion all too readily, to defend a muddle and laxity in their own thinking.
>
> (*Happiness* 271)

Here Munro offers a critical understanding—attributed to Weierstrass—one that recognizes the poetic in Kovalevsky's mathematical abilities, the stunning potential she has and is pursuing.

And in their meeting the next morning after her late arrival in Berlin and a night spent under the Weierstrass roof, Kovalevsky tells her mentor of changes in her life. They have not seen each other for some time, Munro maintains, but that is not necessarily so—she may have visited him en route to Beaulieu (Kennedy 309). She tells him of the death of her husband and her sister, of her coming marriage, and they speak of her literary works, which he has read. Weierstrass is lying abed ill, so Kovalevsky "entered the bedroom smiling at her luck, her coming freedom, her soon-to-be husband." Marrying Maxsim will free her from teaching, from being a professor. Thinking of her own happiness to come, seeing Weierstrass lying ill, she tells him that once married she will live in the south of France "and I shall be healthy there all the time and do all the more work." He wonders though, and she responds, "'*Mein Leiber*' … 'I order you, order you to be happy for me.'" They speak of her literary writings and Weierstrass confesses that "'Truly I sometimes forget that you are a woman. I think of you as—as a—' 'As a what?'" she asks, and he replies "'As a gift to me and to me alone.'" Holding back tears, Kovalevsky kisses him and makes her goodbyes to his sisters: "I will never see him again, she thought" (*Happiness* 279–81). By now, just over midway through "Too Much Happiness," the reader realizes that this will be so.

Thinking of Weierstrass as she makes her way to another train, Kovalevsky considers his situation further:

> Was his life, she thought, so much more satisfactory to contemplate than his sisters'?
>
> His name would last awhile, in textbooks. And among mathematicians. Not so long as it might have done if he had been more zealous about establishing his reputation, keeping himself to the fore in his select and striving circle. He cared more for the work than for his name, when so many of his colleagues cared equally for both.
>
> (*Happiness* 281–2)

Such a passage as this, written when Munro was in her mid-seventies, having been writing seriously and continually for over fifty years, resonates beyond Weierstrass and the specifics of Kovalevsky's life. Much the same might be said of Munro, who has always "cared more for the work than for [her] name," at least insofar as she has been a writer who as much as possible has lived quietly, avoiding rather than seeking out the limelight, focusing ever and always on her work.

Heading to her train, Kovalevsky thinks too of her writings, and Munro details them here within her character's sense that devoting herself to them—"Frivolity to him," Weierstrass—was a failure in his eyes. She recalls too as the fourth section begins that she had failed him before: after she had finished her doctorate she returned to Russia to live a frivolous life not focused on mathematics, living at her parents' estate. "She was too busy, wrapped up in more or less constant celebration" of various things, "but really, it seemed to be, a celebration of life itself": "She was learning, quite late, what many people around her appeared to have known since childhood—that life can be perfectly satisfying without major achievements" (*Happiness* 283). During this time Sophia and Vladimir ceased their previous relation and became a conventional couple; they had a daughter, Fufu, and each pursued activities intended to make money. She wrote "theatre reviews and popular science pieces for the papers," while he ceased teaching geology and took "a job in a company that produced naphtha from a petroleum spring," a company he had to invest in himself as a condition of the job (*Dear Life* 284, 285). These arrangements fail and lead to Vladimir's suicide amid a scandal and legal proceedings. Drawing upon the Kennedys' biography, Munro writes that Sofia "persuaded the magistrate hearing the case to proclaim that all the evidence showed Vladimir to have been gullible but honest" (*Happiness* 286).

With no money left, Weierstrass offered to take Kovalevsky in as a third sister (Kennedy 217). But at the same time his efforts to secure an academic position for her finally bore fruit, when "[t]he new University of Stockholm agreed to be the first university in Europe to take on a female mathematics professor" (*Happiness* 286). Accounting for these changes in Kovalevsky's life, Munro ends her fourth section with a clear image of Sophia setting off into her new life. Once more, her source is *Little Sparrow*, where she is described sailing across the Baltic Sea to Stockholm: "Warmly dressed against the sharp northern airs, she twice watched from the deck as the ship sailed into the setting sun, beyond which lay her future life" (Kennedy 221). Reshaped by Munro, this passage is expanded:

> Then she took a train once more from Moscow to Petersburg to travel to her new and much publicized—and no doubt deplored—job in Sweden. She made the trip from Petersburg by sea. The boat rode into an overwhelming sunset. No more foolishness, she thought. I am now going to make a proper life.
> She had not then met Maxsim. Or won the Bordin Prize.
>
> (*Happiness* 286–7)

This is the apex of "Too Much Happiness," an image on which the story hinges. Munro here reaches and describes the moment which Kovalevsky had worked toward on the trajectory which was her intellectual life. Heading to Stockholm to finally take up a position there, Kovalevsky has the resolve to be the mathematician she is capable of being. This was moment of resolve to make a "proper life" as she "rode into an overwhelming sunset," one in which there would be "[n]o more foolishness." A moment before her accolades as a mathematician and her romance with Maxsim: the life that she intends to pursue, taking each, acclaim and romance—as her life unfolded. Yet this resolve pursued, Maxsim described and the Bordin Prize won, Munro ends the fourth section with Kovalevsky now back on the train traveling from Berlin through Copenhagen to Stockholm, her throat aching.

Having created the contexts of Kovalevsky's situation, Munro has her on an "old and slow" train "after having said that last sad but relieved good-bye to Weierstrass." Beyond the trip itself, Munro has departed from *Little Sparrow* as her source and imagines its circumstances and details. She created a man across the aisle who strikes up conversation, offers her his newspaper, commiserates over "the fine driving snow" they see outside the train, and asks, "'You are going beyond Rostock?'". Munro then gives Kovalevsky's thoughts: "He might have noted an accent that was not German. She did not mind his speaking to her or coming to such a conclusion about her. He was a good deal younger than she, decently dressed, slightly deferential. She had a feeling that he was someone she had met or seen before" (*Happiness* 287). To his question, she replies with her route and he asks, "'Are you satisfied with Stockholm?'" Her response, "'I detest Stockholm at this time of year. I hate it,'" leads to the man's surprising reaction: "he smiled delightedly and began to speak in Russian." She wonders if he had picked up an accent and he explains, "'Not surely. Until you said what you did about Stockholm.' 'Do all Russians hate Stockholm?' 'No. No. But they say they hate. They hate. They love.' 'I should not have said it. The Swedes have been very good to me'" (*Happiness* 287–8).

Munro creates a delightful scene here, one reminiscent of her many meetings on trains and as in past instances this one fulfills a particular purpose. This man, this invented character, is a doctor who recognized Kovalevsky from newspaper photographs. Their continued exchanges are pleasant, but as they approach his destination the man becomes "more and more agitated." He then recommends the route by way of the Danish Islands because of a smallpox epidemic in Copenhagen, one which "'the authorities are trying to keep quiet.'" "'Do not look frightened. I am completely in my right mind.'" Kovalevsky is reminded of her husband Vladimir by this man, by "his beseeching care for her." At this point, as they part, the doctor holds out his hand giving her "a small tablet, saying, 'This will give you a little rest if you find the journey tedious'" (*Happiness* 289–90). This imagined figure is one seen before, since he echoes the shipboard doctor, Mr. Suter, whom Munro imagines delivering Isabel in *Castle Rock*.

What Munro creates in this late-style story, an admitted admixture of fiction and fact, and in this scene with the doctor in particular, is quite precisely the human condition. Fraught in numerous ways by her own hopes and intentions, her good-byes said and any future with Maxsim uncertain, Kovalevsky with her aching throat is journeying back to Stockholm toward her death. And because of Munro's artistry, the reader feels the weight of the journey itself. In the doctor with his "beseeching care," Kovalevsky finds the concern and support she seeks, and his advice that she travel "by the Danish Islands" offers solace along with the mysterious tablet he passes to her. Human connection, a cure, a better direction.

Yet as Kovalevsky journeys on this is not to be. The balance of her trip to Stockholm is difficult: a disgruntled ticket agent, language issues, ferries, trains delayed by snow, a porter who leaves her to carry her own bags in the rain because she does not have the correct currency. She barely makes her train to Stockholm but is helped aboard by a kind conductor. "Once saved, she began to cough. She was trying to cough something out of her chest. The pain and tightness out of her throat. But she had to follow the conductor to her compartment, and she was laughing with triumph in between spells of coughing. The conductor looked into a compartment where there were already some people sitting, then took her along to one that was empty." There is a white-space break here, and Munro continues: "He told her to sit down and save her breath. He went away and came back soon with a glass of water. As she drank she thought of the tablet that had been given to her, and took it with the last gulp of water. The coughing subsided. 'You must not do that again,' he said. 'Your chest is heaving. Up and down'" (*Happiness* 298).

Before the kind conductor leaves her she asks him if he had heard of smallpox in Copenhagen, and he replies in the negative with "a severe though courteous nod." Alone on the train, having taken the tablet the doctor gave her, she recognizes "the extraordinary feeling—the change of perception—which is rippling through her now." She thinks it might have been caused by the stresses of what just happened, her cough, her throat:

> But there is more, as if her heart could go on expanding, regaining its normal condition, and continuing after that to grow lighter and fresher and puff things almost humorously out of her way. Even the epidemic in Copenhagen could now become something like a plague in a ballad, part of an old story. As her own life could be, its bumps and sorrows turning into illusions. Events and ideas now taking on a new shape, seen through sheets of clear intelligence, a transforming glass.
>
> (Happiness 299)⁸

This is an extraordinary passage, focusing Kovalevsky's mind and imagination amid the effects of her journey and of the mysterious tablet the doctor gave her. More than that, the perspective here takes readers back to ballads, old stories, like those seen when Munro was herself just embarked on the Scottish investigations which led ultimately to *The View from Castle Rock*.

As I have said Cox writes about the "fragmentary paragraphs" that Munro uses in "Too Much Happiness," a succession of which, becoming smaller and smaller as the story winds to its end, follow just after the one I have just quoted whole. Thus here, with Kovalevsky still on the train feeling and looking through this "transforming glass," the aura created by the drug the doctor from Bornholm gave her, Munro describes a succession of her character's final "breathing spaces." Moments that most emphatically do "stand out."

Kovalevsky first recalls her discovery of trigonometry when she was twelve, when "she was able to break into this new and delightful language. She was not very surprised then, though intensely happy." "Mathematics," she thought, "was a natural gift, like the northern lights." At one point the Kennedys write of Weierstrass recognizing and responding to his duty to mathematics, and that is what Kovalevsky also recognizes here: mathematics "was not mixed up with anything else in the world, not with papers, prizes, colleagues, and diplomas." Awakened from sleep by the same conductor as the train nears Stockholm, Kovalevsky asks the day of the week and realizes that she may give her lecture. The conductor, as they part, tells her to "[t]ake care of your health, madam." She lectures well, "without any pain or coughing," attends a reception afterwards where she is sociable and, unable to get a cab, walks home in the snow. "Her feet were soaked but she was not cold. She thought this was because of the lack of wind, and the enchantment in her mind that she had never been aware of before, but could certainly count on from now on" (*Happiness* 299–300).

The next day Kovalevsky takes to her bed, a doctor is called and misdiagnoses her, she forgets to ask him about an epidemic going on in Copenhagen, and, when asked about her knowledge of it by her friend and colleague Mittag-Leffler, shows signs of confusion. Having slept, and now with named friends nursing her, "She talked about her novel, and about the book of recollections of her youth at Palibino." She planned for more writing, and "Her hope was that in this piece of writing she would discover what went on. Something underlying, invented, but not." Laughing at this, Kovalevsky is "overflowing with ideas" "of a whole new breadth and importance and yet so natural and self-evident that she couldn't help laughing." She sees her daughter Fufu one last time in the middle of the night. "Sophia could speak just a little. Teresa thought she heard her say, 'Too much happiness'" (*Happiness* 302).

This is followed by eight short paragraphs set off as sections by white-space gaps. Only one has two paragraphs; the others one. The last is a single sentence. So separated by breaks, these are quite fragmentary, just as Cox asserts. They account for Kovalevsky's death and autopsy, her burial, the wreath Weierstrass sent, Maxsim's impersonal speech at the funeral, his subsequent history, Fufu's later life, and this final sentence, a paragraph to end the story and to end the book: "Sophia's name has been given to a crater on the moon." Almost all of this may be found in *Little Sparrow*, cherished facts that Munro has taken to end her story and her book. The single imagined paragraph among the fragmentary concluding ones follows on from Munro's imagined character:

> The doctor from Bornholm read of her death in the newspaper, without surprise. He had occasional presentiments, disturbing to one in his profession, and not necessarily reliable. He had thought that avoiding Copenhagen might preserve her. He wondered if she had taken the drug he had given her, and if it had brought her solace, as it did, when necessary, to him.
>
> (*Happiness* 302–4)

It did, giving Kovalevsky solace and joy just when she was herself about to die. Ending "Too Much Happiness" and ending *Too Much Happiness*, the paragraphs taken from *Little Sparrow* are, just as Munro acknowledged when she sent a draft manuscript of "By the Danish Islands" to Barber, neither just fact nor just fiction, but a "mixture of both." Life that always ends: the cherished fact of mortality: "*Your place left vacant* [or *forgotten*],/*You not there*" (*Happiness* 164; Canadian edition 162; original emphasis).

"Stabbed to the Heart … By the Beauty of Our Lives Streaming By": Munro's Finale

In 1999 Munro published an essay, "Golden Apples," in *The Georgia Review*'s tribute issue on the occasion of Eudora Welty's ninetieth birthday. She begins by invoking the image of her own copies of Welty's books on her shelf; leaving them there but thinking about what they contain, Munro then "sat down to discover what bits of the stories would surface in my mind from all those pages I had read and reread. And so many things came crowding in … that I had to settle on one book, which happened to be the first book of hers that I ever read and the one that has turned out, finally, to be my favorite—*The Golden Apples*" (22). Munro then offers a succession of paraphrased incidents from that book, one made up of interconnected stories and first published in 1949, but then says "I have to stop." Continuing, she writes: "I stop not just because there's so much coming back to me, but because I am overwhelmed with a terrible longing. Stabbed to the heart, as Miss Kate Rainey or perhaps Miss Perdita Mayo would say, by the changes, the losses in our lives. By the beauty of our lives streaming by, in Morgana and elsewhere" (23). Rainey and Mayo are characters in *The Golden Apples*; Morgana, Mississippi is the mythic town where it is set.

Munro discovered and first read *The Golden Apples* during the mid-1950s in Vancouver, a difficult time for her as a writer: her daughters were young so finding time to write was a problem; at the behest of Robert Weaver at the CBC she had been trying to write a novel but the results were always unsatisfactory; she did not much like Vancouver or the neighborhood where she lived (see Thacker *Alice* 141–3). As she explains in the Welty essay, she discovered *The Golden Apples* in the West Vancouver public library and remembered "the quote on the cover, though I don't remember who had provided it: 'She writes exquisitely, she creates a world.'"[9] Munro demurs over the first part of this, "But 'creates a world'—that was more like it" (23). Recalling her discovery of the book within the memories of what she found there as a reader, Munro acknowledges knowing then that what she found Welty doing in *The Golden Apples* was exactly what she wanted to do with her own material: "The story must be imagined so deeply and devoutly that everything in it seems to bloom of its own accord and to be connected, then, to our own lives which suddenly, as we read, take on a hard beauty, a familiar strangeness, the importance of a dream which can't be disputed or explained. Everything is telling you: Stop. Hold on. Here it is. Here too. Remember" (24).

When she found Welty's book and, reading it, discovered its stories to be talismanic, Munro had already been remembering as the basis of her own work. She had written and published stories in which she may be seen creating a world herself ("The Time of Death," "Thanks for the Ride") yet, after her discovery of *The Golden Apples*, there was a shift toward more autobiographical remembrance as the basis of her stories. Munro found a ready outlet for these stories in *The Montrealer* where, between 1961 and 1965, she published five stories and a nonfiction essay—the stories all later included in *Dance of the Happy Shades*, her first book. By the time she was doing this, also, Munro had published "The Peace of Utrecht," the elegiac story based on the circumstances surrounding her mother's death (see Thacker *Alice* 150–4; "This" 17). The first of a succession in Munro's stories where Anne Chamney Laidlaw figures centrally. "Everything is telling you: Stop. Hold on. Here it is. Here too. Remember" (24). Just as Munro wrote in the late 1990s about Welty, just as she wrote then too about her own ongoing practice.

All of this is context: this section examines Munro's "Finale" in *Dear Life*, and in particular the final story, "Dear Life," through two prisms: through Munro's own trajectory as a writer as it has been defined here and, equally, through some of Welty's account of her own trajectory as a writer in *One Writer's Beginnings* (1984). *The View from Castle Rock* reveals Munro recalling and revisiting earlier stories, refashioning them to serve the imaginative and aesthetic needs of that later time in her life and career, complementing them with new stories, newly written and newly researched. Thus Munro's "Finale" is the culmination of a finale she had long been heading toward. The idea of the last four stories in *Dear Life* as a named "Finale" was Munro's alone, for it is both a finale to her last book and a finale to her entire career. And following what she appreciates in Welty, that career has been all about remembering.[10]

One Writer's Beginnings is made up of three sections, "I. Listening," "II. Learning To See," and "III. Finding a Voice." Welty dedicates the book "*To the Memory of My Parents*" to "Christian Webb Welty (1879–1931)" and "Chestina Andrews Welty (1883–1966)," two northerners—the one from Ohio, the other West Virginia, "Yankees"—who moved south to make a home and life together in Jackson, Mississippi ([v]; original emphasis). They had three children, Eudora and two younger brothers. The father died young while the mother lived on into her eighties.

"Learning to See" recounts the vacation the family took in 1917 or 1918—when Eudora was eight or nine—"in our five-passenger Oakland touring car on our summer trip to Ohio and West Virginia to visit the two families, my mother was the navigator. She sat at the alert all the way at Daddy's side as he drove, correlating the AAA Blue Book and the speedometer, often with the baby on her lap" (47). Remembering, recreating the trip in vivid detail, most especially with regard to each of her parents' personalities, Welty continues:

> I rode as a hypnotic, with my set gaze on the landscape that vibrated past at twenty-five miles an hour. We were all wrapped by the long ride into some cocoon of our own.
>
> The journey took about a week each way, and each day had my parents both in its grip. Riding behind my father I could see that the road had him by the shoulders, by the hair under his driving cap. It took my mother to make him stop. I inherited his nervous energy in the way I can't stop writing on a story. It makes me understand how Ohio had him around the heart, as West Virginia had my mother. Writers and travelers are mesmerized alike by knowing of their destinations.
>
> (48)

As she is about to conclude "Finding a Voice," Welty offers two salient passages; the first: "As we discover, we remember; remembering, we discover; and most intensely do we experience this when our separate journeys converge" (112). She then quotes a long passage from her novel *The Optimist's Daughter* (1972)—as *One Writer's Beginnings* makes clear, she is herself her father's "optimist's daughter"—which centers on a character's memory, a remembrance of realizing while looking out the window of a train while heading south to be married, that she is seeing for the first time the confluence of the Ohio and the Mississippi rivers at Cairo, Illinois. This is a literal great confluence which becomes a metaphorical one. After ending the quotation, Welty steps back and elaborates her meaning:

> Of course the greatest confluence of all is that which makes up the human memory—the individual human memory. My own is the treasure most dearly regarded by me, in my life and in my work as a writer. Here time, also, is subject to confluence. The memory is a living thing—it too is in transit. But during its moment, all that is remembered joins, and lives—the old and the young, the past and the present, the living and the dead.
>
> (113–14)

Welty is here referring to her own work and accounting for herself but, even so, what she says points readily to Munro and to her work from the late 1970s on.

The shift in distant memory is marked in *Dear Life* when a reader ends "Dolly" and moves to the book's—and Munro's—"Finale." This shift is something of a whiplash. The changed abrupt ending found in the first published version in *Tin House* sharply asserts that story's toward-the-end-of-life point of view. When that story appears in *Dear Life*, concluding just before the "Finale," the abrupt version is replaced by the narrator's serene assertion of "the rage and admiration" she feels toward her partner Franklin at his willingness to defer to her wishes: "It went back through our whole life together" (*Dear Life* 254). From this moment in which the narrator recognizes their circumstances, Munro shifts back to herself as a child in the "Finale." Whiplash.

In that "Finale" Munro juxtaposes her 2010–12 present with her childhood. Made up of four relatively brief pieces—"*not quite stories*" she writes in the headnote—which revisit her most cherished material: returned to herself as a young girl living in the house in Lower Town Wingham, living within her childhood family. These four pieces are, she believes, "*the first and last—and the closest—things I have to say about my own life*" (*Dear Life* 255; original emphasis). With them, Munro leaves herself as she was as she wrote and returns through memory to the place she started out from, to the place and time so very central to her art.

In them, Munro focuses on four episodes; they reveal the individual situations of each of her parents then, most especially her mother before the onset of Parkinson's disease about 1942, although its ultimate arrival and her struggles are acknowledged presences. Throughout Munro abandons any real pretense of fiction; she has said that they happened as she wrote them, although in her headnote to the section she keeps the fictional door ajar: the four "*form a separate unit, one that is autobiographical in feeling, though not, sometimes, entirely so in fact*" (*Dear Life* 255; original emphasis; Thacker interview September 6, 2013).

Opening "The Eye," Munro goes back to herself at five years old, when her time as celebrated only child ended with the arrivals of her brother and then, about a year later, her sister. "Up until the time of the first baby I had not been aware of ever feeling different from the way my mother said I felt. And up until that time the whole house was full of my mother, of her footsteps her voice her powdery yet ominous smell that inhabited all the rooms even when she wasn't in them" (*Dear Life* 257). Having offered this image, Munro steps back and asks, "Why do I say ominous? I didn't feel frightened. It wasn't that my mother actually told me what I was to feel about things" (*Dear Life* 257–8). Recalling her own feelings then, her uncertainties are genuine. Still, she concludes that "[i]t was with my brother's coming, though, and the endless carryings-on about how he was some sort of present for me, that I began to accept how largely my mother's notions about me might differ from my own" (*Dear Life* 258).

With this "Finale," the gathering she designed as the ending to what she expected to *really* be her last book, Munro returns again and finally to the ending of "The Ottawa Valley": "The problem, the only problem, is my mother" (*Something* 246). This meditation still applies as Munro composed her "Finale" to *Dear Life*: "Why do I say ominous?" Munro asks. She wonders yet and still wants to know, to understand, and is still "trying to get" her mother as she heads toward the end of her own "dear life."

This is so throughout the "Finale" and becomes especially so in the changed ending to "Dear Life." Just before she ends that story, the "Finale," and her career as a writer, Munro recalls a moment occasioned by something she saw in the Wingham paper while she was living in Vancouver and comments matter-of-factly in the face of more wonderment, "But the person I would really have liked to talk to then was my mother, who was no longer available" (*Dear Life* 318).

The focus of "The Eye" is on Sadie, a hired girl the Laidlaws employed to help when the babies came. Munro accounts for Sadie's presence in the house and her activities in the town—working at the radio station and going to dances—before accounting for her death in an accident walking home alone from the Royal-T dance hall. While Munro knows that "[m]y mother wanted something very badly" and suggests possibilities; she also asks if one of the possibilities was "me as I used to be, with my sausage curls that I didn't mind standing still for, and my expert Sunday School recitations." With the babies, her mother has no time, but even so "something in me was turning traitorous, though she didn't know why, and I didn't know why either. I hadn't made any town friends at Sunday School. Instead, I worshipped Sadie. I heard my mother say that to my father. 'She worships Sadie'" (*Dear Life* 263).

Munro establishes all this and then, shifting in time, takes the reader to the viewing after Sadie's death—Munro and her mother went. Upon their arrival her mother speaks to the host, saying that "[s]he hopes it was all right to bring me," "that I was especially fond of Sadie." As they arrive too, Munro notices an older boy from school—she was then in the first grade—"making a disgusted face" at her. She comments that "[t]hen I became aware of my mother's especially gentle and sympathetic voice, more ladylike even than the voice of the spokeswoman she was talking to, and I thought maybe the face was meant for her. Sometimes people imitated her voice when she called for me at school" (*Dear Life* 265). Munro is probing the position of her mother within the society in which they lived—she does so again in the third story in the group, "Voices," here—but while those reflections complement the overall trajectory of the "Finale," the balance of "The Eye" combines remembrance of her mother's behavior while she orchestrated Munro's first sight of a dead body. At the time, a woman who turns out to be Sadie's mother "let out a howl. She did not look at any of us and the sound she made seemed like a sound you might make if some animal was biting or gnawing at you" (*Dear Life* 266).

After describing Sadie's death—she was hit by a car from behind while walking home alone—Munro returns to her own situation:

> Now after the old woman's outburst it seemed to me we might turn around and go home. I would never have to admit the truth, which was that I was in fact desperately scared of any dead body.
>
> Just as I thought this might be possible, I heard my mother and the woman she seemed now to be conniving with speak of what was worse than anything.
>
> Seeing Sadie.
>
> Yes, my mother was saying. Of course, we must see Sadie.
>
> Dead Sadie.
>
> (*Dear Life* 267–8)

Munro details their approach to the coffin, and as she does so her concern is more with her mother's behavior than with her own apprehensions. "'Come now,' she said to me. Her gentleness sounded hateful to me, triumphant. She bent to look into my face, and this, I was sure, was to prevent me from doing what had just occurred to me—keeping my eyes squeezed shut" (*Dear Life* 268). Munro is tracing her mother's efforts to behave appropriately herself and, the more significantly, to force her into the same conventional forms. As she recalls the scene, Munro has them in a confrontation, one that is followed by the revelation of Sadie laid out:

> Then I heard my mother sniffling and felt her pulling away. There was a click of her purse being opened. She had to get her hand in there, so her hold on me weakened and I was able to get myself free of her. She was weeping. It was attention to her tears and sniffles that had set me loose.
> I looked straight into the coffin and saw Sadie.
> … … ….
> The trick was in seeing a bit of her quickly, then going back to the cushion, and the next time managing a little bit more that you were not afraid of. And then it was Sadie, all of her or at least all I could reasonably see on the side that was available.
> Something moved. I saw it, her eyelid on my side moved.
>
> (*Dear Life* 268-9)

This movement of the eyelid was just enough "to be able to see out through the lashes. Just to distinguish maybe what was light outside and what was dark" (*Dear Life* 269). Following this, Munro addresses two changes that, recalled, point to both maturation and change. Focused on the putative movement of Sadie's eyelash, Munro writes: "I was not surprised then and not in the least scared." Then after she and her mother go outside, they "got into the car and began to drive home. I had an idea that she would like me to say something, or maybe even tell her something, but I didn't do it" (*Dear Life* 269-70).

Munro's refusal here toward the end of the first of the "*not quite stories,*" appropriately enough, echoes and reverses another one which appeared toward the ending of "The Ottawa Valley." There her mother refused to answer her daughter's "recklessly, stubbornly" pursued question, "'Is your arm going to stop shaking?'"—a question Munro imagined asking when she was eleven years old during their 1942 visit to her mother's relatives near Carleton Place, Ontario, where Anne Chamney Laidlaw had grown up (see Thacker *Alice* 72–3). Following this earlier exchange, Munro relates:

> I demanded of her now, that she turn and promise me what I needed.
> But she did not do it. For the first time she held out altogether against me. She went on as if she had not heard, her familiar bulk ahead of me turning strange, indifferent. She withdrew, she darkened in front of me, though all she did in fact was keep on walking along the path that she and Aunt Dodie had made when they were girls running back and forth to see each other; it was still there.
>
> (*Something* 244)

Thus in "The Eye" Munro is still probing, wondering about, the mutual refusals which characterized her relationship with her mother. She takes an incident—her visit with her mother to view Sadie laid out—and again examines her recollections of what she saw, her responses, her mother's behaviors, and most especially the changes in her understandings over the decades that have now passed. She does this long after Sadie's death, long after the onset of her mother's disease, long after she married and left her mother to the care of others. Speaking of the supposed movement of Sadie's eyelid that day, Munro writes as the final, matter-of-fact sentence ending "The Eye": "Until one day, one day when I may even have been in my teens, I knew with a dim sort of hole in my insides that now I didn't believe it anymore" (*Dear Life* 270). So saying, Munro's imaginative return to this incident achieves closure within vital personal memories of her mother and, most especially, herself. All these years later, she still recalls the moment—and she is the only one who does.

In the next story, "Night," Munro moves to her teen years, when she had to have her appendix removed and when, afterwards, she learned that the doctor had also removed "[a] growth, my mother said, the size of a turkey's egg. But don't worry, she said, it's all over now" (*Dear Life* 272). Owing to her operation and the inactivity it enforced, Munro had trouble sleeping and was also plagued with terrible thoughts— of strangling her sister in the bunkbed below—so she takes to walking about outside during the twilight of the late-spring and early-summer mornings. "One night—I can't say whether it could be the twentieth or the twelfth or only the eighth or the ninth that I had got up and walked—I got a sense, too late for me to change my pace, that there was somebody around the corner." "Who was it? Nobody but my father. He too sitting on the stoop looking towards town and that improbable faint light." Munro also comments, "Now that I come to think of it, why wasn't my father in his overalls? He was dressed as if he had to go into town for something, first thing in the morning" (*Dear Life* 280, 281).

The two greet each other, he asks about her and she explains her trouble sleeping and her bad dreams, and eventually she tells him that she is walking about because she fears she would hurt her little sister. "'Strangle her,' I said then. I could not stop myself, after all. Now I could not unsay it, I could not go back to the person I had been before" (*Dear Life* 283). Her father is probably surprised by this, but "Then he said not to worry." He said, "'People have those kinds of thoughts sometimes.'" "He did not blame me, though, for thinking of it. Did not wonder at me, was what he said." And as she has done throughout her "Finale," Munro considers what might have happened today (*Dear Life* 283-4).

Just as at the end of "Dear Life" Munro provides a summary assessment of her mother—two, in fact, given the two published endings involved—and here she offers a companion final image of her father: "[O]n that breaking morning he gave me just what I needed to hear and what I was even to forget about soon enough" (*Dear Life* 284). And given her contemplations of her own parenting, she does so with real appreciation. But because this is a finale, her finale, that is not quite enough for Robert Eric Laidlaw. Wondering still why he was not dressed in his accustomed overalls that morning, she thinks "that he was maybe in his better work clothes because he had a morning appointment to go to the bank, to learn, not to his surprise, that there was no extension to his loan. He had worked as hard as he could but the market was not going to turn around and he had to find a new way of supporting us and paying off what we owed at the same time. Or he may have found out that there was a name for my mother's shakiness and that it was not going to stop. Or that he was in love with an impossible woman" (*Dear Life* 284–5).

In "Voices" Munro offers an account of a home dance which she and her mother—her father was not a dancer—attend very briefly; they leave almost at once because Mrs. Laidlaw discovers that a local madam and one of her girls is there. Munro is again remembering each of her parents, making connections, finding the continuities. Thus near the beginning of "Voices" Munro writes, "My father, who was much better liked than my mother, was a man who believed in taking whatever you were dealt. Not so my mother. She had risen from her farm girl's life to become a schoolteacher, but this was not enough, it had not given her the position she would have liked, or the friends she would have liked to have in town" (*Dear Life* 287). Her father "slipped into whatever exchange was going on—he understood that the thing to do was never to say anything special. My mother was just the opposite. With her everything was clear and ringing and served to call attention." As she and her mother arrived at the home dance, Munro knew "that was happening and I heard her laugh, delightedly, as if to make up for nobody's talking to her" (*Dear Life* 290).

For Munro, the whole scene is a wonder—the people, their behavior, the dancing. The madam—whose identity was then unknown to Munro—nevertheless makes a striking impression on her "wearing a dress of golden-orange taffeta, cut with a rather low square neck and a skirt that just covered her knees. Her short sleeves held her arms tightly and the flesh on them was heavy and smooth and white, like lard. This was a startling sight. I would not have thought it possible that somebody could look both old and polished, both heavy and graceful, bold as brass and yet mightily dignified. You could have called her brazen, and perhaps my mother later did—that was her sort of word. Someone better disposed might have said, stately" (*Dear Life* 292). Remembering, Munro recreates her own mystification at the scene along with her long perspective—on both what occurred and how her mother reacted to it. Looking at her description of this notorious woman, Munro also offers a salient comment as something of an aside: "I think that if I was writing fiction instead of remembering something that happened, I would never have given her that dress. A kind of advertisement she didn't need" (*Dear Life* 292).

"Dear Life"—which was first submitted to the *New Yorker* as "Visit" before becoming "A Visitation" before acquiring its title and being first published there as "Personal History" in September 2011—has a similar passage in its midst. Throughout this memoir Munro emphasizes the geography of her childhood—her walks back and forth along the Lower Town Road to and from school—and especially the location of the Laidlaws' house: "It turned its back on the village; it faced west across slightly downsloping fields to the hidden curve where the river made what was called the Big Bend. Beyond the river was a patch of dark evergreen trees, probably cedar but too far away to tell. And even farther away, on another hillside, was another house, quite small at that distance, facing ours, that we would never visit or know and that was to me like a dwarf's house in a story. But we knew the name of the man who lived there, or had lived there at one time, for he might have died by now. Roly Grain, his name was, and he does not have any further part in what I'm writing now, in spite of his troll's name, because *this is not a story, only life*" (*Dear Life* 306–7; emphasis added).

Munro had mentioned Roly Grain previously in just this way in "Working for a Living" (*Castle Rock* 147), but here she asserts the accuracy of the man's name, just as in "Voices" she does with the woman's dress. And the road Munro walks along is "The Flats Road" from *Lives of Girls and Women*; the people who live along it—some of whom, we see again here, are connected to prostitutes—we have seen before as living in Lower Hanratty in *Who Do You Think You Are?/The Beggar Maid*. There are echoes too in "Dear Life" of other stories, fictional but drawn from life: "The Peace of Utrecht," "Boys and Girls," "Red Dress—1946," "Walker Brothers Cowboy" and, repeatedly as she writes of the interior of that house facing west to the room in which the "Royal Beatings" were administered. Beyond these, there are other echoes too.

"This is not a story, only life." "Dear Life" begins: "I lived when I was young at the end of a long road, or a road that seemed long to me. Back behind me, as I walked home from primary school, and then from high school, was the real town with its activity and its sidewalks and its streetlights for after dark" (*Dear Life* 299). Here again is the place Munro started out from where, as Willa Cather wrote to Alexander Woollcott in 1942 about her last novel, *Sapphira and the Slave Girl* (1940), she might have also said, "[M]y end was my beginning" (613).[11] Thus in "Dear Life" there is the walk to and from school, there is the Lower Town school Munro attended for two unhappy years, and there are yet the oddball inhabitants along the Lower Town road—here is "Waitey Streets, a one-armed veteran of the First World War" who "kept some sheep and had a wife I saw only once in all those years …. Waitey liked to joke about the long time I had been at school and how it was a pity that I could never pass my exams and be done with it" (*Dear Life* 302–3). Her parents, their personalities and ambitions, the fox farm, her mother's illness, Munro's increased duties running the household as her mother's health declined: all of this is here, but at the center of "Dear Life" is the visit which gave the memoir its first title.

That visit, a story told Alice by her mother, who called it a "visitation," was paid by Mrs. Netterfield, known as "the crazy woman [who] had pursued the delivery boy with a hatchet" (*Dear Life* 312) because she said he forgot the butter she had ordered.[12] Mr. Laidlaw was gone and Mrs. Laidlaw had left Alice outside in her baby carriage when she saw Mrs. Netterfield "walking down our lane" and, reacting, she ran outside through "the kitchen door to grab me out of my baby carriage. She left the carriage and the covers where they were and ran back into the house, attempting to lock the kitchen door behind her. The front door she did not need to worry about—it was always locked" (*Dear Life* 312–13). Anne Chamney Laidlaw was grabbing her daughter Alice, she always said afterwards as she recounted its events, and as the expression goes, "for dear life" (*Dear Life* 318). Having arrived, Mrs. Netterfield

> was walking around the house, taking her time, and stopping at every downstairs window. The storm windows, of course, were not on now, in summer. She could press her face against every pane of glass. The blinds were all up as high as they

could go, because of the fine day. The woman was not very tall, but she did not have to stretch to see inside.

... ...

I don't know when my mother first told me this story, but it seems to me that that was where the earlier versions stopped—with Mrs. Netterfield pressing her face and hands against the glass while my mother hid. But in later versions there was an end to just looking. Impatience or anger took hold and then the rattling and the banging came. No mention of yelling. The old woman may not have had the breath to do it. Or perhaps she forgot what it was she'd come for, once her strength ran out.

Anyway, she gave up; that was all she did. After she had made her tour of all the windows and doors, she went away.

(*Dear Life* 314, 315)

As ever, in what has been called "the miraculous art" of Alice Munro, "Dear Life" and "Finale" come down to their ending (see Thacker "This"). After she tells the story, Munro writes that "I don't mean to imply that my mother spoke of this often. It was not part of the repertoire that I got to know and, for the most part, found interesting. Her struggle to get to high school" and to become a teacher, her experiences there. "The visitation of old Mrs. Netterfield, as she called it, was not something I was ever required to talk about. But I must have known about it for a long time." At one point Munro asked what happened to Mrs. Netterfield and her mother replied that "'[t]hey took her away' .... 'Oh, I think so. She wasn't left to die alone'" (*Dear Life* 315–16).

But Anne Chamney Laidlaw was "left to die alone," or at least that is how her oldest daughter felt, judging by "Dear Life" and by remembering "The Peace of Utrecht," Munro's first rendering of her mother's sickness and death. As she talks about her mother's repertoire of stories, Munro offers this paragraph that takes us back to the 1940s and her high-school years: "I could always make out what she was saying, though often, after her voice got thick, other people couldn't. I was her interpreter, and sometimes I was full of misery when I had to repeat elaborate phrases or what she thought were jokes, and I could see that the nice people who stopped to talk were dying to get away" (*Dear Life* 315). "The Peace of Utrecht" offers a more elaborated fictional account of the circumstances of Anne Chamney Laidlaw's illness and death, but the narrator Helen and her sister Maddie are interpreters for their mother, who "kept herself as much in the world as she could, not troubling about her welcome; restlessly she wandered through the house and into the streets of Jubilee" (*Dance* 199). Townspeople ask the visiting Helen point-blank "why I did not come home for the funeral" (*Dance* 195) and, later, one of her aunts—the same figures who feature in "Winter Wind" and "The Ticket"—tells her that her mother escaped from the hospital into the January snow. "'Oh, Helen, when they came after her she tried to run. She tried to *run*.' The flight that concerns everybody" (*Dance* 208; original emphasis; see Thacker *Alice* 147–54).

When the *New Yorker* first considered "Dear Life," then entitled "Visit," the next episode after Mrs. Netterfield's visit, her daughter sending a letter including a poem from Oregon and having it published in the Wingham *Advance-Times*, appeared about midway in the narrative. The ending, with some small changes in diction, is as now published, although Munro also wrote just before what is now the last paragraph, "Old Mrs. Nethery who had it in her to become a witch" (Edited typescript, February 4, 2011; *New Yorker* files). Accepted, set in type, and edited by Deborah Treisman—now retitled "Visitation"—the letter to the editor and poem have been moved to their published penultimate position in the text, the previous ending deleted, and this one offered instead: "When my mother herself was dying she got out of the hospital somehow, at night, and wandered around until someone who was not at all connected spotted her and took her in. If this were fiction it would be too much, but it is true" (16, edited proof, July 19, 2011; *New Yorker* files). Although Munro changed the ending between the typescript and the typeset versions, getting closer to the published last paragraph in the *New Yorker* version, Treisman suggests in her edited proof that Munro bring back the first ending and combine it with this new one—she attaches a typed sheet with both to the end of the proof. The next proof—now entitled "Dear Life"—indicates that Munro accepted the suggestion and it ran in the *New Yorker* with both endings (again, but for slight changes in diction) (undated proof [August 26, 2011], author's possession). When "Dear Life" was published in *Dear Life* as the finale to its "Finale," the second ending—the paragraph about Anne Chamney Laidlaw's escape—had been dropped. As both Munro and Close said, it was too late to introduce anything so harrowing.

After Munro recounts her discussion of Mrs. Netterfield, she shifts to her memory of seeing a letter in the Wingham paper from Emma Netterfield Cooper, her daughter, which included a poem about the Maitland River as seen from the Laidlaw farm. Munro quotes three stanzas from the poem, summarizes and comments upon what Cooper says about her relation to Wingham, and writes just before she moves to her ending: "This woman said that she was born in 1876. She had spent her youth, until she was married, in her father's house. It was where the town ended and the open land began, and it had a sunset view. Our house" (*Dear Life* 318).[13] Breaking the narrative, Munro then asks: "Is it possible that my mother never knew this, never knew that our house was where the Netterfield family had lived and that the old woman was looking in the windows of what had been her own home? It is possible." Munro then meditates—as she has throughout her own life—on the possibilities of Mrs. Netterfield's situation:

> Had she been left a widow, short of money? Who knows? And who was it who came and took her away, as my mother said? Perhaps it was her daughter, the same woman who wrote poems and lived in Oregon. Perhaps that daughter, grown and distant, was the one she was looking for in the baby carriage. Just after my mother had grabbed me up, as she said, for dear life.
>
> The daughter lived not so far away from me for a while in my adult life. I could have written to her, maybe visited. If I had not been so busy with my own young family and my own invariably unsatisfactory writing. But the person I would really have liked to talk to then was my mother, who was no longer available.
>
> (*Dear Life* 318)[14]

Munro offers here, just as she reaches the finale of her "Finale," a finale she has been heading toward for some time, a long-considered and deeply felt response to that most essential assertion at the end of "The Ottawa Valley": "The problem, the only problem, is my mother" (*Something* 246). That story, its own finale to the collection in which it first appeared, picks up from "The Peace of Utrecht" and heads through the intervening stories to the finale Munro was about to accomplish in "Dear Life."

Just after she quotes and comments on Emma Netterfield Cooper's poem, Munro writes, "In fact, I had once made up some poems myself, of a very similar nature, though they were lost now, and maybe had never been written down. Verses that commended Nature, then were a bit hard to wind up. I would have composed them right around the time that I was being so intolerant of my mother, and my father was whaling the unkindness out of me. Or beating the tar out of me, as people would cheerfully say back then" (*Dear Life* 317).

One of these poems, published under the pseudonym Anne Chamney, appeared in the *Canadian Forum* before Munro published her first book in 1968. Remember: "Stabbed to the heart … by the changes, the losses in our lives. By the beauty of our lives streaming by, in Morgana and elsewhere" ("Golden Apples" 23). So Alice Munro, the long-contemplated finale achieved, the problem still her mother, her own dear life now a text. "If this were fiction, as I said, it would be too much, but it is true" ("Dear Life," *New Yorker* 47). "But in this book my end was my beginning: the place I started out from" (Cather to Woollcott). So too Alice Munro's end was her beginning: through a shaped late style she returned yet again to her own perpetual imaginary presences, to her home place along the Maitland River in Lower Town Wingham, ever alive, ever beckoning, ever "touchable and mysterious."

Epilogue:
"To Have Got My Chance to Do It, as well as I Could": Alice Munro *Finis*

On November 23, 1995, Alice Munro wrote in response to an inquiry from Eleanor Henderson, her first cousin on her mother's side from Carleton Place, Ontario, who was then assembling genealogical information on the Chamneys. She summarizes her life trajectory and, after listing the years in which her books had been published to date, she steps back and summarizes her career in ways apt, wry, and direct:

> A writer's life is generally pretty boring to describe since it's so much an adventure in solitary imagination and the (hard) learning of a craft. But it's never boring to live, because for one thing, it's so precarious. Sometimes I feel just incredibly lucky—for one thing, to have always known exactly what I wanted to do, and then, to have got my chance to do it, as well as I could.

Having then offered her cousin her personal information, Munro also includes a long postscript paragraph beginning "Here's something about Mother" and details Anne Chamney Laidlaw's career training to teach and then teaching in Alberta and Ontario, ending as "principal of the village school in Merrickville" before she married. Wonderfully treating what she calls "the mother as material" in Munro, Elizabeth Hay ends, as I just have, with the ending of "Dear Life." Hay sees in the two final sentences in *Dear Life* Munro's "unsparing self-knowledge it has taken a lifetime to adequately measure and do so in a voice that is distinctly hers: sober, chastened, wise, and not unkind" (191).

Ending this book on Alice Munro's Late Style I remain ever conscious of what she said to those two interviewers in 2010: "writing is the final thing" (Lahey and Jernigan 52). So Munro has known and done throughout her own dear life, as she wrote to Henderson, and so she continued for over sixty years, moving ever and always from one story to the next, and back and forth between and among stories too. So she has done, productively and continually, from her beginnings until the publication of *Dear Life* in 2012. With its "Finale" to end a remarkable career, that section following on the complexities of the provenance of *The View from Castle Rock* and the considered imaginative departure that *Too Much Happiness* demonstrates through its prior stories preceding the title story and those in *Dear Life* too preceding that "Finale," Munro at last ended the career she has pursued for so very long.

I need finally to call attention to the two photographs I offer in this book: the first, a photograph I took myself of that crypt in Sullivan Township, Grey County, Ontario, the crypt at the heart of "What Do You Want to Know For?". That memoir, and the mysteries at its core, seems to embody—encapsulate and hold—the whole of Munro's late style, and most especially the anticipated "family book" she so long foresaw. A redolent Munrovian phrase, "the rest of the story" may be seen in that crypt, in what she and Fremlin discovered about it, and in her making and shaping their interactions with it, especially her own. Turning ever so briefly to Munro's concurrent—one of the groups that makes up *Dear Life*—fugitive story, "Axis," which likely will never be collected in a Munro volume, I did find myself wishing that I might have found appropriate photographs of the Niagara Escarpment, perhaps along Colpoy's Bay off of Georgian Bay or, equally, of the Frontenac Axis east of Kingston. One of them would have done.

But what I have selected for the frontispiece here, my second photograph (also used on the cover), is one which embodies the drive and desire felt throughout, what seems to me the whole of Alice Munro's last three books, including, and following from, *Castle Rock*: four generations of Laidlaws, photographed by a professional photographer during the summer of 1954 when Alice and James Munro went to Huron County for a visit with their first daughter Sheila. The line of Laidlaws is shown continued in it: Sarah Jane "Sadie" Code Laidlaw, her son Robert Eric Laidlaw, his daughter Alice, her daughter Sheila at about eight months. All of these people headed for literary presence in Alice's works.

Five years later, in 1959, her mother Anne Chamney Laidlaw just dead in February of that year, Alice Munro came back to Huron again, this time on the transcontinental train. During this visit Munro's "first really painful autobiographical story … the first time [she] wrote a story that tore [her] up," "The Peace of Utrecht," was impinging on her imagination (Metcalf interview 58; original ellipsis). There Munro has her narrator, Helen, drive into Jubilee with her children to visit her sister—the sister who had been left behind to care for their now-dead mother, the mother who had fled the hospital during the throes of her last illness. As Helen enters the house, Munro offers this description:

> Then I paused, one foot on the bottom step, and turned to greet, matter-of-factly, the reflection of a thin, tanned, habitually watchful woman, recognizably a Young Mother, whose hair, pulled into a knot on top of her head, exposed a jawline no longer softly fleshed, a brown neck rising with a look of tension from the little sharp knobs of the collarbone—this in the hall mirror that had shown me, last time I looked, a commonplace pretty girl, with a face as smooth and insensitive as an apple, no matter what panic and disorder lay behind it.
>
> (*Dance* 197–8)

Here, in her own words in the critical early story of her career ("a short gallop at full speed"), Munro describes herself in ways both biographically and imaginatively accurate: the trajectory she was embarked on from early style to late. For her, writing is and has always been the final thing: "*maybe* I can do something unexpected with it," she wrote to Gibson from Australia in 1980. So Alice Munro did.

Notes

Preface

1 Focusing specifically on the numerical citation offered for my quotation from the archival manuscript of "The Yellow Afternoon" here, 37.16.34.f1, I need to say a word about the Alice Munro Fonds at the University of Calgary. As here, whenever a numeral citation appears alone without further description the reference is to material held in Calgary as part of the Fonds. The University of Calgary Press published two detailed listings of Munro's papers (First Accession, 1986, Second Accession, 1987); subsequent accessions are described online at https://searcharchives.ucalgary.ca/alice-munro-fonds. The numbering system used there has changed some over the years, but I have endeavored to accurately verify the currently assigned numbers.

    A related point: in holograph compositions and handwritten letters from the Fonds and other archives, Munro ignores the apostrophe in "it's" and also often does not indicate possession nor does she consistently indicate book titles. Quoting such passages, I offer verbatim transcription of what is the archive without use of a "sic." In the same vein, there is also the matter of what Daniel Menaker, one of her editors at *New Yorker*, called "the Munro comma." Munro often chose to use a comma when either a semicolon or period was warranted, and she did not want that comma changed to anything else.

2 On November 5, 1990, Byatt was interviewed on TV Ontario (TVO) by Michael Coren and said this: "my absolute heroine is Alice Munro. I think she is arguably the greatest short story writer I have ever read. I think [of] her mastery of pace and the depth of her understanding of human nature and her absolute mastery of a form which appears simple. But no one of her stories is like the next one and each seems to have made its form exactly as it's required to be to become what it was—to say that thing about those people and at the same time something universally. I admire and envy Alice Munro" (James Adams to Douglas Gibson, n. d., Douglas Gibson Papers, McClelland & Stewart, Box 41, f. 3).

Introduction

1 See signed contract between Alfred A. Knopf, a Division of Random House, Inc., and Alice Munro, December 9, 2003 (947/14.12.1, Correspondence 2001–3, 2 of 4). The contract is for a work entitled "Powers" [*Runaway*] and "Untitled Collection of Stories" [*Castle Rock*]. This was the sole instance of a two-book contract in Munro's career. Explaining it, her editor at Knopf Ann Close said that two-book contracts were sometimes done to ensure the author additional funds or because, probably the case in this instance, the publisher's sense that the second book would not sell as

well as the first. That anticipation was correct. The two books were "joint accounted"; that is, no royalties or subsidiary rights income would be paid until total advances were earned out. Another factor in this was that Virginia Barber retired at the end of 2003, so this contract extended Munro's financial future (Thacker Close interview July 26, 2021).

2. On July 21, 1989, Virginia Barber wrote to Douglas Gibson saying that she was about to send him the manuscript of *Friend of My Youth* and also writes that there "are two extra stories which Alice may decide to include, and I would appreciate your giving her your opinion—'Wood' and 'The Ferguson Girls Must Never Marry.' Otherwise the table of contents represent her selections and her order" (883/11.5). The listing, undated on Virginia Barber Literary Agency stationery as a "proposed table of contents," has the ten stories included in the book. There is a line after which "Wood" and "The Ferguson Girls Must Never Marry" appear with the notation, "Stories which may or may not be included in this collection." A second copy on paper, not stationary, shows the last two titles crossed out (752/04.3.1).

"The Ferguson Girls Must Never Marry" is a particular case. In the second accession of Munro's papers in Calgary there is a great deal of material connected to it, letters and a considerable amount of manuscript, twenty-three files (38.10.8-30). As indicated, after its first publication in *Grand Street* in 1982, Munro worked on it extensively; at one point she has one of its characters, Nola, in Scotland visiting Selkirkshire in a scene she later used in "Hold Me Fast, Don't Let Me Pass" (1988) (38.10.30.3.f1-3). She was still thinking about it in April 2004 when, during an interview, she asked me what I thought the story was about. She said then that she had rewritten it in 2003, saying that "it still doesn't work" and that "it will never see the light of day," explaining that "it has a lot in it that I want to say, but I think when I started writing that I was on the verge of writing complicated stories that came later, and I hadn't quite grasped how to do it." Munro retitled it during that rewrite too, calling it "Souls" (Thacker interview; Munro to Barber November 27, 2003; 947/14.12.1, Correspondence 2001–2003, 2 of 4).

3. Ann Close sees a shift to a more complex style emerging in the *Open Secrets* stories, pointing especially to the ending of "Carried Away" (1991). She thinks that book, and that story in particular, represented "a big change" in Munro's work (Thacker interview July 26, 2021).

4. While characters based on Anne Chamney Laidlaw appear in Munro's early stories, "The Peace of Utrecht" is the first one explicitly about her. Del Jordan's mother owes something to her in *Lives of Girls and Women* (1971), and once Munro returned to Ontario she was the focus of several key stories: "The Ottawa Valley" (1974), "Home" (1974), "Chaddeleys and Flemings: 1. Connection" (1978), "Working for a Living" (1981), "The Progress of Love" (1986), and "Friend of My Youth" (1990). The last story appears first in the book of the latter title, which is dedicated "[t]o the memory of my mother." Throughout, too, more distant characters owing to Munro's mother appear in stories (see, for instance, Thacker *Alice* 448).

Chapter 1

1. This interview is available in two forms, the broadcast audio version on the CBC website and the edited published version in *Queen's Quarterly*. I have used both.

Munro's comment that "there *would* be a book" is on the audio version but not in the published one. The balance of my quotation is from the published version.

2   I treat Welty's influence in Chapter 6, but a comment Munro later made to Ann Close, a person who grew up in South Carolina and Savannah, Georgia, is pertinent: "She told me that she felt closest to her as a writer, and that she'd helped her think that writing short stories was all right to do early on." Close noted that immigration patterns into the South and into Southwestern Ontario were similar, largely Scots-Irish, and continues "I remember reading reviews" of the US editions of Munro's first three books, published and distributed by McGraw-Hill, "and several reviewers thought she *was* a Southern writer. Then both [Virginia Barber] and I were the ones who most 'got' her initially." Barber "grew up in a more rural area [in Virginia] than I did, but the land was / is such an overpowering part of the Southern mythos still" (June 19, 2018; original emphasis).

3   Other stories published after "The Peace of Utrecht" which largely exclude personal material were "The Trip to the Coast" (1961), "Dance of the Happy Shades" (1961), and "Postcard" (1968). All mentioned here are included in *Dance*.

4   While I will return to "Chaddeleys and Flemings" when I take up "The Wilds of Morris Township" in *Castle Rock*, Munro's writing and shaping of it—it is effectively two stories—is germane here as an instance of both her work on personal materials in the late 1970s after moving to Clinton and, ultimately, a key instance of recursion. The story was written as two-part story: the Chaddeleys modeled on her mother's family, the Chamneys, and the Flemings modeled on her father's, the Laidlaws. It was probably written in 1976–7. The two parts together are a forty-one-page typed manuscript, so in effect it has two endings. Through the guise of her narrator, Janet, Munro writes of searching for an unfound boulder—the stone in the field—a headstone for the hermit, Mr. Black, who was buried there, himself an actual person. She writes of her ancestors on both sides: "However they behaved they are all dead. I carry something of them around in me. But the boulder is gone, Mount Hebron is cut down for gravel, and the life buried her is one have to think twice about regretting." After a space, this version of the story ends with the invocation of "Row, row, row your boat" and memories which end "Chaddeleys and Flemings: 1. Connection" (38.8.18.f 40).

This larger story was submitted to the *New Yorker* and rejected in November 1977; Charles McGrath, Munro's fiction editor there, wrote that William Shawn, the magazine's editor, "decided against" the story because "it read more like straight reminiscence than like a story." McGrath demures, saying he thought Munro had "taken the material of reminiscence and turned it into something much stronger—a moving, complicated work of fiction" (November 1, 1977; 37.2.30.5). As *Who* moved into production at Macmillan, Douglas Gibson suggested that Munro split the story in two, a suggestion she took (April 28, 1978; 37.2.20.7). After she pulled the now two stories from that collection, Munro continued to work on them; each was published in a serial. When Munro worked on revisions for each of them, either for the serial publication or for their ultimate appearance in *The Moons of Jupiter*, she revised on original proof sheets from the Macmillan setting dated August 1978 (see Thacker, *Reading* 62–4).

5   Munro referred to the italicized passages in "Home" as "the commentary voice" when she and John Metcalf were rehearsing her presentation of it for a reading at Loyola College in Montreal held on February 7, 1975. The rehearsal and the reading were taped and deposited in the John Metcalf Fonds (24.45.6).

6   This passage becomes "[s]uch unremarkable scenes, in this part of the country, are what I have always thought would be the last thing I would care to see in my life" (*Castle Rock* 286).

7   Not too many years before this John Updike, writing on Borges in 1965, concluded his essay noting "a deep need in contemporary literary art—the need to confess the fact of artifice" ("Books" 246).
8   When I published *Alice Munro: Writing Her Lives: A Biography* I thought this trip took place in 1943, but subsequently proof emerged in the Altamonte Ontario *Gazette* that the visit was the previous year. I again thank Reg Thompson for this information.
9   Another draft, still entitled "Notes for a Work," is dedicated "with love," to Metcalf, signed, and dated October 30, 1973; she wrote "Happy Birthday" on its first page and sent it to him (John Metcalf Fonds 24.48.17).
10 After "Royal Beatings" and "The Beggar Maid" appeared in the *New Yorker* during the first half of 1977, Munro had seven stories published in other serials before she returned to the *New Yorker* in the May 22, 1978, issue with "The Moons of Jupiter." But for "Privilege" in the *Tamarack Review*, all were in commercial magazines.
11 In addition to the three stories that were pulled from *Who*, Munro had another, "Accident," finished and others in process as she looked toward *The Moons of Jupiter*.
12 Barber is here offering a comment as first reader of stories just finished, as agents do. Two facts about her are important: her personal history was like Munro's and, as well, she had a PhD in American literature from Duke University. For Munro at this time the developing friendship between the two was crucial—she had also been developing a close editorial and personal friendship with Gibson, and was doing as well with Ann Close at Knopf and with her *New Yorker* editors.
13 These verbatim archival quotations from holograph preliminary drafts are in notebooks held by the Alice Munro Fonds included in accession 396/87.3, box 6, files 4 and 6. The notebooks are unpaginated. In another draft version of "Hold Me Fast" also in 6.4 notebook, Munro changes some of the detail surrounding the writer McMurchie. The material connected to some of the stories in *The Progress of Love* is also in 6.6. notebook.
14 "Hold Me Fast" was first submitted to the *New Yorker* in early January 1988. Two weeks later Barber reported to Munro that chief editor Robert Gottlieb "isn't keen on" the story and that Menaker was seeking his permission to encourage Munro to revise it (Barber to Menaker January 7, 1988; Barber to Munro January 21, 1988; 752/04.3.1.8).
15 Munro was offered her initial first-reading agreement with the *New Yorker* in December 1977. By then the editors had published just two of the sixty-three Munro stories they would eventually run, but by then they had seen enough and knew what they had. This commitment to writers is justifiably legendary. Talking about it in an interview, Munro commented, "Oh, that's it. Their belief in you, once they've subscribed to a belief in you, they really are going to go the limit with you" (Thacker interview August 2001). Given this respect, rejection letters written to Barber regarding stories that had been decided against, as with Menaker's here, are always rhetorically balanced. Menaker, whom Munro saw as her best editor at the magazine, became a fiction editor there at the same time Charles McGrath did and, together, they found and championed Munro and other younger writers.
16 On February 9, 1989, Munro apparently sent Barber the manuscript of "Friend of My Youth," writing in a cover letter, "Here is what I've been doing—hardly a story, sort of a meditation on story-writing and what I feel about my mother" (847/14.12.1, Correspondence 1989–1990). In the Alice Munro Fonds there is a

typescript manuscript dated (in Virginia Barber's hand) February 26, 1989, as well as proof versions first dated by the *New Yorker* March 8, 1989, and then updated April 18, 1989 (752/04.3.3.2). Thus "Friend of My Youth" seems to have been accepted quickly. On the *New Yorker*'s file-card record, "Friend of My Youth" was bought on March 30, but clearly the decision was made before that (*New Yorker* files). Menaker wrote Munro on March 15, 1989, about the story, saying that he had set it in galleys since they did have "some problems with the last part of the piece." "Not the very last paragraph, though; not a single hair on its head should be touched, as Maxwell used to say)" (947/14.12.1.1). There are slight changes in punctuation between Munro's submitted version of the last paragraph and the final version of the book.

17 Explaining how she came to write "Friend of My Youth" in the Jeanne McCulloch and Mona Simpson interview in the *Paris Review*, Munro confirms the details of Thompson's help with it (242). Further, the detail of the divided and shared house is probably based on Edward and Mary James, relatives of Munro, who lived in Carleton Place, Ontario. They had three daughters, including Sadie, the last, with whom they lived in a divided house (Henderson).

18 In the submitted manuscript typescript Flora's readings to Ellie are described differently: "What did Flora read? More or less what you would expect, to begin with. Those old poems by Sir Walter Scott, that everybody used to have to learn—or learn some passages of—at school. *The stag at eve had drunk his fill. Breathes there a man with soul so dead.* Then she read from novels, also by Sir Walter Scott, which my mother could not follow very well because the characters often spoke in the Scots dialect, or at least with a thick accent" (752/04.3.3.2:10). The quotations here are, respectively, from "The Lady of the Lake" and "The Lay of the Last Minstrel," both well known. Later in the same manuscript, when she is describing the novel about Flora that her mother envisions writing, the narrator refers to another Scott poem, "No more *Marmion* or ancient sermons" (752/04.3:3.2:18). Munro deleted the direct quotations from Scott in on a *New Yorker* galley dated April 18 (752/04.3:3.2:9); the reference to *Marmion* became "No more Scottish, or ancient sermons" in the *New Yorker* first publication (45). Thus using *Wee MacGregor* got her away from Scott as one of the "classics."

In the May 1992 interview with Christopher Gittings, Munro remarks that "[m]y mother did talk about being a writer I remember at one time and she talked a little bit about the kind of novel she would write, so I knew in a way" how she would tell such a story (92).

19 Ten years later, in another first-person story that has autobiographical elements, "Nettles" (2000), Munro does the same thing, ending with a single paragraph set off and describing a subsequent factual discovery relevant to what has just been told (see Thacker Evocative).

20 For an excellent treatment of Munro's use of her religious inheritances throughout her oeuvre, see Somacarrera.

21 During the summer of 2005, when my biography was being completed, Munro was good enough to let me have a manuscript version of *Castle Rock* as it then was. Reading it, I discovered her visit to Joliet in 2004 and her attempt to find her great-great-grandfather's grave there. Following her, I visited the place myself on June 26, 2005, and found it to be just as Munro describes it: set apart unused land with no evidence of graves. The location is technically in Homer Glen, Illinois, at South Parker Road and West 143rd Street.

Chapter 2

1. The manuscript version here is signed and dated "May 2/05" in Munro's hand. It is consistently paginated. I read it in June 2005, just as my biography was in the final phases of production. There was as yet no foreword, and Munro appears to be alternating between the historical pieces and the "special set of [fictional] stories" [x] she subsequently described in the Foreword to *Castle Rock*. Here is the order of its stories in the manuscript as I received it:
    "The View from Castle Rock"
    "Fathers"
    "Men of Ettrick." This was incorporated into "The View from Castle Rock."
    "Lying Under the Apple Tree"
    "Illinois"
    "Hired Girl"
    "The Wilds of Morris Township"
    "Wenlock Edge"
    "Working for a Living"
    "The Ticket"
    "Home"
    "Remnants." This was retitled "Messenger," revised, and some of its material moved elsewhere in the book.
2. While the question of its placement in *Castle Rock* was being considered, "Wenlock Edge" had yet to be seen by the *New Yorker*. It was submitted on August 2, 2005, and published there in the December 5, 2005 issue. Probably because it was not included in *Castle Rock* and did not appear in a book until *Too Much Happiness* in 2009—allowing Munro more time to think about it—there are more variant endings than usual.
3. The word "Nausicaä" has its umlaut in the *New Yorker*, but not in the *Castle Rock* version. In discussing the revised versions of previously published pieces which then were included in *Castle Rock*, my aim is to highlight substantive revisions without accounting for everything that was done to them for the final book version.
4. The writing and publication of *Seven Gothic Tales* are legendary since the author, the Danish Baroness Karen Blixen, created a stir with it. It had been turned down by numerous publishers when it came to the attention of a small US publisher and Dorothy Canfield Fisher of the Book-of-the-Month Club. Its first selection in 1934 drew considerable attention as it launched Blixen's career as a writer (see Atwood, Updike "Divine Swank"). Since "Hired Girl" is set after the Second World War and the reference to it as a Book-of-the-Month Club book seems immediate, the book may have been in the Montjoys' possession for some time or perhaps had been offered as an alternate selection. A copy of it may have been given to Munro in 1948.
5. Ruth Scurr's 2011 *TLS* review of Munro's *New Selected Stories*, "The Darkness of Alice Munro," needs to be noted here in relation to the difference seen in the two published versions of "Hired Girl" between "brutality" and "cruelty." With rapt discernment as she reviews the late-style selection before her, Scurr delves immediately into the presence of another book—like *Seven Gothic Tales*—specifically mentioned in a story, this time E. R. Dodds's *The Greeks and the Irrational* (1951) which Juliet in "Chance" is reading on a train traveling west across the Canadian Shield in winter. Scurr notes Dodds's epigraph to his first chapter, a quotation from William James: "The recesses of feeling, the darker, blinder strata of character, are the only places in the world in which

we can catch real fact in the making" (Dodds 3). As she begins her precisely sharp readings of late-style Munro, Scurr asserts that she "centres her fiction on catching real fact in the making in just this Jamesian sense" (3). Thus the difference between "brutal" and "cruel" in the versions of "Hired Girl." The darkness of Alice Munro in fact.

6   In an unusual typographic mistake in first editions (Knopf, McClelland & Stewart) of *Castle Rock*, the family name "Montjoy" is twice offered as "Mountjoy" on the last page of the story (254). This is carried into paperbacks as well. I have ignored this mistake and used "Montjoy."

7   This reference to "a muddled trance" is both an instance of Munro making fun of herself and also germane. Over the years in published profiles Munro talked about her writing as concentrated thinking, often done early in the morning, still in a housecoat, looking out the window (see Thacker *Alice* 378–81).

8   Having myself twice set out to find this crypt without luck in the mid-2010s, I acknowledge and thank Reg Thompson for his help and excellent directions toward finally finding it on September 12, 2019.

9   Just as she begins her discussion of the glacial history of the area, Munro remarks that a "glacial landscape such as this is vulnerable. Many of its various contours are made up of gravel, and gravel is easy to get at and always in demand" (*Castle Rock* 318). This passage is, with a few small revisions, the 1994 version. In *Castle Rock* she has again added material, including this about gravel: "it's a way for farmers to get hold of some cash. One of my earliest memories is of the summer my father sold off the gravel on our river flats, and we had the excitement of the trucks going past all day, as well as the importance of the sign at our gate. *Children playing.* That was *us*" (*Castle Rock* 318–19; original emphasis). When I visited the former Laidlaw fur farm in Lower Town Wingham along the Maitland River in 2004, the evidences of that summer's gravel removal were still there. Munro used this episode in "Nettles" (*Hateship*) and *Dear Life* contains a story entitled "Gravel" (2011).

10 Revising this passage for *Castle Rock*, Munro shifted the years of these deaths to a decade earlier, the phrase there being "a date in the sixties or seventies of the nineteenth century" (324). This may have been a correction or, perhaps, Munro phrased it this way to be closer to her ancestors who came to Huron County in the 1850s.

11 In the source Munro was likely looking at here, *A History of Sullivan Township 1850-1975*, the relevant description of the Mannerow Cemetery (Cedardale) reads:

Around the middle 1800's, the Mannerows came to this country from Germany. They settled in Sullivan on Lot 19, Con[session] 4. Mr. Mannerow gave one-half acre near the southeast corner for a burying ground. His son, Henry, was the next owner of the farm, He received his deed to the S ½ of the S ½ Lot 19, Con[session] 4 on September 16, 1880 for 50 acres.

So this burial plot has since been known as the Mannerow Cemetery even though the name was changed to Cedardale Cemetery at a meeting on June 26, 1922 on a motion by Henry Kreutzkamp seconded by John Minke.

This cemetery is well known for the two vaults in it. The large burial vault in the centre was built by Henry's son, John, in the year 1895–96. It is constructed of stone and mortar now grown over with grass. The interior is all cement. The door is locked by means of an intricate device which was fashioned by John's son, Theodore (Ted).

The first one to be buried in this vault was John's son, William, who died at the age of 3 years at the time the vault was built.

(78–79)

12 The three assertions that I have pointed out in "What Do Want to Know For?"—"It's the fact you cherish," "There are always puzzles," and "The past needs to be approached from a distance"—may well be connected with the fact that Munro waited until just before *Castle Rock* to include (and presumably revise) the memoir or, as she called it, the memorial. Only "It's the fact you cherish" is in the 1994 version.

13 This letter has the date of its receipt, June 18, 2003, written on it in Barber's hand, along with the title of the manuscript, "The View from Castle Rock" (947/14.12). While Barber retired as an agent at the end of 2003, she continued to serve as first reader and respond to Munro's work throughout the making of her last three books.

14 On August 17, 2008, I visited the Boston Presbyterian Church and its cemetery and saw the Laidlaw tombstones, including Isabella's. It notes that she was "Wife of Thomas Aiken" and that she died "30 December 1891 Aged 73 years." No birth date appears. On the Laidlaw stones, both Andrew and Walter separately memorialize their parents by name.

15 Just as she told Sheila Munro in 1997, during our 2010 interview Munro told me that these letters had come down to her through the Laidlaws. She also said some of the letters she used are in an archive in Toronto. None of the family letters, nor Walter's journal, are in the Laidlaw papers in the Archive of Ontario.

16 The list of stories designated "memorish" is, in the order as written with Barber's further notes: "'Working for a Living' (Grand St) / 'Hired Girl' (N. Yorker) / 'The View from Castle Rock' -unpublished / 'Fathers'—unpublished New Yorker / 'Lying Under the Apple Tree' New Yorker." There follows a line with "'Wood' (New Yorker) / 'The Ferguson Girls Must Never Marry' (Grand St)." Another line, and two characterized "memorial": "'Home'—New Statesman (get that version) / 'What Do You Want to Know for?—unpublished' / published in a book in Canada" (947/14.12.1, Correspondence 2001–3, one of four). Writing to her colleague agent Abner Stein, who handled Munro's work in Britain, Barber gives him an overview in fall 2002: "She also has some pieces she refers to as "memoirish" which more or less go together for another volume. So, in the next year she'll be working on these. Her health is good, and she may be coming around to the idea that she has more time than she thought before the by-pass operation" (October 29, 2002; 947/14.12.1, Correspondence 2001–3, one of four).

17 The photograph was provided by Munro. In the *New Yorker* files it is attached to an internal art traffic / credit and caption sheet dated May 30, 2002. A reproduction of it is found as the fifth photo in the gathering following page 246 in Thacker *Alice*.

18 While I will not belabor editing details as stories moved from submission to first publication (usually, though not always) in the pages of the *New Yorker* here, I will discuss such matters with reference to "Fathers" and "Lying Under the Apple Tree" in order to establish a baseline.

19 Munro drew here on an actual incident of near-electrocution involving her father. The June 3, 1943, issue of the Wingham *Advance-Times* carried this headline and story: "COWS ELECTROCUTED ENTERING BARN / Second Cow To Meet Similar Fate / The fact that they were wearing rubber boots probably saved Robert Laidlaw and Lloyd Cook of town from receiving severe electric shock or worse. Mr. Thos. Thompson a short distance from Ripley called them to salvage a cow which had died in the doorway of his barn." "The rubber boots they were wearing no doubt did them

a good turn" (1). Cook worked with Munro's father; they collected dead livestock as a food source for the foxes.

20 For many years at the corner of the road Munro describes there was a Lower Wingham grocery—I have a photograph of its storefront from the 1920s. It was across the road from the Lower Town school, which Munro attended 1937–9 for grades one and three, skipping grade two. She recalled that by then the store was closed and a family lived there, but there was still some commercial advertising on the building. It is the basis of Flo's store in *Who / Beggar Maid*.

21 While beyond the scope of my discussion here, I would nevertheless note that this narrator's avowed and deep interest in movies and movie stars is one she shares with Munro herself.

22 With regard to this passage, see DeFalco 44, that article, and the whole of the volume in which it appears, *passim*, as well as my review of that book. Also, some critics have seen in "Fathers" the possibility that Dahlia had some hand in her father's death by intentionally hiding his boots. Be that as it may, there is no question but that the story offers something of the murder mystery about it.

23 The editing Munro's stories received at the *New Yorker* is itself a story, but there is no question but that the editors' responses to her work played a key role in its development. That said, and certainly as time went on, editors would require alterations that once the story ran in its pages Munro ultimately rejected for the subsequent book version. For example, here Munro's preferred description of the blossoming apple trees seen from a distance, "clotted with snow" (a version is in the submitted manuscript, "like clots of snow") becomes "like trimmings of snow" (*Castle Rock* 197; submitted manuscript 1; *New Yorker* 88). In another instance here, Treisman suggests that they cut a passage which begins "Now that my father had to be at the foundry by five o'clock …" and details the changes in the narrator's family life caused by the progress of her mother's illness; biographical facts. Munro agrees, for the passage is not in the *New Yorker*, but she reinstated it to *Castle Rock* (*New Yorker* proof, May 20, 2002 14; *New Yorker* files; *Castle Rock* 214).

24 The mention of Lucy Maud Montgomery's work here is telling, since Munro has been drawn to her from an early age. In 1989 she published an afterword to a new edition of *Emily of New Moon* (1923) in which she emphasizes its effect on her when she first read it as a girl.

25 Throughout Munro's work the reading and appreciation of poetry are a continual presence and, as well, she has spoken of it in interviews. As a girl she was attracted to Tennyson and, as a young woman, she wrote poetry, publishing just one poem using her mother's name, after her death, as a pseudonym (Thacker *Alice* 125–6, 611). As early as 1951 she wrote a polished unpublished story entitled "The Return of the Poet," one drawing from her intellectual discoveries of poetry and its traditions while a university student. It focuses on a young man, another student poet who shares a similar background with Munro, who returns his hometown Maitland (the name of the river which flows by the Laidlaw farm in Lower Town Wingham) and who sees the distinction between his poetic attractions and the realities of the hometown he has left. It builds to a two-sentence quotation from early in Walt Whitman's *Song of Myself*, "*Stop this day and this night with me and you shall possess the origin of all poems*"; skipping a line Munro continues, "*You shall no longer take things at second or third hand, nor look through the eyes of the dead, nor feed on the spectres in books*" (37.16.5.f10; original emphasis; Whitman l. 33, 35). Home again, the poet writes no more poems.

Throughout Munro's publications, several characters are poets and particular poems are invoked. The title of the Canadian edition of her fourth book, *Who Do You Think You Are?*, owes to an incident involving poetry. And the best-known invocation of poems and poetry is found toward the end of "The Ottawa Valley" when three characters take turns reciting passages memorized years before in school. Thus this narrator in "Lying Under the Apple Tree" may well be seen as Munro herself, "rampaging through [her] school texts" for poems. Ontario used standardized texts when Munro was school, books like W. J. Alexander's *Shorter Poems* published in 1924 by the T. Eaton company in Toronto. This book may have been the one Munro used as a student.

26   When I published the first edition of *Alice Munro: Writing Her Lives: A Biography* in late 2005 I reported *Power in the Blood*—a title Douglas Gibson particularly liked—to be the forthcoming book's title. It was changed to *The View from Castle Rock* in November 2005 after Barber wrote to Gibson explaining Munro's thinking, writing "It's my genuine belief that Alice is no longer happy with it." "Yes, there are great story-tellers even from generations ago in her family, but she's not going to want to make that claim in a title, however subtly" (November 15, 2005; M&S Z106.8).

Chapter 3

1   These generalizations are based on a well-timed interview. In April 2004 Munro explained to me that "in the last book which I shall publish, I'm planning on publishing 'Working for a Living,' and a long story—I think it's a seven-part story—I've written about the Laidlaw family coming out on the boat, which nobody has seen at all, and then some other stories like 'Hired Girl.' Autobiographical stories like that and the more recent ones like 'Lying under the Apple Tree.'" I then asked her about the disclaimer in that story's first publication in the *New Yorker* and she responded, "actually the disclaimer was okay. I mean it was true—it was a story in the sense that it was really about the first boyfriend I had, so it was okay. But all the circumstances surrounding him, the Salvation Army, his job at the horse stable, the horse stable woman—that was all fictitious, so it was a story made the way most of my stories are." Hearing this, I asked if it was going to be included in *Runaway*: "No, because I'm keeping all these autobiographical-based story to come out in another book. The story 'Fathers' is coming out in that book too. I like that story a lot."

Elsewhere in the same interview, I asked her, "Is this the first time when you've been consciously thinking about two different books at the same time?" She replied, directly addressing her methods: "No. Well, when I had those leftover stories—like 'Accident' was a leftover story, and 'Queenie' was a leftover story, then I know I've got to write another book, because I want that story in it. Those were not throwaway stories, so they launched me on to the next step, and the same thing has happened now because I've got two lots of stories, one of which is ready for a book and one of which isn't enough. But this is the first time I've had as much left over" (Thacker interview April 2004).

2   Gorra's excellent review of *Too Much Happiness* has always struck me as recompense on the part of the editors of the *TLS*; the review they published of *The View from Castle Rock* is among the weakest and wrong-headed that the book received (see Thacker *Alice* 545–7, *Reading* 227–30).

3   My argument here focuses on the making and shaping of *The View from Castle Rock* through its archival provenance, so what has already been discussed and will continue to be central here are those materials. That said, I acknowledge that the book has received significant critical attention and, as well, I believe I have read most everything in print. But because most critics know very little of the book's long provenance nor, for that matter, have many looked at prior serial versions, I do not much critique criticism focused on *Castle Rock* here.

4   Edel continues, "It is the quest for this secret that I regard as the justifiable aim of literary biography. All the rest is gossip and anecdotage" (17). Lyall Powers, a close colleague and collaborator of Edel's, considered this passage Edel's clearest statement of biographical theory.

5   "Remnants," the last section here, was later retitled "Messenger" and designated as the book's epilogue. Also, by this time Munro had added to the ending of "Working for a Living"—an account of Robert E. Laidlaw's late-life writing and containing a long quotation from one of his articles.

6   This image, with this caption written on it in an anonymous hand, is in the Library of Congress collection, number LC-USZ62-7307 (see Thacker *Reading* 217–26).

7   Munro adapts the text from the original slightly. There in the first quotation Laidlaw wrote "all through North America before *that* I knew" and the phrase he used was "Coining Lies," not "conning Lies." In "Changing Places" she uses "coining" (200). Also, her first ellipsis is not needed after "Home" since "Hogg poor man" follows immediately after.

As these comments suggest, there are copies of James Laidlaw's two autograph letters to William Lyon Mackenzie (January 8, 1827, and March 17, 1827) in the Laidlaw Family Fonds at the Archives of Ontario, apparently part of materials collected for a family history circa 1970. Additionally, there are two typed transcriptions, one dated February 28, 1919, of James Laidlaw's September 19, 1819, letter to his eldest son Robert in Scotland, which Hogg got published in *Blackwood's* and Munro also quotes from (F230, File: Settlement F230-1, B437613; see Hogg Letter). Among these materials also there are two letters from James Laidlaw (1796–1886), third son of Munro's Old James, a person whom she mentions. He preceded the family to Canada in 1817, to Economy, Nova Scotia, where he taught school. His first letter is addressed to his father and is dated December 5, 1817; it offers an account of his own voyage, the nature of the country, and reports his prospects. The second letter was written on September 30, 1819, and is addressed to a Mr. Thomas Shortreed in Lyonstown, Ontario County, New York. James does not know Shortreed, but he writes to try get word to his family, who were in Lyonstown staying in Shortreed's house over their first winter in America. He intends to join them once his teaching term is done and he has looked after his affairs. When James wrote from York to Robert, he comments that they "like this place better than the States" (James Laidlaw to Robert Laidlaw, September 9, 1819; *Blackwood's* 631–2). His brothers in Scotland had told him that the family stayed with Shortreed and that they had gone to York (F230, File: James, uncle to RL, first of family to Canada, F230-6, B437613).

When I asked Munro about archival research she said she knew that there were Laidlaw Family papers in Toronto—but for those cited here, most of these had to do with Laidlaws descended from Walter Laidlaw, one of whom founded a prosperous lumber company in partnership with a Thomas Shortreed, perhaps the same man James addressed from Nova Scotia in 1819. In 2010 she told me that she had not consulted them (Thacker interview 2010; see also Gilbert and Zemans, eds.)

8   I am quoting here from Miller's 2007 essay, "The Passion of Alice Laidlaw"; the same sentences are to be found in his review of *Castle Rock* in the *Guardian Review*.
9   While it is certainly the case that the reviews Munro received for *Castle Rock* were not as lyric as those gotten two years before for *Runaway*, and for the volumes which preceded it, they were only a bit snarky here and there rather than fully negative. Clearly, this was a book in which readers found a Munro different from the author they were used to. That said, there was a sharp difference here in the reviews it got; Good, for instance, calls the book "coy" and Munro's agent, Jennifer Rudolph Walsh, told me that the foreword was a mistake, one reviewers seized upon (Thacker interview July 20, 2010; see also Thacker *Alice* 544–9). *Castle Rock* sold about half the number hardback copies in the United States that *Runaway* did (Thacker Close interview July 26, 2021).
10 By way of clarification on this point: while Gibson remained Munro's Canadian editor throughout and so oversaw the editing and shaping of the Canadian editions of her books from *Who Do You Think You Are?* (1978) on, as her career developed much connected to her book production was in New York. From *The Progress of Love* (1986) on Knopf handled the typesetting and, with the *New Yorker*, Close, and Barber there too, many editing decisions were made there.
11 As explained above, Munro's first visit to Ettrick was in late January or early February 1982. Additionally, she and Fremlin spent January through part of March 1990 living there. Given these facts and that she was there during "very early spring," her reference here could be to either trip or both.
12 Engraved on the tombstone in the Ettrick Kirk cemetery:

Here Lyeth
William Laidlaw
The far-famed Will O'Phaup
Who for feats of frolic agility strength
Had no equal in his day
He was born at Craik in 1691
And died the 84th year if his age
Also Margaret his oldest daughter
Spouse to Robert Hogg & Mother of
The ETTRICK SHEPHERD
Born at old Over Phaup in 1730
And died in the 83 year of her age
Also Robert Hogg her Husband
Late tenant of Ettrick Hall
Born at Bowhill in 1729
And died in the 93 year of his age
And three of their sons (Photograph: Laidlaw Family Fonds F-230-4: B437614)

13 Munro has been drawn to such religiosity. When she was writing to Gittings in late 1992 about "A Wilderness Station," she identifies its title as coming from Boston, as acknowledged there, and comments that "His whole crazed life is remarkable—somebody should write about him" (November 16, 1992). So she later did in *Castle Rock*. In the same way, one of Munro's mid-career signature stories, "The Progress of Love" (1986), there is a similar passage about religiosity (*Progress* 4; see Thacker *Alice* 21–6).

14 Discussing Munro's writing in *Castle Rock*, and as will be considered at greater length presently, Hadley notes that Munro is writing "about things she can't quite know, but always with a proviso, a sign in the text that she's guessing" (17). An examination of preliminary production versions of *Castle Rock* in the Alice Munro Fonds at Calgary shows Munro sharpening factual materials—various short phrasings are added and some are rewritten (see Knopf copy-edited manuscript dated January 12, 2006 [MsC 323.1.1]; first-pass author's proof [April 27, 2006, [MsC 323.1.1]; and second-pass author's proof [June 13, 2006, MsC 323.1.2]).

15 In a newspaper profile published concurrently with *Castle Rock*, Munro made her personal feeling for the book apparent, and commented too on her purposes within the text:

Writing this book was really important to me, she says. "I felt it wouldn't be popular but at my age you don't care. You do what you need to do. I was encouraged by reading William Maxwell. He was the fiction editor at *The New Yorker* but also wrote books about his ancestors and his childhood. It made it legitimate to write about ordinary family relationships, ordinary human life. The stories about myself are totally factual; I wrote them over a long period of time. The old stuff I discovered and wrote about recently," she says.

(Stoffman H10)

16 The manuscript version of "Remnants" which concludes the 140-page version of "Laidlaws II: The View from Castle Rock" that was submitted to the *New Yorker* in March 2005 is seven pages long. After a brief discussion of changes to the land in Huron County since her father was a boy, it concentrates on Munro's 2004 visit to Joliet, Illinois, in search of William Laidlaw's 1839 or 1840 grave there. The version in the May 2005 book manuscript, also seven pages, expands this, and introduces some elements that are ultimately retained in "Messenger," but its central incident remains the visit to Joliet. Once she had decided on "What Do You Want to Know For?" over "Wenlock Edge," Munro initially thought to use only part of it in the epilogue, apparently thinking that using the whole memoir with "Remnants" would give the book two endings (Munro to Gibson September 10, 2005; M&S Z106.5). Also, the Knopf copy-edited version of the book, dated January 12, 2006, reveals that the "No Advantages" section was initially called "Family History" while the "Home" section was originally "Stories" (MsC 323 1.1).

17 A comparison of the *New Yorker* version of "The View from Castle Rock" with that published in the book suggests Munro added blocks of prose to the early portions of the piece, expanding detail regarding characters and circumstances. These are found on pages 33, 34–5, and 36–7. Walter's journal, quoted from throughout, must have come down in the family; it is not in the Laidlaw Family Fonds in the Archives of Ontario.

While it does not appear that Munro herself was interested in discovering the vessel the family sailed on, a likely candidate is the *Agincourt* of Leith captained by a man named Mathwin. That ship, a three-masted vessel square rigged on all masts, was built in 1804 in North Shields, England; it carried 400 passengers and made three crossings (1817, 1818, 1819) between Leith and Canada (Halifax and Quebec). Rated a second-class vessel—meaning that it was unfit for carrying dry cargoes—it was fit for long sea voyages (Campey 246). I thank Douglas Gibson for pointing this material out.

18 In "Changing Places," Munro wrote that "The baby Isabella had six children and lived to be an old woman. On her tombstone is written *Born at Sea*" (192; original emphasis). The first sentence is factual, although one genealogy puts the number of children at five. After "Changing Places," Munro changes her name to Isabel, although there are references to her as Isabella in the family papers; her nickname was Tibby (see Laidlaw Family Fonds, F230, File: NP Dates on Family Tree, Settlement F230-1, B437613). Her gravestone does not say "*Born at Sea*," however, a fact I verified myself. Munro evidently learned this and revised the *New Yorker* and *Castle Rock*—in each case she uses "*Born at Sea*" but does not claim it is engraved into Isabel's gravestone (*New Yorker* 77, *Castle Rock* 87).

19 As the family story was published, there were differences. In "Changing Places," Munro did not know which brother traveled to Illinois to collect Mary Scott Laidlaw and her children. By 2005 she knew it was Andrew. Similarly, in "Changing Places," Munro dates Will's death and Jane's birth on January 5, 1839 (204). In *Castle Rock* she changed the year to "either 1839 or 1840" (88), the latter year also turning up in some family genealogies.

20 Robert B. Laidlaw's memoir also appeared in the *History of Morris Township and Stories Relating to Pioneer Days, 1856-1956* under the heading "Trials and Tribulations of the Early Settlers." Munro may well have seen it there, but she apparently wrote to the editor of *Blyth: A Village Portrait* asking after a personal copy in early 1978 (see Susan Street to Munro, February 15, 1978; 38.2.37). In addition to Robert B. Laidlaw's memoir (17–21), the book includes a section entitled "The Laidlaw Settlement" (14–15) with background on the family provided by "The late Robert Laidlaw, of Lower Wingham, [who] was a descendant of the family, and the following is taken from his outline of his forebears' history" (14).

21 There is a note attached to the reprinting of Big Rob's memoir in *History of Morris Township* saying "The James Laidlaw who was killed was buried in Lot 7, Concession 10, but about 1900 the family had the body re-interred in Blyth Union Cemetery where it still rests." This location of the original grave was on Thomas Laidlaw's land. A list of gravestones in the Blyth Cemetery made by the Ontario Genealogical Society in 1983 does not include James Laidlaw. His mother Mary Scott Laidlaw's grave is listed, and its details are consistent with what Munro writes; on the stone after her death date she is listed as "Relict of / William LAIDLAW. Who Died / in Illinois U. S. / Jan. 5, 1839: / Aged 41years. / Natives of the / Parish of Ettrick / Selkerkshire [sic], Scotland."

22 A typescript genealogy dated July, 1937 held in the Laidlaw Family Fonds states that "'Big Rob' married Christian [also Christina in other sources] McCollum and they had 11 children": Susan (1859–c. 1935), Andrew (1860-1934), Duncan (1862-1932), James (1865–), George (1866-7), Agnes (1867–c. 1905), John (1869–), William (1870, died), Annie (1872–), Mary Ellen (1874, died), and Findlay (1876–) (F230, File: Family Tree, F230-6, B437613). Given this, there does not appear to have been either a Forrest or a Lizzie.

23 The *New Yorker* rejected "Chaddeleys and Flemings," then a two-part single story, on November 1, 1977, so composition earlier that year is likely (Charles McGrath to Munro; 37.2.30.5).

    Regarding the three deaths by cholera the father mentions after James Laidlaw's accident, this too is part of family lore, as Munro explains as she visits the Blyth Cemetery in "Changing Places" when she visits Mary Scott Laidlaw's grave there. The latter was the grandmother who died of cholera. "And nearby are two grandchildren of Mary's—a girl of thirteen and a boy a year old—who died the same year she did, 1868. I had heard all my life, it seemed, the story of the two children and the grandmother who died at the same time, of cholera, in the hot weather, and how in haste to bury them, the lace curtains in the house were taken down and used for shrouds" (205). But in the cemetery she sees that the three died at different times, so she realizes that part of the story cannot be truth. The deaths were though: "Little Rob" Laidlaw (1832–96), third son of William and Mary Scott Laidlaw, and his wife Euphemia (c. 1839–1905) were the children's parents.

24 The complicated details surrounding the publication of *Who Do You Think You Are?* may be found in Thacker *Alice*, 341–52. Briefly, after the book was late into production at Macmillan, Munro decided to take it off the press and restructure it. The original version was in two parts, a set of Rose stories in third person and a set of Janet stories in first with, at the end, the revelation that Janet wrote the Rose stories. Restructuring it, Munro eliminated Janet's presence altogether and rewrote some of the latter's as Rose stories. Three Janet stories—both "Chaddeleys and Flemings" and "The Moons of Jupiter"—were taken out of *Who*, saved, and after further revision published in *The Moons of Jupiter* in 1982. This quotation is from a bound proof of the first version sent to reviewers. It is held in the John and Myrna Metcalf Collection at McGill University, Montreal.

25 In addition to "Home" and "Working for a Living," Munro was also working on "Wood" (1980) and "The Ferguson Girls Must Never Marry" (1982). As in the Edemariam profile, she told me that she had taken up this work in the spirit of doing it herself rather than letting others do it after she was gone. Regarding "Home," she was quite adamant about removing the author's commentary, asking "who cares how you feel about what you have just written?" (Thacker interview August 2001).

26 Comparing the two versions of "Working for a Living," it is clear that while Munro lets some portions of the 1981 version stand, the changes at the level of punctuation and syntax suggest that her revisions were thorough. The version published in *Castle Rock* shows her still striving to get each parent exactly right, and to get their partnership even more so. That said, Munro's relations with her father emerge as the more significant.

27 Laidlaw published six pieces between May 1974 and August 1976 in the *Village Squire*, a magazine published by the Blyth *Citizen*. The memoir Munro calls "Grandfathers" (November 1974) actually has in the title position "Robert Laidlaw Relects [sic] on Grandparents, His and Others." For more on Laidlaw's writing and the circumstances surrounding the posthumous publication of his *The McGregors*, see Thacker *Alice* 315–16, 336–8. Also, at one point in the composition of *Castle Rock* Munro placed this section on her father's writing at the end of "Home."

28 "The Ticket," along with "Dimension," and "What Do You Want to Know For?," was submitted to the *New Yorker* by an assistant to Munro's agent on November 30, 2005, so it had been written by then (*New Yorker* files). It is also included in the May 2, 2005, version of the book manuscript.

29 Both of these stories resonate within "The Ticket." Each deals in spontaneous class-differentiated romances from the point-of-view of the man. In Coppard's case, the attraction is mutual but there is no sexual union. Munro's early story, "Dulse" (1980) echoes "Dusty Ruth" (see Thacker *Reading* 115–31, 277–8). With Galsworthy's "The Apple Tree" there is a sexual union under the apple tree and, like the narrator in "The Ticket," they make plans for a life together. Drawn by circumstances to friends, the narrator abandons this young woman of a lower class and that leads to her suicide, something the narrator only learns years later when he stops at the same place by happenstance to celebrate his wedding anniversary with his wife of the same class. The epigraph quotes a classical tale in which tragedy occurs because characters

have no empathy. Munro points to the same class configurations—something she never forgot with her husband's family—and has her narrator eschew love for sex. In each case the narrator is cold-hearted.
30   Munro added "those cows …. someone died" to the master proof of *Castle Rock*, one dated June 16, 2006 (see MsC 323 1.3).

Chapter 4

1   In addition to this letter, Barber prepared a list titled "Short Stories since Friend of My Youth" dated November 4, 1992; it includes page lengths and former titles and has the first six stories in *Open Secrets* on it (883/11.5.3). While Munro was writing these stories she regularly pronounced them "weird" (883/11.5.2). While it is not clear which stories she sent, the ending of "Carried Away" (1991) deals in what Munro in the *Paris Review* interview called "alternate realities," and there too she calls it "weird" (256). When asked about the beginning of Munro's late-style Ann Close, her editor at Knopf, said the "big change" came into Alice's work about this time and that they—Munro herself, Barber, and Close—ascribed it to "Carried Away." She said that *Open Secrets*, the book, was "kind of on the borderline" of the big change (Thacker Close interview July 26, 2021).
2   In this version Munro has shifted from Janet as a first-person narrator to third person. The cited typescript page reads "When the bus pulled into Dalgleish tonight, she had looked out at the streets with an emotion that owed something to *Winesburg, Ohio*, something to Spoon River, quite a lot to Chekhov. The real town was not much like a town in Ohio or Illinois and surely less like a village in Russia" (38.10.37.f5).
3   "The Ticket" was not published serially before its appearance in *Castle Rock*, although it was considered twice at the *New Yorker*—in an initial submission and a revision (Treisman email May 15, 2022).
4   This title echoes that of Munro's first published story, "The Dimensions of a Shadow" (1950), which appeared in *Folio*, the undergraduate literary magazine at the University of Western Ontario.
5   The magazine version of "Wood" was reprinted in both *The Best American Short Stories 1981* and *Best Canadian Stories, 81*.
6   This sentiment about "Wood" was shared by readers. After it had been published in the *New Yorker*, McGrath inserts this parenthetical into a letter: "(Speaking of attention, I'm also enclosing some 'Wood' fan mail; it's amazing how that story seems really to have touched some people at a very fundamental, practical level.)" (December 11 [1980]; 38.2.4.13).
7   Roy's changed occupation returns recursively to *Who Do You Think You Are?/The Beggar Maid* where Rose's father runs a "furniture and upholstery repair business" (*Beggar* 3).
8   Others agreed regarding the *New Yorker* version of the story. Although John Metcalf was keen to have a Munro story in *Best Canadian Stories, 81*—he wrote her an emphatic, even begging, letter requesting "Wood" on January 8, 1981—to which she agreed, he also expressed doubt about it; as he was putting the book together Metcalf wrote his coeditor, Leon Rooke, that he "still found Alice's story ['Wood'] obscure and *flat*" (Metcalf to Rooke January 28, 1981; John Metcalf Fonds 24.14.19.7).
9   Editors at the *New Yorker* are known to engage in fastidious, detailed editing for clarity and coherence. While there was a particular period during the late 1990s

when Munro was not happy with the editing her work got there—she felt it was being cut too much—most of the time she has agreed to suggestions, although, as indicated, she often reverted to her submitted text after a serial has appeared in the magazine (see Thacker *Alice* 474–8).

10   Probably more than any single early Munro story, "Material" has been the site of considerable disagreement as to the veracity and motivation of the narrator. See McGill "Daringly."

11   The ending of "Fiction" when it was originally published in *Harper's*—so the *New Yorker* passed on it—had a different final paragraph: "This could turn into a fairly funny story someday. Joyce would not be surprised. That's what she often does with her life" (80). By the time that ending got to the typed setting copy of *Too Much Happiness*, that paragraph became three (see Thacker "Stabbed" 439, n. 10).

12   Munro's zeal for her endings brought about an anomalous one in "Deep-Holes." In the *New Yorker*, after Sally leaves Kent, Munro offers this penultimate paragraph: "There is something, anyway, in having got through the day without its being an absolute disaster. It wasn't, was it? She had said 'maybe.' He hadn't corrected her." This paragraph is the same in *Too Much Happiness* but for a dropped set of quotation marks. As usual, it was the final paragraph that drew Munro's attention. This is final paragraph in the *New Yorker*: "And it was possible, too, that age could become her ally, turning her into somebody she didn't know yet. She had seen that look of old people, now and then—clear-sighted but content, on islands of their own making" (73). This wording was suggested by Treisman (*New Yorker* proof; June 10, 2008). Revising this for the book, the final sentence becomes: "She has seen the look on the faces of certain old people—marooned on islands of their own choosing, clear sighted, content" (Canadian M&S *Happiness* 115). As she was working toward this ending, Munro tried and rejected this version of the paragraph, turning her hand to: "~~And it was possible, wasn't it, that age could get to be her ally, turning her into somebody she didn't know yet. She had seen the look on faces of certain old people—marooned on islands of their own choosing, clear sighted, reckless merry, free of loss~~" (May 14, 2009, 117; MsC 343.1.5). Owing to the timing of printing (Knopf published two months after McClelland & Stewart), irrespective of the exact wording, the final paragraph was dropped from the Knopf edition. There "Deep-Holes" ends with "He hadn't corrected her" (Close to Thacker December 20, 2012).

13   While I have no direct evidence that Munro knew Cather's "The Profile," she has long been a close reader of Cather's work (see Thacker *Reading* 115–31, 277–8).

14   Munro's placement of this apartment "on the Square," as well as the reference to the narrator's Victorian home being located "on the cliffs above Lake Huron," indicates that "Face" is set in Goderich in Huron County. In the same vein, the narrator's purpose in coming home seems parallel to Fremlin's return to Clinton in the early 1970s. After his father died, and after he had retired from the civil service in Ottawa, he returned Clinton to help his mother and put things in order; he did not intend to stay. Once he was there and had done that, though, he realized that his mother could not live there alone, so he stayed (Thacker interview April 2004).

15   The exact submission chronology for "Face" is not clear. On the same day Munro wrote Treisman with this "possible clearing up," Jessica Almon, assistant to Munro's agent Jennifer Rudolph Walsh, submitted "a revised version of Alice Munro's story, *Face*, for your review" to Treisman. Presumably, this means that the editors there had seen it before, or that Munro was still revising.

16 When Treisman sent her edits to Munro, she asks for clarification on the provenance of the slip of paper the narrator finds in the Hutchinson book. She also writes that she "wondered about including the Hutchinson book there—there are so many references in that passage, from the de la Mare to all the other poems they choose to recite, that it starts to feel a little overburdened to me" (August 15, 2008 proof; *New Yorker* files). Munro evidently agreed, for the reference to Hutchinson is deleted in the magazine and in the book. That said, Munro's choice of Huchinson's book seems just as conscious as her quotations from de la Mare and others in "Face." *The Happy Warrior*—its title taken from Wordsworth's "The Character of the Happy Warrior" (1807)—is a sentimental romance.

17 de la Mare's "Away" was first published in his *Memory and Other Poems* (1938). In his *Collected Poems* (1979) the poem is punctuated. Both the *New Yorker* and Knopf checked and so ran the poem with punctuation. Douglas Gibson acceded to Munro's preference to go without, so it appears without end punctuation in the McClelland & Stewart edition. In the *Collected Poems*, the penultimate line is "Your place left vacant" (used in the *New Yorker* and by Knopf) rather than "Your place forgotten" in the Canadian edition; also in the *Collected Poems* there is an "or" in the line she offers as "On love, on duty" in all three versions.

18 In first edited proof, Treisman asks about cutting the last two paragraphs of the story. She writes, "not sure what these lines do—my suggestion would be to end it on 'dying to get away.'" Munro apparently rejected this idea, since Treisman has written the published ending on the last page of the proof. This likely means that Munro gave her the new wording of the last paragraph—the one changed—on the telephone (22–3, edited proof, August 14, 2008; *New Yorker* files).

19 Munro's ending here, with its use of the de la Mare poem, is reminiscent of the ending of "Chaddeleys and Flemings: 1. Connection" (1979) which uses "Row, Row, Row Your Boat" to similar effect as it ends, emphasizing "Life is but a dream" (see Thacker *Alice* 369–72, *Reading* 45–64, 272).

20 One of the unusual aspects of "Some Women" is its metaphorical imagery and innuendo. When Rozanne offers to shave Bruce, Munro uses the word "undertake." The narrator, when she waited on Bruce, "avoided looking at him. And this was not really because he was sick and ugly. It was because he was dying." She likens his sickroom to the Catholic Tabernacle, the center of "an atmosphere of death in the house." "He was the one stricken." Thus throughout there are references and phrasings reminding readers of his impending death. Equally, in describing Roxanne, Munro alludes to the sweetness of candy: this reference to toffee is followed by Roxanne being likened to "a chocolate bunny on Easter morning," and there is mention of her "candy lips" too, connected to her "sumptuous bottom" and so to her sexuality. The celebratory macaroons Mrs. Crozier buys and the narrator surreptitiously eats—although Roxanne refuses them—are at the center of her meditations. After the altercation at the locked door, the narrator goes downstairs and eats two without pleasure, shoving the box into the refrigerator "so I would not hope to turn the trick by eating more" (*Happiness* 173–4, 178). Sexual inuendo again.

21 As was her usual practice, Munro continued to think about "Some Women" after it had been submitted to and bought by the *New Yorker*. On August 14, 2008, Munro sent Treisman two revised pages, commenting that she wanted her to have "these slight changes in case I fall off a cliff or something." Treisman's edits for clarity in two sets of proofs are thorough, and some which Munro retained into the book

version—the fact checker corrected Munro that "Tabernacle" is where Catholics keep the host; she initially had "Sepulcher" (*New Yorker* files).

Chapter 5

1. My reference to Munro's renamings of Wingham-like towns bears comment. In the fragment used as epigraph here the town is Dalgleish, a name Munro used but, hometowns are also Carstairs, Hanratty, Jubilee, Logan, and Walley. These are the most frequently used names. Jubilee is the name Munro used early on—in *Dance of the Happy Shades* and *Lives of Girls and Women*—and Hanratty follows—in *Who Do You Think You Are? / The Beggar Maid*. Dalgleish is in *The Moons of Jupiter* and the others appear later. She seems to have associated particular town names with individual characters and, as well, keeping a name allowed her to tell something of the business history of the town.
2. Two other comments Munro made during our 2010 interview are notable here. When I asked her about the autobiographical implications of opening sentence in "Some Women," she replied, "I am totally amazed ['to think how old I am']. The amazement is just going to get worse and worse until I die. Unless the Alzheimer's takes everything away and then I won't be amazed at anything."
3. While published by the *New Yorker* as an interview, Munro and Treisman did not sit down and talk in the usual way. Instead, Treisman sent her questions and Munro wrote her answers. These were slightly edited, the questions interspersed, and published online (see "For Deborah [,] Answers from Alice?," holograph, n.d., [circa November 2012]; *New Yorker* files).
4. "Axis" was ultimately withheld from *Dear Life* either because of Fremlin's objection after he read it—as Munro told me on September 6, 2013—or because she did not want him to read it—Ann Close's recollection of the decision (Close to Thacker August 30, 2013). Apparently he did not regularly read her stories in magazines, waiting for the book versions instead. The story clearly draws on his life: he flew in the RCAF as a bomb-aimer and saw action during the Second World War; returned to Canada, he studied philosophy and political science at Western Ontario, and drove a taxi before turning to further study in physical geography and a career in that field with the Canadian government in Ottawa. Like Royce, he never married. Given Munro's use of information she got from him in other stories and her decision to withhold "Axis" from *Dear Life*, it seems reasonable to infer that Fremlin's discovery of the Niagara Escarpment may well have occurred in much the same way it is described in "Axis." His M.A. thesis at Western was entitled "Geomorphology of the Niagara Escarpment, Niagara River-Georgian Bay" (1958).
5. In addition to its first publication in the *New Yorker*, "Axis" was included in *The Best American Short Stories 2012*. Though edited slightly, this discussion of "Axis" and its provenance is substantially the same as that found in my 2016 introduction to the Bloomsbury collection, *Alice Munro*.
6. The interrupted sex scene in "Axis" echoes that between Del Jordan and Jerry Storey in *Lives of Girls and Women* where Jerry asked Del to take off all her clothes and she complies. They are interrupted by Jerry's mother's return (*Lives* 200–2). So too the scene in "Lying Under the Apple Tree." There and in "Axis" the sex scene is a plot device—the story's focus is elsewhere.

7   A word about the archival versions of "Axis." Working with Ann Close after the publication of *Dear Life*, I helped arrange the donation of these materials by Knopf to the Alice Munro Fonds, making copies for my own use. While largely arranged and described the work on them is not completely finished as I write in 2022. In verifying the holdings, the archivists have not been able to locate the materials connected with "Axis" I am describing here, so I am differentiating the four typescript copies of "Axis" I have, one of which appears to be the original submission to the *New Yorker* (obtained from the *New Yorker* files); the other three show holograph signs of Munro's work on revisions, with some commentary by Close, so they were among the *Dear Life* papers Knopf donated to the Fonds.

8   While Munro is more precise about geography in this revision, naming Wiarton as the place where Royce notices the cliffs of the Niagara Escarpment and indicating that Royce drove taxis in and around London, she collapses distances from London.

9   This autograph page is accompanied by a clean typed version of the same page, suggesting that it was retyped at Knopf without the final phrase. The deletion of that last phrase was made after July 9, 2012, when Munro faxed Close corrected pages of typeset proofs of *Dear Life* dated June 29, 2012. There the autograph substitute page (176) is included without the strikeout, and Munro added the white-space break just before "The briefest note, the letter tossed" on the previous page (175). So this strikeout was probably made in the second-pass proofs, although Munro may have decided against it as a decision apart from formal proofing.

10 The circumstances Munro assigns to the mother in "Gravel" echo Munro's own during the ten years she still lived with James Munro and their daughters in Victoria (1963–73). They had moved there to open Munro's Books and, after the first several good years of shared mutual enterprise, they drifted apart, Alice finally leaving for good in 1973. After the Munros had been in Victoria for a time and gotten the store established, they bought and moved into a grand Tudor style house on Rockland Avenue; it was James' preference, and Alice, who was eight months pregnant with their youngest daughter when they moved in, capitulated. She always hated it (see Thacker *Alice* 183–4). The cultural turmoil of the 1960s played a part here too, with Alice more liberal than her husband; various stories reflect this rift. The William Maxwell reference is to his *So Long, See You Tomorrow* (1980), where a dog is a substantial character; Munro articulates her admiration for that novel and Maxwell generally in her essay, "Maxwell" (see Thacker *Alice* 224–36; "Alice Munro's Victoria"; "As Truthful").

11 Following this chronology is, again, instructive as to Munro's productivity making *Dear Life*. As I tried to ascertain what was yet coming during the summer of 2011, Close confirmed that *Harper's* bought "Train" before "Alice's wonderful editor there," Ben Metcalf, resigned. "She's written another couple stories recently—one that she describes as 'autobiographical'—that I haven't seen yet" (August 3, 2011). Given timing, this one was probably "Dear Life" but, in any case this remark confirms that the "Finale" to *Dear Life* emerged concurrent amid its other stories.

12 In addition to this archival evidence, there is an (apparently) finished typescript story, "Married People," dated in Munro's hand October 10, 1974, and dedicated to "my husband Jim." She sent to John Metcalf. It begins "One day in the winter when Norah was crossing a street she met a man who looked familiar. This did happen to her, she had come to that time of life." The two also find a place to sit down and catch up with one another; it may be related to this holograph draft, but there are echoes in

it of "Material," which had already been published by 1974, and various other Munro stories yet to be written (John Metcalf Fonds 24.48.16).

13   This version of the ending of "Dolly" is more equivocal and less abrupt than the *Tim House* ending—this one has been developed, added to—through the narrator's certainty that Franklin would not open any letter that turned up after she died—and smoothed out. It is an apt prelude to the "Finale" that follows. Franklin's character is another recognition of Fremlin who, like Franklin was practical (he bought Dolly a car to drive to North Bay) and also a poet. Stolid. Himself. Here is the ending in *Tin House*:

Of course, I would have to be on the lookout for the letter I had written him. What a joke it would be—well, hardly a joke—if I should die in the meantime.
   That made me think about the conversation we'd had earlier in the fall and our notion of being beyond all savagery and elation.

(80)

Commenting on the distance between the *Tin House* version and the *Dear Life* version, Close said that "She started rewriting it, and as she did, over several versions, both the order of the ending paragraphs and to some extent their tone began to change. At some point, I asked her if she meant to do that, and she said yes, that this current version, or one of the versions heading toward the current version was what she had in mind" (September 4, 2013). It was during these rewrites that Munro dropped the phrasing, "a perfectly ordinary and savage woman."

14   Close is recalling that the final words of the *Tin House* version are "savagery and elation" (80). Regarding that line, Close also said that "Aware that she had been trying to 'end' her writing career for the past several books, I think I questioned whether she really wanted" to put the ongoing relations in, specifically the phrase, "ordinary and savage woman," "there or not, but she was very definite about it" (September 6, 2013).

Chapter 6

1   I saw an advance proof of "Dear Life" on August 11, 2011, so that, at Munro's suggestion, I could provide the *New Yorker* with photographs to accompany the piece. They used an image captioned "Alice Munro, at the age of two or there, in her hometown of Wingham, Ontario" (*New Yorker* 40; Thacker *Alice* facing 246).

2   A November 27, 2007, cover letter to Deborah Treisman from Jennifer Rudolph Walsh confirms that she did submit "Too Much Happiness" to the magazine along with "Free Radicals." Treisman consulted her notes on my behalf, writing that they "took [the latter story] in early December of 2007, and I would have turned down 'Too Much Happiness' at that point." Her notes indicated too that "Too Much Happiness" was "likely more than 20,000 words long and thus it wasn't possible for us to do. We were not publishing online novellas at that point, and there was really no way to get that amount of space in a regular issue. We had done one fiction issue with three Munro stories ('Chance,' 'Soon,' 'Silence') that would have added up to 25,000 words or so, but it was a feat to get that done, and I don't think

I would have been given the space to do it a second time" (emails; see Thacker *Alice* 514–15).

3   In May 2010 I had an exchange with David Sanders, the Director of Ohio University Press, seeking to contact Don H. Kennedy; he confirmed the author was deceased. He said that they had tried to contact his heirs but to no avail. At that time the lowest price for a used copy of the out-of-print *Little Sparrow* was about $200.

4   Stillman writes in her 1978 introduction to *A Russian Childhood*: "Before Christmas Sofya and the newly married Anne-Charlotte, who had never met Maxim, had arranged to spend New Year's day together in Genoa. Because of a misaddressed telegram the meeting never took place, and Sofya and Maxim spent the day alone in a Genoa cemetery, wandering among gravestones and rehashing old differences" (35). The Kennedys, for their part, write:

Upon learning that Anna Charlotte and her husband would be returning shortly after Christmas [1890] to Naples, Sophia conceived the idea of meeting them in Genoa to introduce Maxsim to the Count and probably also for a *tête-à-tête* with Anna. Unfortunately, because of a misdirected telegram, the couple passed right through Genoa while Sophia and Maxsim waited in vain. They went sightseeing there, and on New Year's day walked among the monuments of the old cemetery, which were of interest to Maxim in his study of custom. While there, Sophia half-whispered to him, superstitiously but not entirely seriously: "One of us will not survive this year, because we have spent the first day in a burial ground."

(310)

5   Toward the beginning of the chapter in *Little Sparrow* on Kovalevsky's literary writings, "Her Literary Life," a chapter that breaks the biography's chronology, the Kennedys point to and quote a letter Sophia wrote to A. S. Montvid in late 1890 in reply to her surprise over Kovalevsky's two realms of accomplishment. She begins with the passage that Munro edited to use as an epigraph to "Too Much Happiness," continuing to write "'and one of the first mathematicians of our century very correctly said that it is not possible to be a mathematician without having the soul of a poet. Of course it must be understood that one must abandon the old supposition that a poet must compose something non-existent, that fantasy and invention are one and then same'" (Kennedy 264). Beyond her epigraph, Munro takes this rendering of the mathematician and the poet by Kovalevsky and largely assigns it to her mentor Weierstrass.

Kovalevsky wrote verse but began writing seriously in 1886 when she published "Recollections of George Eliot" along with other articles and reviews after she earned her doctorate and returned to Russia. In 1887 she collaborated with Anna Charlotte Leffler as co-author of two plays together entitled *The Struggle for Happiness*. She is most prominently known for a memoir, *Recollections of Childhood*, first published in Swedish in 1889 as *Our Russian Life: The Raevsky Sisters* as apparent fictions and translated into English as *A Russian Childhood*. A revised Russian translation was published in 1890 with the fiction guise dropped (see *Happiness* 282; Kennedy 274). The Kennedys assert that it "is worthy to stand beside Tolstoy's *Childhood, Boyhood, and Youth* and similar works by Aksakov and Turgenev" (263). There is also her posthumous novel (or novella), *The Nihilist* (in English *The Nihilist Girl*).

It was published in Swedish in 1892. The Kennedys maintain that had she focused on fiction, Kovalevsky could have been a significant novelist.

6. I acknowledge Cox's 2013 reading of *Too Much Happiness* through Munro's late style as forerunner here. Arguing that "Munro's approach to her subject matter has remained consistent," Cox notes "an authorial standpoint firmly based in old age, [where] there is a changed emphasis in Munro's handling of time" (277).

7. When following a source document often what an author does not use is as illuminating as what she does use. Munro very clearly shaped Kovalevsky's travels—she stopped in Berlin to visit Weierstrass on her way to Maxim's place in Beaulieu in addition to the stop Munro uses on the return trip. Also, the Kennedys speculate that Kovalevsky may have had thoughts of suicide about this time, "which more than once she had discussed in a theoretical way with Anna Charlotte" (Kennedy 309). Munro makes no mention of this possibility.

8. Munro had initially written the final sentence here as follows: "As if she saw everything now through clear sheets of intelligent glass." In a manuscript containing numerous edits and additions in Gibson's hand—some of these may have been his, but it is more likely Munro phoned in her own changes and he transcribed them when the book version was being prepared—this sentence is edited to as published. This edit is followed by the addition of the paragraph describing Kovalevsky's remembrance of her discovery of trigonometry and the nature of pure mathematics (M&S Z119.13.60-60a).

9. This quotation is by Lewis Gannett of the New York *Herald Tribune*. It is on the back cover of the Harvest Book edition of *The Golden Apples*.

10. Regarding the archival evidence of Munro's perpetual work on the endings of her stories, I make the same point—using some of the same languages—in *Alice Munro: Writing Her Lives* (563). Both Ann Close and Douglas Gibson, Munro's editors, have told me that the idea for the finale grouping was Munro's alone, although Gibson suggested the need for a title for the section and an author's note—this was mentioned in Close's cover letter for the copy-edited manuscript, so this would have been spring 2012 (Close to Munro n.d. [spring 2012]).

11. In 1942, writing to the critic and editor Alexander Woollcott, Cather comments that she is glad he likes the last chapter—the epilogue—of *Sapphira*, saying "Many people didn't. But in this book my end was my beginning: the place I started out from." She then offers an account of the memory of "the thrill that went through me" whenever she recalled the scene of Nancy's return which she used to end the novel. Cather's ending and Munro's "Finale" seem to emerge from the same methods; they are borne of a similar place in each career, and create quite similar effects.

12. Owing to the people who lived along Munro's walk to school and back through Lower Town Wingham to Wingham—a daily three-kilometre trek she began in Grade Four when she was eight—Munro's archival manuscripts and some of her published works are frequented by odd characters (see Thacker *Alice* 53, 65–6). Mrs. Netterfield in *Dear Life*—whom Munro presents as a real person, remembered—may well have been the basis for characters in draft stories. In one titled "The Heart of an Executioner," for example, a fragment dating from the 1950s, there is an elderly woman, Mrs. Farr, who though feeble is in the habit of wandering off (37.15.6.1.f1). Mrs. Netterfield, with her hatchet, is a similar character, and they are frequent in Munro's writings, especially in her early work.

13 The letter Munro refers to was dated January 31, 1955, and it was also republished locally in a volume devoted to Huron County with the notation, "This poem is describing the Laidlaw farm." I have a copy of the letter from this source but no record of its original publication. Munro renders the letter's information accurately, although Emma Netterfield Cooper says she was born in Wingham in 1875, not 1876.

14 In the *New Yorker* version of "Dear Life," the phrasing here is "my own invariably torn-up writing" (47).

Works Cited

1. Archival and Unpublished Sources

Alice Munro Fonds. Special Collections Division, University of Calgary Libraries, Calgary, Alberta.
Canadian Broadcasting Corporation Archives. www.cbc.ca.
John Metcalf Fonds. Special Collections Division, University of Calgary, Calgary, Alberta.
John and Myrna Metcalf Collection McGill University Archives, Montreal, Quebec.
Laidlaw Family Fonds, F 230 Archives of Ontario, Toronto, Ontario.
Macmillan Company of Canada Archive. William Ready Division of Archives and Research Collections, McMaster University, Hamilton, Ontario.
McClelland & Stewart Archive. William Ready Division of Archives and Research Collections, McMaster University, Hamilton, Ontario.
New Yorker Files. 1 World Trade Center, New York, New York.
New Yorker Records (*c.* 1924–84). Center for the Humanities, Manuscripts and Archives, New York Public Library.
Robert Kroetsch Fonds. Special Collections Division, University of Calgary, Calgary, Alberta.
Robert Weaver Fonds, R5318-0-4-E Library and Archives Canada, Ottawa, Ontario.

2. Published Sources, Interviews, Letters, and Emails

The Alice Munro Papers: First Accession: *An Inventory of the Archive at the University of Calgary Libraries*. Compiled by Jean M. Moore and Jean F. Tener, edited by Apollonia Steele and Tener, biocritical essay by Thomas E. Tausky. University of Calgary Press, 1986.
The Alice Munro Papers: Second Accession: *An Inventory of the Archive at the University of Calgary Libraries*. Compiled by Jean M. Moore, edited by Apollonia Steele and Jean F. Tener. University of Calgary Press, 1987.
Atwood, Margaret. "Margaret Atwood on the Show-Stopping Isak Dinesen." *Guardian*, November 29, 2013, www.theguardian.com. January 13, 2022.
Awano, Lisa Dickler. "Kindling the Creative Fire: Alice Munro's Two Versions of 'Wood.'" *New Haven Review*, May 30, 2012. https://www.newhavenreview.com/blog/index.php/2012/05/kindling-the-creative-fire-alice-munros-two-versions-of-wood.
Awano, Lisa Dickler. "The Tremendous Importance of Ordinary Events: An Interview with Alice Munro about Two Versions of 'Wood.'" *New Haven Review*, issue 9, Winter 2011, pp. 46–67.
Barber, Virginia. Emails to Robert Thacker, August 24, 2005, and April 18, 2010. Author's possession.
Bell, J. J. *Wee MacGreegor: A Scottish Story*. [1902]. Grosset & Dunlap, [1903].

Berry, Wendell. "Sweetness Preserved." *Imagination in Place*. Counterpoint, 2010, pp. 87–101.
Berryman, John. "Shakespeare at Thirty." 1953. *The Freedom of the Poet*, preface by Robert Giroux. Farrar, Straus and Giroux, 1976, pp. 29–55.
Butt, William. "Messengers and Messaging in Alice Munro's *The View from Castle Rock*." Struthers, *Alice Munro Everlasting*, pp. 345–66.
Byatt, A. S. "Alice Munro: One of the Great Ones." Review of *Selected Stories* by Alice Munro. Toronto *Globe and Mail*, November 2, 1996, pp. D14, 18.
Campey, Lucille H. *An Unstoppable Force: The Scottish Exodus to Canada*. Natural Heritage Books, 2008.
Carrington, Ildikó de Papp. "Other Rooms, Other Texts, Other Selves: Alice Munro's 'Sunday Afternoon' and "Hired Girl." *Journal of the Short Story in English*, vol. 30, Spring 1998, pp. 2–8.
Cather, Willa. Letter to Alexander Woollcott. December 5, 1942. *Selected Letters of Willa Cather*, edited by Andrew Jewell and Janis Stout, Knopf, 2013, pp. 612–14.
Cather, Willa. *Sapphira and the Slave Girl*. 1940. Willa Cather Scholarly Edition. Historical Essay and Explanatory Notes by Ann Romines. Textual essay and editing by Charles W. Mignon, Kari A. Ronning, and Frederick M. Link. University of Nebraska Press, 2009.
Close, Ann. Emails and letters to Robert Thacker. Author's possession.
Close, Ann. Letter to Alice Munro. N. d. [spring 2012]. Author's possession.
Cohen, Leah Hager. "Object Lessons." Review of *Too Much Happiness* by Alice Munro. *New York Times Book Review*, November 29, 2009, pp. 1, 9.
Coppard, A. E. "Dusky Ruth." *Adam & Eve & Pinch Me*. Project Gutenberg.
Cox, Ailsa. "'Age Could Be Her Ally': Late Style in Alice Munro's *Too Much Happiness*." *Critical Insights: Alice Munro*, edited by Charles E. May. Salem Press, 2013, pp. 276–90.
de la Mare, Walter. "Away." *The Collected Poems of Walter de la Mare*. Faber and Faber, 1979, p. 281.
DeFalco, Amelia. "The Shame of Affect: Sensation and Susceptibility in Alice Munro's Fiction." *Ethics and Affects in the Fiction of Alice Munro*, edited by Amelia DeFalco and Lorraine York. Palgrave Macmillan, pp. 35–56.
Delbanco, Nicholas. *Lastingness: The Art of Old Age*. Grand Central, 2011.
Dinesen, Isak. *Seven Gothic Tales*. 1934. Vintage, 1991.
Dodds, E. R. *The Greeks and the Irrational*. 1951. Martino Fine, 2020.
Duffy, Dennis. "Alice Munro's Narrative Historicism: 'Too Much Happiness.'" 2015. Struthers, *Alice Munro Everlasting*, pp. 367–86.
Edel, Leon. "Introduction." *Henry James: The Treacherous Years, 1892-1901*, vol. 4 of *The Life of Henry James*. J. B. Lippencott, 1966, pp. 14–17.
Edemariam, Aida. "Alice Munro: Riches of a Double Life." *Guardian*, October 3, 2003.
Eisenberg, Deborah. Review of *The View from Castle Rock*, by Alice Munro. *Atlantic*, December 2006, p. 128.
Findley, Timothy. "The McGregors." Review of *The McGregors*, by Robert Laidlaw. Toronto *Globe and Mail*, May 19, 1979, p. 45.
French, William. "Annual Blooms." Review of *74: New Canadian Stories*. Toronto *Globe and Mail*, September 26, 1974.
Galsworthy, John. "The Apple Tree." *Five Tales*. Scribner's, 1921, pp. 199–278.
Gilbert, Nathan and Joyce Zemans, editors. *Making Change: Fifty Years of the Laidlaw Foundation*. ECW Press, 2001.

Gittings, Christopher E. "The Scottish Ancestor: A Conversation with Alice Munro." *Scotlands*, vol. 2, 1994, pp. 83–96.
Good, Alex. Review of *The View from Castle Rock* by Alice Munro. *Quill & Quire*, October 2006, p. 41.
Gorra, Michael. "Crossing the Threshold." Review of *The Love of a Good Woman* by Alice Munro. *New York Times Book Review*, November 1, 1998, pp. 6–7.
Gorra, Michael. "Mortal Fear: Love and Death, History and Destiny: The Late Mastery of Alice Munro." Review of *Too Much Happiness* by Alice Munro. *TLS*, August 21 & 28, 2009, pp. 3–4.
Hadley, Tessa. "Dream Leaps." Review of *The View from Castle Rock* by Alice Munro. *London Review of Books*, vol. 29, no. 2, January 25, 2007, pp. 17–18.
Hay, Elizabeth. "The Mother as Material." *The Cambridge Companion to Alice Munro*, edited by David Staines. Cambridge, 2016, pp. 178–92.
Henderson, Eleanor. Email to Robert Thacker, January 17, 2004. Author's possession.
Henighan, Stephen. "The Sense of an Ending." Review of *The View from Castle Rock* by Alice Munro. *TLS*, October 27, 2006, pp. 21–2.
A History of Sullivan Township 1850 to 1975. Sullivan Historical Society [Desboro, Ontario], 1975.
Hogg, James. "Letter from the Ettrick Shepherd." *Blackwell's Magazine*, March 1820, pp. 630–1.
Hogg, James. "Odd Characters." "The Shepherd's Calendar," *Blackwell's Magazine*, March 1820, pp. 440–8.
Hutcheon, Linda and Michael. "Historicizing Late Style as a Discourse of Reception." *Late Style and Its Discontents: Essays on Art, Literature, and Music*, edited by Gordon McMullen and Sam Smiles. Oxford University Press, 2016, pp. 51–68.
Kakutani, Michiko. "The Delicate Arithmetic of Love and Independence." Review of *Too Much Happiness* by Alice Munro. *New York Times*, November 30, 2009, pp. C1, C9.
Kennedy, Don H. *Little Sparrow: A Portrait of Sophia Kovalevsky*. Ohio University Press, 1983.
Kovalevskaya, Sofya [Sophia Kovalevsky]. *Nihilist Girl*, translated by Natasha Kolchevska with Mary Zinn, introduction by Kolchevska. MLA, 2001.
Kovalevskaya, Sofya [Sophia Kovalevsky]. *A Russian Childhood*, translated, edited, and introduced by Beatrice Stillman. Springer-Verlag, 1978.
Lahey, Anita and Kim Jernigan. Interview with Alice Munro. *The New Quarterly*, no. 119, Summer 2011, pp. 43–53.
Laidlaw, James. Letter to Robert Laidlaw. *Blackwell's Magazine*, March 1820, pp. 631–2.
Laidlaw, Robert [E.]. *The McGregors: A Novel of an Ontario Pioneer Family*, introduction by Harry J. Boyle. Macmillan, 1979.
Laidlaw, Robert B. "Diary of Robert B. Laidlaw." In *Blyth: A Village Portrait: 1877-1977*, edited by Sandra Street, Blyth, Ontario, pp. 17–21.
Lee, Monika. "Fractal Fiction in Alice Munro's 'Too Much Happiness.'" Struthers, *Alice Munro Everlasting*, pp. 387–407.
Luft, Joanna. "Boxed In: Alice Munro's 'Wenlock Edge' and *Sir Gawain and the Green Knight*." *Studies in Canadian Literature / Études en littérrature canadienne*, vol. 35, no. 1, 2010, pp. 103–26.
Lurie, Alison. "The Lamp in the Mausoleum." Review of *Carried Away* and *The View from Castle Rock* by Munro, *Lives of Mothers and Daughters: Growing up with Alice Munro* by Sheila Munro, *Alice Munro: Writing Her Lives: A Biography* by Robert Thacker. *The New York Review of Books*, December 21, 2006, pp. 22, 24, 26, 28, 30.

Martin, W. R. and Warren U. Ober. "Alice Munro as Small-Town Historian." *The Rest of the Story: Critical Essays on Alice Munro*, edited by Robert Thacker. ECW Press, 1999, pp. 128–46.

Martin, W. R. and Warren U. Ober. "Alice Munro's 'Hold Me Fast, Don't Let Me Pass' and 'Tam Lin.'" *ANQ*, vol. 13, no. 3, Summer 2000, pp. 44–8.

May, Charles E. "The Short Story's Way of Meaning: Alice Munro's 'Passion.'" *Narrative*, vol. 20, no. 2, May 2012, pp. 172–82.

McCulloch, Jeanne and Mona Simpson. "Alice Munro: The Art of Fiction CXXXVII." Interview. *Paris Review*, no. 131, 1994, pp. 226–64.

McGill, Robert. "Alice Munro and Personal Development." *The Cambridge Companion to Alice Munro*, edited by David Staines. Cambridge, 2016, pp. 136–53.

McGill, Robert. "'Daringly Out in the Public Eye': Alice Munro and the Ethics of Writing Back." *University of Toronto Quarterly*, vol. 76, no. 3, 2007, pp. 874–89.

McMullen, Gordon. *Shakespeare and the Idea of Late Writing: Authorship in the Proximity of Death*. Cambridge University Press, 2007.

Metcalf, John. "A Conversation with Alice Munro." *Journal of Canadian Fiction*, vol. 1, no. 4, 1972, pp. 54–62.

Miller, Karl. "Lives and Letters: Humble Beginnings." Review of *The View from Castle Rock* by Alice Munro. *Guardian Review*, October 28, 2006, p. 21.

Miller, Karl. "The Passion of Alice Laidlaw." *Changing English*, vol. 17, no. 1, April 2007, pp. 17–21.

Millgate, Michael. *Testamentary Acts: Browning, Tennyson, James, Hardy*. Oxford University Press, 1992.

Mitchell, Lee Clark. *More Time: Contemporary Short Stories and Late Styles*. Oxford University Press, 2019.

Munro, Alice. Afterword. *Emily of New Moon* by Lucy Maud Montgomery. 1923. McClelland & Stewart, 1989, pp. 357–61.

Munro, Alice. "Amundsen." *New Yorker*, August 27, 2012, pp. 58–69.

Munro, Alice. "Axis." *New Yorker*, January 31, 2011, pp. 62–9.

Munro, Alice. "Axis." *The Best American Short Stories 2012*, selected by Tom Perrotta with Heidi Pitlor, introduction by Perrotta. Houghton Mifflin Harcourt, 2012, pp. 122–37. Munro comment on story p. 329.

Munro, Alice. "A Better Place than Home." *The Newcomers: Inhabiting a New Land*, edited by Charles E. Israel. McClelland & Stewart, 1979, pp. 113–24.

Munro, Alice. "Changing Places." *Writing Home: A PEN Canada Anthology*, edited by Constance Rooke. McClelland & Stewart, 1997, pp. 190–206.

Munro, Alice. "Characters." *Ploughshares*, vol. 4, no. 3, Summer 1978, pp. 72–82.

Munro, Alice. "Child's Play." *Harper's*, February 2007, pp. 73–84.

Munro, Alice. "Connection." *Chatelaine*, November 1978, pp. 66–7, 97–8, 101, 104, 106.

Munro, Alice. "Corrie." *New Yorker*, October 11, 2010, pp. 94–101.

Munro, Alice. "Corrie." *The Pen / O. Henry Prize Stories 2012*, chosen with an introduction by Laura Furman, with essays by jurors Mary Gaitskill, Daniyal Mueenuddin, and Ron Rash. Anchor, 2012, pp. 392–409. Munro comment on story p. 427.

Munro, Alice. *Dance of the Happy Shades and Other Stories*. 1968. McGraw-Hill, 1973.

Munro, Alice. "Dear Life." *New Yorker*, September 19, 2011, pp. 40–2, 44–7.

Munro, Alice. *Dear Life*. Manuscript. March 2012. Knopf. Author's possession.

Munro, Alice. *Dear Life*. Knopf, 2012.

Munro, Alice. "Deep-Holes." *New Yorker*, June 30, 2008, pp. 66–73.

Munro, Alice. "Dimension." *New Yorker*, June 5, 2006, pp. 68–79.

Munro, Alice. "Dolly." *Tin House*, vol. 13, no. 4, issue 52, 2012, pp. 65–80.
Munro, Alice. "Dulse." *The Moons of Jupiter*. McClelland & Stewart, 1982, pp. 36–59.
Munro, Alice. "Everything Here Is Touchable and Mysterious." *Weekend Magazine* [Toronto *Star*], May 11, 1974, p. 33.
Munro, Alice. "Face." *New Yorker*, September 8, 2008, pp. 58–66.
Munro, Alice. *Family Furnishings: Selected Stories, 1995-2014*. Foreword by Jane Smiley. Knopf, 2014.
Munro, Alice. "Fathers." *New Yorker*, January 22, 1990, pp. 64–71.
Munro, Alice. "The Ferguson Girls Must Never Marry." *Grand Street*, vol. 1, no. 3, Spring 1982, pp. 27–64.
Munro, Alice. "Fiction." *Harper's*, August 2007, pp. 73–84.
Munro, Alice. "Free Radicals." *New Yorker*, February 11 and 18, 2008, pp. 136–43.
Munro, Alice. "Friend of My Youth." *New Yorker*, January 22, 1990, pp. 36–48.
Munro, Alice. *Friend of My Youth*. Knopf, 1990.
Munro, Alice. "Golden Apples." *Eudora Welty at Ninety: A Tribute. The Georgia Review*, vol. 53, no. 1, 1999, pp. 22–4.
Munro, Alice. "Good-By, Myra." *Chatelaine*, July 1956, pp. 16–17, 55–8.
Munro, Alice. "Gravel." *New Yorker*, June 27, 2011, pp. 64–70.
Munro, Alice. *Hateship, Friendship, Courtship, Loveship, Marriage*. Knopf, 2001.
Munro, Alice. "Haven." *New Yorker*, March 5, 2012, pp. 66–73.
Munro, Alice. "Hired Girl." *New Yorker*, April 11, 1994, pp. 82–8.
Munro, Alice. "Home." *74: New Canadian Stories*, edited by David Helwig and Joan Harcourt. Oberon, 1974, pp. 133–53.
Munro, Alice. "Home." *New Statesman*, December 17, 2001–January 7, 2002, pp. 84–93.
Munro, Alice. "Introduction." *The Moons of Jupiter*. Penguin, 1986, pp. xiii–xvi.
Munro, Alice. Introduction to the Vintage Edition. *Selected Stories*. Vintage, 1997, pp. xiii–xxi.
Munro, Alice. "Leaving Maverley." *New Yorker*, November 28, 2011, pp. 64–71.
Munro, Alice. "Leaving Maverley." *The O. Henry Prize Stories 2013*, chosen with an introduction by Laura Furman, with essays by jurors Lauren Groff, Edith Pearlman, and Jim Shepherd. Anchor, 2013, pp. 85–105. Munro comment on story, p. 437.
Munro, Alice. Letter to Christopher Gittings. November 16, 1992. Author's possession.
Munro, Alice. Letters to Douglas Gibson. Macmillan Company of Canada Archive, William Ready Divisions of Archives and Research Collections, McMaster University.
Munro, Alice. Letters to Douglas Gibson. McClelland & Stewart Archive, William Ready Divisions of Archives and Research Collections, McMaster University.
Munro, Alice. Letter to Eleanor Henderson. November 23, 1995. Author's possession.
Munro, Alice. Letters to Robert Weaver. Robert Weaver Fonds, R5318-0-4-E, Library and Archives Canada, Ottawa.
Munro, Alice. Letters to Virginia Barber. Virginia Barber Papers. Alice Munro Fonds, Archives and Special Collections, University of Calgary.
Munro, Alice. *Lives of Girls and Women*. McGraw-Hill, 1971.
Munro, Alice. *The Love of a Good Woman*. Knopf, 1998.
Munro, Alice. "Lying under the Apple Tree." *New Yorker*, June 17 and 24, 2002, pp. 88–90, 92, 105–8, 110–14.
Munro, Alice. "Maxwell." *A William Maxwell Portrait: Memories and Appreciations*, edited by Charles Baxter, Michael Collier, and Edward Hirsh. Norton, 2004, pp. 34–47.

Munro, Alice. *The Moons of Jupiter*. 1982. Knopf, 1983.
Munro, Alice. "Night." *Granta*, no. 120, summer, 2012, pp. 59–71.
Munro, Alice. *Open Secrets*. Knopf, 1994.
Munro, Alice. [pseudonym Anne Chamney]. "Poem (Untitled)." *Canadian Forum*, February 1967, p. 243.
Munro, Alice. "Pride." *Harper's*, April 2011, pp. 59–60, 62–7.
Munro, Alice. *The Progress of Love*. Knopf, 1986.
Munro, Alice. *Runaway*. Knopf, 2004.
Munro, Alice. "Some Women." *New Yorker*, December 22 and 29, 2008, pp. 69–77.
Munro, Alice. *Something I've Been Meaning to Tell You: Thirteen Stories*. McGraw-Hill, 1974.
Munro, Alice. "Spaceships Have Landed." *Paris Review*, no. 131, 1994, pp. 265–94.
Munro, Alice. "The Stone in the Field." *Saturday Night*, April 1979, pp. 40–5.
Munro, Alice. "To Reach Japan." *Narrative*, Winter 2012, https://www.narrativemagazine.com/issues/winter-2012/fiction/reach-japan-alice-munro.
Munro, Alice. "Too Much Happiness." *Harper's*, August 2009, pp. 53–72.
Munro, Alice. *Too Much Happiness*. Knopf, 2009.
Munro, Alice. *Too Much Happiness*. McClelland & Stewart, 2009.
Munro, Alice. "Train." *Harper's*, April 2012, pp. 48–58.
Munro, Alice. "Train." *The Best American Short Stories 2013*, selected by Elizabeth Strout with Heidi Pitlor, introduction by Strout, Houghton Mifflin Harcourt, 2013, pp. 145–72. Munro comment on story, p. 333.
Munro, Alice. *The View from Castle Rock*. Manuscript version. May 2005. Author's possession.
Munro, Alice. "The View from Castle Rock." *New Yorker*, August 29, 2005, pp. 64–77.
Munro, Alice. *The View from Castle Rock*. Knopf, 2006.
Munro, Alice. "Wenlock Edge." *New Yorker*, December 5, 2005, pp. 80–91.
Munro, Alice. "What Do You Want to Know For?" *Writing Away: The Pen Canada Travel Anthology*, edited by Constance Rooke, McClelland & Stewart, 1994, pp. 203–20.
Munro, Alice. "What Is Real?" *Making It New: Contemporary Canadian Stories*, edited by John Metcalf, Methuen, 1982, pp. 223–6. Also *Canadian Forum*, September 1982, pp. 5, 36.
Munro, Alice. "Wood." *New Yorker*, November 24, 1980, pp. 46–54.
Munro, Alice. "Wood." *The Best American Short Stories, 1981*, edited by Hortense Calisher with Shannon Ravenel, introduction by Calisher, Houghton Mifflin, 1981, pp. 241–54.
Munro, Alice. "Wood." *81: Best Canadian Stories*, edited by John Metcalf and Leon Rooke, Oberon, 1981, pp. 93–110.
Munro, Alice. "Working for a Living." *Grand Street*, vol. 1, no. 1, Autumn 1981, pp. 9–37.
Munro, Alice. "Writing. Or, Giving Up Writing." *Writing Life: Celebrated Canadian and International Writers on Writing and Life*, edited by Constance Rooke, McClelland & Stewart, 2006, pp. 297–300.
Munro, Alice. "The Yellow Afternoon." Manuscript. Alice Munro Fonds, University of Calgary. 37.16.34.f1-11.
Munro, Alice. "The Yellow Afternoon." *Anthology*, CBC Radio, February 22, 1955.
Munro, Sheila. Interview with Alice Munro. March 1997. Author's possession.
Munro, Sheila. *Lives of Mothers and Daughters: Growing Up with Alice Munro*. McClelland & Stewart, 2001.
Redekop, Magdalene. "Alice Munro and the Scottish Nostalgic Grotesque." *The Rest of the Story: Critical Essays on Alice Munro*, edited by Robert Thacker, ECW Press, 1999, pp. 21–43.

Reeves, Eric. Email to Robert Thacker. October 18, 2021. Author's possession.
Riddell, Elizabeth. "To Alice Short Is Beautiful." *The Bulletin* [Australia], April 17, 1979, p. 52.
Roberts, Deborah. "The Sublime Munro." Letter. *New York Time Book Review*, December 20, 2009, p. 4.
Ross, Val. "Lunch at Alice's Restaurant." Toronto *Globe and Mail*, October 28, 2006, pp. R1, R8.
Said, Edward W. *On Late Style: Music and Literature against the Grain*, foreword by Mariam C. Said, introduction by Michael Wood. Pantheon, 2006.
Said, Edward W. "Thoughts on Late Style." *London Review of Books*, vol. 26, no. 15, August 5, 2004, pp. 3, 5–7.
Salter, Mary Jo. "In Praise of Accidents." Review of *Friend of My Youth* by Alice Munro. *New Republic*, May 14, 1990, pp. 50–3.
Sanders, David. Email to Robert Thacker. May 26, 2010. Author's possession.
Scott, Sir Walter. *Minstrelsy of the Scottish Border*. 1802. Revised and edited by T. F. Henderson. Oliver and Boyd, 1932.
Scurr, Ruth. "The Darkness of Alice Munro." Review of *New Selected Stories* by Alice Munro. *TLS*, September 30, 2011, pp. 3–4.
Shorter Poems, selected by W. J. Alexander, revised edition. T. Eaton Company, 1924.
Somacarrera, Pilar. "'The Unavoidable Collision of Religion and Life' Scots Presbyterianism in Alice Munro's Fiction." *Studies in Canadian Literature / Études en littérature canadienne*, vol. 40, no. 2, 2015, pp. 88–107.
Stillman, Beatrice. Introduction. *A Russian Childhood* by Kovalevskaya, pp. 1–45.
Stoffman, Judy. "Making a Short Story Long." Toronto *Star*, October 28, 2006, pp. H1, H10.
Struthers, J. R. (Tim). Email. April 1, 2021. Author's possession.
Struthers, J. R. "The Real Material: An Interview with Alice Munro." *Probable Fictions: Alice Munro's Narrative Acts*, edited by Louis K. MacKendrick. ECW Press, 1983, pp. 5–36.
Struthers, J. R. "Traveling with Munro: Reading 'To Reach Japan.'" *Alice Munro: Hateship, Friendship, Courtship, Loveship, Marriage, Runaway, Dear Life*, edited by Robert Thacker. Bloomsbury Academic, 2016, pp. 163–83.
Struthers, J. R., editor. *Alice Munro Everlasting: Essays on Her Works II*. Guernica, 2020.
"Tam Lin." *The Oxford Book of Ballads*, selected and edited by James Kinsley. Oxford, University Press, 1969, pp. 13–21.
"Tam Lin": Meta Version. *Tam Lin Balladry*, tam-lin.org. Accessed September 14, 2020.
Thacker, Robert. "Alice Munro Country." *Dalhousie Review*, vol. 98, no. 3, Fall 2018, pp. 412–18.
Thacker, Robert. "Alice Munro's Victoria." *Canadian Literature*, no. 236, spring 2018, pp. 177–81.
Thacker, Robert. *Alice Munro: Writing Her Lives: A Biography*. Revised ed. Emblem, 2011.
Thacker, Robert. "'As Truthful as Our Notion of the Past Can Ever Be': William Maxwell, His *Ancestors*, and Alice Munro's *The View from Castle Rock*." *Authorship*, vol. 10, no. 1, 2021, pp. 1–16.
Thacker, Robert. Email to Charles May. June 27, 2011.
Thacker, Robert. "'Evocative and Luminous Phrases': Reading Alice Munro's *Hateship, Friendship, Courtship, Loveship, Marriage*." *The American Review of Canadian Studies*, vol. 45, June 2, 2015, pp. 187–95.

Thacker, Robert. Interviews with Alice Munro. August 21–22, 2001, Clinton, Ontario.
Thacker, Robert. Interviews with Alice Munro. June 19–20, 2003, Clinton, Goderich, and Wingham Ontario.
Thacker, Robert. Interviews with Alice Munro. April 23–24, 2004, Comox, British Columbia.
Thacker, Robert. Interview with Alice Munro. June 14, 2010, Goderich, Ontario.
Thacker, Robert. Interview with Alice Munro. September 6, 2013, Bayfield, Ontario.
Thacker, Robert. Interview with Ann Close. July 21, 2010, New York City.
Thacker, Robert. Interview with Ann Close. July 26, 2021, Telephone.
Thacker, Robert. Interview with Ann Close. November 10, 2021, Telephone.
Thacker, Robert. Interview with Ben Metcalf. July 27, 2010, Telephone.
Thacker, Robert. Interview with Deborah Treisman. July 19, 2010, New York City.
Thacker, Robert. Interview with Jennifer Rudolph Walsh. July 20, 2010, New York City.
Thacker, Robert. Interview with Virginia Barber. November 20, 2000, New York City.
Thacker, Robert. "Introduction: 'Durable and Freestanding': The Late Art of Munro." *Alice Munro: Hateship, Friendship, Courtship, Loveship, Marriage, Runaway, Dear Life*, edited by Thacker. Bloomsbury Academic, 2016, pp. 1–20.
Thacker, Robert. *Reading Alice Munro, 1973-2013*. University of Calgary Press, 2016.
Thacker, Robert. Review of *Ethics and Affects in the Fiction of Alice Munro* edited by Amelia DeFalco and Lorraine York. *The American Review of Canadian Studies*, vol. 49, no. 3, September 2019, pp. 464–6.
Thacker, Robert. "'Stabbed to the Heart … By the Beauty of Our Lives Streaming By': Munro's Finale." Struthers, *Alice Munro Everlasting*, pp. 409–42.
Thacker, Robert. "'This Is Not a Story, Only Life': Wondering with Alice Munro." *Alice Munro's Miraculous Art: Critical Essays*, edited by Janice Fiamengo and Gerald Lynch. University of Ottawa Press, 2017, pp. 15–40.
Thompson, Reg. Email. November 16, 2021. Author's possession.
Treisman, Deborah. Emails to Robert Thacker. May 12 and 15, 2022. Author's possession.
Treisman, Deborah. "On 'Dear Life': An Interview with Alice Munro." November 20, 2012. newyorker.com.
"Trials and Tribulations of the Early Pioneers." *History of Morris Township and Stories Relating to Pioneer Days, 1856-1956*. Blyth *Standard* [Blyth, Ontario], 1956, pp. 28–30.
Trumpener, Katie. "Annals of Ice: Formations of Empire, Place and History in John Galt and Alice Munro." *Scottish Literature and Postcolonial Literature: Comparative Texts and Perspectives*. Edinburgh University Press, 2011, pp. 43–56.
Turbide, Diane. "The Incomparable Storyteller." *MacLean's*, October 17, 1994, pp. 46–9.
Updike, John. "Books: The Author as Librarian." *New Yorker*, October 30, 1965, pp. 223–4, 226–8, 231–6, 238, 241–6.
Updike, John. "Late Works: Writers Confronting the End." Review of *On Late Style* by Edward W. Said. *New Yorker*, August 7 and 14, 2006, pp. 64–71.
Updike, John. "'Seven Gothic Tales': The Divine Swank of Isak Dinesen." *New York Times*, February 23, 1986, sec. 7, p. 3.
Ventura, Héliane. "The Female Bard: Retrieving Greek Myths, Celtic Ballads, Norse Sagas, and Popular Songs." *The Cambridge Companion to Alice Munro*, edited by David Staines. Cambridge, 2016, pp. 154–77.
Ventura, Héliane. "The Legacy of the Forest: A Source Study of 'Wood' (2009) by Alice Munro." *Textual Practice*, vol. 36, no. 3, 2022, pp. 422–37.
Wachtel, Eleanor. "Alice Munro: A Life in Writing: A Conversation." *Queen's Quarterly*, vol. 112, no. 2, Summer 2005, pp. 266–80.

Wachtel, Eleanor. Interview with Alice Munro. "Writers and Company." November 2004. https://www.cbc.ca/player/play/2411628438.
Ware, Tracy. Emails to Robert Thacker, June 4, 2020 and September 17, 2022. Author's possession.
Ware, Tracy. "Tricks with 'a Sad Ring': The Endings of Alice Munro's 'The Ottawa Valley.'" *Studies in Canadian Literature / Études en littérature canadienne*, vol. 31, no. 4, 2006, pp. 126–41.
Weaver, John. "Society and Culture in Rural and Small Town Ontario: Alice Munro's Testimony on the Last Forty Years." *Patterns of the Past: Interpreting Ontario's History*, edited by Roger Hall, William Westfall, and Laurel Sefton MacDowell. Dundurn, 1988, pp. 381–401.
Welty, Eudora. *The Eye of the Story: Selected Essays and Reviews*. 1978. Vintage, 1979.
Welty, Eudora. *The Golden Apples*. 1949. Harcourt, Brace & World, 1962. A Harvest Book.
Welty, Eudora. "The House of Willa Cather." 1974. *The Eye of the Story*, pp. 41–60.
Welty, Eudora. *One Writer's Beginnings*. 1984. Warner, 1985.
Welty, Eudora. *The Optimist's Daughter*. 1972. Vintage, 1978.
Whitman, Walt. *Song of Myself. The Norton Anthology of American Literature*, vol. B (1820–1865), edited by Robert S. Levine and Arnold Krupat. Norton, 2007, pp. 2210–54.
York, Lorraine. "Retrospective Recursion." Review of *Alice Munro*: Hateship, Friendship, Courtship, Loveship, Marriage, Runaway, Dear Life edited by Robert Thacker, *The Cambridge Companion to Alice Munro* edited by David Staines, and *Reading Alice Munro, 1973-2013* by Thacker. *Canadian Literature*, no. 233 summer, 2017, pp. 164–7.

Index

Agincourt (Leith) 195 n. 17
Alexander the Great 122
Alexander, W. J. 116, 117, 191–2 n. 25
Alfred A. Knopf, Inc. x, xiii, xiv, 3, 4, 183–4 n. 1, 186 n. 12, 189 n. 6, 194 n. 10, 195 n, 16, 198 n 1, 199 n. 12, 200 n. 17, 202 n. 7, 202 n. 9
Alice Munro Book Club xv
"Alice Munro Country" 111
Alice Munro Fonds (University of Calgary) xiii, xiv, 2–3, 41–2, 127
Alice Munro: Writing Her Lives: A Biography (Thacker) viii, x, xii, 72, 90, 186 n. 17, 197 n. 24, 197 n. 26, 199 n. 9
Almon, Jessica 199–200 n. 15
Anthology (CBC Radio) xii
"The Apple Tree" (Galsworthy) 95–6, 197–8 n. 28
The Atlantic Monthly 23, 29
Awano, Lisa Dickler 104–5
"Away" (de la Mare) 117–18, 163

"Ballad of Sir Patrick Spens" 116
Barber, Virginia ix, x, xiii, xiv–v, 18–9, 20–1, 30, 36, 42, 43, 48, 57, 61, 62, 73, 74, 93, 149, 156, 159, 169, 183–4 n. 1, 184 n. 2, 185 n. 2, 186 n. 12, 186 n. 14, 186 n. 15, 186 n. 16, 190 n. 13, 190 n. 16, 192 n. 26, 194 n. 10, 198 n. 1
Bayfield, Ontario 110, 111
"The Beauty of Death" (Gibran) 105
Berry, Wendell 128
Berryman, John 10, 11
Besser, Carin 73–4, 75
Best American Short Stories 1981 ("Wood") 198 n. 5
Best American Short Stories 2012 ("Axis") 201 n. 5
Best American Short Stories 2013 ("Train") 150

Best Canadian Stories, 81 ("Wood") 105, 198 n. 5, 198–9 n. 8
"The Birthmark" (Hawthorne) 114
Blackwood's Magazine 59, 76, 78, 81, 137, 193 n. 7
Blyth *Citizen* 197 n. 26
Blyth Union Cemetery 38, 75, 86–87, 99, 196 n. 21, 196–7 n. 23
"Blyth: A Village Portrait" 87, 196 n. 20
Book-of-the-Month Club 45, 188 n. 4
Bordin Prize (French Academy of Science) 157, 161, 166
Boston, Thomas 37, 80, 81, 88, 194 n. 13
Boston Presbyterian Church Cemetery (Halton, Ontario) 58, 75, 78, 84, 190 n. 14
Brontë, Charlotte 74
Brontë, Emily 70
Bruce Peninsula (Ontario) 131
Butt, William 72, 75
Byatt, A. S. xii, 183 n. 2

Callil, Carmen 36
Cameronians 31–2, 35, 36, 59
Canada-Australia Literary Award 24
Canadian Broadcasting Corporation (CBC) xii, 11, 149, 170
Canadian Forum 7, 180
Canadian Shield 130, 132, 188–9 n. 5
Carleton Place, Ontario 16
Carrington, Ildikó de Papp 43–44, 48
Cather, Willa xii, 20, 114, 177, 180, 199 n. 13, 205 n. 11
Chapman, Lyman 51
"The Character of the Happy Warrior" (Wordsworth) 200 n. 16
Chatto & Windus 36
Close, Ann x, xii, xiv, 104–5, 106, 110, 129, 131, 132, 133, 146–7, 149, 152–3, 155, 159, 179, 183 n. 1, 184 n. 12, 185 n. 2, 186 n. 12, 194 n. 10, 198 n. 1,

201 n. 4, 202 n. 7, 202 n. 9, 202 n. 11, 203 n. 13, 203 n. 14, 205 n. 10
Code, Thomas 94
Cohen, Leah Hager 103, 106
Collected Poems (de la Mare) 163, 200 n. 17
Colonial Advocate (York, Upper Canada [Toronto]) 59, 76, 84
Colpoy's Bay (Wiarton, Ontario) 131, 182
Confessions of a Justified Sinner (Hogg) 82
Cooper, Emma Netterfield 178–80, 206 n. 13
Coppard, A. E. 95–96, 197–8 n. 28
Cox, Ailsa x, 163, 168–9, 205 n. 6

de la Mare Walter 117–18, 163, 200 n. 16, 200 n. 17
DeFalco, Amelia 191 n. 22
Department of Creative Writing (University of British Columbia) 107
"The Diary of Robert B. Laidlaw" 87, 196 n. 20
Dinesen, Isak 42, 44–5, 188 n. 4
Dodds, E. R. 188 n. 5
Dostoevsky, Fydor 157
"The Dreamers" (Dinesen) 45, 47
Dryburgh Abbey 36
Duffy, Dennis xi, xvi, 74–5, 76, 79, 83, 137, 157, 158–9, 163
"Dusky Ruth" (Coppard) 95–6, 197–8 n. 28

Edel, Leon 72, 193 n. 4
Edemarian, Aida viii, 5
Eisenberg, Deborah ix, xi, 23, 72, 75
Emily of New Moon (Montgomery) 191 n. 24
Esquising, Halton County, Upper Canada (Ontario) 60
Enigma of Arrival (Naipaul) 24, 72, 75
Ettrick Kirk Cemetery 75, 78, 80, 194 n. 12
Ettrick Valley (Scotland) 23–4, 25–32, 36, 72, 77, 78–9, 80–2
Evans, Mary 8

Findley, Timothy viii, 14
Fisher, Dorothy Canfield 188 n. 4
Fitzgerald, F. Scott 133
Folio 198 n. 4

Fremlin, Gerald xv, 3, 4, 24, 25, 32, 36, 38, 48–56, 79, 91, 98, 104, 129, 143, 144, 151–3, 159, 182, 194 n. 11, 199 n. 14, 201 n. 4
French, William 14–15
Frontenac Axis xiv, 130, 132, 182

Galsworthy, John 95–6, 197–8 n. 28
Gannett, Louis 205 n. 9
The Georgia Review 169–70
Gibran, Khalil, 105
Gibson, Douglas ix, xiii, 3, 13, 22, 41, 78–9, 83, 146, 182, 184 n. 2, 185 n. 4, 186 n. 12, 194 n. 10, 195 n. 17, 200 n. 17, 205 n. 8, 205 n. 10
Gittings, Christopher xv, 36–8, 41, 87, 102, 187 n. 18, 194 n. 13
Goderich, Huron County, Ontario 199 n. 14
The Golden Apples (Welty) 12, 169–70
Gone with the Wind (Margaret Mitchell) 70
Good, Alex 76–7, 194 n. 9
Gorra, Michael 24, 72, 75, 103, 111, 118–19, 125, 128, 192 n. 2
Gottlieb, Robert 186 n. 14
Grand Street 8, 14, 39, 90–2, 93, 184 n. 2
"Grandfathers" (Robert Eric Laidlaw) 94
Granta 143, 147
The Great Gatsby (Fitzgerald) 133
The Greeks and the Irrational (Dodds) 106, 188–9 n. 5
Guardian viii, 5
Guardian Review 194 n. 8

Hadley, Tessa 23, 77, 83, 195 n. 14
The Happy Warrior (Hutchinson) 117, 200 n. 16
Harper's 8, 112, 135, 137, 140, 143, 147, 156, 199 n. 11, 202 n. 11
Harvard Classics 120–1
Hawthorne, Nathaniel 114
Hay, Elizabeth 181
Henderson, Eleanor 181
Henighan, Stephen 77
"Hippolytus of Euripides" 96
History of Morris Township of Morris Township and Stories Related to Pioneer Day 1856–1956 196 n. 20, 196 n. 21

A History of Sullivan Township, 1850-1975 189 n. 11
Hogg, James ("Ettrick Shepherd") 28, 59, 76–7, 80–2, 83–4, 193 n. 7
Hogg, Margaret Laidlaw 28, 36, 80, 82
Hogg, Robert 80
Horace 106
Housman, A. E. 106, 108
Humpty Dumpty 132
Huron County Ontario ix, xv, 2, 3, 4, 24, 30, 36, 37, 57, 66, 79, 83, 99, 103, 110, 129, 141, 157, 159, 182, 206 n. 13
Hutchinson, A. S. M. 117, 200 n. 16

I Promessi Sposi (*The Betrothed*) (Manzoni) 120–1
Ibsen, Henrik 157

James, Edward and Mary 187 n. 17
James, Sadie 187 n. 17
James, Williams 188–9 n. 5
Jane Erye (Charlotte Brontë) 74
Jernigan, Kim ix
Joliet, Illinois 85, 187 n. 21, 195 n. 16
Joyce, James 44

Kakutani, Michiko 103, 151
Kennedy, Don H. and Nina 157–9, 160–2, 164, 168, 204 n. 3, 204 n. 4, 204–5, n. 5, 205 n. 7
Kilgour, David Goldie 53
Kincardine, Ontario 111
Kingston, Ontario 130
Kovalevsky, Maxsim Maxsimovich 158, 159, 161, 166, 169
Kovalevsky, Sophia 103, 106, 156–69
Kovalevsky, Vladimir 161, 165–6, 167

Lehey, Anita ix
Laidlaw, Andrew (1794–1874) 60, 76, 84–5
Laidlaw, Anne Clarke Chamney (1898–1959; mother) ix, xii, 6–7, 16–17, 20, 89, 91–3, 96, 120, 149, 155–6, 170, 172–5, 176, 177–80, 181–2, 184 n. 4
Laidlaw, Euphemia (c. 1839–1905) 196–7 n. 23

Laidlaw, Isabel (Isabella) (1818–91) 58, 140, 167, 196 n. 18
Laidlaw, James (1763–1829) 59–60, 76, 78, 81–2, 84, 137, 193 n. 7
Laidlaw, James (1796–1886) 193 n. 7
Laidlaw, James (1816–18) 74, 75, 84
Laidlaw, James (c. late 1820s–1853) 13, 38, 50, 60, 85, 86–7, 89, 196–7 n. 23
Laidlaw, Jane (c. 1840–66) 85, 86, 196 n. 19
Laidlaw, John (c. 1830–1907) 86–7
Laidlaw, Mary Scott (1800–68; great-great grandmother) 59–60, 85–6, 94, 196 n. 21, 196–7 n. 23
Laidlaw, Robert (1728–1800) 37, 80
Laidlaw, Robert (1792–?) 59, 6, 192 n. 7
Laidlaw, Robert B. (1828–1908; "Big Rob") 87–9, 196 n. 20, 196 n. 21, 196 n. 22
Laidlaw, Robert (1832–96; "Little Rob") 196–7 n. 23
Laidlaw, Robert Eric (1901–76; father) ii, viii, 14, 17, 19–20, 66, 89, 90–4, 97–9, 175–6, 177, 180, 182, 190–1 n. 19, 196 n. 20, 197 n. 26
Laidlaw, Sarah Jane "Sadie" Code (1876–1966; grandmother) 16, 90–1, 95–7, 182
Laidlaw, Thomas (1836–1915; great grandfather) 86, 94
Laidlaw, Walter (1799–1873) 60, 71, 75–6, 84, 195 n. 17
Laidlaw, William (1691–1775; "Will O'Phaup") 36, 80–2, 194 n. 12
Laidlaw, William (1780–1845) 23, 28
Laidlaw, William (1798–1839 or '40; great-great grandfather) 38, 58–60, 73, 84–6, 94, 99
Laidlaw, William Cole (1864–1938; grandfather) 90–1, 96–7
Laidlaw Family Emigration (1818) 22, 38, 195 n. 17
"The Lamp in the Mausoleum" (Lurie) 56
Lanark County Ontario 32
Larsen, Joan xv
"Late Works: Writers Confronting the End" (Updike) 5
Lee, Monika 156–7
Leffler, Anna Charlotte 157, 160, 204–5 n. 5
Lehey, Anita ix

Leyshon, Cressida 73-4
Lives of Mothers and Daughters (Sheila Munro) 71
Little Sparrow: A Portrait of Sophia Kovalevsky (Kennedy) 157-9, 160-2, 164, 166, 169, 204 n. 3, 204 n. 4, 204-5 n. 5, 205 n 7
London *Free Press* ix,14
London Review of Books 23
Longinus 106
Lower Town Wingham Ontario 4, 62, 64, 66, 91, 97, 103, 172, 177, 180, 189 n. 19, 191 n. 20, 191-2 n. 25, 205 n. 12
Lurie, Alison 56

Mackenzie, William Lyon 59, 76, 82
MacLean's 37
Macmillan of Canada 3, 13, 22, 185 n. 4, 197 n. 24
Maitland River (Ontario) 62, 103, 109, 153, 180, 191 n. 25
Making It New (Metcalf) 7, 8
Mannerow Cemetery (Cedardale) 48-56, 189 n. 9, 190 n. 11
Manzoni, Alessandro 120
Martin, W. R. 27-8
Marx, Karl 91
Maxwell, William 135, 186 n. 16, 195 n. 15, 202 n. 10
May, Charles E. xi, 135-6, 137
McCall's 8
McClelland & Stewart x, xiii, 189 n. 6, 199 n. 12, 200 n. 17
McCulloch, Jeanne 101, 187 n. 17
McGill, Robert x, xv
McGrath, Charles 8, 18-9, 21, 103-4, 185 n. 4, 186 n. 15, 198 n. 6
McGraw-Hill 185 n. 2
The McGregors (Robert Eric Laidlaw) viii, 14, 197 n. 26
McMullen, Gordon 5, 7
Melrose, Scotland 36
Memory and Other Poems (de la Mare) 200 n. 17
Menaker, Daniel 29-30, 36, 186 n. 14, 186 n. 15, 186-7 n. 16
Metcalf, Ben 202 n. 11
Metcalf, John 7, 17, 185 n. 5, 186 n. 9, 198-9 n. 8

Miller, Karl 77, 193 n. 8
Millgate, Michael 4-5
The Minstrelsy of the Scottish Border (Scott) 28, 82
Mitchell, Lee Clark 3-4, 5, 132
Mitchell, Margaret 70
Montgomery, L. M. 191 n. 24
The Montrealer 170
Montvid, A. S. 204-5 n. 5
More Time: Contemporary Short Stories and Late Styles (Lee Clark Mitchell) 3-4, 5, 132
Mosses from an Old Manse (Hawthorne) 114
Munro, Alice Ann Laidlaw (1931-) xiii, x, xi–xii, xiii, xv, 1, 4, 5–6, 7–9, 11–13, 14, 18, 24–5, 28–32, 36–7, 38, 41–2, 44, 46–57, 58–61, 62–3, 65–7, 70, 71–2, 76–82, 83–4, 87–9, 90–5, 96–9, 104–5, 106–8, 110–11, 115–16, 117, 118, 119, 120–1, 123–5, 127–9, 130, 132–3, 134–6, 138, 140, 141, 142–3, 145, 147, 149, 151, 155–6, 157, 161, 165, 169–70, 172, 176–80, 181–2, 187 n. 18, 189 n. 7, 189 n. 10, 190 n. 12, 190 n. 15, 190–1 n. 19, 191 n. 21, 192 n. 1, 193 n. 7, 194 n. 11, 195 n. 17, 199 n. 14, 200 n. 18, 200–1 n. 21, 201 n. 2, 201 n. 3, 202 n. 9, 202 n. 10
Books and Stories (books listed chronologically):
Dance of the Happy Shades 12, 43, 70, 140, 150, 170, 201 n. 1; stories: "Boys and Girls" 12, 86, 177; "Dance of the Happy Shades" 185 n. 3; "Day of the Butterfly" (Good-By, Myra) 64-5; "Images" 12, 137; "The Peace of Utrecht" 7, 12-13, 16, 31, 94, 124, 155, 170, 177, 178, 180, 182, 184 n. 4; "Postcard" 124; "Red Dress—1946" 12, 177; "Sunday Afternoon" 43-4, 48; "Thanks for the Ride" 170; "The Time of Death" 47, 135, 147, 170; "The Trip to the Coast" 185 n. 3; "Walker Brother Cowboy" 12, 52, 64, 120, 177
Lives of Girls and Women 13, 64, 69, 138, 150, 177, 201 n. 1, 201-2 n. 6;

stories: "Baptizing" 69, 201–2 n. 6; "The Flats Road" 64, 177
Something I've Been Meaning to Tell You 2, 14, 115; stories: "Material" 2, 16, 39, 112–13, 124, 149, 164, 199 n. 10, 202–3 n. 12; "The Ottawa Valley" 3, 15, 16–17, 35, 105, 115, 116, 125, 151, 155, 157, 172, 174, 180, 184 n. 4, 191–2 n. 25; "Something I've Been Meaning to Tell You" 25, 115; "Winter Wind" 3, 15, 16–17, 94, 178
Who Do You Think You Are? / *The Beggar Maid* viii, xiv, 3, 6, 7, 13, 14, 17–18, 22–3, 24, 39, 64, 89, 94, 95, 98, 107, 146, 150, 177, 191 n. 20, 191–2 n. 25, 194 n. 10, 197 n. 24, 197 n. 28, 198 n. 7, 201 n. 1; stories: "Privilege" 186 n. 10; "Royal Beatings" 7, 14, 17, 65–6, 177, 186 n. 10
The Moons of Jupiter 7, 11, 17, 19, 146; stories: "Accident" 61, 186 n 11, 192 n. 1, 201 n. 1; "Chaddeleys and Flemings: 1. Connection" 13–14, 18, 19, 21, 95, 124, 147, 184 n. 4, 185 n. 4, 196 n. 23, 197 n. 24, 200 n. 19; "Chaddeleys and Flemings: 2. The Stone in the Field" 11, 12–13, 14, 19, 21, 22, 35, 86, 88–9, 120, 124, 185 n. 4, 196 n. 23, 197 n. 24; "Dulse" xii, 18, 19, 20–1, 104, 147, 197–8 n. 29; "Labor Day Dinner" 19; "The Moons of Jupiter" vii, 186 n. 10, 197 n. 24; "Mrs. Cross and Mrs. Kidd" 22; "The Turkey Season" 18, 19, 56
The Progress of Love 6, 26, 134, 186 n. 13, 194 n. 10; stories: "Circle of Prayer" 134, 168; "Miles City, Montana" 42, 56, 113, 135, 149, 150; "The Progress of Love" 150, 184 n. 4, 194 n. 13; "White Dump" 6, 26, 129, 134
Friend of My Youth 6, 23–36, 38, 41–2, 105, 184 n. 2, 186 n. 16; stories: "Friend of My Youth" 25, 30–6, 94, 184 n. 4; "Hold Me Fast, Don't Let Me Pass" 25–32, 35, 36, 82, 184 n. 2, 186 n. 13, 186 n. 14; "Meneseteung" x, 6, 57, 158–9, 163

Open Secrets 6, 37, 38, 42, 72, 87, 101, v133, 138, 184 n. 3, 198 n. 1; stories: "The Albanian Virgin" 42; "Carried Away" 133, 163, 184 n. 3, 198 n. 1; "Open Secrets" 111; "Spaceships Have Landed" 101, 125; "Vandals" 101; "A Wilderness Station" 13, 37, 38, 57, 60, 76, 87, 138, 194 n. 1
Selected Stories xii, 2, 38, 72, 101, 125
The Love of a Good Woman x, 6, 24, 37, 38, 156; stories: "The Children Stay" 135; "My Mother's Dream" 135
Hateship, Friendship, Courtship, Loveship, Marriage vii, x, 1, 5, 6, 10, 38; stories: "The Bear Came Over the Mountain" 5; "Hateship, Friendship, Courtship, Loveship, Marriage" 106; "Nettles" 5, 136; 187 n. 19, 189 n. 9; "Post and Beam" 5; "Queenie" 192 n. 1; "What Is Remembered" 5
Runaway xi, 4, 6, 10, 11, 38, 72, 76, 83, 98, 194 n. 9; stories: "Chance"106, 188–9 n. 5, 203–4 n. 2; "Juliet Triptych" (three connected stories) 106, 134; "Powers" xi; "Runaway" 110; "Silence" 113–14, 134, 203–4 n. 2; "Soon" 134, 203–4 n. 2
The View from Castle Rock ix, x–xi, xii, xiv, 1, 3, 4, 5–6, 9–10, 11, 13–14, 16, 17, 20, 23–5, 28, 30, 34, 36, 37–9, 41–2, 44–9, 56–7, 58, 61, 66, 70, 71–3, 74–99, 102–3, 106, 109, 110, 119, 125, 156, 157, 158–9, 167, 168, 170, 181, 182, 185 n. 4, 187 n. 2, 188 n. 1, 188 n. 2, 188 n. 3, 189 n. 9, 190 n. 12, 191 n. 22, 191 n. 23, 193 n. 3, 194 n. 9, 196 n. 19; stories: "Fathers" xi, 48, 61–7, 70, 82, 99, 188 n. 1, 190 n. 16, 192 n. 1; "Hired Girl" xi, 41–9, 76, 94, 119, 122; "Home"viii–x, xi, 1–2, 3, 13, 14–17, 42, 52, 56, 61, 75, 82, 90, 94; 97–9, 110, 127, 184 n. 4, 185 n. 5, 185 n. 6, 188 n. 1, 188–9 n. 5, 190 n. 16, 197 n. 25, 197 n. 26; "Home" (*Castle Rock* section) xi, 43, 66, 83,

94, 106, 119, 195 n. 16; "Illinois" 84–6, 188 n. 1; "Lying Under the Apple Tree" xi, 43, 48, 61–2, 67–70, 81, 82, 93, 115, 188 n. 1, 190 n. 16, 190 n. 17, 191–2 n. 25, 192 n. 1, 201–2 n. 6; "Men of Ettrick" (*Castle Rock* section) 78, 80–2, 188 n. 1; "Messenger" ("Remnants") 37–8, 56, 78, 83–4, 87, 98–9, 188 n. 1, 193 n. 5; "No Advantages" (*Castle Rock* section) xi, 39, 43, 57, 66, 73, 77, 78–80, 90, 94, 195 n. 16; "The Ticket" xi–xii, 14, 16, 43, 48, 82, 90, 94–7, 102, 178, 188 n. 1, 197 n. 27, 197–8 n. 29, 198 n. 3; "The View from Castle Rock"39, 57, 58, 59, 61, 73–6, 78, 80, 82, 83–4, 137, 188 n. 1, 190 n. 16, 196 n. 18; "What Do You Want to Know For?" xi, 3, 10, 38, 41–3, 48–57, 61, 65, 76, 78, 79, 83, 90, 91, 98, 102, 129, 159, 182, 189 n. 9, 190 n. 12, 190 n. 16, 195 n. 16, 197 n. 27; "The Wilds of Morris Township" 13, 60, 87–9, 90, 185 n. 4, 185 n. 4, 188 n. 1; "Working for Living" 3, 6, 7, 13, 14, 17–24, 28, 39, 42, 56, 77, 82, 85, 89, 90–4, 102, 127, 177, 184 n. 4, 188 n. 1, 193 n. 5, 197 n. 25, 198 n. 2

Too Much Happiness ix, xiii, xiv, 2, 4, 9, 10, 19, 24, 72, 102–25, 146, 151, 156–7, 159, 163, 169, 181, 192 n. 2, 199 n. 11; stories: "Child's Play" 111–12; "Deep-Holes" 106, 113–14, 199 n. 12; "Dimensions" ("Dimension") 102, 110–11, 159, 197 n. 27; "Face" 105, 113–18, 119, 124, 128, 137–8, 139, 163, 169, 197 n. 28; "Fiction" 2, 112–13, 120; "Free Radicals" 111, 156, 203–4 n. 2; "Some Women" 118–25, 135, 143–4, 200 n. 20; "Too Much Happiness" xi, 2, 6, 9, 56, 106, 118, 156–69, 203–4 n. 2, 204–5 n. 5, 205 n. 7, 205 n. 8; "Wenlock Edge"41–3, 56, 83, 102, 105–10, 111, 115, 125, 129, 152, 188 n. 1, 188 n. 2, 185 n. 16, 195 n. 16;"Wood" 6, 19, 61, 102–6, 116, 125, 159, 184 n. 2, 190 n. 16, 197 n. 25, 198 n. 5, 198 n. 6

Dear Life ix, xiii, xiv, 1, 2, 3, 4, 6, 9–10, 12, 52, 65, 192, 102, 103, 120, 127–53, 155–56, 159, 172–80, 181, 202 n. 11; stories: "Amundsen" 2, 114, 128, 143, 145–6; "Corrie" 132–5, 138, 144; "Dear Life" 12, 18, 64, 65, 66, 92, 120, 128, 135, 140, 155–6, 170, 176–80, 202 n. 11; "Dolly" 4, 56, 65, 143, 147, 151–3, 159, 172 102 n. 13; "The Eye" 68, 172–5; "Finale" (*Dear Life* section) 4, 6, 7, 9–10, 56, 65, 68, 102, 103, 120, 128, 129, 135, 141, 143, 153, 155–6, 170, 172–80, 181, 202 n. 11, 203 n. 13, 205 n. 11; "Gravel" 135–7, 138, 140, 189 n. 9, 202 n. 10; "Haven" 143–5; "In Sight of the Lake" 143, 147; "Leaving Maverley" 140–3; "Night" 143, 175–6; "Pride" 115–16, 128, 135, 137–40, 151; "To Reach Japan" 2, 130, 141, 143, 147–50; "Train" 2, 143, 147, 150–1, 202 n. 11; "Voices" 120, 129, 176

Fugitive or Manuscript Short Stories: "Axis" 52, 69, 79, 106, 127–8, 129–32, 137, 143, 182, 201 n. 4, 201 n. 5, 201–2 n. 6; "A Better Place than Home" 61, 86; "The Boy Murderer" 2, 150; "Characters" 129; "The Dimensions of a Shadow" 198 n. 4; "The Ferguson Girls Must Never Marry" 6, 7–9, 61, 184 n. 2, 190 n. 16, 197 n. 25; "The Heart of an Executioner" 205 n. 12; "The Man Who Goes Home" 2, 3; "Married People" 202–3 n. 12; "Places at Home" 3, 13, 98; "The Return of the Poet" 191–2 n. 25; "The Yellow Afternoon" xii, 96

Essays and Script: "Changing Places" (*Writing Home*) 38, 57–61, 66, 71–2, 76, 84, 86–7, 193 n. 7, 195 n. 18, 195 n. 19, 196–7 n. 23; "1847: The Irish" (CBC script) 24; "Everything Here Is Touchable and Mysterious" ix, x, 153, 180; "Golden Apples" 169–70, 180; "Maxwell" 202 n. 10; "What Is Real?" 7, 8–9

Munro, James 1, 94, 95, 97, 107, 135, 182, 202 n. 10

Munro, Jenny 149

Munro, Sheila ii, xv, 1, 2, 71–2, 149, 182, 190 n. 15
Murray, Annie xv
Murray, Gilbert 96

Naipaul, V. S. 24, 72, 75
Narrative 143, 147
The Newcomers / Les arrivants (CBC) 24
New Selected Stories (Munro) 188 n. 5
New Statesman viii, 90, 97–8
New Yorker xiii, xiv, xv, 5, 6, 7, 8, 9, 12, 14, 17, 18–19, 21, 22, 29–30, 31, 36, 37, 39, 42, 44, 46–7, 57, 59, 61–3, 67–8, 69–70, 72, 73, 75, 83, 84, 87, 89, 101–3, 104, 106, 196–8, 109, 110, 116, 117, 118, 127, 128, 129–32, 134, 135–6, 137, 140, 142–3, 146, 155–6, 178–9, 186 n. 10, 186 n. 12, 186 n. 14, 187 n. 16, 188 n. 2, 188 n. 3, 190 n. 16, 190 n. 18, 191 n. 23, 193 n. 23, 194 n. 10, 195 n. 16, 196 n. 18, 197 n. 27, 199 n. 9, 199 n. 11, 199 n. 12, 200 n. 17, 200 n. 18, 200–1 n. 21, 201 n. 3, 202 n. 7, 203 n. 1, 206 n. 14
Niagara Escarpment 130–1, 182, 202 n. 8
The Nihilist Girl (Sophia Kovalevsky) 204–5 n. 5
Nobel Prize in Literature (2013) x, xiii, xiv

O. Henry Prize Stories 2013 ("Leaving Maverley") 141
Ober, Warren 27–8
Odyssey (Homer) 44–5
On Late Style (Said) xi, 4
On the Sublime (Longinus) 106
One Writer's Beginnings (Welty) 170–2
Ontario Northland Railway 145
The Optimist's Daughter (Welty) 171
Osler Bluff (Niagara Escarpment) Ontario 113
Ottawa Valley (Ontario) 30–5
Ozick, Cynthia 157

Paris Review 101–2, 125, 187 n. 17, 198 n. 1
PEN Canada 42, 57

PEN / O. Henry Prize Stories 2012 ("Corrie") 132, 134–5
The Physiography of Southern Ontario (Chapman and Putnam) 51
The Pirates of Penzance (Gilbert and Sullivan) 64
Plimpton, George 101
Poincaré, Jules 162–3
Pointe au Baril, Ontario (Georgian Bay) 42
Porterfield, Maud Code (178–1976; great aunt) 95
Power in the Blood 69, 192 n. 26
Powers, Lyall 193 n. 4
"The Profile" (Cather) 114, 199 n. 13
Putnam, Donald 51

"Recollections of George Eliot" (Sophia Kovalevsky) 204–5 n. 5
Redbook 8
Redekop, Magdalene 25, 28
Reeves, Eric xv, 31–3, 35
Remnick, David 74
Rooke, Leon 199 n. 8
Royal Canadian Air Force (RCAF) 25, 201 n. 4
A Russian Childhood (Sophia Kovalevsky) 204 n. 4, 204–5 n. 5

Said, Edward xi, 4–5
Salter, Mary Jo 29
Sanders, David 204 n. 3
Sapphira and the Slave Girl (Cather) 177, 205 n. 11
Scotlands 36
Scott, Sir Walter 28, 36, 76, 80, 82, 151, 187 n. 18
"The Scottish Ancestor" 36
Scurr, Ruth 188–9 n. 5
"The Second Coming" (Yeats) 9
Selkirk, Scotland 24, 36
Seven Gothic Tales (Dinesen) 42, 44, 47, 188 n. 4, 188–9 n. 5
74: New Canadian Stories viii, ix, 14, 17
Shakespeare, William 10, 11
Shakespeare and the Idea of Late Writing (McMullen) 5
"Shakespeare at Thirty" (Berryman) 10
Shawn, William 185 n. 4

Shorter Poems (Alexander) 116–17, 191–2 n. 25
Shortreed, Thomas 193 n. 7
Simpson, Mona 101, 187 n. 17
A Shropshire Lad (Housman) 106–10
Sir Gawain and the Green Knight 107, 109–10
So Long, See You Tomorrow (Maxwell) 202 n. 10
Somacarrera, Pilar 78, 187 n. 20
Song of Myself (Whitman) 191–2 n. 25
Statistical Account of Scotland (1799) 75
Stein, Abner 190 n. 16
Stillman, Beatrice 204 n. 4
Stoffman, Judy 195 n. 15
The Struggle for Happiness (Sophia Kovalevsky and Leffler) 204–5 n. 5
Struthers, J. R. (Tim) ix, xv, 14, 30
Sullivan Township, Grey County, Ontario 49, 53
"The Supper at Elsinore" (Dinesen) 47, 48

"Tam Lin" 25–8
Tamarack Review 21–2, 149, 186 n. 10
Tennyson, Alfred Lord 191 n. 25
Testamentary Acts (Millgate) 3–5
Thompson, Alice Mary 32
Thompson, Reg xv, 31–3, 50, 186 n. 8, 187 n. 17, 189 n. 8
Thoreau, Henry David 72
Times Literary Supplement (TLS) 24, 188–9 n. 5, 192 n. 2
Tin House 143, 151–2, 203 n. 13, 203 n. 14
Toronto *Globe and Mail* 14
Toynbee, Arnold J. 121
Treisman, Deborah xiii, xiv, 61–3, 67–8, 70, 73–4, 109, 113–14, 116, 118, 132, 136–7, 139, 140, 143, 145, 179, 191 n. 23, 199 n. 12, 199–200 n. 15, 200 n. 16, 200 n. 18, 200–1 n. 21, 201 n. 3, 203–4 n. 2
Trevor, William 102
Trumpener, Katie 78–9
Turbide, Diane 38, 87
Turgenev, Ivan 157

Ulysses (Joyce) 44, 45
University of British Columbia (UBC) 107
University of Western Ontario (Western University) 2, 106, 129, 198 n. 4
Updike, John 5, 186 n. 7
Upper Canada (Ontario) 59

Ventura, Héliane 28, 104–5
Village Squire (Blyth *Citizen*) 94, 197 n. 26
Virginia Barber Literary Agency 17
Voltaire 91

Wagner, Allison xv
Walsh, Jennifer Rudolph 73, 156, 194 n. 9, 200 n. 15, 203 n. 2
Ware, Tracy xiv, 77, 115–16, 119
The Wars of the Three Kingdoms 31–2
Weaver, John 77
Weaver, Robert 11–12, 21–22, 149, 170
Weierstrass, Clara 166
Weierstrass, Elisa 161
Weierstrass, Karl Theodore William 161, 162–6, 168, 169
Welty, Eudora xii, 12, 44, 169–72
Whitman, Walt 191–2 n. 25
Wiarton, Ontario 131, 202 n. 8
Will County, Illinois 60, 86
Wingham *Advance-Times* 178–9, 190–1 n. 19
Wingham, Ontario 109, 127, 133, 140, 155, 179
Woollcott, Alexander 177, 205 n. 11
Wordsworth, William 200 n. 16
"Writers and Company" (CBC) 11, 184 n. 1
Writing Away (Constance Rooke) 42, 48
Writing Home (Constance Rooke) 57
Wuthering Heights (Emily Brontë) 70

Yeats, William Butler 9, 127–8
York, Lorraine x, xv

www.ingramcontent.com/pod-product-compliance
Lightning Source LLC
Chambersburg PA
CBHW071831300426
44116CB00009B/1511